Privilege & Poverty

THE LIFE & TIMES OF IRISH PAINTER & NATURALIST

ALEXANDER WILLIAMS RHA

1846–1930

To the memory of
Robert Duke Williams
(R.D.W.)

Privilege & Poverty

THE LIFE & TIMES OF IRISH PAINTER & NATURALIST
ALEXANDER WILLIAMS RHA
1846–1930

GORDON T. LEDBETTER

The Collins Press

First Published in 2010 by
The Collins Press
West Link Park
Doughcloyne
Wilton
Cork

British Library Cataloguing in Publication Data
Ledbetter, Gordon.
Privilege & poverty : the life and times of Irish painter
and naturalist Alexander Williams RHA (1846-1930).
1. Williams, Alexander, 1846-1930. 2. Painters--Ireland--
Biography.
I. Title
759.2'915-dc22
ISBN-13: 9781848890343

Design and typesetting by Burns Design
Typeset in Times New Roman
Printed in Spain by GraphyCems

Jacket photographs

Front flap: ink sketch of a barefoot woman carrying turf, *c.* 1890 (courtesy David Britton). *Front jacket and spine*: pastel of the artist in old age, *c.* 1925, signed E[dward] J[ames] Rogers, (1872–1938) (author's collection). *Back jacket*: (top) 'Toilers of the Sea', oil on canvas (*courtesy John O'Shea*); (bottom, l–r): photograph of the artist in academic robes from an advertising booklet among his papers; paper label of Williams & Son (courtesy Darren Stone); postcard showing the shopfront of Williams & Son, Dame Street (*courtesy Darren Stone*); taxidermy specimen from the Williams studio (Golden Eagle), 1887 (*courtesy of The National Museum of Ireland*). *Back flap*: St Patrick's Close (courtesy of Whyte's Fine Art).

CONTENTS

ACKNOWLEDGEMENTS

A LEXANDER WILLIAMS' LIFE was one of many parts, interwoven of course, but for the benefit of the reader and indeed myself, his several careers, so far as possible, are dealt with in separate sections in the book. Beginning with Williams' singing career, I am very grateful to Paul Arbuthnot, himself a cathedral alto, for answering my many queries on choral singing in the nineteenth century and for providing me with a copy of his M. Litt thesis on the Vicars choral of the Dublin cathedrals.

The legacy of the taxidermy studio, founded by Alexander and his brother Edward, among public collections, is to be found primarily in the Natural History Museum in Dublin and also the Ulster Museum in Belfast. At both institutions I received the most generous help. Dr Nigel Monaghan, Curator of the natural history collection in Dublin, gave me access to the museum's records and suggested to me many useful avenues for exploration concerning taxidermy in general and the Williams' business in particular. At the Ulster Museum, Angela Ross, Vertebrate Curator, took time out to show me the work of both Williams and the Sheals brothers, pointing out in the process the finer details of both. Labhras Joye of the Art and Industrial Division at Collins Barracks, National Museum, demonstrated the technicalities of nineteenth-century firearms that Williams refers to in his writings. Catherine de Courcy, historian of Dublin Zoo, illuminated for me the important connection between the Zoo and the Williams family.

Distinct from taxidermy was Williams' life-long interest in birdwatching and ornithology. To Angela Ross and the Trustees of the Ulster Museum, I am indebted for making available to me two ornithological diaries of Alexander Williams. I greatly valued the help of expert ornithologists in BirdWatch Ireland, in particular Niall Hatch who was unstinting in answering my many queries on bird life in Ireland and who kindly reviewed some of the artist's work; also Brian Caffrey, Irish Atlas Project Co-ordinator; Paul Milne, Secretary of the Irish Rare Birds Committee; and Tim Gordon, for his knowledge of corncrakes.

Painting was, of course, Alexander Williams' primary career and I am enormously grateful to Dr Brendan Rooney, Curator of Irish Art at the National Gallery of Ireland, for looking at part of the script in progress and for making many useful suggestions. Also at the National Gallery Niamh MacNally of the prints department not only showed me work by the artist held by gallery, but generously took the time and trouble to source other visual material for me.

At the Dublin City Gallery, the Hugh Lane, I am very grateful too to Jessica O'Donnell for making available to me correspondence relating to the artist and his large watercolour of Greenwich.

Achill was an abiding centre for the artist's activities through the greater part of his life. On the island itself, local historian and long-time family friend, John O'Shea of Dooagh, was a major source of help and encouragement on this project from the start. A long-time admirer of the artist, he generously put his own extensive collection of papers and paintings at my disposal, kept up a flurry of correspondence and opened up for me a number of lines of research which proved invaluable. At the artist's home, Bleanaskill Lodge (www.achill-art-garden.com), Doutsje Nauta and Willem van Goor proved to be delightful hosts and provided me with much useful information, as did Sheila McGinty. To Elizabeth Morgan JP (née Scanlon), who was born on Achill and brought up at Bleanaskill Lodge, I am indebted for sharing her and her family's memories of their time there. At Keel, Brian Sheridan, great nephew of John Sheridan of the Slievemore Hotel, Dugort, kindly provided me with useful background information.

The Dublin Sketching Club, now the Dublin Painting & Sketching Club, of which Williams was a founder member, has fortunately preserved important archive material and I am most grateful to the Club and the present secretary, Patricia McGloughlin, for permission to examine the collection in the National Library of Ireland and for kindly providing me with much additional information. To Fred Pfeiffer I am indebted for information on George Prescott, and his boat *Iris*, which forms a part of the early history of the Sketching Club.

Williams spent much time painting around the coasts of Ireland and I depended greatly on the knowledge of marine historian Cormac Lowth, who provided me with much information on the history and lore of Irish ships and shipping. Conor McHale very generously undertook genealogical and related research on my behalf; and Kieran McGovern kindly made available to me his research on Williams' friend, Charles J. Patten. Martin Dwan too helped on the project in a variety of ways, and it was in conversation with him that the title for the book emerged. Warm thanks are due to Patricia Butler who kindly took time out from her own book on the history of the Water Colour Society of Ireland to answer many queries on both the artist and on Irish art history.

(In passing I would like to acknowledge the kindness of photographer Mark Boland of Silver Image Photography who came to my house on an errand for the Society and spent more time sharing his knowledge of photography with me.)

The largest collection of Williams' paintings on public view is to be seen at the Lake Hotel, Killarney, where the artist often stayed. They would have remained out of reach, high on the walls of the hotel, had not proprietor Niall Huggard kindly arranged to have the pictures taken down to facilitate photographing them.

I much appreciated the unfailing help of staff at the libraries I used. I should particularly like to mention Liz Gleeson and Andrew Isley, Dr Charles Benson and Helen Beaney of the library of Trinity College, Dublin. To the staff of the National Library of Ireland I am indebted, especially to Avice-Clare McGovern. (The NLI, incidentally, has sketches by the artist, as does the Crawford Gallery in Cork). Gearoid O'Brien of the Athlone Public Library and Mary Furlong of the Representative Church Body Library, Braemor Park, greatly facilitated my research. My thanks too to the staff of the New York Public Library. With only half a day to spare I was astonished and grateful to find the speed at which the library could expedite order slips. Thanks are due to Jason D. Stratman, archivist at the Missouri History Museum for material on the St Louis World Exhibition; and to the Minnesota Historical Society. Garry Haines of the Whitechapel Gallery, London, kindly made available material relating to the Irish Exhibition of 1913.

I was generously supplied with material from the archives of Dublin fine art houses. David Britton of Adam's Fine Art with great kindness made available to me his own personal and extensive collection of Williams' sketches; and Kieran O'Boyle with much patience delved back into the records at Adams for me. Likewise I am most grateful to John de Vere White and Rory Guthrie of de Veres Fine Art; and to Sir Robert Goff of the Cynthia O'Connor Gallery who kindly gave me access to the gallery's records on the artist. It is with pleasure that I express my gratitude to James and Thérèse Gorry, who in addition to restoring several of Williams' paintings for me, gave me access to their library of books and catalogues and generously provided me with images of 'Old Dublin'.

To Koraley Northen I owe a debt of thanks in painstakingly working with Photoshop on quite a number of images. It was to Koraley too that I turned to have the considerable number of catalogues sorted and edited. Similarly, I offer my sincere thanks to Susan Maxwell, who checked and rechecked the financial figures in the appendices, dealing heroically with the artist's often haphazard bookkeeping, and who patiently assisted me on a number of photographic trips.

I should also like to acknowledge the help provided by: the Duke of Abercorn KG; the Marquess of Aberdeen; the Earl Annesley; the Lady Ashtown; Elizabeth Augereau; John Beaumont; Anthony Berry; Dr Albert Bradshaw; Frank Brannigan; Laura Summerton of Bridgeman Art; Norah Castle; Finbarr Connolly; Noel O'Hara of the Central Statistics Office; Colette Ding; Stuart Kinsella, Christchurch Cathedral; Jill Cerasi of Christie's Fine Art, London, and Bernard Williams, Christie's, Edinburgh;

Professor Richard Clarke; Sean Collins; Bernard Comie; Patrick Corkey; Professor Anne Crookshank; Father Patrick Crowe SJ; Deirdre Daly; Gabrielle de Freitas; Pat and Marita Doherty; Captain Martin Donnelly; the Earl of Drogheda; the late Jim Garry, historian of Drogheda; Dr Terence Grimes; Leo Oosterweghel, Director Dublin Zoo; Brendan Delaney, Archive & Heritage Manager, ESB; Mark Fennell; Andrew D. Watt of Finnegan Menton; Michael O'Keeffe, manager Ferrycarrig Hotel; Andrew Glenn-Cragie; the Knight of Glin; Austin Greene; Allyson Lee, Grogan & Co.; Barry Healy-Doyle; Rowena Fisher; Paul Gilmore; the Rev. Ruth Griffiths, Inverchaolain Church; Robert Jennings; Barry Lacey, Irish Labour History Society; Ann Kennedy, Gerry Kennedy; Dr Paddy Kineen; Dr Gabrielle Langdon; Dr Martyn Linnie; John Logan; Professor David McConnell; Niall McEvoy; Dr P. A. Morris; the Marquess of Londonderry; Mary Jacinta Lynch; Donal MacNally; Maeve Madden; Donal O'Brien; Daphne Pfeiffer; Rev. Dr Michael Piret, Dean of Divinity, Magdalen College; Dr Robin Darwell-Smith, Archivist Magdalen College; Denis Magee; Standish Mason; Brendan Matthews; Shân McAnena, Curator of Art, Queen's University, Belfast; John McCullen, *Drogheda Independent*; Pamela McDonough; the late Vi McDowell; James McGuire, editor *Dictionary of Irish Biography*; Sean McManmon; Lindy Meyer; Padraic Moore; Elizabeth Butler, archivist Muckross House; Sandra Morgan, St Patrick's Choir School; John Mulcahy, *Irish Arts Review*; Padraic Conneely MIHI, National Yacht Club; Jack Nolan; John Nolan; Phil Nolan; Paula Norris; Maeve O'Connell; Eddie O'Connor; the Lord O'Neill; Rita O'Regan; Tom and Rosemary O'Reilly; June Peard; the Earl of Portarlington; Professor Frank Geary; Paddy Quill; Christopher Ashe, Wellesley Ashe Gallery; Gerard Whelan, Librarian RDS; Calvo Ranedo and Marianne Ranedo-Klein; Charles Reede; Gerald and Veronica Roden; Judith and Peter Rowe; Pat Ruane; Irene Scanlon; Anne Lyons, Smurfit Kappa Group; Dr Michael Smurfit; the late Dr Philip Smyly; Darren Stone; Anne Dillon, Sotheby's Dublin; the Dean and Chapter St Patrick's Cathedral and administrator Gavin Woods; Hilary Stevenson; Top Hat Taxidermy; John Tierney; Norman Ludgate of Treasure Chest Antiques; the Rt Hon. Roderick Trench; Dr Robert Trys-Jones, the Natural History Museum at Tring; Patricia de Montfort, Department of History of Art, University of Glasgow; Aubrey Fennell, Tree Register of Ireland; Gerry Kelly, Valuation Office; John Ward; the Marquis of Waterford; Professor Gail Gráinne Whitchurch; Sarah Gates and Adelle Hughes of Whyte's Fine Art; Dr Bryan Wilkinson; Dr Peter Wilson, and the Marquess of Zetland.

Permission to quote from the following publications is gratefully acknowledged: Academic Press for *The Bird Collectors* by Barbara and Richard Mearns; Clogher Historical Society for *History of Monaghan for Two Hundred Years, 1650–1860* by Denis Carolan Rushe; Institute of Professional Auctioneers and Valuers for *Anatomy of an Irish Country House and Garden c.1730–2004. The Altamont Estate Co. Carlow* by Ann O'Dea; Smurfit Communications for Smurfit Art Collection 2001, with introduction by Aidan Dunne, and Yale University Press for *Paul Henry with a catalogue of the Paintings, Drawings, Illustrations* by S. B. Kennedy.

Try as I might there were a number of pictures I could not find. Top of the list was the oil of Queen Victoria at Kingstown Harbour, 1900. It was last sold at Adam's in 1992 but I could not trace it further. Nor did a single picture of the gardens at Altamont, County Carlow, which the artist exhibited in 1892, turn up. Colm MacElwee very kindly made a search through the house for me but without success. Somewhere there are likely be studies of fish and birds, of plants, even perhaps of butterflies, work on porcelain, and perhaps oil or watercolours of street scenes in the provinces as well as old Dublin studies. It was disappointing not to have been able to identify with certainty the panoramic backdrop of any taxidermy case as indisputably by Alexander Williams. Paintings apart, it is possible that further memorabilia may yet be found in private hands. There is reason to believe that there were other diaries and that just possibly the records of Williams & Son survive somewhere. I should be most interested to hear from anyone who knows of any such material.

In conclusion I wish to thank my sister, Audrey Baker, for reading the manuscript in progress and providing useful criticism. Sadly, not one of the four members of the Williams family, whom I knew and who knew the artist, is still alive. It was Alice, the artist's daughter who had the foresight to preserve her father's papers. On her death, they went to her first cousin, Robert (Bob) Williams, who so often referred to Alexander that it almost seemed his uncle remained a presence to him. Perhaps of the three children of Alexander's brother, Willie, he most closely resembled the artist by temperament through his exuberance and sheer love of life, which was frequently remarked upon by those who knew him. Teddy Williams as a leading taxidermist and museum painter had a career that came closest to that of his uncle. The artist's niece, Florence Ledbetter (née Williams), my mother, the third sibling, knew the artist less well than her two older brothers, but all provided me with information for which I am grateful.

I also wish to acknowledge the painstaking work of editor Aonghus Meaney and designer Alison Burns; and to express my gratitude to the staff of The Collins Press for their unfailing help.

Gordon T. Ledbetter
Dublin 2010

www.privilegeandpoverty.com
www.alexanderwilliamsrha.com

PART I

BEGINNINGS

Watercolour over pencil. The village of Dugort, Achill Island, with St Thomas' Church in the foreground, and Slievemore rising behind. Dugort was established as a mission settlement in the 1830s and most of the buildings seen here still exist. The Slievemore Hotel (now an apartment complex) is the main building in the centre. Signed. Late nineteenth century. 23¼ x 17¾ in. (59 x 45 cm). The picture was featured in an edition of the *Dictionary of British Water Colour Artists* up to 1920 (Vol. III) by H. L. Mallalieu.

Oil on board sketch. Signed. 'Minaun Cliffs from Keel Strand' (Achill) written on back. 7 x 13¾ in. (8 x 35 cm). Note the sheaves of oats made up as stooks in the foreground, with lazy beds, used since time immemorial, beside them.

Watercolour over pencil of Monkstown, County Dublin (detail), looking northwards, showing the Martello tower at Seapoint. A large part of the artist's output was of the Dublin coast, both north and south, and Martello towers were often featured in his coastal sketches and pictures (see also p. 269). Signed. 12½ x 25½ in. (32 x 65 cm).

CHAPTER
1

Origins

Watercolour of family crest from one of the artist's sketch books.

An abiding impression of Victorians is of their sheer industriousness. In that respect, and in others, Alexander Williams and his first cousin Sir William Whitla seem to fit the mould perfectly. Sir William, in writing his best-selling medical books, is reputed to have worked eighteen-hour days, not to mention the effort he put into his medical practice and sundry other activities, religious and political. Alexander Williams, at one period of his life, was a hatter, taxidermist and singer, and still managed to indulge his abiding passion – painting. Add teaching and he may be said to have had five careers. He had tenacity and staying power too, working right to the end of a long life. He held popular solo exhibitions nearly every year during his prime, and sometimes more than one in a year. No other painter has matched his record of exhibiting at the Royal Hibernian Academy (RHA) for *sixty-one continuous years*. He was nothing if not prodigious; good for his bank balance perhaps, but not always good for the work he produced, which could be uneven. Astonished at first, the press grew used to the size of his exhibitions. In his day his standing was high, the press not only generally lauding his one-man shows – which became a regular and eagerly anticipated Dublin social fixture – but recognising him as the artist who more than any other opened up the west of Ireland, and most especially Achill Island, to a wider and increasingly appreciative public. As such, his work has a historical niche, but one that became quickly overshadowed, indeed forgotten, as the next generation of Irish artists emerged, whose aspirations for a truly Irish, nationalist or Celtic identity led to the common perception that the authentic painting of the 'real Ireland', much of it focused on the west of Ireland, arrived only with the twentieth century. A revision of his reputation is overdue.

Williams was an inveterate hoarder and collector. Over a lifetime he kept all sorts of material relating to his painting career, including printed catalogues of his solo exhibitions, a number of which have fancy covers and illustrations, innovations at the time. He also kept handwritten versions of his catalogues, which show not only the prices he was charging but the names and addresses of the buyers written alongside the number and title of the pictures. Evidently the handwritten catalogue was laid open on a table in the exhibition room available for those who wished to mark their purchase. The visitors' books of his first solo exhibitions have survived, and tell much about the sort of people who turned up for his shows. Remarkably, the financial accounts of many of his exhibitions have survived, and even accounts of his yearly earnings. Williams filled notebooks with copious and carefully pasted news cuttings – reviews mainly, but leavened with bits of tittle-tattle from the social columns. He kept innumerable letters, both business and personal, bread-and-butter sales for the most part but with here and there a comment, a little nugget among the bland business that provides a window on how things were done in those days. Countless letters are preserved from Dublin Castle informing the artist, waiting no doubt with bated breath, of when the Lord Lieutenant or his wife, or both, were intending to put in an appearance at his exhibition. Better still were the letters from the Castle that accompanied the cheques for pictures his lord or ladyship and their circle had bought. Williams also wrote memoirs and kept volumes of diaries.

In all the surviving papers of the artist, preserved by his family for over a century, is a rare cache – possibly the largest of its kind – as much a record of Ireland in the late nineteenth century as it is of Williams himself.

Painting was the most central and enduring feature of his life, but not the whole of it. Williams was also an expert ornithologist and taxidermist, and his house, in true Victorian fashion, was filled with mounted taxidermy specimens and skins, birds of all kinds. He wrote copiously on bird life, both privately and publicly. He forsook taxidermy, however, to make a living from singing while he established himself as a painter.

Williams had an evident taste for writing. In manuscript he left two volumes of memoirs and also kept many diaries and journals, sometimes jotting day-by-day notes about brief excursions in whatever sketchbook he had to hand. In what he called his 'Chronicles & Memoirs' he kept year-by-year notes of what he was doing and where he travelled, a record that he maintained fairly steadily up to the 1920s. The last entry of all was in 1930 when he noted, in a spidery and uncertain hand, his eighty-fourth birthday. His earliest signature is to be found on a watercolour from 1866, when he was twenty. A year later he started what he called his 'Ornithological Notes & Shooting Diary, 1867' in a distinctive and fine copperplate hand. His Achill diary, a rare day-to-day account of life on the island before the First World War, he wrote up in a separate volume, as he did extensive ornithological diaries.

Williams was neither a cerebral writer nor an introspective one. The diaries were not an outlet for angst, still less for scandal; bereavements he noted with the briefest or no comment. There was unquestionably a melancholic side to his nature which is hardly apparent among his writings but marked in his paintings. He was more outward than inward looking. The memoirist Diana Athill once observed that 'One of the things that make me love writing or looking at pictures is that you become unconscious of yourself. Anything absorbing makes you become not "I" but "eye" – you escape the ego.'[1] This approach applies precisely to Williams. It was the world around him that caught his attention much more than himself.

Against the odds his papers survived. On his death they passed to his only surviving child, Alice, who, penniless and without a home of her own in the latter part of her life, and with no obvious skills or qualifications, took on housekeeping duties for elderly and retired clergy and perhaps others. Until well into middle age she had lived at home with her parents, until their deaths in the 1930s. It is hard to know how happy she was or if she was lonely during her later years. Her goddaughter[2] recalled visiting, as a child, the home of one such elderly clergyman. She remembered entering a dark, gloomy house that she found 'spooky'. This particular clergyman, perhaps as mad as he was evidently eccentric, apparently enjoyed mimicking the sounds of a hen triumphantly laying an egg while sitting on the lavatory. (This party piece, however, was not performed during the visit of the goddaughter.) When one job ended Alice would valiantly pack up her worldly goods, including her father's memorabilia, and move on. No doubt some of the material got jettisoned along the way; she may have lent diaries and sketchbooks, and perhaps, more may yet turn up in private hands. A large number of sketchbooks which went for auction some years ago in Northern Ireland, and which were subsequently broken up for the purpose of framing and selling the sketches individually, may have originally belonged to Alice. In total she held on to thirty-five volumes of papers, including her father's very first Achill sketchbook and another of Donegal, and pictures besides. It is a tribute to Alice Williams that through a disjointed life she managed to preserve so much.

Certainly the papers were worth preserving. There is material here about Victorian Ireland that is to be found nowhere else. The breadth of Williams' life was unusual; the papers illuminate that diversity. *En passant* his writing evokes a world that was often unfeeling in regard to the animal kingdom and indeed to humanity in general. His papers take us into the world of musical Dublin and elsewhere, and relate what it was to make one's way as a singer. Most interesting of all he has left a record, in rare detail, of what it was to make one's way as a painter in Victorian Ireland. Diverse as his activities were, the papers show how close-knit and overlapping was the Dublin society that took an interest in these things.

Remarkably for a man who made such efforts to cultivate titled patronage and was enduringly successful in doing so, he was equally at home physically working with Achill Islanders. At a time when class was so rigidly defined, the fact that he so insouciantly spanned the divide was more remarkable then than it might seem now. He had a string of titled patrons and constantly sought Castle patronage. Yet when it came to it, he preferred to stay put on Achill than accept an invitation to Dublin Castle, even when it was a royal visit that was on offer: 'Just now the exquisite delights of my "Island Home" compensate me for my absence from Dublin and I simply revel in it although I feel I ought to be in town and attend the King's Levee.'[3]

The painter, who was to sign himself Alexander, Alex, sometimes Alec and on rare occasions A. Williams, was born, unintentionally, in the house of his uncle Robert Whitla. In the spring of 1846 Alice Williams went from her house in Drogheda to visit her sister-in-law, Anne Whitla, who was living in the Diamond, Monaghan town. Both women were heavily pregnant and went into labour almost simultaneously. Each produced a baby boy within a few minutes of each other, but separated by a day; Williams arrived just before midnight on 21 April, while his cousin Robert Jones Whitla made his appearance early on the morning of 22 April. In time-honoured fashion, the two babes were placed on plush cushions to be admired by one and all, and when the babes were removed, so family legend had it, each mother took up the wrong baby. An amusing tale but no more than that. There were two girls as well, bringing the Williams' siblings to the unexceptional number of five, but all survived into adulthood and indeed into old age. Anne Whitla produced a family of twelve, William being her seventh child, but few were long lived. Had Alexander really been swapped, then we may believe it was he, rather than Robert Whitla, who emigrated to Canada and got a commission as a major in the Canadian Rifles. Not a few of the family down the generations emigrated to North

America. Williams' own uncle, John Williams, with his son, John Alexander, fetched up at Cincinnati but with less success than Robert Whitla. In an ill-judged baptism requiring total immersion in the Ohio River, first the father was swept away, then his son in attempting to save him. Many of the Williams clan prospered in America. But the line of the family through the painter went no further than the generation after him. Neither of his two children had issue themselves.

The first immigrant in the line of this particular family of Williams settled just three and a half miles outside Monaghan town where Alex Williams was born, but nearly 200 years earlier. Taking the third-class road east out of the town, one is quickly enveloped in deep and isolated countryside even before reaching the picturesque spot where the little Ballyclareen bridge crosses the River Cor. Just beyond the bridge, to the left as the ground rises, it is easy to miss a narrow boreen as thickly lined now with thorn trees as it has probably been for centuries. All around the land undulates, but looking diagonally to the right it is easy to pick out a prominent hill about half a mile distant. At the top of that hill once stood The Groves, while a short distance up the boreen was Lappan; The Groves and Lappan, within sight of each other across the valley, were probably once a single estate. The Groves is believed to have been the older house and so the first homestead of the immigrant Williams family.

Such rural peace is misleading in relation to the arrival of the first of the family, John Williams, in about 1649. His trade was innocuous enough; living near Neath, in Glamorganshire, he was a feltmaker, a hatter, a trade he would ply in Ireland once he was settled. What brought him to Ireland was not his trade but his support for Oliver Cromwell, as a result of which he was rewarded with The Groves and Lappan estate.

Cromwell arrived in Ireland to take over the parliamentary forces in August 1649 and with a single-mindedness that was his hallmark routed most of the rebel and royalist forces, leaving others to deal with residual pockets of resistance and mop up the ensuing political and social mess. His taking of Drogheda and Wexford, key towns for the loyalists among other resisting strongholds, where every inhabitant was put to the sword, are remembered yet.

Cromwell still remains a figure that can give rise to strong feelings. In the Dáil, a deputy, if driven to it, may still occasionally be heard to hurl the accusation of 'Cromwellianism' across the floor at any policy regarded as intolerably harsh or authoritarian. More generally, undercurrents of an unspoken and residual sense of grievance at what had taken place all those years ago are present even still in the Irish psyche and, by the same token, a distaste towards those perceived to have benefited, even at a remove, from Cromwell. The prevailing view of Cromwell as a figure of unparalleled savagery has, predictably, a counterpart among revisionists who argue that he was a man of his times, if more able and effective than most; the times were harsh and brutality was meted out by whoever had the means to do so. The Irish were unfortunate to be at the sharp end of things.

Whatever view one may take of the man, the consequences of Cromwell's Irish policy are hardly in dispute. It caused the single greatest dislocation of Irish society up to and including the Great Famine of the 1840s. The Protestant faith became the Established Church while Roman Catholics were banned from holding land or political office. The administration of Ireland was now securely held in Protestant hands and what came to be called the Ascendancy remained in the ascendant, the privileged minority ruling class, for generations to come. Contrary to what is sometimes thought, it was the rebel and royalist forces who were targeted for land confiscation, not the populace at large. Those who were dispossessed were deported to the West Indies and sold into slavery or were forced to cross the Shannon into Connaught and make the best they could of the poor soil in the west. Cromwellian settlements took their place.

By this means were the campaign soldiers and supporters rewarded. Parliament had had insufficient funds from taxation alone to meet the costs of the campaigns, so money was raised by subscription. Those who subscribed were known as 'the Adventurers'. This was where John Williams enters the story. He became one of the Adventurers, contributing £50 which suggests he was an unusually well-to-do maker of hats. What he was like as a soldier, indeed whether he ever saw active service, goes unrecorded but he held the rank of Lieutenant and Commissary in Cromwell's army and is later mentioned as serving as a soldier of the Commonwealth in County Louth. He was a late subscriber to the cause, 919th on the list of Adventurers. This leaves open the question as to whether Williams was only prepared to commit his money after Cromwell had taken control of the campaign. Among later members of the Williams family, there was speculation, amounting even to belief, that John Williams was actually a relative of Oliver Cromwell. The reason for this belief is tenuous, based on the little-known fact that Cromwell's family name was originally Williams. The family took a new name, a common enough occurence in Wales at the time, from their patron, no less a figure than Thomas Cromwell (c.1485–1540), a court favourite, who oversaw the destruction of the monasteries for his sovereign Henry VIII, before falling out of favour and losing his head.

That John Williams was a late subscriber on its own says very little and much cannot be hung on it. Still, the notion that the Williamses were related to Cromwell stuck around for several generations. Cromwell would have been regarded as a Puritan hero to earlier generations, a defender of the truth faith, a figure with which to identify. It is said Cromwell's name once appeared on family trees alongside John Williams, although in what relationship is not known; and none of these family trees is known to have survived. Tradition does often contain the truth. On the other hand, family trees sometimes preferred the conceits of good breeding and the right connections to lowly truth. There is no hard evidence to resolve the matter one way or another and it has to be said that Williams is an exceedingly common name in Wales.

By a law enacted on 1 January 1652 it was decreed that the land promised to the Adventurers since 1642, now comprising about 1 million hectares, should be drawn by lots. This process took place in the summer of the following year and the estate comprising the lower Groves and Lappan in County Monaghan thus came into the possession of John Williams. It is unlikely that the unfortunates removed by force or who departed under the press of circumstances would have willingly left a house and home intact for a settler to inhabit. Either John Williams built The Groves from scratch or rebuilt what the natives had torn down or torched.

In the nearby Tyholland churchyard was found the grave of another John Williams, most likely the settler's son, but conceivably his grandson, the inscription stating that he had been born at The Groves and died aged seventy on 14 February 1723, which meant he had been born on the property in the year in which the lots were drawn, 1653. He is reputed to have taken part in the Siege of Derry in 1688–9. 'On the Protestant side of course,' commented John Fletcher Williams who wrote up a family history, ignoring or not knowing that just three generations down the line another family member took the opposite side. This was Mathew Williams (b. 1773), great uncle of the painter, who aligned himself with the United Irishmen of 1798, albeit not very reliably. Despite being the chosen leader for the rebellion among the men of Tyholland and the old town of Castlemaine, at the appointed hour Mathew failed to show up.

How quickly do planters establish themselves! With the exceptions of the Siege of Derry on the one hand and the botched efforts of the United Irishmen in Monaghan on the other, the Williams family seem to have led a peaceful existence. The two John Williams, father and son, established the pattern: farming the land and plying their trade of making hats. In the absence of shops they went to market, in Monaghan town no doubt, and to big annual fairs such as the one at Ballinasloe, County Galway. So the family continued their trade, passing down secrets of hat-making developed and known only to themselves, so it was said, living at The Groves and Lappan through six or seven generations, until well into the nineteenth century.

But as of the millennium a visit to the area revealed that nothing was left of The Groves: not a single stone, not a hint of a farmyard. It is all meadow now. The only evidence left of The Groves and the generations raised there is a telltale depression of a short entrance drive from the road to where the house must have stood.

Up the boreen, however, are still the remains of the Lappan house. Among scrub and

twisted trees, the doorway remains, a window and part of another, a couple of crumbling stone walls, just enough to identify it from a floor plan fortuitously made before the house fell into ruin.

In 1888 an American member of the family, John Fletcher Williams, on a European tour, decided to visit the haunts of his forefathers. The following year he wrote up the history and genealogy of the family and published privately 150 copies of a little book of his researches. He had the advantage of having access to anecdotal memoirs, written by a Samuel Williams,[4] much of which he was able to confirm.

Carte-de-visite of John Fletcher Williams (1834–1895).

Fletcher Williams' sketch of
The Groves

On arrival in Dublin on 13 September Fletcher Williams teamed up with William Williams, father of the painter, and headed straight for The Groves. To his delight he was greeted by the owner, a Mr Samuel Gilliland, who immediately 'asked us if we were Williamses. On replying "yes", he said he had suspected it from our personal appearance, and that the idea came to him who we were, and our object, when he saw our car approaching the old place.' But Fletcher Williams' delight in meeting the farmer was tempered when he saw the house: 'As I dismounted from the car, at the site of the old house, on the summit of the eminence, a painful feeling came over me, as I saw its ruinous condition.'[5]

Still, what was no longer visible the farmer was able to recall and Fletcher Williams provided this description of The Groves:

I drew a plan of the house, which he pronounced correct. I also made a pencil sketch of the ruins, which is herein copied by the photo engraving process. The house was probably 40 feet front, and 24 deep. It was well and thoroughly built of hewn stone, and had been stuccoed both outside and inside. It was 1½ stories high, and had (as do all the houses in the region) a thatched roof. Mr Gilliland says it was a well finished and comfortable residence and looked very neat on the outside. To the north of the main house was an addition quite spacious in size, one story in height, which, I have no doubt, was used for the hat shop. Still north of this, down the slope a little and detached from the house, was a large barn, built of stone, which is still standing in good condition. Wm. Williams asserts that his grandfather, Mathew Williams, built this. The second floor of this barn, when not occupied by grain, or other products, was used for a ball room, and was very suitable for that purpose. Here the country beaux and belles used to tread the rustic dances, set in motion by some rural fiddlers, and the rafters of the old structure have doubtless resounded many a time with the musical laughter of the buxom Irish lasses, and their brawny laddies.[6]

Cromwell would hardly have approved of such carryings-on, no matter how innocent.

Fletcher Williams and his cousin had better luck when they turned their attentions to Lappan as it was still inhabited. On arrival, 'Mr James Hughes, the present tenant of the farm, advanced to meet us. He had already suspected who we were and our purpose, and when we alighted remarked, "I think your names are Williams?"' Visitors to that lonely spot must have been few and far between. 'It was a neat looking residence outwardly,' Fletcher Williams recalled, 'but showed marks of antiquity,' by which he meant it was near dereliction. This was a solemn moment for Fletcher Williams:

> I entered this venerable house of our ancestors through the low doorway, with feelings such as became the occasion, and sat down in the main family room. Inside it was poorly lighted, and the rafters and ceiling above were absolutely ebonized by the smoke from the fireplace where peat had been burned for 150 years, and by lamp smoke, etc. A woman was leaning over the fire-place, cooking, probably – a woman with some traces of intelligence and beauty, but showing the marks of hard work and hopeless poverty. There was no wooden floor in the entire house, and perhaps there never had been one. The floor was paved with stone and brick, and it appeared very old and much worn. It was undoubtedly the one which was put down when the house was built. An old staircase, not enclosed, ran from the rear of the room, to the attic above. It looked more ancient than anything else; the oaken planks seemed worn hollow by the footsteps of a century and a half. The walls were roughly plastered, and had been white once.[7]

It is evident that the Williamses never rose to the rank of Anglo-Irish grandees. The Groves and Lappan were a far cry from the 'Big House' beloved of Irish novelists. As John Fletcher pointed out, the two houses were typical of farmsteads around about. We know from the will of John Williams (c. 1708–95),[8] written the year he died, that he held land distinct from his own farm, which was occupied by tenants. This put him above the small farmer subsisting on his own smallholding but well below fulfilling the common notion of the Anglo-Irish, being of independent means with a household of servants, and riding to hounds. The will gives a good idea of John Williams' worldly goods. In addition to the farm, farmhouse and cow house, he leaves to his wife 'two cows and my mare, my chest of drawers, my bed and bed clothes, and my kitchen furniture'. He also left his wife 'all the turf bog I now possess'. His desk, perhaps an unusual item to be found in such a farmhouse at the time, he left to his son Mathew.

Unlike the Normans who came, saw and having conquered, then intermarried with the native population and as such merged with it, the settlers for generations remained a people apart. They bred among themselves; Protestants they were and Protestants they remained. John Fletcher Williams remarked on it: 'During their residence in Ireland of about a century (or more in some lines), the Williamses do not seem to have intermarried with the native race, at all. This may have been largely owing to differences in religion, nationality, or social position.' He is right of course in what he says, so far as it goes, but he is rather missing the point. Where religion, nationality and social identity represent one side of a dividing line, those who hold them important generally have underlying economic reasons for doing so.

With remarkable Victorian certitude, not to say complacency, John Fletcher took the opportunity of drawing attention to the virtuousness of his Irish cousins. 'It is gratifying to know,' he wrote, 'that our ancestors were devout and pious people. The influence of heredity is very powerful. "Bon sang ne peut mentir." Good progenitors generally have good descendants, and their best traits are thus perpetuated from generation to generation. All the Williamses that I have ever heard of are religious people, many of them intensely so. I do not believe that there is a skeptic or atheist in the entire sept, or ever was.'[9]

Maybe so or maybe not, but this line of Williamses was no more immune to dysfunction than any other family. Moving down the line to Mathew (father of the rebel Mathew), he and his eldest son, Alexander, had a serious falling out, leading to Alexander turning his back on The Groves forever:

> Pausing only after he left the old house, in the beautiful alley lined with hawthorns, and looking around, from that lovely eminence, over the fertile paternal acres which had slipped from his grasp, the natural and excusable feelings of his heart overcame him, and he raised his hand, exclaiming, 'the curse of God be upon this house.'[10]

Make what one will of the curse, the remaining history of The Groves is a tragic one. It is at this point that Elizabeth, sister of Alexander (the painter's grandfather) and born about 1780, comes into the story. Disappointed in love, she was said to have drowned herself in the well adjacent to the house. Rumour quickly spread that the spirit of the unfortunate girl came back to haunt the place. This rather offended the religious orthodoxy of Fletcher Williams, who dismissed the ghost story, but he was well aware that: 'Among a people as superstitious as the rural population of Ireland was at that time, it was easy for any foolish story of anything supernatural to gain full credence.' The result was that when the family not long after vacated The Groves it was impossible to find another tenant for it and the house fell into ruin.

Meanwhile, Alexander, the wronged or errant son, had gone to Dublin, taking with him his hat-making skills if nothing else. These he plied, as did his son William who became the father of Alexander, the subject of this book. In his turn, the young Alexander, long before he became a professional painter, would learn how to make hats just as his forebear John Williams from Glamorganshire did in what is thought to be an unbroken line of hatters. In 1845 William Williams had married Alice West from Drogheda, County Louth. He moved there, possibly because she came into property or had family commitments. At any rate William established a hat-making business in his wife's town rather than his own. So it was that Alexander the painter was to spend his first fifteen years in Drogheda.

CHAPTER
2

A Drogheda Boyhood

Baltragh on the River Boyne, County Louth. Oil on paper, signed. 4 x 16 in. (10 x 40.6 cm). Exhibited at The Modern Gallery, London, 1906. The artist did a number of similarly elongated landscapes.

Williams described his boyhood in Drogheda as halcyon days. Here it was that sketching became an early preoccupation and he would take himself down the quays entranced by the busy river traffic on the Boyne. Just four miles upstream from the mouth of the river and the open sea, Drogheda did much trading with Liverpool. In 1852 the population of Drogheda was 16,000. The town is built on a hill overlooking the river, and is said to have more steps than any other town in Ireland. Its medieval layout remains; and Williams, were he to walk around the town today, would have no difficulty finding his way about the narrow streets, the little nooks and crannies and its hidden lanes and byways. In his day it was all cut limestone, giving the town a subdued and rather austere charm. On the outskirts of the town were terraces of cottages of thatch and whitewash. 'Dear quaint old Drogheda and its picturesque river Boyne,' Williams commented with evident affection in his memoirs, pondering the imprint of memories clustering

> . . . around its many historic landmarks. The Boyne obelisk, how proud and stately it used to look on its rocky pedestal before its solitary grandeur was destroyed by the building of the ugly wooden bridge so close to it. Was there no spot up or down the river where it could have been placed except alongside the famous old monument? Then the interesting boating trips one had along the river, till arriving at the crumbling old town one viewed its ancient blackened walls, gay with wallflowers all the year round, revealing glimpses of St Mary's Abbey and away beyond on the higher ground St Magdalen's Steeple, still bearing the marks of Cromwell's battering heavy shot . . . Then on under the old bridge close to the Bullring. The river walls here dank and brown and covered with green moss and the curious old quays crammed with collier brigs and schooners. Alas! How changed and gone nowadays.[1]

Of the great obelisk only the plinth now remains and the Bullring has long since been demolished. Today the buildings of glass and steel and painted concrete seem like intruders in the old city. Modernity has lifted some of the austerity but perhaps removed much of the town's charm in the process. If Williams found any irony in his family fetching up in Drogheda he made no mention of it. The family lived over their shop, which was situated at the junction of St Peter's Street and Lawrence Street, in the town centre, opposite the Tholsel. By this stage the Williamses were no longer farmers, still less landowners. They could fairly be described as petite bourgeoisie: having a shop and being an employer put William Williams a step above being merely a tradesman. Hardly a family of influence, then. Still, being Protestant at any level in the pecking order of things counted for something; it could open doors and facilitate networking. The Williamses were Methodists at this stage, while the Whitlas were Presbyterians. Both families had ardent religious members. William Williams was a Methodist lay preacher. The artist's first cousin, Sir William Whitla (1851–1933), was an eminent physician and professor of medicine (the Whitla Hall at Queen's University Belfast is named after him).

Timbered medieval bathe house at the corner of Shop Street and Laurence Street, Drogheda, demolished 1825. Pencil copy by the artist, probably based on an original by Robert Armstrong.

Early in his life he became an evangelical Methodist, preached in church and in retirement occupied himself with publishing a commentary on Sir Isaac Newton's 'Daniel and the Apocalypse', translating into English Newton's Latin for his own pleasure. Such high Victorian earnestness in the family Williams did not seem to find onerous. He remained a churchgoer all his life, often referred to doing so in his writings and clearly enjoyed both church music and ritual. He was easy-going too and far removed from the unbending temperament required of the true fundamentalist. His faith, if he pondered it, was probably what it is for most people – an amalgam of personal and cultural identity as well as belief, custom, affection for what is familiar, and for its social and business ramifications. Both Alexander and his younger brother, Willie, would revert to being what the family had been earlier: members of the Church of Ireland. This had less to do with dogma than circumstances; marriage may have been one influence, as both their wives were members of the Established Church, and the fact that both men became cathedral choirmen in Dublin.

In passing, it is interesting to note that religion was not always the dividing line that one would expect it to have been. At one time the Williamses had the contract to supply top hats for Maynooth College, now a constituent college of the National University of Ireland, but originally set up by Grattan's parliament in 1795 'for the better education of persons professing the popish or Roman Catholic religion'.

Set in the centre of Drogheda, the hat shop was well placed to take advantage of passing trade and William Williams seems to have prospered, but he knew grim times and had stories to tell of the Great Famine raging at the time of Williams' birth, 'when it was a common sight to see the bakers' carts on their rounds protected from the violence of the starving people by guards of soldiers'. The Famine brought disease in its wake. There was a particularly virulent visitation of cholera that struck with force between April and October 1849, but William and his family survived the epidemic unscathed this time around. Epidemics were common, however, and it was an outbreak of a no less dreaded disease, typhus fever, that would carry away his wife, Alice, some years later.

Williams' schooling began at a now long-forgotten establishment, Miss Horan's School for infants, where he suffered an early childhood embarrassment that no child could experience today:

> One incident connected with my time there made an unpleasant impression on my childish mind. Our servant always escorted me to the school door but after a while I insisted on going by myself and it was when I was wending my way one morning that a dreadful accident befell me. My petticoats gave way and hung in folds around the tops of my little shoes. I can distinctly remember the feeling of deep humiliation that came over me at my utterly helpless condition, and I must have shown it for a kind woman took compassion on me, and taking me into the shelter of a doorway produced some pins and fixed me up so that I went on my way rejoicing.[2]

Apart from the old fashioned dress code, what a contrast to our own times that at such a tender age he would have been allowed to walk to school unaccompanied. Outgrowing his petticoats, he next went on to another long-vanished school, Leonard's in Paradise Row. It was hardly the kind of place to which any parent would want to send their child today:

> There I recollect one day we had a serious mutiny. Some of the scholars took exception to the severity of the punishment inflicted by the master on one boy as being excessive and they openly gave vent to their opinions. The master tried to chastise several and then the fun began. Some of the older scholars went for him, glad to get the opportunity of paying off old scores as he was detested by them. Uproar was the result, school slates, ink bottles, furniture and everything portable was hurled in the direction of the master's head and the school was 'shut down' early that day.[3]

An event of that kind today would probably get headlines in the national press if not questions raised in the Dáil. Whether it was the lack of discipline that prompted another move Williams does not say, but from Leonard's he was transferred to the Rev. Thomas Logan's Academy, a somewhat grand title for a school which consisted of no more than a schoolroom tucked beneath the Presbyterian church. It too is long gone. His time at Logan's Academy appears to have been uneventful.

His final move was to the famous Drogheda Grammar School, then located in the town. It was presided over by the formidable Rev. Dr E. H. Goslett, LLD, 'a gentlemen who was a strong believer in the benefits of corporeal [sic] punishment, and indeed his appearance gave one the impression that he was exceedingly well qualified to carry out his theories', and carry them out he did. Williams may have escaped the worst of his excesses, but not so a schoolmate by the name of Jack Ball, an evident hero of Williams'. 'Feared by all the masters but idolised by the boys, Jack was the terror of the school . . . he was daily the chief actor in some escapade. His muscles were like steel, his hands as hard as hickory, and in fact he seemed to be hickory all over for no punishment appeared to take any effect on him.' But Goslett certainly tried:

> The Rev. Doctor would cane him all round his study, lashing his hands, legs and back until he could hardly stand over him, and at the end of the castigation Jack would gather himself up, make a profound bow in his killingest style and calmly wish the doctor 'good morning'. The next time that he would be introduced for punishment the doctor would greet him coldly with 'Well Stick, what are you up for today?'[4]

Unfortunately, we are left with no idea as to what became of the fearless Jack Ball.

Goslett may have been a man to instil discipline but not necessarily a love of learning. 'I always detested both Latin and Greek,' Williams confessed, 'and my brother excelled in both, and they proved of the greatest use to him in after years, and the easy way in which he used to roll off the generic and specific terminology of birds and plants was ever my envy.' The comment suggests Edward was the more bookish of the two.

There was plenty that Williams remembered about Drogheda apart from his school experiences. We get a glimpse of how divisive religion could then be, with religious tension flaring up from time to time. His own father feared for his life during one of the elections in the 1850s when feelings ran high. An elderly shopkeeper, a Methodist with more courage than commonsense known as 'Holy Harry', paraded himself provocatively in his white choker, an article of dress associated with Methodism, and made no secret of voting for the Conservative candidate. Williams recalled how his behaviour had

> . . . incurred the bitter hostility of the mob . . . in broad daylight they assembled opposite his premises and whilst the police stood by drawn up under arms I saw every pane of glass in the front of his house flittered with stones to atoms. My father had great difficulty on that occasion to 'keep an even keel' . . . and on that particular night it was lights out early and a retirement was made to the basement, after securing all the window shutters above, and there we sat till early morning, listening to the wild shouts of the rival mobs, the dull sound of the crashing of whole windows of glass, the hoarse cheering, the heavy tramping of the soldiers and the police charging the mobs on each side of our house, followed by the clatter and jingling of the cavalry clearing the streets.[5]

The Williams' shop looked directly down Shop Street with a view towards the Bullring on the far side of the river. One form of entertainment had been to tether a bull which was then baited by dogs, one after another, until the tormented creature was exhausted – 'pinning the bull' it was called. Williams never saw the spectacle but his mother may well have done so. The sport was abolished by Act of Parliament in 1835. Thereafter bulls did rather better than common criminals – it would take another thirty-three years before hanging in a public place was prohibited by parliament. Sheep, horse and cattle stealing were still all capital offences in 1835, as was sacrilege. Whatever about abolishing bull baiting and curtailing the grounds for capital punishment, it was still an authoritarian society and by modern precepts a brutal one. It is hardly surprising therefore if schoolchildren were generally more violent and less sensitive to suffering than might be expected of children today. Williams tells a childhood tale which appears to have amused him to recall. Although it had a fortunate outcome, it is a repulsive story nevertheless:

> My brother and self had been reading a book describing the adventures of 'Trappers' amongst the North American Indians which we greatly admired, and we longed to have some experience in that particular line, and our wishes were gratified shortly after. We were staying at that time renting a cottage near the Tower [Mornington at the mouth of the Boyne] and had been hearing sad complaints from our mother and the servant of the depredations of some 'varmint' that had on several occasions made raids on our stores of provisions, so we proceeded to track it, and having discovered a broken pane in the cottage window we agreed that the animal must be a cat. Not taking into account the probable after effects, we got a piece of our stout fishing line and fastened a strong cod hook on to the end of it, and after baiting it with a tempting piece of meat, which we took the precaution of tying on securely, we made the other end fast to a stout nail in the window sill, and placing the baited hook in the hole in the window pane we retired to bed and soon fell sound asleep. The result exceeded our most sanguine expectations. About midnight the household was disturbed by the most astounding cat calls and noises and I heard my Father lumbering out of bed and shuffling about the door of his room in a pair of slippers, endeavouring to come at the source of the music . . . Presently the situation dawned on him, for he made use of some forcible remarks (he was too pious a man to use sulphurous language) and came into the house, and we knew by the rattling noise that he was feeling about in the knife box for a weapon to cut the line . . . I will pass over the 'court martial' next morning and the punishment meted out to the offenders. I was exceedingly curious as to what became of that cat. It happened that a few mornings after that eventful night I stepped into a neighbour's house with a companion to shelter from rain, and whilst sitting at the fire the good woman of the house told us mournfully that her favourite cat had met with an accident, and that somebody had stuck a large fish hook into her. She volunteered to show her to me and I fully expected to see a half yard of fishing line hanging out of her mouth. I was immensely relieved when she appeared with pussy looking in the best of health; and she drew my attention to a large cod hook, which had passed through her forearm between the bone and the muscle.[6]

Williams headed down to the village shoemaker for a pair of pliers with which he removed the barb and the shank of the hook, earning the lady's undying gratitude. The cat was apparently none the worse for its ordeal.

Other pranks were more innocent and innovative. Immediately across the road from the shop was the towering Tholsel or law court, now a bank which, with the addition of a clock tower, is still one of the chief landmarks of Drogheda and one with which Williams would have been very familiar. The law, then as now, took itself very seriously, not lessened by these still being days of empire. Even the entry into the Tholsel was a matter of some ceremony:

> It was the custom in those days at the assizes to receive the Judges with some show of state and a Trumpeter was employed to stand outside the door of the courthouse 'The Tholsel', and as the judge in his robes emerged from his carriage door, the Trumpeter played the first part of the National Anthem. His trumpet was kept ready in a niche, just inside the door. One of the 'boys' watched his opportunity and contrived to fix a cork into the large end of the instrument, just before it was required. This day the alarm was given, the escort of mounted constabulary rode up followed by the Judge's carriage, the Sheriffs with their wands took their places on each side of the steps. The carriage door opened, the venerable judge made his appearance, his robes supported by an attendant. The musician put the bugle to his lips and drew a full breath but alas not a sound could he make, and as the judge passed in he gave the unfortunate fellow with the purple face one of his most scathing glances.[7]

A wonder of the age was the building of the huge railway viaduct over the Boyne at Drogheda; it is easily the most dominant structure in the locality. When it was completed in 1855 it had a span of 250 feet and was 90 feet high. It was said to be the seventh largest bridge in the world and to have been built more economically than any comparable structure in the British Isles. But such economy came at a price.

> When the building of the Viaduct to connect the two railway lines was commenced, my Father as a geologist was greatly interested in the stupendous excavations made in the bed of the river and elsewhere for the foundations of the stone piers, as they revealed to him many interesting facts in his favourite science. He had permission from the engineers to take me with him into the immense coffer dams where myriads of workmen were digging and filling barrows with earth which were wound up by steel wires to the top along inclined planes. On one occasion when we were present a part of the dam gave way and a tremendous rush of water mixed men, barrows and implements with the thick yellow mud and all were floating and swirling about until rescued.[8]

They were the lucky ones. Health and safety were far from being the issues they have since become. While the engineers expended energy bickering over who deserved most credit for the great achievement, a hidden cost went almost unnoticed:

A sad part of the undertaking was the number of workmen who were injured or lost their lives during their work. The melancholy processions of stretcher bearers wended daily through the streets of the town to the hospital. One day the bearers, resting, laid down their burden, a fine specimen of an English navvy on the street opposite our door, and whilst we boys were looking on in silent awe, a poor woman advanced and reverently lifted the covering from the then dead man's face. Crossing and blessing herself she made the remark which to this day I [have] never understood: 'It was the Lord that saved his eyes'![9]

Not all his boyhood memories were so morbid or so eventful. For boys some things never change. There were, predictably, 'glorious times' playing at Red Indians in favourite haunts – Babington Woods, now a housing estate, and Beaulieu Woods, which still survives as part of Beaulieu House close to the Boyne. In the absence of toys, Alexander and his brother Edward improvised with what materials they could lay their hands on, commandeering an 'American bacon box' large enough to accommodate one of them at a time. It served as a makeshift rowing boat for adventures along a stream near Mornington at the mouth of the Boyne. Capsizing was an ever-present problem, Williams recalled. Presumably the stream was innocuously shallow water. But the water in which he and his friends disported themselves was not in fact always shallow, and there were no adults around when Williams made an attempt to teach himself to swim:

Some corks which I had arranged, as I thought, to keep their place under my arm pits shifted their position to my knees, with the result that my head got down near the bottom and my feet waved wildly over the surface of the water; fortunately one of my companions promptly came to the rescue, but I was as near gone as ever I felt in my life. After a couple of summers I became an expert swimmer and used to cross and recross the Boyne at Maiden Tower with ease.[10]

What seems remarkable now is the degree to which Alexander and his brother Edward were given the run of the town and its environs free of parental supervision. Both boys became keen shots and, from their early teens, the pair were let loose to shoot over the extensive mudflats and reed beds flanking the Boyne and the meadows and woodlands beyond, all within easy reach of where they lived and which abounded in wildfowl and game. The hammerless breech-loading shotgun, the forerunner of the standard weapon today, was only being developed in the 1860s. Williams and his companions would have used old-fashioned muzzle loaders, first stuffing the gunpowder down the barrel, followed by the shot and wadding. It is not known how sophisticated were the mechanisms of the guns the boys had; the earliest muzzle loaders had no safety catches to prevent the hammers snapping forward and discharging the gun. But even on muzzle loaders fitted with safety catches, it was all too easy to discharge them accidentally. Frozen, wet or careless fingers slipping off a hammer while in the process of cocking it, or catching the hammer in clothing or surrounding bushes, or tripping in the undergrowth were ever-present hazards. Not just in imagination but in reality, Williams knew exactly what it was like to get shot:

It was near Mornington that I had a narrow escape from being shot dead. With a companion I had gone out very early in the morning shooting as I wanted to get a snipe to set up. Whilst standing in a marsh spot looking about me my companion was making his way down a little wooded hillock and tripped in some brambles and as he stumbled his gun which was cocked and pointed in my direction exploded. I must have been about 60 yards off and I received thirty grains of no 6 shot all over my left shoulder blade. Had they struck my head I believe I should have been killed. The sensation was just like having a bucket of ice cold water dashed over my back, followed by a deadly sick fainting feel[ing]. I was able to stagger to a bank and lay down for a few moments, and then got my clothes removed. My companion I think was more alarmed than myself and his distress and exclamations when he saw the damage was pitiful. I fortunately had a very sharp penknife with me and I got him after much trouble to dig out the shot grains at once, which at last he accomplished and we started to walk the three miles back to Drogheda. I decided not to tell my parents of the accident fearing they would deprive me of my gun and prohibit any further shooting. I got a friend to rub oil into my wounds to relieve the stiffness and I soon became all right again.

Curious to say when bathing in the sea months afterwards two grains of shot came away in my hand from the deep flesh at the back of my left arm.[11]

There was more than an element of *The Boys' Own Magazine* about Williams' adventures which, it should be remembered, took place from when he and Edward were in their early teens. A memorable character he and Edward befriended was a poacher by the name of John Henry Hudson and it is easy to understand Hudson's appeal. He was a 'bluff, hearty middle aged man who led a kind of Robinson Crusoe existence that we boys greatly admired, near Mornington. He had built himself a comfortable sort of wigwam in the side of a steep bank beneath the public road not far from Mornington Church, overlooking the river, and spent all his time shooting and fishing and denouncing the "Game Laws" and the fishery Conservators at every opportunity.' Williams relished the opportunity of doing the same:

In the olden days the Boyne was a splendid salmon river. I was present one day near the Tower when a 52 pounder was netted but at that time boats shot their nets as far as the Bar Perch at the entrance to the river. Hudson had boats and a net of his own, and hired a crew each season, and it used to give me great delight when I was invited and got a seat in the boat to go fishing with them. The Fishery Conservators decided to curtail the fishing area and closed the river from the Bar Perch to a point higher up

opposite to Baltray. In this 'still water' no boats were permitted under a heavy penalty
. . . One day, it was the last of the fishing season, we were all on the river with the
other boats, and not having much luck. This temptingly fine sheet of water lay in the
sunshine without a single boat on it and the salmon leaping in plenty. The sight was
too much for the rebellious Hudson and he announced to us all that he had made up
his mind to take one shot of the net in the forbidden water . . . the boat was rowed
down a few hundred yards and the net shot in a wide sweep was brought to the bank
. . . and we could see as the net was slowly pulled in that it was full of fish. There was
great excitement as the bag with fourteen fine salmon and a heap of white trout was
pulled up on the bank and we all set to work to knock them on the heads. We had just
settled the last one when three men emerged from behind the wall, they were the
dreaded Water Bailiffs, and the chief officer advancing, said 'I seize this boat! This
net! And these fish in the name of the Queen, and Mr Hudson I warn you that you will
be prosecuted.' Whereupon he and his men put all the lovely fish as well as the net
into the boat and getting in themselves took to the oars and rowed away off to
Drogheda. Poor Hudson was prosecuted and in addition to losing the fish, had his
boat and net confiscated, and himself heavily fined.[12]

No doubt the water bailiffs made a good thing out of the confiscated fish.

Williams remembered that the south side of the river was nearly all slob and was
exposed at low water, and 'along the entire river from the Viaduct at Drogheda to the Bar
Perch at the entrance to the river a wall of wattles was constructed protected on each
side by blocks of stones to keep the river channel free from the silting sand of the slob
lands. This was a famous shelter for sportsmen endeavouring to approach the sea fowl
by day and also a convenient place for lying up at night waiting for duck to cross to the
feeding grounds.' If using an old-fashioned shotgun was not dangerous enough, Williams
records that he also learned to use a 'fowling piece' for duck shooting, a firearm with a much
longer barrel and fire power, and a more powerful recoil. He seems to have managed well
enough with such an unwieldy weapon; but the unreliability of all firearms was
demonstrated to him in spectacular fashion when his friend Hudson was out on the river.

On a desperately cold frosty night in his shooting punt, my friend Hudson nearly
came to an untimely end. There was no moon in sight and he had let fly at some ducks
going overhead. There was a terrific report and a blinding flash of light in his face and
he discovered that he held the stock of the gun in one hand and the barrel in the other,
all the intervening portion owing to the bursting of the gun barrel had been blown
away apparently without doing him injury.[13]

For all that William Williams allowed his sons what seems like almost unlimited freedom
at an age that now seems unthinkable, he was not at all a remote Victorian paterfamilias;
to the contrary in fact. While hat-making was the father's bread and butter, he had an

abiding and wide-ranging curiosity in natural history and was very much in the Victorian tradition of the amateur naturalist and collector. He had left school at thirteen, with no formal qualifications, in order to provide for his widowed mother. His father compensated for his scant education, according to Williams, by being an avid reader with a special interest in geology, zoology and the now discredited pseudoscience of phrenology. He studied at the Drogheda Mechanics Institute at night, taking courses which specially provided for those with minimal education intent on bettering themselves. It was perhaps because William Williams was largely self-taught that he had a gift for sharing his enthusiasms with his sons. When the boys were young he was particularly enamoured with geology and made a habit of taking them on trips out to a fruitful spot for fossils called Cruicerath (at the time of writing, a Roadstone quarry), about six miles from Drogheda: 'A day spent with him carrying our wallets of hammers and chisels for digging them out of the rocks was always hailed with delight, and the evening found us homeward bound and loaded with very interesting and sometimes valuable forms of extinct animals, some of which required much skill and patience to detach them from the solid rock without injuring them.'

What most captured Williams' interest and that of his two brothers, however, was not geology but their father's knowledge of birds and taxidermy. 'My earliest recollections, vividly impressed on my memory', Alexander wrote, 'are connected with natural history rambles, when my father used to take my brother and myself out for walks in the environs of Drogheda pointing out the different birds we met with and telling us particulars about them, and after a lapse of over half a century I can see the place vividly impressed on my mind like a picture, where I first was pointed out a common "Willy Wagtail". Those early rambles laid the foundation for that passion for natural history which has been all my life a source of the keenest enjoyment.'[14]

William Williams had picked up the techniques of preserving skins and of mounting them as taxidermy specimens from an old friend, a member of the Evatt family from Mount Louise, County Monaghan. He joined forces with Robert J. Montgomery of Beaulieu House and together they listed the avifauna of Drogheda and its environs. Making lists, however, was rarely where things ended in those days. It was almost de rigueur in demonstrating your interest to set up a collection, the rarer the specimens the better. Both men made their own collections of skins and provided material for what was formerly the Dublin Natural History Society, now the Natural History Museum of Ireland.[15]

In those days, boys in general were actively encouraged to hunt birds, to trap them for keeping in an aviary or kill them to make a collection of skins or, better still, as mounted specimens. These were pastimes as respected a publication as *The Boy's Own Magazine*, established in 1855, went to some lengths to promote. For instance Volume V, published in 1859, contained – along with breathtaking narratives on the Crusades (all four), an article headed 'Clean within or clean without?' (the importance of moral cleanliness as well as physical cleanliness), mathematical puzzles and poetry – a feature on

'How to preserve birds'. But there was little point in learning how to preserve bird skins if you did not also know how to procure them. So the magazine featured another article entitled 'Birds: how to trap and catch them' and then, having found a better recipe, an additional article devoted to 'Bird lime'. The magazine did not refrain from describing how a caged chaffinch might be encouraged to sing by blinding it, the object of the exercise being to attract other chaffinches which might then be caught. The method of blinding was with a red-hot needle, attached to a stick, so you would not be in danger of hurting your fingers. There were two methods: if the needle was plunged right through the eye, then blindness was permanent; if only held close to the eye until the lens turned white, a method called 'scaling', then, according to the article, the sight of the bird would return in a few months. The magazine prefaced this despicable technique with the comment that it would be carried out only 'if you have sufficient cruelty and hardness of heart (which we believe not one of our readers has)'.[16] Then why describe the technique at all?

With apparently no intended irony, the article on trapping began by describing birds as 'our feathered friends' and ended by saying that: 'Cruel as it appears to slay and take prisoners the minstrels of the air, yet there is good in it; for is it not written of man on the very threshold of the Holy Book – "Let them have dominion over the fish of the sea, and over the fowl of the air . . ."' Of course every well brought up British child would have known that the Holy Book was the Holy Bible – reference to which could justify a lot more than the Crusades. Whether Williams ever read *Boy's Own* is not known; but the magazine is indicative of the prevailing culture of the time.

It is probably fair to say that the young Alexander learned more outside the classroom than he ever did within. His interest in natural history had been sealed at the tender age of nine by an enforced holiday, when for health reasons unspecified, but a chest ailment most likely (childhood ailments run to fashion, and to have a 'bit of a chest' was once commonplace), the family doctor advised 'that I should be taken to the sea shore for three months'. So a thatched cottage was rented at Mornington on the Boyne estuary during the summer. The experience was one Alexander never forgot, and nearly sixty years later the memory of this enforced holiday prompted some purple prose:

> Here for the first time my brother Edward and myself were brought into daily communion with nature, rambling about the sea shore, or over the wild thyme covered sand banks in our bare feet, chasing the wild bee to its nest, listening to the glorious singing of the skylarks everywhere, watching the White Winged Terns or Gulls wending along the sands, and the Curlew and Oystercatchers feeding about the mussel banks, and to this day the weird call of the Curlew at night in the city revives in my memory the place where I first heard it, where the placid Boyne in slowly curling eddies flowed toward the sea and here we often during the long days of summer threw our fishing lines into the deeps.[17]

Sketch made at the
mouth of the Boyne and
Mornington, evocative of
his boyhood memories.

William lost no time in imparting his taxidermy skills to his three sons, all of whom were eager to learn. As boys it all went together; being keen shots they got their own specimens and in the process became proficient in identifying birds. Once they had learned to stuff specimens and mount them on twigs and artificial rocks, putting them in glass cases and making an attempt at painting backdrops was a natural progression.

After some practice at skinning we made efforts to stuff birds and after a lot of attempts my brother succeeded, greatly to his delight, in getting a starling fitted up and placed it on a twig of a tree; he fixed two small black beads into the apertures where the eyes had been, and it was so well done that my Father to encourage him allowed it to be placed in the shop window. It had not been there long when a person came in and offered my brother two shillings for it which my Father allowed him to accept, and the boy's delight at finding that by his skill he was able to coax money out of a stranger's pocket was unbounded . . .

I remember once I did get ahead of him when a pretty specimen of a "Willy Wagtail" was given to me which I determined should be a stunner. I set up the handsome little bird in my best stile and gave the dainty tail a suitable upward angle. Then I procured a small box from our grocer that once contained starch, I carefully lined this with white paper and imitated the artist [Bernard] Tumalti by painting with very indifferent water colours a view of sea and sky in which our beloved 'Maiden Tower' was a conspicuous object. Having prepared the box I got some fine sand and gravel and glued it on to the bottom and having decorated it with dried grass, I put my Willy Wagtail on the bottom. I got a piece of glass and fastened it into the front

Sketch made at the mouth of the Boyne showing the beacons which warned ships of shallow water.

and carefully papered and painted the outside. This *chef d'oeuvre* I proudly exhibited to my astonished brother. His surprise was a great delight to me, but the effect of it was to make him keener in his desire to outdo me and this friendly rivalry was the source of much pleasure, leading to our rapid improvement in the art.[18]

What turned a passing childhood interest in art into something more ambitious for Williams was seeing at first hand the work of this local artist, Bernard Tumalti, and that of his brother, Thomas, apparently the only two artists in the town. Little is known about them. They were Irish, the small alteration from Tumalty an innocent little conceit to give themselves a continental cachet. Alexander remembered Thomas Tumalti as specialising in portraiture and Bernard in landscape and still life. Their studio was responsible for the portraits of at least two mayors of Drogheda. William Williams sat for Thomas in the 1850s but the portrait is now lost. Bernard, in fact, did landscape, portraiture and some interiors, exhibiting at the Royal Hibernian Academy on seven occasions between 1827 and 1847, portraits primarily. If Williams remembered Bernard for his landscapes only, it was probably because Bernard picked up work from William Williams painting scenic backdrops for his taxidermy cases. Such embellishment was something of an innovation at the time. Bernard Tumalti is also said to have taught drawing.[19] Williams makes no mention of having ever received formal lessons from him but surely picked up tips from him and perhaps his brother on their visits to the hat shop.

The two painters were well known to William Williams as they both lived in a house owned by Bernard, at No. 6 School House Lane, one of the narrow medieval lanes behind the hat shop. When William brought his young son around to see Bernard in his studio the experience amounted almost to an epiphany:

I well remember the impression made when my father took me one day to see him and I viewed with awe the contents of his humble studio. One painting I considered most lifelike and natural, that was a dead canary painted on a cabbage leaf. I looked with veneration and admiration at the artist, and wondered if it might be possible one day for me to attain to similar exalted talent.[20]

To say the least, it seems a curious combination to put a canary with a cabbage. However, it was clearly a spur to Williams' ambitions, for he tried his hand at still life and, as we shall see, a picture he exhibited at the RHA was at least as anomalous as Tumalti's canary and cabbage.

William Williams usually had a number of skins in various stages of preservation and mounting in his shop, which included 'pheasants, grouse, blackcock partridge, quail, woodcock and snipe'. You would be hard pressed to find a grouse, quail or partridge around Drogheda today. But Williams could remember when the quail was 'exceedingly common [when] all along the sloping valley of the Boyne white smiling fields of wheat spread out as far as the eye could travel, and here in the summer evenings as one walked along the river everywhere the loud whit, whit, whit call of the birds might be heard. All this is now changed, it does not pay to grow wheat and whether or not that is the cause, the quail is now almost extinct in Ireland.' Rarer still is the bittern; no longer a resident, it is now seen only very rarely as an occasional visitor to Ireland, but according to Williams, in his youth it was 'not uncommon . . . and I have often seen it brought in to my father's shop by shooters coming home after a day's snipe shooting in the bogs near Drogheda.'[21]

Bittern (*Botaurus stellaris*) bought from the Williams studio for £2.5.0 in 1880 by The Natural History Museum of Ireland.

In those days arsenic was much used in the preservation of skins. Bernard Tumalti had a horror of the poison that amounted to a phobia:

My father often had his shop full of idlers calling in to have a chat, but whilst he never idled and kept on at his work he used to carry on long arguments on politics, religion, science etc. Some of the young men were fond of joking and knew Bernard's failing. On one occasion when Bernard and others were present and my father was busy preparing a pheasant's skin some of the 'boys' got between poor Bernard and his retreat by the door, and when the dreadful 'poison pot' made its appearance he made several ineffectual attempts to escape but was always foiled by the wags; his discomfiture kept on increasing and, little boy as I was, never did I see such abject terror depicted before on a human face; his eyes became dilated and seemed ready to burst, his face crimson and the perspiration poured down from under his tall hat until the boys, becoming alarmed, allowed him out. It was a cruel but interesting example of the force of imagination.[22]

William would mount the specimens in glass cases along with artificial rockwork and Bernard would provide the finishing touch, painting in an appropriate background, a *trompe l'oeil*, of sky and mountains. 'Generally the birds did not long remain in his [William's] hands, as they were often purchased at good prices by the surrounding admirers, so that what he had followed at first as a hobby and amusement became afterwards a source of income.' Williams watched the artist with boyish fascination and recalled that Bernard Tumalti, 'working at those backgrounds painted in tempera gave me the very earliest inkling of what was in after years to become with me the ruling passion'. It was a passion that expressed itself early. Even at the age of eight or nine:

> I used to attempt to draw the red sailed fishing boats that passed up and down the river and with a penny box of clay colours, the earliest form of art material that I was acquainted with, tried to imitate the colour of the sails and the green of the sea, certainly the valuable faculty of observation became early developed with me, for the birds, the flowers, the sunlight and all the objects of the landscape impressed themselves on me, and I could enjoy equally days when the sky frowned and the wind carried storm clouds across the sky. The fishing boats lying motionless on the sea, or scudding into the river on a bad day, always appealed to me.[23]

All in all it would seem to have been an exceptionally happy boyhood. Williams himself looked back upon 'fifteen halcyon years', with activities that were decidedly hands-on rather than passive, indoor or bookish. None of the sketches he did as a child have survived. The earliest picture known is a postcard-size watercolour of a sunset over a bay from 1866, when he was twenty. He pasted it into the front of his notebook, 'Chronicles & Memoirs', describing it as 'my first sunset water colour'. Precocious in his drawing and painting skills he was not; the execution is scrappy, the coloration crude. Evidently he kept the little picture for sentimental reasons. Beneath it is a fading sepia photograph, taken maybe fifty or more years later, of the artist in late middle age or even old age, entering the sea naked, off rocks, smiling directly at the camera and seeming not to feel the cold. Recalling Drogheda, he could muse that 'on looking back at those early days I fancy I must have been developing some of that tireless energy, that desire always to be occupying my time and exercising my fingers which has been one of the leading features of my life.' It was fair comment.

On the balance of probability Alexander Williams would never have become a painter had he remained in Drogheda. The opportunities would simply not have presented themselves. How great a part of life is chance! His boyhood came to an abrupt end at the age of fifteen when his father decided to up sticks and move to Dublin. He was removed from school at the same time and was required to start work. Apart from attending evening classes in drawing at the Royal Dublin Society (RDS), he would receive no further formal education. He was to spend one more year in Drogheda, in the shop, after which Dublin would become and remain the centre of his life.

Oil on paper. Exhibited at RHA, 1881, and at the Dublin Sketching Club the year before, as 'Bullfinch, Apple Blossom and Hedge-Sparrow's nest'. 9 x 12 in. (22.9 x 30.5 cm). Unsigned. Provenance: Williams family collection.

smooth overall texture. The bulk and structure of the outside of the nest do fit quite well for dunnock, perhaps the artist did a rough painting of the nest and neglected properly to depict the inside. It is also possible that the cushioning material inside the cup of the nest had been removed prior to painting. It can sometimes come out as a single piece of matted material, leaving the bare twigs visible beneath.[31]

Exhibiting at the RHA was still some way off. While Williams toiled away at making hats, his artistic aspirations were nearly dashed before they were born. His father had attended drawing lessons at the RDS and naturally enough showed interest in his son's efforts in that direction, that is, until William Brocas (c. 1794–1868) entered the hat shop one day in 1864:

Whatever encouragement my Father might feel disposed to give me in my artistic longings was effectually dispelled by the outcome of an interview he had with a Dublin artist, Wm Brocas, a member of the Royal Hibernian Academy of Arts, who sometimes came into our shop to have a chat with him. Art and artists was the subject of conversation on one occasion, and my Father had been telling the old man how clever I was with my pencil, and that I was always making sketches; finally he called me and introduced me to him and I heard him say 'What would you think if I made an artist of him?' Brocas gazed at me intently, brushing back with his hand the thick hair on my forehead and remarked, 'He has a fine head! Make an artist of him is it?' Then in a tone of withering contempt that I have never forgotten, he added: 'Make a sweep of him first.' This pronouncement from a well-known Dublin artist, who my Father considered eminent in his profession, was a finishing stroke and I need hardly remark that my Father seem[ed] inclined to throw cold water on my further efforts.[32]

To his credit, although he evidently remembered the slight for the rest of his life, as well he might, Williams had the necessary tenacity – or perversity – to continue despite such a dismissive judgement: 'The many difficulties I met with then and afterwards did not damp too much my ardour, but only served to whet my appetite and made me more determined, for the very love of the pastime, to avail myself of every possible opportunity for study.'[33] He followed in his father's footsteps in taking drawing lessons at the RDS for a short period. Beyond that he was self-taught, and by dint of his own perseverance, Brocas notwithstanding, he would establish himself as an artist among his peers and with the public at large.

PART II

THE TAXIDERMIST

Watercolour signed and inscribed: 'Old Wormwood Gate – A vanished Dublin Slum.' 10 x 14 in. (25.5 x 35.6 cm). Of the artist's solo exhibition in the Leinster Hall in 1908, *The Irish Times* wrote: 'No 30 – Wormwood Gate, a water-colour of considerable size – has attracted a good deal of notice, both on account of its historic value and the contrast it presents to the other pictures. The Gate was formerly a small bye-way leading from the quays to Cook street, but the locality is quite altered, the old houses have been swept away, and substantial warehouses now occupy the old site.' (25 January 1908).

Facing page: A case of sparrowhawks, *Accipiter nisus*, from the Williams studio, nineteenth century, and still displayed in the Dublin Pet Stores, Capel Street, the oldest pet shop in the city (dating from the early 1800s).

CHAPTER 4

The Battle of the Hats and Birds

A fter six years in Dublin the hat business was prospering, Williams recalled, '. . . and we seemed to be on the flowing tide, when like a thunderbolt from a blue sky an appalling catastrophe fell upon us.' A catastrophe indeed, but it was nothing as compared with what happened to their landlord and his family next door.

On the evening of 7 June 1866, Williams and his father were attending a meeting of the Dublin Natural History Society at the Royal Irish Academy in Dawson Street when word came through that their premises were on fire. 'Never shall I forget the paralysing feeling those few words made on me. Hurrying out, we jumped on an outside car and dashed off. At Trinity College we saw immense volumes of smoke rising in Westmoreland St and blotting out the light of a fair summer evening. Thousands of people running from every direction converged between the college railings and the Bank of Ireland, and Westmoreland Street was a surging mass of people so dense that it was impossible to get near our premises.'[1] At least there was no one inside, unlike next door, No. 20, where William Williams' landlord, Delaney, and his family lived over their tailoring business. Delaney himself happened to be out, but his wife, three daughters, a gentlemen friend of one of the girls and a maid were all in the building and none managed to get out.

Six deaths made it one of the worst fires in the centre of Dublin at the time. What had caused the fire? It was widely reported in the press that it had started in No. 19, the hat shop, which would, of course, have meant the Williamses had been responsible for the terrible loss of life. Williams was circumspect in what he included in his memoirs. The extract he chose to transcribe from *Saunder's News Letter* makes no mention of what was generally said in the press, that the fire had started in the Williams' basement.

Inexplicably, in the ensuing public enquiry, Williams' father was not called as a witness despite there being QCs representing all sides. However, William insisted on putting himself forward. He said he wanted to have his testimony heard to counter what had appeared in the press. His case was hardly strengthened when it emerged that a fire had taken place in his shop a year earlier. William testified that: 'It occurred between nine and ten o'clock on Saturday night; I always believe it was through my son's carelessness; I suspect he lit a piece of paper to look for something, and that he incautiously dropped it.' It was a minor fire, William said, with an insurance claim of about £7. Alexander then took the stand and agreed that he had indeed probably dropped a candle. The question of what they kept stored down in the cellar was also raised. Calico was mentioned but there was only a small quantity of it; there was shellac and some spirits of wine and a stove, in which coal and anthracite were burnt, and which was always kept lit during the day. They also had something much more inflammable, naphtha, which they used for cleaning the feathers of birds. Asked if they were in the habit of putting out the fire last thing in the evening, William replied, somewhat ambiguously: 'We looked at it; the draft was very strong and if the fire was not slacked it would be out in twenty minutes.' On the evening in question it was Edward who left last and who would have attended the fire and locked the workshop. He does not appear to have been called as a witness. William asserted that if the fire had started in his cellar it would have been immediately noticed: 'If the fire occurred in my workshop, Mr Delaney's family in passing down through their trap door to get to the cellar could not have but smelt the smoke; besides, it must have come through the railings to the street.'[2] In this he was supported by Thomas Delaney, son of the landlord, who in his evidence said he '. . . saw the shop shut up by the porter on the night of the fire; when he put up the last shutter he went home; I then closed the shop door, used no light or fire either that day or night on the premises, left the shop by the trapdoor, and passed Mr Williams's workshop, which was then locked; when I went out it was about quarter to eight o'clock . . . there could not be a fire in Mr Williams's shop without my seeing it when I was passing.' It could be argued that that proves very little. Might not the fire have started between when Thomas Delaney left the building and when it was noticed around nine o'clock? A small, smouldering fire may go unnoticed and take time to reach some more combustible material. The stove of anthracite might have emitted a fatal spark after Thomas had left the building.

Among much contradictory and confusing evidence, there was a consensus among eyewitnesses that the fire had started in some lower part of the building and burnt upwards. In the event, the enquiry concluded that the cause of the fire and precisely where it had started could not be determined. At this remove, is it possible to add anything further to that conclusion? In fact, a case can be made for arguing that the fire, wherever it did start, did not start in the Williams' basement. There was an interesting piece of evidence given by the supervisor of the Waterworks, a man by the name of Mervyn Paget Crofton. On the night of the fire he had to be summoned from some distance and was a late arrival at the scene. In his evidence he stated that he '. . . was struck on first arriving at the fire with the extraordinary appearance [in No. 19] of something like ignited Roman candles, so much so that I at once said there must have been fireworks kept in the house; I never saw an appearance like that at a fire before.'[3] William had acknowledged the presence of naphtha and a pervading smell of the liquid was commented on in evidence presented to the enquiry. Whether or not there were fireworks in the building, there is little doubt that the supervisor witnessed the explosive effect of naphtha. Clearly, had the fire started in the basement, those explosions, certainly naphtha, perhaps in combination with fireworks, would have been seen at the beginning of the conflagration, not near its end.

'Our feelings may well be imagined as we stood in mute helplessness gazing at the complete destruction of our premises and the accumulated property it contained, much of it irreplaceable and my Father's distress was acute when he told me that he was very much under-insured, and that practically he was a ruined man.' There was nothing for it but to start over again and William Williams lost no time in finding alternative premises. The following month he rented the ground floor of 27 Bachelor's Walk, picking up the pieces of the business as best he could.

Rough legged buzzard, *Buteo lagopus*, (rare in Ireland), Williams & Son. In Ulster Museum.

Troubles, they say, do not come singly and six months after the devastating fire, on 12 January 1867, Alice Williams died in one of the periodic outbreaks of typhus. Williams had been close to his mother and her death prompted him to a passage of Victorian prose and sentiment in which, as many a son has been inclined to do, he expressed some personal regrets: 'Hers was a pious, gentle, unassuming nature, and in my exuberance of youth, I often sorely tried her patience, but her tender admonitions and the lessons learned at her knee sank into my heart and my great and enduring regret since has been that I was deprived of the opportunity of repaying her in some degree for the unspeakable affection she lavished upon me. If ever a saint trod this earth, she was one, and the gentle little Robin Redbreast that perched on a tombstone beside her grave in Mount Jerome Cemetery during the interment in deep snow and sang so touchingly was an emblem of her sweet and loving spirit.'[4] It was his mother who had shown enduring faith in his painting abilities and he never forgot it.

Bachelor's Walk proved a disappointment. It was a question of so near and yet so far. Only a short distance from Westmoreland Street, regarded as second only to Sackville Street for trade at the time, Bachelor's Walk lacked the trading vigour of either; and the unfortunate William Williams, now newly widowed, had barely enough money to support himself and the family still at home, never mind the two boys who were part of the business.

It was at this point that Williams and Edward took some of the pressure off their hard-pressed father with a business idea of their own. 'We boldly got business cards printed announcing that Messrs A. and E. Williams had commenced the business of Naturalists. We however did not make the mistake of Mr Brown in an advertisement that ran thus: "Mr Brown, 'Furrier', begs to announce that he will make up gowns, capes, etc for ladies out of their own skins." We did not confine ourselves altogether to setting up birds but we attempted other branches of the taxidermist's art,' by which presumably he meant the preparation of mammals and fish skins.

Their card and a prominent notice they displayed immediately attracted attention. 'In addition to native birds we obtained specimens from Africa, America and Australia from time to time and we arranged some brightly coloured foreign birds with humming birds in glass shades, making artificial trees and arranging dyed grasses and mosses naturally about them. We suggested to our parent that he should allow us to exhibit one of these attractive objects in the centre of the large plate glass window of our shop and he complied, and here surrounded by head gear of various kinds, our first combined composition was publicly displayed. It attracted much notice by the novelty of its surroundings and was at last purchased and the money divided between us.'[5] Thus encouraged, they continued to exhibit their wares among the hats.

From the start the boys called themselves naturalists rather than taxidermists or mere bird stuffers. The term naturalist was more prestigious and would, in context, be understood as someone who removed the entrails of birds and fish, preserved their skins and mounted them in lifelike poses. The two boys had been doing this for years and had a good working knowledge of Irish birds. The young men however were not infallible. They got publicity, and gained a valuable friend, by writing to *The Irish Times* in connection with a long-tailed duck (*Harelda glacialis*) which had been shot at Irishtown. Speaking with the voice of authority they declared that the appearance of such a rarity 'presaged an early and severe winter'. The letter was picked upon by Robert Warren, a noted ornithologist of the day, living at Moyview, Ballina, County Mayo, who replied to the paper pointing out that this species was in fact a regular visitor and not a rarity at all. Curious to see what the two young men were about, he took the opportunity when in Dublin of calling on them. From this first meeting developed a lifelong friendship. Warren was notably generous in the way he was prepared to share his knowledge as his letters to Alexander show, and offered the two boys every encouragement.

Not long after, another noted ornithologist came to show an interest in their work – Richard M. Barrington, who lived at Fassaroe, near Bray, County Wicklow. This was the

Purple sandpipers, *Calidris maritima*, Balbriggan, 1900. Williams & Son. The artist's predilection for painting Martello towers suggests the backdrop might be his.

Widgeon, *Anas penelope*, by Williams & Son. Langham Collection in the Ulster Museum.

beginning of a wide network of contacts which would include such names as A. G. More of the Natural History Museum (then called the Dublin Museum of Science and Art), R. J. Ussher, living in Waterford, and Professor Charles J. Patten, originally from Dublin but living in Sheffield, names remembered yet in the history of Irish ornithology. In time the Williams' taxidermy business would became a locus for collectors, sportsmen and naturalists calling in and exchanging information.

In about 1870 William Williams moved the business yet again, this time to No. 3 Dame Street. Whatever about the importance of location to selling hats, so labour intensive an industry as making them was clearly ripe for automation, and so it proved. Times were changing in the hat trade and the move to Dame Street was no answer to what was taking place:

> At this time English manufacturers were making great headway and combining to employ costly machinery which tended to do away with a great deal of hand labour and cheapened the products of manufacture. Pushing travellers were employed and gradually the Dublin employers were undermined and outsold with the result that some of them closed down and gave up hat manufacturing. My Father with dogged determination stuck to the business but in the meantime we were advancing rapidly in our art of setting up natural history specimens and were becoming known through[out] Ireland.[6]

The new premises had the advantage of windows on either side of the entrance. The boys persuaded their father that one window be given over to birds and the other to hats. William had to recognise that Williams and Edward were making a success of their sideline, even to the point that they were now beginning to supply the Natural History Museum[7] (previously known as the Dublin Museum of Science and Art and then the Natural Museum of Science and Art) with specimens. So began what Richard M. Barrington in the *Irish Naturalist* dubbed 'the battle of the hats and birds':

> . . . one could readily perceive that Mr Williams senior, while proud of his sons' achievements, was most reluctant to permit his own occupation to be interfered with, for Edward was anxious to banish the hats and fill the window with birds. The struggle between the hats and birds was renewed with the result that there were two windows, one for hats and another for birds. Gradually however (fortunately for Irish naturalists) the birds, assisted by the beasts and fishes, swept their enemies the hats away altogether, and when another change of residence was made to the adjoining premises, No. 2 Dame Street, the entire front was filled with interesting and attractive specimens so lifelike and natural that their novelty in Dublin attracted the attention of many foot passengers, and a group was always collected on the pavement outside the window. It is unusual for a competition such as I have described to terminate so conclusively in favour of natural science.[8]

Established 40 Years.

2. WILLIAMS & SON, NATURALISTS. 2.

SKINS
DRESSED
AND
MOUNTED

2 DAME STREET

From

WILLIAMS & SON

NATURALISTS and FURRIERS,

2 Dame St., DUBLIN

Skins Dressed and Prepared as Rugs.
Horns and Hoofs Mounted.

ALL WORK OF THE HIGHEST CLASS.

All Specimens sent for Mounting should have Owner'
Name enclosed.

To...

.... *19*

Memorandum showing the shopfront of Williams & Son, 2 Dame Street.

In Dublin the family were well placed to exploit the exponential increase in interest in taxidermy. There were plenty of moneyed people around of the hunting, fishing and shooting variety, with the 'Castle set' an obvious ongoing source of clients. Moreover, as the family business was just around the corner, so to speak, from the Natural History Museum, it made it the obvious choice from which to obtain material and to have specimens mounted. There does not appear to have been too much in the way of competition. Certainly there would have been any number of bird stuffers and taxidermists around, but few local names made it into Thom's *Official Directory of the United Kingdom of Great Britain and Ireland*. In 1866, the year the two Williams boys started their business, there were but two: a Mrs Sarah Glennon (possibly the widow of a Richard Glennon who had been a taxidermist) of 22 Frederick Street South and a John Glennon of 46 Wicklow Street, who was probably the son. But the Glennons were gone by 1877. Thereafter, in Dublin at least, the Williams family had no serious rivals and so it remained. At the turn of the century just twenty-three people were listed under the census heading of 'Animal, bird etc – Preserver; Naturalist'. Of these, eleven were in Leinster. One was a female and she was the only other naturalist to have a place in *Thom's Directory* at this time. She sounds rather more like a clairvoyant than a taxidermist: 'Madame Margoth, naturalist and importer of foreign birds. No. 1 Dame Street and No.1 Exchange Court.' As there appears to be no record of her in the Natural History Museum nor of cased specimens bearing her name, the likelihood is she was primarily involved with the millinery trade.

Although the hat trade might have been on the wane, William Williams stuck with it for some years. While the family remained at 3 Dame Street, the only entry in Thom's, 1869–71, was 'William Williams, hatter'. Alexander says they moved next door, their last move, to No. 2 Dame Street in 1872. *Thom's Directory* suggests that for a transitional period they may have kept both premises, hats in one and birds in the other. At any rate the first appearance of 'A. & D. [an evident misprint] Williams, naturalists' first appears in 1872 with William Williams still down as a hatter, at No. 3 Dame Street. Not until 1876 do all three appear as naturalists at No. 2. In fact at this point Williams had probably left or was at the point of leaving the business; trade directories tend to show a time lag. William and Edward traded thereafter under the name of Williams & Son, even after young Willie had joined them.

Alexander and Edward had established their business during what is often described as the golden age of the Victorian collector. Despite mummification and desiccation having been practised since time immemorial, bird skins and their feathers have always proved vulnerable to decay and destruction by insects and mites (an ever-present problem), so that little taxidermy from even as late as the eighteenth century remains. Not until the French apothecary Jean-Baptiste Bècoeur (1718–77) began to use an arsenical soap of his own devising did taxidermy specimens become relatively permanent. His recipe was not published until the early 1800s, after which its use became widespread despite getting a less than enthusiastic press in some quarters. 'What is the consequence of this to the user of wet or dry arsenical preparations?' asked Montague Browne in *Practical Taxidermy*, who unsurprisingly favoured other preparations. 'Coughs, colds, chronic bronchitis, soreness of the lips and nose, ugly ulcers, brittleness of nails, and partial or complete paralysis.'[9] There is no reason to believe that William Williams used gloves or a dust mask, and whatever effects arsenical soap may have had on William, premature death was not one of them. He lived to the exceptional age of eighty-eight and there are many examples of taxidermists of earlier days living to a ripe old age.

As the century progressed, bird-stuffers sprang up all over the British Isles and Ireland with probably the majority of towns, of any size, boasting at least one taxidermist or bird-stuffer. While the firms of James Sheals in Belfast and Williams in Dublin became the two most prominent taxidermists in Ireland from the latter part of the Victorian age until well into the twentieth century, they were by no means the earliest in the field. In Belfast it is said that the first taxidermist was a James Nicholl, listed as both gunmaker and bird-stuffer in the *Trades Directory* for 1835. The connection between gunsmithing and taxidermy is self-evident; less clear is why a preponderance of hairdressers should have been attracted to the business, but such was the case. Perhaps dealing with ruffled feathers is a natural extension of dealing with unruly hair, with the undeniable advantage that dead birds do not argue.

James Sheals was into his thirties before he started his business as a full-time taxidermist in 1856, ten years before Alexander and Edward. (Leaving no ambiguity as to what he was about, James Sheals is described in the *Trades Directory* for 1885 as a naturalist, bird-stuffer *and* taxidermist.) His two sons Alfred and Thomas, especially the former, developed the skills their father had taught them and were regarded as pre-eminent in their field. Birds in particular and small mammals were their speciality, as was the case with the Williamses, who also did much work on fish. In London it was the firm of Rowland Ward that was unmatched for setting up big game in dramatic poses

Silver medal awarded by the Royal Zoological Society to William (Willie) Williams in 1913.

of unrivalled realism, even to the point of once showing a tiger in the act of savaging an unfortunate African boy. The tiger was a real specimen, the black boy was surely a sculpture, an art in which Rowland Ward himself also excelled. It takes a lot of space to work on big game such as giraffes and elephants, and having prepared a large specimen, you need to be able to get it out on the street for transport to its final destination. Even Rowland Ward was continually pressed for space.

As might be expected, the Williams family had a close connection with the Royal Zoological Gardens, now called Dublin Zoo, in the Phoenix Park, from which, as the records in the Natural History Museum show, came a continuous supply of dead animals. The zoo, the museum and Williams & Son would all have been in close contact. The museum would most likely have been given an option on dead specimens and no doubt would have expressed an interest in particular species, with Williams & Son being notified when the death of a sick animal was anticipated. Arrangements could then be made for the animal to be skinned and preserved before decay set in. Visits to the zoo to observe living specimens so as to be able to model them in lifelike poses was doubtless regularly undertaken by all three brothers. There is a reference, for example, in the minutes of the zoo in 1878 to Edward Williams wanting to obtain as authentic an expression of birds and animals as he could manage. Although the family business was perfectly placed in being so close to both the zoo and the museum, it did not have a monopoly. A record in 1869 shows that 'Mr Williams' was notified about the carcase of a tiger, but other interested parties were also informed, as the zoo wanted to get the best possible price.

Once the small bore rifle and shotgun, not to mention arsenical soap, became available, the Victorian obsession for collecting took off in earnest:

Collecting provided a convenient and socially acceptable excuse for respectable grown men to climb trees, scramble down cliffs, go camping and roam freely out of doors, pitting themselves against the terrain, the weather and wary, elusive quarry.

Success demanded physical fitness, endurance, patience, skill with guns and a level of field craft now rare among birdwatchers. In short, it was considered good, manly fun – and whether practised as a hobby, lifestyle or profession it was dominated by men – female bird collectors were few and far between.[10]

As a result rooms, even rooms especially designed and built for the purpose, were filled with taxidermy specimens of all kinds. There was not necessarily much science or order to the collecting. Acquisition was the thing, and birds that would have never met in real life found themselves perched together, a dozen at a time, in large glass cases, with not a thought of how anomalous they might look. As the fashion for taxidermy took hold, collectors were limited not by the opportunity to shoot – there were few laws to contend with – so much as limitations of space in which to display what they had shot. Exhibits were rarely confined to drawing rooms or studies. It made sense to begin with some specimens in the entrance hall, the better immediately to impress the visitor as to how far-flung had been the travels of the owner.

Carcases, improperly cured and in a state of putrefaction, were often spoilt before reaching Europe, but parts might be saved. Elephants' feet became ink stands and drinks cabinets, rhinoceroses' feet became doorstops and umbrella stands, exotic birds were fashioned into firescreens and table lamps; indeed the uses to which mammal parts and birds might be put around the house, from ashtrays to paper weights, bookends and doorstops, were limited only by the ingenuity of the taxidermist. Rowland Ward in Lomdon took the lead and advertised all manner of domestic bric-a-brac, but Williams & Son would have done their share of such work too.

Nothing equalled the prestige of bringing home a tiger. If space was at a premium at home – and if the wife objected to the idea of sharing her drawing room with a three-dimensional stuffed tiger – there was always the option of having your tiger skin splayed out on a wall or laid down as a conspicuous if inconvenient rug on the drawing room floor. The glaring, threatening eyes and snarling jaws provided the visitor with a little frisson of excitement while taking a cautious step sideways to avoid snagging an ankle or tearing a stocking on tooth or claw, before waiting patiently upon yet another inevitable favourite story from the proud sportsman of derring-do against the odds in some faraway savannah.

The typical Victorian fisherman might be expected to have a selection of glass cases containing his specimen catches. In many a house and hotel salmon, trout and pike lurked among rushes and reeds, set over a base of small rocks and gravel and a watery backdrop painted on the timber back. Well preserved, such trophies can last a long time. A number of specimen trout caught in the early 1900s and stuffed by Williams & Son still adorn the walls of the Lake Hotel, Killarney, and a century later still look as shiny as if newly caught, although the original settings have been replaced. Each taxidermist had his own techniques: dried grasses were often used along with real stones and pebbles; sometimes vegetation was made with dyed wood shavings and rocks made artificially of

A prodigious pike, *Esox lucius*, 48 lbs in weight and 4 ft 3½ in long (21.8 kg; 151 cm). Williams & Son, nineteenth century.

Exhibition room in the Natural History Museum. All around are to be seen taxidermy specimens and tableaux by Williams & Son.

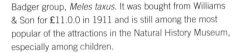

Badger group, *Meles taxus*. It was bought from Williams & Son for £11.0.0 in 1911 and is still among the most popular of the attractions in the Natural History Museum, especially among children.

Fox group, *Canis vulpes*, bought from Williams & Son in 1910 for £11.0.0.

semi-crumpled paper, painted in suitable shades of grey, sometimes varnished to give a watery, aquatic effect, and touched up to suggest algae and lichen.

Sadly, no company records of Williams & Son are known to have survived as they have in the case of both Sheals and particularly Roland Ward. However, records held by the Natural History Museum of nineteenth-century taxidermy running into the twentieth do provide an idea of the work carried out for the museum by the Williams family and others. In the scheme of things, a taxidermist rated rather lowly and often received no credit. Presentations to the museum of skins usually acknowledged the donor and less reliably the taxidermist for the simple reason that he was regarded as a tradesman. His position was somewhat analogous to that of a gardener; prize-winning tomatoes at a flower show would be credited as having been grown by Lady so-and-so in even though her delicate hands might never have touched the tomatoes, which had, of course, been assiduously cultivated by her gardener. At least the donor to the museum had probably shot the specimen, even if its perfect state of preservation and realistic mounting were the work of his often unacknowledged taxidermist. Williams & Son in this respect did themselves no favours in seemingly often failing to label their own cases. Many examples around Ireland of what appears to be their work lacks the final confirmation of their stamp or label. Nevertheless, information about the firm can be gleaned from what records there are. To give a comparison of prices, a memo from Williams & Son to the Natural History Museum in 1909 gives the following costs for a variety of birds: 2 Peregrine Falcons 15/- each; Nightjar 7/6d; 1 Eagle Owl 12/6; 1 Young Skylark 3/6; 1 Martin 3/6.[11] Prices would reflect not only the size of the mammal or bird involved but also its relative scarcity; and no doubt what the taxidermist felt the museum and the market in general would bear. By way of comparison with the cost of taxidermy, a proposal to the museum from Williams to fill a corner of the hall in 1906 by constructing artificial rockwork to represent a sea cliff came with a price tag of £10, indicating the much greater time and labour involved. (In this instance the word 'postponed' was noted against the proposal.)[12] The Natural History Museum in Dublin in particular and also the Ulster Museum in Belfast, quite apart from private collections, contain numerous displays of naturalistic tableaux by the Williams brothers, where the aim was to show both mammals and birds, not only naturally posed but in habitats matching as closely as possible to those where they would be found in the wild. At this level of work, taxidermy perhaps moves across the dividing line from craft to art. Williams & Son proudly advertised themselves as 'Designers of the Life Groups in the National Museum, Kildare Street'.[13]

Alexander described the firm as world famous. It was no idle boast since the family dealt with skins collected from across the globe. Records in the Natural History Museum illustrate the range of material passing through Dame Street. There is a note from Williams & Son to Dr R. F. Scharff, enclosing accounts and promising to 'send in the Jungle Fowl, an oriental pheasant, tomorrow'.[14] A list of birds sent in on approval mentions a bird of the genus *Polypectron*, common to the Malay Peninsula and the Philippines.[15] To Mr A. R. Nichols there is a request from Williams & Son to provide the common and Latin name of a Ceylonese bird and the Latin name for Leadbeater's Cockatoo, an Australian species.[16] Another communication to Nichols requests the correct name of a small African antelope and more surprisingly Williams & Son ask for the Latin name for a pine martin, which would suggest a paucity of books and reference material at Dame Street.[17] In a letter to Scharff, Samuel Houghton mentions that he caught forty Pacific salmon in Canada and has had three mounted for himself by Williams of Dame Street who still have a 'King Salmon' and a 'Cobo' which the firm has cured and painted.[18] If the museum is prepared to pay for mounting them, he will be glad to present them to the museum. An appended note says the museum promises to recommend acceptance. Material that the museum itself required or accepted seems surprisingly random, the unusual with the commonplace, to judge from one particular delivery note to the museum's storekeeper from Williams & Son, which listed: '2 Glacuous Gull skins; 1 Iceland Gull skin; 1 Chaffinch, 1 Pipit [Museum notes this as a Male Meadow Pipit]; 1 Oriole, Stuffed pheasant; Buzzard; 2 Weaver Birds; Blackbird; Jay; Snow Bunting; Raven, and a hare'.[19] The weaver birds were the gift of an H. B. Rathbone, and depending upon the species might have come from sub-Saharan Africa, Asia or even Australia. It is not clear where H. B. Rathbone's wanderings had taken him. No doubt the taxidermist left the definitive identification of exotic species, such as the weaver birds, to the museum.

Not all offers were accepted. When Colonel James D. Day wrote to the museum offering his St Bernard, stuffed by Williams, the museum declined on the grounds of space. There was once a fad for having your beloved pet dog stuffed. In such instances Willie always made sure to take a down payment, as such commissions were notoriously unreliable – affectionate memories could be displaced by a new pet before the stuffing was done.[20] Space was not a problem for another curiosity, this time offered by Lord

Headley writing from the wilds of Illaunaguini, Lough Corrib, Headford, County Galway, to describe three skins of the buff- or cream-coloured rat caught on his island on the Corrib. They are with Williams & Son where they are being set up for the museum, he says. The interesting point is that these rats were not known on the mainland. The first his lordship caught had pink eyes, then he caught four more with eyes of normal coloration.[21]

Another curiosity was what was said to be a giant stuffed rat. When it was exhibited in the shop window in Dame Street it caused a sensation. Word had spread that the rat's prodigious size was the result of drinking stout and it quickly came to be known as the 'Guinness Rat'. It is even said that the police were required to control the gullible crowds that gathered to see the creature. It was in fact a coypu, a rat-like creature, that came from the zoo.[22]

William Williams made something of a speciality in researching the extinct Irish deer, more commonly, if misleadingly, referred to as the Great Irish Elk. The firm advertised that they had the 'head and antlers of the great extinct Irish deer, *Cervus giganteus*, generally in stock'. It is clear from a communication sent from Williams & Son to Walter Rothschild (who formed an unrivalled natural history collection, especially birds, at Tring, Hertfordshire, with little consideration as to cost) that the Williamses actively went after business. It is curious that the communication to so important a collector was done with what can best be described as memo, rather than by formal letter with a printed letterhead. However, the memo indicates the firm had done business with Rothschild before.

The Hon. Walter Rothschild

Some time ago we had the honour of supplying you with a skeleton of the Irish elk which we trust has met your approval.

We now have a very curious head of a similar animal, a photo of which we enclose, it is abnormal in form and unique we never met the like of it and we think never shall, one palm is the usual form the other the right antler is exceptional it is 26 inches across in the widest part and the whole head is of a large class far above the average, as you purchased the skeleton from us we give you the first offer of it at 60 guineas & no matter for what amount you <u>could not get one like it</u>.

We have the honour to be yr obt servant
Williams & Son

We may remark that this head is <u>unusually sound</u> it will last for thousands of years, and will increase in value as they are getting very scarce. As far as we can learn they have nothing like this head in the British Museum.[23]

The style is rather pressing. Across the top of the memo is written 'Answer – not required'. One wonders if the final price achieved was anything like what was asked from Rothschild, a considerable sum.

Common to all forms of collecting, be it stamps or bird skins, the rare has a cachet all of its own. The Victorian appetite for killing fauna and avifauna of any kind seems, in retrospect, to have been as insatiable as it was indiscriminate, or if discrimination was practised it was in regard only to the pursuit of the rare and the exotic. Once seen, the rare and the unusual was as good as done for.

The *Irish Naturalist* magazine which ran from 1892 to 1924 gives a vivid idea of the prevailing culture and attitudes to wildlife during the period. It was once the official organ of the Royal Zoological Society of Ireland, the Dublin Microscopical Club, and the Belfast Natural History and Philosophical Society, among other bodies. All three brothers, Alexander, Edward and Willie J., contributed articles and nature notes to it from time to time, with Alexander continuing to publish articles on bird life, and even observations on butterflies and moths, in the *Irish Naturalist* and elsewhere long after he had severed his connection with taxidermy. The magazine provided readers with information on natural history – some of it scientific and much of it anecdotal; if all you wanted to know, month by month, was who had shot what rarity, when and where, you could not do better than turn to the *Irish Naturalist*. Naturally enough, many rarities passed through the workshop of Williams & Son, and announcing their arrival provided free advertising:

> A very fine specimen of the Snowy Owl (*Nictea scandiaea*) was shot in the vicinity of Belmullet on the 13th December. The bird measures five feet to the extreme tip of wings, and twenty-five inches from beak to tail; weighing four pounds four ounces. The specimen has come into the possession of Mr J. T. O'Reilly, Carne House, Belmullet, who has forwarded it to us for preservation.
> Williams & Son, Dublin.[24]

Though his livelihood depended on what clients brought him, Edward perhaps pointed to a change of attitude in himself if not in others when he wrote: 'A very fine female Osprey, *Pandion haliaetus*, was shot in the neighbourhood of Cahir, Co. Tipperary, on 10th October. It was in company with another which fortunately eluded all efforts to capture it.'[25] However, it was certainly not the usual thing to take one rare specimen and leave the rest. Rare was the occasion when an opportunity to shoot a novelty was resisted, but the *Irish Naturalist* did manage to record at least one instance, when Willie spotted a nuthatch in Malahide:

> Mr Trumbull kindly offered to shoot the bird, but I thought it was unnecessary, as I was absolutely certain of the species. Since then I have had a letter saying the bird is still about the garden.[26]

There was long resistance to giving up on the old dictum that 'what is killed is history, what is missed is mystery'. The idea of birdwatching with the aid of telescope or binoculars as a pastime and a means of identifying species in preference to shooting and collecting took a long time to catch on. Meantime, as the new century progressed, there was a growing awareness that shooters might be eliminating native species, provoking a *cri de coeur* from one of the best-known collectors, Richard M. Barrington in an article in the *Irish Naturalist* in 1915 headed, with a question mark, 'The last (?) Golden Eagle':

Golden Eagle, *Aquila chrysaetos*, taxidermy specimen from the Williams studio, 1887. Natural History Museum, Dublin.

> Early in January, happening to call at Messrs Williams & Sons [*sic*], No. 2 Dame street, Dublin, the well-known taxidermists, I saw, to my surprise and horror, a freshly killed Golden Eagle – a fine old male, weighing 8½ lbs, and whose extended wings measure 6ft 3 in. It had been shot near Ardara, Donegal. This is no doubt the Eagle which my old friend Mr Ussher told me he had seen on the Donegal coast, north of Slieve League in 1913. It has had no mate for some seasons, and is said to have inhabited the district for forty years. The middle toe of one foot was missing – showing that it had been trapped – but the wound was perfectly healed. After diligent search and enquiry this was the only Golden Eagle which Mr Ussher could then trace with certainty as existing in Ireland – though he had heard rumours of one in Mayo. What are we to think of those who are responsible for the extermination of this magnificent bird – whose powerful flight amidst the wildest glens and loftiest precipices added an irresistible charm to some of the grandest Irish scenery?[27]

Legislation begun towards the end of the nineteenth century started giving protection to birds and birds' eggs with, initially, protection being provided for some species on a county by county basis, before a blanket ban was introduced for most species, excluding those regarded as pests. Williams' attitude evidently underwent change too from the days of his Clontarf diary when he recorded shooting anything and everything. In a long article for the *Irish Naturalist* in 1908 he reported with approval the effect protective legislation was having on bird populations around his favoured haunts of Bull Island, Clontarf, and beyond. Shopkeepers might not have been equally pleased, however.

It is not so very many years since the poulterers' shops in the City of Dublin often contained in the last week of April numbers of Golden Plover in the handsome black, white and yellow full summer plumage, together with specimens of the fine White-fronted Goose, a sight that often grieved humane bird lovers. The law which fixed the end of the killing season nearly two months earlier has saved the lives of a great many more of our beautiful shore birds and put a stop at the same time to what was a crying evil, the constant Sunday shooting that was carried on at Clontarf, Dollymount, Sutton, Baldoyle and different parts of the bay of Dublin.[28]

There was little reason to deplore eating Golden Plover and the White-Fronted Goose per se if you were in the habit of eating other fowl, although the inference here appears to be that the birds had previously been killed while they were trying to breed. All three brothers, Alexander, Edward and Willie, made a habit of going out birdwatching on the Sabbath, the one full day off they had in the week. It was their form of recreation, to which Sunday shooters were, of course, a nuisance, as on the report of a gun the birds rose to the air and were gone.

Much of this shooting was evidently a form of recreation, with often no other object in mind than to shoot, not to add a skin to a collection nor obtain food for the pot, or even to look for a few pence from a local poulterer. This was what the so-called Sunday shooters were about, often leaving their kill where it lay dead or, when the bird was not killed, even leaving it where it had fallen injured, to die. To give an instance, on 1 August 1910 Williams recorded that he walked from town to the Shelley Bank where he saw: 'Two men shooting. Saw them kill a bird and throw it away. Searched for it and got it, an immature Lesser Tern in interesting plumage. Set it up for my collection.' The incident was not an isolated one:

Lovely clear sunny frosty morning. Walked from Haddington Road to the Shelly Bank . . . Walked out on the Bank past the Island. Counted 100 Godwits looking beautifully golden and white in the winter sun. 40 Oystercatchers. I carefully stalked a very large flock of Ring Plover. Sanderling and Dunlin all assembled on the raised middle part of the sandy point . . . Dead birds rather numerous, I examined the remains of 4 Herring Gulls 2 adult and 2 immature, one Common Gull and one Black Headed – on my way back I found a perfect immature Herring gull quite recently shot which I took home and also a very fine curlew also quite recently killed.[29]

The issue appeared in the press from time to time. Williams saved this news cutting:

Last Sunday the writer came across three wounded gulls on the strand; in two cases the wing was broken, and in the other case there was a broken leg. This wanton destruction of our birds deserves the severest censure. Besides it is illegal to shoot on Sundays.

Surely it is time that the authorities did something to put an end to this most cruel 'sport' – Yours etc, A. R. Sandymount, November 9, 1909.

At the other end of the spectrum were those who assembled collections to make systematic studies of birds in the field, of their breeding habits and habitats, their migration patterns, their calls, their morphology and taxonomy. In its day Williams & Son was an important source for records. 'The firm's books contain a large amount of information relative to the identity and place and date of capture of interesting specimens,' recalled Robert Lloyd Praeger (1865–1953), 'and were often consulted by ornithologists.'[30]

With the death of William Williams in 1901 and of Edward a few years later, the business passed into the sole hands of Willie, who ran it until his death in 1937. Despite the Victorian era being regarded as the heyday for taxidermy, Willie made a good thing out of the family business until well after the First World War. Edward, a rather diffident personality, had claimed that even at the height of the fashion for taxidermy, 'the remuneration obtained for stuffing animals has not been sufficient to secure the services of persons trained to produce high class work.'[31] That may have been true for Edward, but Willie took a more enterprising view and managed to find full employment for three in addition to himself. There may have been others employed too at one time or another. With no other income, Willie lived all his married life in some prosperity, raising a family of three, at 'Flax Bourton', No. 1 St Kevin's Park, Dartry, in what is now Dublin 6.

In passing it might be mentioned that 'Flax Bourton', although the family has long left the house, may yet contain a souvenir from the Williams' studio in Dame Street. On one occasion Willie took home on the tram, which ran as far as the terminus at Dartry, the head of a hippopotamus in a state of putrefaction that made preserving and stuffing it impossible. He dealt with the sizeable skull by burying it in the back garden. His intention may have been to have it picked clean by insects and then to mount the skeletal head. However, according to family lore he never did dig it up. This little aside is offered to any enterprising archaeologist who might come upon the skull in years to come and, putting two and two together, as archaeologists are wont, draw the conclusion that once upon a time, not long past, hippos were happily disporting themselves down on the banks of the nearby River Dodder.

To Willie is attributed the introduction into Ireland of 'bones', the practice of drawing serrated bones across each other in imitation of the craking sound of the mating corncrake who may thus be tempted to respond and put in an appearance. Corncrakes are notoriously shy and difficult to see. On one occasion while trying the technique at Baldoyle Racecourse, he heard an answering call drawing close and closer. Going discreetly in pursuit he found another birdwatcher doing the same, also 'craking' with a pair of bones.[32]

After Willie Williams died in 1937, his elder son, Teddy, an avid birdwatcher and taxidermist, ran the business until he joined the British army as a volunteer in 1942.

He never returned to the business in Dame Street, which was wise. Besides taxidermy being no longer fashionable, no more than the unworldly Alfred Sheals, Teddy had no head for business. He was spared the possibility of a similarly impoverished old age by joining the Leicester Museum in 1946, becoming the museum's chief taxidermist and leaving with a pension.

After the Second World War the business at No. 2 Dame Street stumbled on under Walter Connolly, Willie's former employee. Connolly was now getting on in years but he had the assistance of one if not two daughters.[33] The premises under his care are just within the orbit of the childhood memories of the author. At the top of what seemed endless narrow stairs, in a carpeted hall or annexe with light flooding in from a glass dome, you were confronted by a collection of stuffed dogs, pets of years ago, uncollected and forgotten. In the last years of the business, Mr Connolly, suited, gave the impression of not so much working as presiding over the establishment attended by his two daughters, notable for their hair dyed jet black, cheeks rouged to the last and lips of fire-engine red; they were well disposed to a wide-eyed child, smiling broadly at him, but they both looked incongruous in a taxidermy studio. However, it was Connolly, sitting there as if holding court, that was the most memorable of the three. He was a small, dapper man, quite elegant, with a pair of waxed moustaches, perfectly horizontal at the ends, that he twirled and caressed, in retrospect obviously for effect and his own pleasure, watching with amusement the interested gaze of the boy; the points of each moustache, left and right, being as sharp as if they had been through a pencil sharpener. The silence up there, so far above street level, with the heavy enclosing walls was intense and the atmosphere airless. The annexe or hall ended in a few steps boldly framed by a plaster arch beyond which was a receptionist's table and beyond that again one entered the taxidermy room itself. It seemed immense, with small low windows and a huge table that just about filled the room. The smell of must, dust, decay, of age and preservatives was suffocating and unforgettable, a smell like no other, and experienced neither before nor since. There was a huge skate hanging from the ceiling, suspended over a bucket or container of some sort. It had a particularly revolting smell, perhaps of formaldehyde. It was a record and recent catch. Otherwise everything else seemed old and withered and untouched. Every inch, it seemed, of the table and every other available surface, the window ledges included, and the ceiling, had birds and skins in every conceivable state of composition and perhaps of decomposition, some hanging from perches, some lying flat, eye sockets repulsively filled with cotton wool, awaiting glass eyes that they would never now receive. One could imagine that half of the skins and trophies and exhibits and bits and pieces had not been touched since before the First World War, maybe there were skins that went back to the last century, who was to know? To a small child it was an unforgettable and unique sight. But it is long gone. No. 2 Dame Street and the entire beautiful terrace of which it was once a part was pulled down in the 1970s for the purpose of widening the street.

Times change and so do attitudes. Few museums nowadays have an active policy for the acquisition of skins. Taxidermy is out of fashion and a licence is required to kill most species of birds and mammals, other than those regarded as vermin or pests. The common view of the Victorian collector and the associated art of skin preservation is generally one of distaste for its rapaciousness and to the fashion for collecting is attributed the depletion and in some instances the extinction of avifauna and fauna. There is an element of truth in this view, but it is a partial view. While there are attested cases where a collector killed the last bird or collected the last eggs of a particular species, or more commonly the last specimen within a given locale, it is by no means so clear the extinction was due exclusively, or even in part, to the activities of sportsmen and collectors. A hypothetical figure of 150,000 bird species has been put forward as having once inhabited the earth. If this figure has any meaning then well over 90 per cent have since disappeared, the majority in prehistoric times, and we are dependent upon fossil records for information about them. Perhaps in the greater scheme of things, we are at the tail end of biodiversity, the result of a natural process of elimination as well as a self-inflicted one. To take a convenient recent date, the relationship between mankind and avifauna is relatively well known from the 1600s. In the 400 years that have elapsed since then, in the order of ninety bird species and perhaps sixty subspecies have become extinct. Taking this period as a whole, in the opinion of Eric Fuller in his book *Extinct Birds*:

> Most recent bird extinctions are due to human intervention. Yet the kinds of intervention resulting in extinction are not always those that might be popularly supposed. Hunting and shooting, for instance, often make little overall difference to bird populations. Bird lovers might find these activities morally distasteful but there are fewer cases than might be imagined – although the passenger pigeon, the dodo and the great auk are celebrated ones – where extinction can be directly or solely related to them. Similarly, egg collecting, one of the great *bêtes noires* of the bird protection movement, is largely blameless in terms of actual extinctions – even though it is such an unpleasant activity.[34]

What did for some bird populations in Victorian days, much more than taxidermy and collecting, was the millinery business. Members of the 'gentler sex' were much given to embellishing their heads with feathers, or sometimes the wing or the head of a bird, and truth to tell some women were satisfied with nothing less than adorning their heads with a whole bird. The absurdity of it all was well captured by George Bernard Shaw in a letter he wrote to *The Times* following a visit to the Royal Opera, Covent Garden, London:

> At 9 o'clock (the opera began at 8) a lady came in and sat down very conspicuously in my line of sight. She remained there until the beginning of the last act. I do not complain of her coming late and going early; on the contrary, I wish she had come later and gone earlier. For this lady, who had very black hair, had stuck over her right

Ostrich feathers were the thing, here dyed black for the bridesmaids on account of Queen Victoria's recent death. Alexander is second from the left, his wife near centre behind the old lady in the striped dress. Willie Williams' wedding party, Bristol, 1901.

ear the pitiable corpse of a large white bird, which looked exactly as if someone had killed it by stamping on its breast, and then nailed it to the lady's temple, which was presumably of sufficient solidity to bear the operation. I am not, I hope, a morbidly squeamish person; but the spectacle sickened me. I presume that if I had presented myself at the doors with a dead snake round my neck, a collection of black beetles pinned to my shirtfront, and a grouse in my hair, I should have been refused admission. Why, then, is a woman to be allowed to commit such an outrage?

But they were and they did. It was something like a mania while it lasted. So much so that at one time in Britain 'the plumage industry was an important part of the national economy and it has been estimated that from 1870 to 1920 twenty thousand tons of ornamental plumage entered the country each year'. There was an obvious tie-in between taxidermy and the millinery business, with some firms advertising themselves as suppliers to the millinery trade. The Williamses were never milliners but they were in the thick of the supply line, advertising themselves as suppliers of 'women's plumes'. Williams' wife, Kitty, very likely helped herself to what was available for up-to-the-minute fashion; the *Irish Society and Social Review* on one occasion admiringly reporting on her 'bodice finished with a lovely feather boa'.[35]

Millinery became a special concern of the Irish Society for the Protection of Birds with Fr O'Ryan, a colourful member of the society, going on record at the AGM of 1911 to say that 'he had been accused of saying that a woman who wore an osprey should be hanged. He pleaded guilty to the charge. He thought that ospreys would be worn as long as they continued in fashion. As a bachelor, he could say without fear that if it were the fashion for women to wear newly born babies stuffed in their hats they would do it (laughter).'[36] In 1910 the British army banned egret feathers which were used by some regiments, giving rise to the banner in one newspaper: 'Women less humane than army.'

The range of birds with which women saw fit to adorn their heads was considerable; 'the most popular species were herons and egrets (for "osprey" plumes), birds of paradise, cock o' the rocks, parrots, toucans, trogons and hummingbirds.'[37] The best time to kill egrets was during the mating season when they develop decorative plumage; a consequence was the number of chicks left to die helplessly on their nests. Kittiwakes fared worse: 'After capture birds had their wings cut off and were then thrown back alive into the sea.'[38] This barbarous practice was still taking place at Bempton, Yorkshire, in the second half of the nineteenth century. It was such activities that eventually prompted bird protection acts, although economic rewards meant there was considerable resistance. The market for feathers for the millinery trade, while it lasted, was voracious. One dealer alone, in London, sold 2 million wild bird skins in just one year. Compare that with the number of preserved museum skins. Worldwide there is reckoned to be approximately 10 million bird skins in public institutions; the figure is, of course, but a fraction of the number of birds killed in the process of building collections, both public and private, over the last couple of centuries. Nevertheless, it has been suggested that:

> Whatever the figure may be for the past *200 years* it is still small when one considers that the world's motorists and domestic cats each kill over a million birds *every day* and billions more are killed each year by hunters, collisions with man-made structures, pollution, habitat destruction and pest control.[39]

Indeed current habitat destruction has incomparably more far-reaching consequences than bird collecting ever had, and worse, it is continuing at an exponential rate, to the point where many scientists would share the view that: 'The extinction of species is probably something that is now quite out of control and no-one can realistically predict what the consequences of this may be.'[40]

The impact of the collector and hunter of old, and even the millinery trade, pale into insignificance compared with what is happening today. It is easy to denigrate Victorian and Edwardian attitudes to collecting and taxidermy, but a more considered view recognises the value of their legacy. While it is self-evident that the observation of living creatures is necessary for their study, the converse is true also, that dead specimens, particularly where date and place of death and other details are properly recorded, yield information that no living bird can. As techniques for analysis of the past become ever more sophisticated, museum collections become of increasing value to research. Whatever else one might want to say about collectors and taxidermists, museum collections of skins, represent, in the literal use of the word, an incomparable scientific and educational resource. Although it was not to be his life's work as it was to be for his two brothers, Williams was proud of what he had started with his brother Edward: 'Little did we imagine at the time that we were laying the foundation for what was destined afterwards to turn into a most important Dublin naturalist's business of world wide reputation,'[41] he wrote in his memoirs of Williams & Son with justifiable pride. The Natural History Museum in Dublin contains some 20,000 bird skins as well as a large collection of mammals, a significant part of which was prepared by this one taxidermy firm over the best part of a century.

A tuatara, a rare and endangered New Zealand reptile. This specimen lived in Dublin Zoo for some thirty years from the 1890s. It died in 1941 and it may have been the last creature from the zoo preserved by Williams & Son while it remained a family business.

CHAPTER
5

The Ornithologist

'Near Raheny' (on back label). Watercolour 10 x 14 in. (25.4 x 36 cm). Signed and dated 1885.

Williams retained his interest in the 'bird world' long after he had left the taxidermy business in the 1870s, keeping up with the latest news, swapping information in the way that any group with the same abiding interest will do. He found an outlet for his enthusiasm with the Dublin Naturalists' Field Club, and served on its committee. As he went about Ireland on his sketching trips he would make calls on fellow ornithologists; and as it was a widely scattered brotherhood, correspondence was the main method of communication; many of its members were energetic letter writers.

It is interesting how many of those who made names for themselves as naturalists had no formal scientific background. They were self-taught, spurred by curiosity to observe and record, often in painstaking detail, the natural world around them. Many of their names are remembered yet: Richard John Ussher (1841–1913), who lived in some style at the family seat, Cappagh House in County Waterford, is often cited as the leading ornithologist of the day. He, like many among Victorian naturalists, belonged to the landed gentry. He was the proverbial poacher-turned-gamekeeper in having once been an enthusiastic collector of birds' eggs before reacting against the practice and thenceforward becoming a prominent champion of conservation causes, notably with the Irish Society for the Protection of Birds. He is remembered as the chief author, with Warren, of *The Birds of Ireland* (1900). Robert Warren (1829–1915), also from a landowning family, was an avid birdwatcher all his life, spending his early years at Castle Warren in County Cork and subsequently almost all of his adult life at Moyview on the River Moy, County Sligo, both excellent locations for the observation of birds. Prior to Ussher's famous work, in the nineteenth century there were few reference books on Irish birds to which the enthusiast or serious ornithologist could turn. Between 1849 and 1851 William Thompson (1805–1852) published in parts what was a major scientific study, unfinished at the time of his death. This was *The Natural History of Ireland*, in which his work on birds formed a part. In 1853 a smaller work in a more popular style was published by a friend of Thompson's, John J. Watters, who acknowledged his debt to the earlier work in *The Natural History of the Birds of Ireland, Indigenous and Migratory*. Curiously, in addition to the English and Latin names for bird species, Watters went to the trouble of including the common French names. It would be more than thirty years later before Alexander Goodman More (1830–1895), who joined the staff of the Dublin Museum of Science and Art in 1867, published a list of Irish birds in 1885, which he updated in 1890. A.G. More, as will become apparent, became a valuable friend to Alexander.

Another was Richard Manliffe Barrington (1849–1915), who lived in Fassaroe, County Wicklow, where he had extensive lands. Although he qualified as a barrister, he had wide-ranging interests far beyond the law, including zoology and ornithology. While he wrote on many natural history subjects, he is best remembered for his groundbreaking work *The Migration of Birds as Observed at Irish Lighthouses and Lightships* (1900) which included 'the measurement of about 1,600 wings'. Barrington's extensive collection of skins he left to the Natural History Museum in Dublin, part of which still forms a section of the permanent display. For all his weight of learning Barrington was by all accounts the most genial of companions and an amusing person to be around, to judge from a letter he wrote to Williams, which is as striking as it is unintelligible. It begins: 'My dear Porous Plaster, I could stand anything except being called a "Turnip" – an "individual" is bad enough but a turnip! – a bloodless turnip!! – without fear of favour or affection – is a gross libel.' It goes on to say: 'Of course Hatch St is Hatch St & the people in it are not quite fledged so allowance must be made for them & other bloodless operators.'[1] In the way that friends can sometimes develop private wordplay, Barrington and Williams seem to have worked up a private language all of their own and which was probably understood only between themselves. Barrington appears to be making a pun on Hatch Street, where Alexander lived with his family; but beyond that, at this remove, it is impossible to as much as hazard a guess as to the rest of the meaning of the letter.

There was always a cleric or two around with an interest in bird life. Once such was the Rev. Charles Benson (1836–1919), who had at one time the benefice at Balbriggan, County Dublin, and who wrote *Our Irish Song Birds* (1886 and reprinted since), an evocative book of much charm. He and Alexander had in common not only their love of birdwatching, but the melancholy fate of losing their only sons at an early age. Indeed Benson was prompted to write his book on the death of his fifteen-year-old son, to whom the book is dedicated, and among its chapters are references to field trips father and son shared together.

A notable academic and as such something of an exception within this circle of naturalists whom Williams had befriended was Dr Charles J. Patten (1870–1948). He qualified with distinction in medicine from Trinity College Dublin and became Professor of Anatomy at Sheffield University. A prolific writer on birds, among much else he produced a speculative study on bird psychology, and at least one definitive work, *The Sea Birds of Great Britain and Ireland* (1906), the text of which, for its engaging detail and descriptive passages, repays reading today. Apart from a number of superb line drawings (the author of which for some reason remaining unacknowledged) the book is profusely, if quaintly, illustrated with black-and-white photographs of taxidermy specimens. Patten, as one might expect of an anatomist, was capable of fine taxidermy and used his work in the book as well as photographs of specimens mounted by Williams & Son. Patten was a frequent visitor to the studio in Dame Street. He was a lively correspondent, demanding of himself and others in his approach to ornithology as much as in his medical activities.

Socialising in naturalists' circles was not necessarily time out from his painting career for Alexander, as many of these friends clearly supported him in his art endeavours. We find Ussher writing on birds and pictures in the same letter: 'Your beautiful view of Glena and the Tomies has arrived safely and I send you a cheque for £10. Would you send me 2 rings to hang it with screw shanks I have none. There is a pair of 18 Pochards [and] 2 Tufted Ducks on an adjoining lake and I saw a ♂ Shoveler yesterday week – and a Raven Saturday.'[2]

Williams enjoyed writing articles for magazines mainly on natural history, such as the *Irish Naturalist* and *The Field*; more surprisingly he also contributed an article or two for a short-lived humorous magazine called *Pat*, published in Dublin. This was a profusely illustrated political magazine with topical jokes, many of which are difficult to fathom today. Contributors were not named so it is not possible to identify what he wrote for *Pat*. Unlike his personal writings which show scant regard for punctuation and few corrections, his named published pieces and letters are well crafted.

If Williams was not a scientist, he was nevertheless an acute observer of birds and a reliable witness of bird behaviour. A case in point was his study of sanderlings in which he raised the issue as to why some birds around Dublin Bay did not conform to the usual migratory patterns. Food, he reckoned, was at the heart of the matter. We find him in 1910 writing a letter of enquiry to the museum addressed to J. N. Halbert (author of *List of the Beetles of Ireland* with Rev. W. F. Johnson) and an authority on water mites, asking him to identify what he describes as flies on which Williams had found some sanderlings feeding. He explains he is writing a paper on the sea birds in question.[3] (The answer is noted on the letter. The mites are *Fucellia fucorum*.) His article duly appeared in the *Irish Naturalist* in October of the same year as 'Observations on the Sanderling of Dublin Bay'.

His interest in sanderlings may have been prompted by studies being made on the same species by Charles J. Patten, who was nothing if not methodical in his field studies and with his anatomical and medical knowledge he was rather better equipped than most to delve into the innards of birds. The migration patterns of sanderlings were of particular interest to him and on which he sought Williams' help. Patten was very specific in what he required and how it should be supplied. This letter gives a flavour of his style:

My dear Williams

I hope you will collect all the Sanderling you can during the height of the summer season, and if you let me have their bodies <u>with full data of plumage</u> I shall be delighted to work up the minute anatomy of generatives. The bodies should be placed in formalin <u>immediately after death</u>. I am working away at the generative organs just now and only the other day made sections of the specimens you sent me from Iniskea, on the 21st Aug. 1900 . . . Unfortunately most of the birds were females, but I have a few very interesting testicles under observation. If you get the opportunity you ought to collect <u>all the sanderlings possible</u> and make skins. I will help you if you are overworked, as I believe between us we will settle the question beyond dispute regarding the age of these summer birds. I go to Clare Island about the end of [the] month for a fortnight, and I hope again in September. I must tarry at Achill if you are there. The last body you sent is under way but it is a ticklish piece of work owing to the fact that it was dried up somewhat. Have you any reprints of your paper recently published in *The Field*?

Kindest remembrances and best wishes
Ever Sincerely
C. J. Patten[4]

Evidently Williams was able to supply what was wanted and in the required condition. Patten wrote again two months later:

My dear Williams,
Many thanks for your letters and sanderling bodies. I was very interested to get further evidence on the question of fertility. Fortunately one was a male and the testes have been minutely examined. As far as I can find the bird never bred & was one of the pre-nuptials stage. Shall be delighted to have other bodies at once for investigation. It is splendid that you can get Sanderling. We should examine birds shot every month in the year. When the quite immature birds come [?] to the Bull will you try and get me about half a dozen . . .[5]

You knew where you stood with Patten. He was a man who was unequivocal in his views. Shooting and collecting was justified in the name of science, but not otherwise. He wrote in his preface to *The Aquatic Birds of Great Britain and Ireland*: 'A naturalist who kills for the mere sake of collecting deserves to rank lower than one who does not collect at all.' This would have been regarded as rather radical thinking at the time in some quarters. It would have ruled out virtually all the mounted specimens prepared for private houses, collecting for collecting's sake. It comes as a surprise to discover that having been so supportive in garnering sanderlings for Patten, Williams should suddenly baulk at obtaining a single specimen of a white wagtail for the museum in Dublin:

The spring migration of the White Wagtail along the East Coast of Ireland has now been established as far as authentic observations have taken place, but science demands that there should be proof in the shape of a real bird. Much as I dislike to kill there was no option, so I procured one of the birds, an adult male in excellent plumage which I showed to Dr Scharff and Mr Nichols at the museum during the day, in the flesh. I also procure[d] the male whinchat.[6]

Was it the fact that the white wagtail is less commonly met with than the whinchat that gave him misgivings? Or was he objecting to making the kill for the museum because it was required merely for identification? It is doubtful if he ever had a consistent position. It is also of interest in that, although both Scharff and Nichols knew Williams well, the word of a reliable witness was not regarded as sufficient evidence. A bird in the hand was still required. Old habits died hard.

DAILY MAIL, WEDNESDAY, JANUARY 9, 1907.

FIELD CLUB DEVASTATION.

PHOTOGRAPHY VERSUS COLLECTING.

It sounds like a paradox, like the unintelligent action of some savage nation.

We approve and cultivate the love of Nature; we think it good and desirable above most things. Therefore we encourage children to love Nature by teaching them to kill birds and insects and flowers, and to put them in boxes with little labels. We call it Nature study, and give prizes for it. We look with favour on field clubs that carry devastation among the less common fauna and flora of the countryside. We speak respectfully of wealthy collectors who employ a multitude of agents to deprive the country of its rarest and most beautiful species. We call these people lovers of Nature because they destroy it with enthusiasm.

We admire evolution and arduously trace it out. Yet we praise collectors for stealing its most wonderful results from us. We forget that evolution will never re-create a species we destroy. A species that is dead is gone.

THE VICTIMS OF GREED.

That humane naturalist, Mr. W. H. Hudson, says, in speaking of the Dartford warbler ("Birds and Man," Chap. XII.):

Down to within thirty years ago it was 'airly common, though local, in the South of ... north as the bor... has

Newspaper clip from the *Daily Mail* kept in the 'Ulster Diaries'. The paper is proposing that photography should supersede the collecting of skins, which the paper deplores: '. . . we encourage children to love Nature by teaching them to kill birds and insects and flowers, and to put them in boxes with little labels.' (9 January 1907).

Even after he left the taxidermy business Williams collected skins both for himself and for others, and clearly science was not always in mind. He shot occasionally and evidently kept up his skills in taxidermy. 'You set up and mounted your White Wagtail in a style that I never saw equalled,' Warren wrote to him, 'except by your brother Edward, and in fact I have never seen anything to beat it, either in stuffing or attitude. It is as if the bird was actually standing alive.'[7] Williams certainly had an eye for verisimilitude, noting 'a beautiful Greenshank, graceful and lively . . . I could see that the feathers of the head and neck were ruffled and standing on end and not all carefully smoothed as one sees in the stuffed specimen.'[8]

It is hard to see any pattern to his collecting. He finds that 'Window Martins [house martins] are very plentiful at Skerries, and I obtained one for my collection, the first for years.'[9] Science of sorts breaks in when Williams wants to make a comparison between sanderlings in Youghal and those in Dublin Bay. 'I think there can be little doubt that they are non-breeding birds that have remained in this fine bay extending for over 3 miles from Youghal and which then turns inland a long way. There is an absence here of the immense quantities of sand hoppers and the food cannot be so rich as that of the Bay of Dublin.'[10] More often the entries suggest collecting for collecting's sake. On a visit to Trumbull's, Beechwood, Malahide, he found '3 magpies had been killed and I was sorry

I missed getting one of them for my collection. In the garden I saw a pair of Bullfinches and as the gardener had orders to shoot them I secured a female, also a common wren, a song thrush, and a great tit.'[11]

It was not only bird skins that Williams and Willie collected but occasionally eggs too. On 12 June 1910, Williams records: 'With Willie took walk along Balbriggan. We discovered tree sparrow's nest in the thatch of a deserted cottage. We took clutch of five eggs. Terns passing and repassing along the coast. We saw several tree sparrows drinking at a rivulet close to the road. Walked in through the fields for a while, common buntings everywhere.'[12] Just a fortnight earlier at Skerries they again 'examined the old Lime Kiln on the shore, where my brother took a nest of tree sparrows last year'.[13]

However, collecting was secondary to his main preoccupation of birdwatching, and the occasional articles that he wrote on birds and wildlife form only a small part of what he wrote on the subject. In the early 1900s he wrote up at least three birdwatching diaries. Two belong to the Ulster Museum and for want of a title are referred to here as the 'Ulster Diaries'. How they came into the possession of the museum is not known, but possibly through the naturalist Robert Patterson (1863–1931) who at one time lived at Holywood, County Down. An exhibition of material collected by Patterson was exhibited at the People's Palace, Belfast, and was later transferred to what was then called the Belfast Municipal Museum and Art Gallery, now the Ulster Museum. Patterson died just a year after Williams. It is possible the diaries were among his effects. It is intriguing that neither volume bears either the artist's name or a title, as he was much given to putting both titles and his signature to what he wrote. This suggests the possibility that the two volumes were once part of a larger number of birdwatching diaries and others may yet remain in private hands.

Ornithology aside, the diaries clarify a social issue. Williams and his younger brother met up almost weekly to go birdwatching, but rarely visited each other's houses. There was a chilly stand-off between 4 Hatch Street and 'Flax Bourton' in St Kevin's Park. There were dark murmurings from Flax Bourton that the Hatch Street lot were snobs. Whatever else Williams was, he was not a snob. A snob does not forego a king's levee in favour of staying put, gardening on Achill Island. Nor does a snob acknowledge his lack of education; and no middle class Victorian with notions about himself would revel in manual labour as Alexander clearly did, as we will see, when working on Achill. There was no lack of harmony between the two brothers. Seemingly it was the two wives who could not 'hack it'. The perceived social chasm between art and trade may have been at the heart of the matter.

One volume of the 'Ulster Diaries', which runs from 1 August 1909 to 28 March 1911, contains more than 200 pages of closely written text. The other, slimmer volume has but a single entry for 1906, a second for 1907 and then runs from 2 April 1911 until 2 May 1915. Separate from the two is a day-to-day diary that Williams kept for a number of years on Achill Island. He was almost as compulsive in jotting down bird observations as he was in making sketches.

The diaries make clear that Williams was a birdwatcher rather than what is now known as a twitcher, which is to say he was not in active pursuit of rarities. The pleasure he got from birds lay in observing them, their behaviour, their habits and their calls, whatever those birds might be. Like all naturalists he was keenly tuned in to the changes of the seasons and an intrinsic part of the pleasure of birdwatching and listening lies in observing the seasonal changes in vocal song, in breeding patterns, in noting the contrast between summer and winter dress, in the immature plumage of the young, and not least the arrival and departure of migrants. (The term twitcher, as a matter of interest, was coined only in the 1950s and did not appear in print, it is said, until the magazine *World of Birds* first used it in 1972).[14]

That said, few birds would have been rarer than the nuthatch which put in an appearance in north County Dublin in 1911, and Williams took time and trouble to see it for himself. From Robert Warren came a swift letter of congratulations: 'You must be delighted at your good fortune in seeing and identifying the first nuthatch in Ireland, your friend afterwards seeing the bird running down a tree fully corroborated your identification.'[15] Whatever news Warren had received, it was actually Willie who first saw the bird in Trumbull's garden in Malahide. Williams recorded in his diary that, having been notified by Willie of the bird's appearance, he had to pay two visits himself to Trumbull's before he managed to see it.[16] There is no doubting that the bird the brothers identified was indeed a nuthatch, but the sighting has since been discounted as a probable introduction from across the water where it is a common enough species. 'A bird so notably sedentary is most unlikely to have undertaken, unaided, the crossing of the Irish Sea.'[17] Previous appearances had also been discounted by both A. G. More and Ussher.

The bird Willie and Williams saw could have been an escape. An attractive, well-marked species, the bird in question might have been brought over for keeping in a birdcage. Birdcatchers were busily occupied in satisfying a large market. The old Bird Market off Francis Street was once a landmark in the centre of Dublin city, and features among the artist's sketches of old Dublin. On a visit to Youghal, County Cork, Williams remarks in his diary, without further comment, that in the county 'the goldfinch must be a common bird as I noticed 12 caged in one street.'[18]

It was not only for the domestic trade that wild birds were captured. The Royal Zoological Gardens in Phoenix Park had a display of wild birds – with the assistance of Williams and Willie. If Williams was not a tick-hunter or twitcher, one passage migrant in particular caught his fancy: the white wagtail, or Ray's wagtail as he often called it. Ever since the antics of the willy wagtail had been pointed out to him, as a child, by his father, Williams was intrigued by this group of birds in particular. He looked for white wagtails around Kilbarrack and adjacent spots, initially without success as he confessed to Robert Warren in Cork. This was just the kind of subject on which birdwatchers enjoy exchanging information, with Warren writing back to say: 'You express surprise that neither you nor your brother Edward ever met them in his lifetime! But I think that is easily explained. Although I shot the first in April 1851, yet it was not till 1893 I met them again.' Birdwatchers and hunters have keen memories. Robert Patterson was in on this subject too, writing from County Down: 'I am very glad you have this season again met with the White Wagtail; I have only seen the bird once here.'[19] By persistence Williams and Willy had found where and when to observe them and caught them live: 'During the week the 3 Ray's Wagtail we noticed on last Sunday, we captured with a clap net as they were flying low over a field at Baldoyle and the birdcatcher brought them into my brother Willie who purchased them and sent them out to the Zoological Gardens for the aviary.'[20]

A rare species Alexander mentions in the 'Ulster Diaries', having seen it twice by sheer chance, was the goosander, *Mergus merganser*, once at the Bull and once on a lake in Killarney, the sightings being twenty-five years apart. Robert Warren confessed that in fifty years of living by the River Moy in Ballina he had never seen one.

When his days of choral singing were behind him, it was Williams' habit on a Sunday morning, more often than not, to join forces with Willie and walk out, or take the tram from Dublin to a favoured haunt to do their birdwatching. They would do so Sunday after Sunday, as his diaries indicate. During the week he might cover similar territory painting and sketching. It was an easy matter to get to the coast from the centre of the city, particularly after the turn of the century. There was a horse-drawn tram service from the centre of Dublin to Clontarf which began in 1873, and from 1900 a full tram service as far as Howth with convenient stops along the way. It was these Sunday morning trips that make up the bulk of the diaries.

Fairview at the time was pushing out into the sea. The new area, which was to become Fairview Park, was then also known as 'the promised land'. Williams kept an interested eye on developments: 'Walked with Willie to Annesley Bridge and visited the new plantation on the filled in works at Fairview. The trees & shrubs are very interesting, one that we saw a great many of *Salix jasmonoides* with rich and dark red bark seemed of most vigorous growth.'[21] Sallies were always of particular interest to him and he made a collection for his garden at Bleanaskill Lodge, Achill Island. The 'promised land' having been examined, the pair then headed off to what was perhaps their favourite haunt of all: 'Tram to Dollymount and we walked out on the Bull Wall and sat on the stones in the brilliant sunshine watching the waves reflecting the blue sky and rolling in on the flat sandy strand. A very high tide.' The North Bull Island represents an outstanding habitat for sea birds, being a combination of mudflats, salt marshes and sandflats. It is not a natural island, but developed as a result of human intervention in the area. With the aim of keeping the mouth of the River Liffey free of silt, massive bulwarks were built in the eighteenth and nineteenth centuries, notably what are known as the Great South Wall and North Bull Wall. These protective walls in combination with natural tidal scouring led to the deepening of the mouth of the river. Conversely, it was the silting up of the area beyond the mouth of the river, a process that still continues, that led to the creation of what is the elongated North Bull Island (currently about 5 km long by 1 km wide) which stretches in a line parallel with the shore towards Sutton and Howth. The Bull Bridge which joins the island with the mainland was built in 1907 and is still in use. Bull Island is a site of national and indeed international importance for both breeding birds and winter visitors. Among species that occur in internationally significant numbers are knot, pale-bellied Brent geese and redshank.

Of local historical interest today is an article that Williams wrote for the *Irish Naturalist* and which was subsequently printed in booklet form, with the title of 'Bird Life in Dublin Bay: The Passing of Clontarf Island'. Where was the island? One might well ask. Williams answered the question in some detail:

> This place was a conspicuous object and of considerable dimensions, measuring about 400 yards wide and 16 feet in height. It was situated close to the road which bounds the City on the east, and which extends from the Alexandra Basin, North Wall as far as the River Tolka at Annesley Bridge, Fairview. Today at high water the sea-mew swims over its ancient site.
>
> The highest part of the island was composed of coarse banks of yellow clay, full of pebbles and layers of sea-shells, and those banks bore a thick covering of grass, which with a profusion of Sea-pink made the place look gay and bright. Here the fishermen used to spread their nets on poles to dry, and various kinds of craft were hauled up on the grassy banks out of the reach of the tide during the winter.
>
> There were two picturesque wooden cabins where the men lived all the year, and a large covered bathing-shed stood close to the big swimming-pond, which was enclosed by wooden stakes and tree stumps. The bath was about 30 yards long, and here many youngsters learned to swim in safety, as the bottom sloped gently from one end, to about a depth of 7 feet. During the long warm summer evenings there was plenty of animation as the boats full of bathers were ferried across from the city side, and the grassy banks were a favourite resting place for tired artisans.

It had been a favourite haunt for Williams and his brother Edward in their youth, enabling them to become 'acquainted with the appearance and habits of nearly every species of bird that frequented the shores of Dublin Bay'.

> The early frosty mornings of September used to find us wading along the sandy margins of the streams that skirted the island, searching closely among the flocks of Dunlins for the Little Stint or the Curlew Sandpiper, and sometimes late into the moonlight nights lying among the long grass and listening to the confused cries of the multitudes of sea-fowl spread all over the island to the water's edge.

Alexander recalled the island with affection all his life:

> Those who remember the charm of the place cannot banish a feeling of regret that this romantic spot, so easy of access to the Dublin people, so splendid a recreation ground, where the artist found so many subjects for his pencil, where the naturalist could so

Picture of Clontarf Island by Williams featured in the *Irish Naturalist* magazine.

conveniently study the aquatic birds of Dublin Bay, and where the fowler exercised his ingenuity amongst the great flocks of sea-fowl, has disappeared as completely as if the sea had swallowed it up. At high water the moonlight is reflected over the glassy tide where once the weather beaten old wooden houses stood, and the tops of a few blackened and decayed stakes are all that now remain to mark the site.

The demand that sprang up for the materials to make concrete led to the sale of the island, and long strings of carts and horses conveyed away the gravel, of which it was composed, at low water to the Clontarf shore, and at high water iron and wooden barges came sailing round the Liffey and anchored, and when the tide fell, leaving them high and dry, were filled with gravel of all sizes, and sailed away with their cargoes when the sea returned. This work was carried on for so many years that, almost imperceptibly and apparently unnoticed, the whole place became flattened down and brought level with the surrounding mud at low water, and even at the present time barges may daily be seen slowly carrying out the process of destruction, and scraping away anything that may still remain to show the site of 'Old Mud Island'.

A sketch from 1878 accompanied the article, showing a sloping wooden jetty leading up to a quite substantial fisherman's hut with nets drying beyond it, and plentiful gulls overhead. The whereabouts of the original sketch are unknown.

Changes along soft coastlines can be rapidly affected by weather patterns as well as human interference. As a regular visitor to the North Bull, Williams was very conscious of such changes. An entry for 18 June 1911 illustrates how quickly natural changes can occur:

Near the end of the Bull noticed a curious change in the storm beach. Some years ago the sea threw up a considerable extent of sand at some distance from the tidal mark

'Goodbye', oil on board, inscribed and signed. 7¾ x 14½ in. (19.6 x 37.1 cm). The boat and the building suggest this might be Clontarf Island, although the woman's dress is more typical of the west of Ireland.

proper. The water at high tide was deep between this sandbank covered at full tide and the beach of the Bull. Latterly this long ridge, over a mile in length, has been accumulating and is now above water except at very exceptional high tides. A zone of sand covered with short marin [marram] grass extends along the Bull beach now, to the seaward of this there is a bare zone, and recently has been formed between this and the water a long strip of fresh green marsh covered by ordinary stunted grass quite out on the sea shore and which must be inundated at times to depth of nearly three feet. This long zone of verdant grass extending for about a mile presents a curious sight as the whole of this recent addition now appears at a place which only a few years ago was part of the bare wave-worked sandy beach, and the channel between the raised sandbank seaward which used to be deep enough to bathe in is now filling up rapidly.[22]

There are plenty of observations of this kind in the diaries.

Williams often recorded the numbers of each species of birds he saw and one might wonder how he went about counting them. In one entry he tells of his own rough and ready method of making computations where large numbers were involved. Here he is on a December morning in 1909 at Malahide:

Coming out on the estuary close to the water we heard a great confused noise in the distance and saw a great flock of 300 Brent Geese on [the] wing. They settled on the water and with the glass we had a splendid view of this great army just arrived from Arctic solitudes where perhaps the foot of man has never trodden. There they were full of life & activity, all in movement swimming in and out in one great extended line. Their bright white sides and black necks flashing in the water and reflecting the frosty morning sun. I counted by a favourite habit of the birds of swimming out in an extended line and separating so that I could easily count up to 50 and then comparing them with the length of the rest of the birds and their crowd of heads came to the conclusion that their numbers were over 300. Away beyond this great flock and closer to the opposite shore and extended along the shallow water were black masses of Baldcoots at rest. It would be difficult to tell the exact number, but there were certainly over 1000 birds in extended formation here thinned out and there in closer clumps.[23]

How accurate was his method of counting? According to Niall Hatch of BirdWatch Ireland:

The counting method that he describes is very similar to those employed by wetland bird counters today, where a group of a known size is used to estimate a flock total, though with modern optical equipment (especially high magnification telescopes), these estimated counts are probably a bit more accurate today. We actually train our counters to do this using a special computer program, and it has regularly been found that when people try this estimating trick, to begin with they usually underestimate the number of birds present, sometimes by a huge amount: it takes a lot of practice.[24]

On another occasion, having to take shelter against the rain and with the tide receding, on a whim Williams decided to record not only the order in which species were arriving on the mudflats, but the numbers in each cluster of arrivals. It made for an unusual diary entry:

The rain getting worse my brother and self made for the shelter of the coastguard station and ensconcing ourselves in the lee of the Bull Wall for an hour I watched the ever increasing numbers of waders flying up the stream against the wind and rain and crossing the Bull bridge, mak[ing] their way farther up the exposing mud flats of Clontarf . . . Two redshanks were the first to arrive here as on the shores of Achill Sound in Co. Mayo. This bird is the very first to watch the fall of the tide and makes its way to where the first submerged mudflat becomes visible. Birds now follow in their order: Curlew 2.13; Seapie 2; small parties of Dunline; Curlew 3.3.4.5.3.1.1.1.4. Whimbrel 2; Redshanks 3; Curlew 8.14; Whimbrel 1; Curlew 4.3.4.1.1.11. Redshanks 1.3; Dunlin 2.5.6; Curlew 1; Dunlin 10; Curlew 1.8; Redshanks 1; Dunlin 10.20; Curlew 3.1.34. Redshanks 2; Dunlin 4.9. Small waders Dunlin & Ring Plover 30.23; Redshanks 1; Curlew 1; Redshanks 2; Curlew 10.1.6. Dunlin 8.15.30; Redshank 1; Ring Plover 13; Curlew 4; Ring Plover 4; Redshank 10; Dunlin 6; Curlew 11; Redshanks 2; Dunlin 8; Ring Plover 2; Curlew 3; R. Plover 1; R. Plover 15; Curlew 5; Redshank 2; Dunlin 8, Redshanks 2, Curlew 5; Redshanks 6; Curlew 11; Ring Plover 17.15; Curlew 40; Redshanks 5; Dunlin 3.12; Curlew 2; Dunlin 6.3.3; Curlew 2; Dunlin 13.10; Herring gulls 2; Dunlin 6; Curlew 7; Dunlin 8; Curlew 2.2.4.60.30;

Dunlin 12.4.10; Curlew 1; Blackheaded gull 2. Plenty of these birds could be seen all along the edge of the stream for miles . . . Through the misty rain flocks might be seen still approaching, but I came away about 1pm by the Tram to Nelson's Pillar.[25]

Happily, a birdwatcher today, if so inclined, could do the same thing and with the same species.

Young Willie had some curious habits when out on his rambles, if they can be described as habits. Williams recorded his brother sowing seeds of what he calls Escholtzia (actually *Eschscholtzia*), on or in the vicinity of Bull Island;[26] adding nonchalantly that 'they may puzzle some future botanists to account for their appearance if they grow.' A week later Willie is at it again, only this time at Portmarnock: 'We crossed the sand dunes, plenty of breeding lapwings . . . Willie sowed a variety of seeds he brought with him for the purpose.'[27] But what was the purpose and what were the seeds? More poppies? *Eschscholtzia* is the genus name for poppies found along the North American coast, the best known of which is *E. californica*. This common garden species, an import of course, may be the one Willie was intent on sowing, but the species or hybrid name that Alexander has written is illegible. What is significant is that the plants appear not to have been indigenous. What was Willie's purpose? It is possible that the poppies, were they to grow, might attract moths or butterflies. Perhaps that is what he had in mind. But exotics, if not actually pernicious, usually contribute less to the environment than native plants. On another occasion, as Williams records, Willie went to the trouble of transplanting thistles to the sand hills along the Bull. These he and Willie had previously removed from Portmarnock golf links. Native thistles would be rather more useful than Californian poppies – thistledown is a favourite food of goldfinches for instance – but interfering with the native flora of wild places would create consternation today and would not have found favour then.

There were plenty of opportunities, sometimes on trips with the Dublin Naturalists' Field Club, sometimes with the Dublin Sketching Club as well as on private jaunts, for Williams to visit islands off the east coast. His own little crafts were not up to it – he used them only for paddling around the mudflats on the Bull – but he had friends with much larger boats. There was Trumbull's 'tight little racer' the *Ixia* of 6¼ tons, on which he mentions going to Lambay Island, and George Prescott (of which more in the chapter on the Dublin Sketching Club) had a 'commodious motor boat' moored at Kingstown, on which Williams was often a guest. Sketching could be combined with birdwatching on such trips, sometimes providing opportunities not available to the shore-bound. En route to Ireland's Eye he mentions passing 'The Home Fleet under the command of Sir Wm May, [which] lay off Kingstown. 8 vessels: [including] The Lord Nelson, Flag Ship; Dreadnought; St Vincent; Bellerophon; Collingwood and the Hospital ship Marie'.[28] Williams was in his element on such trips. Arriving on the island:

. . . we were soon up to our knees in bluebells extending in long streaks like blue smoke from the upper rocks down to the edge of the sandy shore, and interspersed with the young, tender shoots of bracken . . . From every part of the island could be heard the loud, angry scolding of a fine male peregrine . . . he was flying in circles round the highest part of the cliff, sometimes within 60 yards of us. It was beautiful to watch him after a wide circle high over the cliffs poise on perfectly motionless wings . . . using his broad fanned tail, he rose or fell and sheared off over the blue sea, again coming in a wide sweep round and fiercely calling, his quickly repeated and incessant Cae! Cae! Cae! Cae! Cae! Before we left he alighted on the topmost pinnacle of the detached rock known as the Stag and here at a distance of only 150 yards, with the glass I studied every detail of his plumage . . . his splendid dark eyes were very visible, and often he turned his head a little aside and looked down on the ledges below him packed closely with black and white bodies of the razorbills and guillemots, whilst herring gulls and kittiwakes crossed back and forward . . . Sometimes the wings and tail would droop and his head would project forward, the back well arched and in this position he would continue calling, his cream coloured throat and barred breast showing out well against the dark violet blue of the sea. Parties of puffins were dispersed all about the sea near the base of the rocks. I counted 30 in one patch . . . We bore away for the Home Fleet off Kingstown and sailed round them, seeing them to much advantage.[29]

Inland the city was rapidly spreading out but beyond Clontarf there were still great swathes of farmland, wild meadow and extensive hedgerows. Baldoyle, Kilbarrack and Swords were still rural villages. Places familiar to Williams have now disappeared under concrete and housing. One such favourite haunt on account of its diversity of plant and bird life were the so-called Pits of Baldoyle, an expanse of marshy hollows and reed ponds where sand martins once nested. Having taken the tram to Dollymount and walked to Kilbarrack:

I struck into the fields at the old Abbey, crossed the railway and admired the advancing growth so perceptible all over the Pits of Baldoyle, the blazoning of the gorse, the bright green hedges, and the new green flaggers[30] starting out of the water helped by the balmy sweetness, warmth and light of this beautiful May morning. I notice the babbling of the Sedge Warblers in the scrubby undergrowth, the roving call of the Redpolls, the Hedge Sparrows' song and the Willow Wren's delightful singing, but all outdistanced by the soul inspiring melody of the skylarks overhead.[31]

From the old mill near Portmarnock Bridge he could see scoters, not by the naked eye he notes but with a 'glass', and in season there would be reed buntings 'in full summer dress'. Three weeks earlier, in April, he had been to the Pits of Baldoyle and found 'the tall gorse bushes that appear between the pools of water have been all fired,

'The Glare of Summer sketch from nature Portmarnock nr Dublin April 1893' (written on back).
Oil on board. 10 x 18 in. (25.4 x 46 cm). Signed.

the undergrowth burnt away and the tall blackened stems of the gorse are all that is left.'
That seemed to trouble Williams more than the wrens:

> We are surprised to find that the burnt bushes are full of them, evidently just arrived.
> We walked quietly through them and note that they keep very low down near the
> roots . . . Lying down in shelter again we are pleased to hear the song of the Chaffinch
> in the thinly covered green thorn hedge, and also note the jerky music of the Reed
> Buntings, and from the other side of the hedge a flock of over 200 Greenfinches
> mount up and away. Amongst them we detect a few yellowhammers. A grey wagtail
> in graceful swoops comes over the fields to the ponds, and from an adjacent farm the
> domestic fowl can be distinguished, mixed with the music of the thrush and robin. But
> the bird we love to hear is the common linnet, so sweetly and suddenly singing,
> almost to itself, from a spray of yellow gorse.[32]

He had a permit from Lord Ardilaun to enter his estate at St Anne's, Clontarf, now a
public park, and he made much use of it:

> I have never seen so many flocks of fieldfares, starlings and redwings all making for
> the trees at St Anne's and on entering [I saw] they were in abundance, especially the
> missel thrushes and fieldfares quarrelling over the berries in the fine yew trees
> abounding in the demesne. A mantle of fine snow covered the ground and picked out
> the tracery of leaves and stems on the trees and thick as they could walk, starlings
> were searching the ground under the trees in company with blackbirds, thrushes,
> redwings, missel thrushes and fieldfares, all keeping up a lively chatter. I made my

way along past the house and into the Dingle and the walk here was enchanting. Bamboos, ornamental plants, ferns and all the beautiful foliaged plants standing out in perfect outline silhouetted with snow. Noticed a party of longtailed tits in the tall trees. Stealing up quietly I peeped out on the lake where 6 swans in company with an Australian swan [*Cynus atratus*, black with a conspicuous red bill] were in the immediate foreground . . . Lord Ardilaun in severe weather feeds the wild birds and his servants boil potatoes and spread them about the grounds with other food which is greedily devoured.[33]

Trees and shrubs are often remarked on, side by side with the birds.

Farming practices were becoming more efficient with a corresponding loss of avian habitat. Williams watched while favourite spots, including the water meadows at Baldoyle, were changed irreversibly: 'The owners have been filling in the hollows and sandpits and smoothing the surface for cultivation and we fear that the gorse bushes we love and admire may soon follow – man's hunger for land. We walk through fields where long tracts of soil have been carted away from the base of the stone walls. These parts used to be covered with a dense growth of weeds affording food and shelter for birds.'[34] At Portmarnock, 'The Dublin Co. Council have been ruthlessly slaying the thorn hedges and cutting them down almost to the roots everywhere along the public roads.' A local stud farmer, Williams records, successfully sued the council and obtained damages for loss of shelter. No such recourse was open to the birds: 'We must "wait and see" and hope that the course of time may even improve the new growth, making the hedges thicker than before.'[35]

If the reckless pruning of hedges was one thing, the erection of barbed wire was quite another and Williams was perfectly capable of taking matters into his own hands: 'Glad to see that the farmer has taken the hint to remove all trace of barbed wire from the public stile leading to the path to Baldoyle which has been a right of way in my recollection for over 40 years,' he writes with satisfaction in an entry for May 1915, 'and which he attempted to stop by heavily interlacing the entrance with barbed wire. This I cut a passage through with a strong wire snippers. The old stile is in the next field to Kilbarrack Church ruin, and I see now he has taken away all trace of the impediment.'[36] But he could not persuade the farmers to retain the natural vegetation: 'Regret to see so much of the gorse has been cut away in recent years.' Such a comment from a bird lover is predictable but his next comment takes us by surprise: 'The Howth Estate people have built a splendid concrete wall reaching from the Graveyard of Kilbarrack as far as the next farm on the Howth side. Great improvements have been carried out and old fences levelled and hollows filled in fields and now turned into pasture – at great expense. Favourite pools where snipe used to be regularly flushed have gone forever and given way to husbandry.' This is less than a lamentation. Loss of avifauna habitat is measured here against a Victorian faith in progress, as yet untroubled by the knowledge of how far such progress would take us.

Whatever the great R. J. Ussher may have thought of some of the practices that Alexander and Willie indulged in is not recorded. Maybe the topic of what was procured for Williams & Son in Dame Street was off limits but could hardly have been a secret. A visit to Cappagh House, Cappoquin, County Waterford, in the summer of 1910 was a memorable event for Alexander:

> Mr Ussher met me at Cappoquin and after service at the church there drove me through a lovely country . . . soon the woods of Cappagh appeared on our left. There are 150 acres of hill clothed to the top with trees. A pond of considerable size and other bits of water are near to the house and after luncheon Mr Ussher took me down to the boat to have a row and look round. He also showed me his other sanctuary of which he is proud and jealously guards the spot, access is through a rustic gate and paling extending into the water on both sides of the path. The whole place is delightfully tropical, overgrown with underwood, and covered with trees and shrubs; underneath these in a dark secluded spot is the lair of the otters. Several holes in the dark peat and leaf mould showed where the animals enjoyed the owner's protection. We rowed on the pond which is deep but densely filled with green weed stuff which provides a splendid resort for water snails and other insects on which the birds and trout feed.
>
> After dinner we proceeded to the 'Badger Sanctuary' in a thick wood on the slope of the hill, of which the owner is also proud. The creatures had thrown up an immense heap of clay and appeared to have several entrances to their den. Proceeding up the hill we came out on to a clear tract free of trees, where a plantation of Japanese fir trees had been made. The little trees seemed to be doing very well, some were nearly 2 feet high but were nearly lost in the long grass in some places. The evening was closing and we wanted to hear the nightjars 'charring'. We had not long to wait as one started in a group of fir trees its uncanny sounds. Mr Ussher crept up close to the tree which it left and flew away over the meadow between us. We heard others, and we got into a very dark corner and waited for some of the birds to come up close to us without success. Coming down the hill amongst the trees to the farm yard the sound of young owls screeching reached us and one ghostly form we discerned flying softly over a shed and looking startlingly white in the darkness. I had a great treat afforded me by being allowed most kindly by my host to read the manuscript of many of his Tours in Ireland in search of bird life. His many cave digging searches for mammoths and extinct animals and his successful searches in 'kitchen middens' for bones of the Great Auk. I retired to rest and left my bedroom window wide open and was lulled to sleep by the hissing screech of the owls in the fir trees.[37]

As revealing of the drift of Williams' mind as his diary entries are the numerous news cuttings he pasted in with them. On the lighter side, there were curiosities that caught his attention: a hawk that swooped down on a golf ball; a starling with seventeen catch phrases; a bird porridge (with a scientific recipe) which was administered by daubing over small trees; 'Lightning as a song stimulant' – for nightingales; a preventative against gnat bites in a letter from the Dean of Clogher (*Oleum betulae*, the oil of the white birch mixed with a little olive oil is the answer apparently – but useless if you have already been bitten, the dean thoughtfully added); and the 'Great Auk's Egg Romance', the egg in question having been bought in 1894 for 36s and sold a few weeks later for a whopping £183.15.0. It was up for sale again in 1912, while being 'safely guarded and kept at Messrs Steven's auction rooms, Covent Garden'. More sober news cuttings covered such topics as reports from the Tuscar lighthouse by C. J. Patten; 'winter' butterflies making an appearance due to unseasonal warmth, and the migratory patterns of birds. But by far the most numerous of the news clips Williams kept show a preoccupation with conservation and related issues of the day. Clips on the millinery trade; a leaflet listing what birds were protected and where; annual reports from the Irish Society for the Protection of Birds (which had a membership of 227 in 1910), one lamenting that Kerry County Council refused to pass any resolution protecting the eggs of choughs; another recording that the extension of the closed season for goldfinches 'had done a great deal of good' – in Killarney the work of birdcatchers had almost exterminated them – but trappers were thought to be decreasing in numbers generally. Ussher came in for praise in the protection he had organised for the phalaropes breeding in the west, while in Donegal C. W. Wright reported likewise the successful protection of the red throated diver after years of failure.

As conservation became more of a public issue, it gave rise to strong feelings. An acrimonious debate erupted in the press over the shooting of a rarity, a bar-tailed godwit, in Youghal, County Cork, in 1909. Williams saved three news clips on the subject. Two of the contributors dismissed the fuss over the bird. Fergus McClean came to the sportsman's defence asserting that identity of the bird was not known until after the bird had been shot and sarcastically ventured the question, 'Is your correspondent a vegetarian? I fancy he must be.' Another correspondent writing anonymously as 'A Sportsman' was even more sarcastic: 'When Ireland becomes prosperous, sober, and contented under Home Rule, and there is no longer any ordinary crime, it is pleasing to imagine the almost useless RIC [Royal Irish Constabulary] employed (about Youghal at least) in protecting rare little birds from your correspondent and his friends.' The third letter to the editor, as one might expect from R. J. Ussher, was a well-considered one in which he took the middle ground: 'I beg to offer some remarks on the birds that ought chiefly to be spared. These are species that either breed in Ireland in very small numbers, like the beautiful kingfisher, which is everywhere shot, or would breed if they were spared, like the bittern.' (Ironically, the bittern is no longer a breeding species in Ireland.) Ussher then provides a list which includes rarities such as the bar-tailed godwit, before mentioning a few species he would not protect, such as hawks, magpies, and grey crows, which are 'enemies of the feathered race'. He concludes: 'We need to discriminate what should not be shot, and to learn what great enjoyment and benefit may be derived from encouraging most birds.'[38] In the light of population changes we might differ with Ussher over which species need protection, otherwise to many his letter would sound remarkably modern.

Such a letter could hardly have been written when Williams was a youth. Back in the 1850s and 1860s conservation and bird protection hardly impinged on public consciousness. That was a time when Williams hunted kingfishers along the Tolka.

But times were changing. 'Warren,' wrote Williams after visiting his friend at his house at Monkstown, County Cork, with its view across to Spike Island, 'greatly deplores the scarcity of birds, sea and land, compared to what he remembers 50 years ago when he lived here.'[39] That was written in 1910. Warren put it down to changing agricultural practices and an increase in maritime traffic. For all that there was still an abundance of wildlife in a land less sullied, and a landed gentry who maintained their woodlands and hedgerows, their lakes and water meadows, and became naturalists in the process.

Alexander did not belong to that leisured class of Victorians whose time was their own. But he was one of those rare fortunates for whom between work and leisure there was no conflict, indeed no dividing line. Where he went to sketch, he could watch birds; where he went to watch birds, he could sketch. We take leave of him absorbed in painting the world around him on a warm summer's day in July 1910, by the Lake Hotel in Killarney:

> Numbers of birds come to feed on the grasses in profusion. Reed buntings, yellow buntings, greenfinches, chaffinches and sparrows, bullfinches – nothing could look better than they did, on a small wild rose bush in full flower. Steel black and red and white. Siskins came in livery of black, gold and green, and perching on a plant of the tall buttercup exhibited their harmonious colouring, set off with a background of white marguerites and mauve and white orchis, springing out of emerald grass with many coloured wildflowers. Many were the pleasing little incidents I witnessed as brush in hand I patiently portrayed a lovely scene of sylvan beauty with a background of purple green mountains and blazes of hot sun between showers. Dancing over the meadow comes a lovely azure winged dragon fly, but the keen willow wren with her little ones hid in the thick of the wild rose bush has seen it. She swoops down and flutters to right and left and in an instant returns to the spray, in her mouth the luscious morsel, and the two folded azure wings only project as she jigs head downward in search of her young. The spotted flycatcher also sits on the fir tree bough in the shade. He comes launching out into the warm summer air in semi-circular curves over the meadow, snaps right and left. There is food for all and to spare . . . I was charmed with the singing of the greenfinch, one was only a couple of yards away behind a bush and its song was particularly sweet.[41]

Sketching and birdwatching . . . few vocations and pastimes combine so well together. Alexander well recognised his good fortune.

PART III

THE SINGER

Boats in all their manifestations greatly appealed to the artist. This pencil sketch is inscribed 'Torpedo catcher Kingstown'. 4 x 7 in. (10 x 17.8 cm). Early twentieth century.

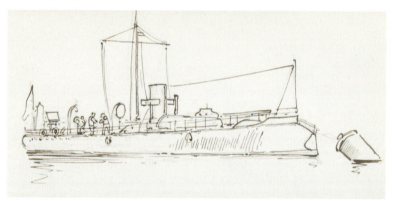

Pencil sketch inscribed 'Torpedo boat Kingstown'. A preparatory sketch, among several, used for drawings for the *Graphic*. Torpedo boat was the original name for a submarine. 4 x 7 in. (10 x 17.8 cm). Early twentieth century.

Oil on canvas. Dublin Bay with an impending storm. Poolbeg is at the extreme right of the picture. The main boat is a brigantine, once a very familiar sight along the Dublin quays where they would deposit and collect cargo, typically coal. The boat to its left is a lugger used for herring fishing. Signed and dated 1880. 12 x 22 in. (30.5 x 55.9 cm).

CHAPTER
6

Parallel Lives

Watercolour signed, dated 1892 and inscribed 'Old Canon St. St Patrick's Close, Dublin'. 10 x 12¼ in. (26 x 33 cm).
The artist returned to this subject again three years later, *The Irish Times* commenting: 'This is a bit of Dublin now
passed away, for Old Canon street, with its quaint curio shops, was part of the site taken in by St Patrick's Park.
Mr Williams took this sketch on the very last day of the existence of Old Canon street in the form here pictured.'

D uring the period that I was steadily settling down to the study of the art of painting I was dabbling off and on in music'.[1] Whatever about pursuing two careers, clearly there was no possibility of indefinitely sustaining three, although for a period he did just that: combining painting with singing on top of going into the shop in Dame Street for a day's work in taxidermy. Ironically, the one Williams jettisoned was the one which would have best sustained him into old age – taxidermy.

There was no music in the Williams household apart from his mother singing about the house in 'an attractive voice'. She had no formal training and there is no reason to believe Williams had either. He does mention having had some singing lessons as a child but it is unlikely they amounted to much. His real start in music began through his friendship with Ivor McDonnell, once a boy soprano at the Chapel Royal, now a tenor of unbounded ambitions. It was Ivor who introduced Williams to the musical scene in Dublin. There was plenty of it about. Anyone with pretensions to a bit of gentility and the makings of a voice might be expected to participate in musical evenings at home or at grander and more formal salons and soirées. Music making was still part of the weft and weave of the social fabric of the day, with the division between amateur and professional musician much less well defined than it has since become.

Not one to shirk a challenge, Alexander began working up a duet or two with Ivor McDonnell before joining forces with another friend, Tom Large, and attempting a trio. This was Haydn's serenade 'Maiden Fair', except their version was one with a difference. Amateur dramatics were as popular as music, and the three friends concocted what sounds like a typical piece of Victorian drawing-room malarkey: 'Whenever we performed, we fixed up a screen, behind which the bass Tom Large in a night shirt and red sleeping cap waited, whilst we sang the first verse of the duet. At the commencement of the second verse he made his appearance and delivered himself in abusive music which never failed to bring down the house.' By abusive Williams presumably meant hamming the thing up for all it was worth. The trio became a popular party piece.

There was another aspect to these amateur frolics which was almost certainly pivotal to his subsequent career as a professional singer. As Williams tells it, he found he had a gift for ventriloquism. It was an entirely accidental discovery:

I had been to hear a ventriloquial performance at the Rotunda Rooms in company with some friends, and next day we were discussing the performance, and we all tried to make our voices appear up in the chimney from the fire place. All had a go at it, and when I tried, I asked a question in my natural voice, and replied by employing some kind of constriction in my throat. My listening companions shouted out in excitement 'You can do it Williams' just like the fellow we heard last night. I need hardly say that no-one was more surprised than myself at the possession of such [a] gift . . . I continued to practise and took considerable pains to construct a figure of a 'shock headed' boy, with a large head and small body which I modelled in gutta percha and made the chin to move up and down to imitate speaking by an internal

Pencil sketch, inscribed 'Burris Court near Christchurch Cath^d'. The cathedral towers behind. Note the Georgian doorway set in the remains of a derelict house on the right. 7 x 8½ in. (17.8 x 21.6 cm).

arrangement which I manipulated with one hand behind whilst the figure was seated on my knee. It was a fiendish looking creature with stiff red hair, and large human looking eyes that stared in a vacant gaze. The dress was short knickerbocker, with bare legs modelled in gutta percha, stockings and little shoes completed the impish look of what our domestic termed 'a little divil'.[2]

What is one to make of this? The artist's nephew was sceptical that his supposed skill amounted to anything.[3] Against that we have Williams' testimony of the number of times he performed with 'Master Johnny Gogarty' as he called the little devil and the success he had with him. Audiences were then no doubt more amenable to suspending disbelief and more easily amused by amateur theatricals. He first tried out Master Johnny at a children's party, '. . . where I produced him from a small carpet bag; seating myself on a chair at one end of the drawing room I placed him on my knee. To this day I can vividly recall the expressions on the faces of the children as they crowded round and watched with absorbing interest and open mouths . . . and the vociferous laughter that greeted one of Johnny's little songs 'The Cuckoo' given in a small piping voice.'[4] Never mind that one child burst into tears in terror. Williams had more reason to remember that 'amongst the older visitors one very pretty young lady attracted my attention, owing to her radiant face, her golden hair and her infectious hearty laughter'. This was Miss Catherine Gray from Monkstown, then aged about ten. She would become something of a Dublin beauty, and the artist's wife.

There were plenty of musical engagements for Alexander and his friends; events with such aspiring titles as 'Grand Conversazione' held by the Telegraph branch of the civil service and 'Grand Soirée Ball' of the Independent Order of Rechabites, among them. The term 'soirée' was giving way to 'conversazione' in the 1870s, according to Williams, the distinction in meaning becoming blurred. Be that as it may, at any of these events Williams and company were expected to provide entertainment.

Master Johnny Gogarty made his public debut at the Antient Concert Rooms at 28 Great Brunswick Street (now Pearse Street) on 4 September 1871 in a concert given by the Total Abstinence Society. Hardly the most promising of audiences, one might have thought, but the performance went well enough for Master Johnny to be invited for a return visit some time later. His second appearance was even more successful. This was for a civil service soirée in the Round Room of the Rotunda and Master Johnny triumphed: 'The floor was crowded . . . Master Johnny was in very good form that evening and the "gags" and impromptus frequent. After his song was over and the applause died out, Johnny suddenly squeaked out "Look Sir at the soldier in the gallery!" In an instant every head in the audience turned, and every eye was directed toward the empty gallery, and when everybody saw the sell the applause was deafening.'[5] Things went rather differently at Swift's Hospital (now known as St Patrick's Hospital) in Kilmainham: 'When a number of the lunatics were allowed into the drawing room and mixed with the guests, the appearance of Master Johnny seemed to quite upset their equilibrium and they became so terribly excited at the little divil's appearance that I think they would have gone for me, only that numerous attendants were close at hand to remove the most obstreperous quickly.' The patients of Swift's Hospital aside, there seems no doubt that Master Johnny was a popular turn in Dublin.

In mixing in the milieu of choirmen it was a natural progression for Williams to think of choral work himself. He had chosen an opportune time. In the face of increasing civil unrest in Ireland, the British Prime Minister, W. E. Gladstone, had set about introducing reforms. Among such measures was the disestablishment of the Church of Ireland, the official Church of state since the 1600s. The bill was drawn up in 1869 and came into law in 1871. Anticipating the need to make economies, St Patrick's Cathedral formed what was known as the Amateur Choir, referred to by Williams also as the Voluntary or Gentlemen's Choir. The idea was that unpaid amateur singers would supplement the vicars choral. After Disestablishment there was a third category, the stipendiary choirman, the term vicar choral becoming an honorary title.

The Voluntary Choir St Patrick's National Cathedral 1871. Dublin

G. H. WONFOR

DUBL

Photograph of the Voluntary Choir, St Patrick's Cathedral, 1871. Williams is centre under the picture of the cathedral.

When Williams was offered a place among the baritones in the amateur choir, he seized it:

> I thoroughly entered into and enjoyed the services, sitting amongst others of the same voice, one leaning on another, and singing together; it was a delight to stand in the choir and see the glorious morning sun streaming in many coloured beams across the grand old building, and it was a joy during the week looking forward to Sunday morning, and its voluntary devotional exercises.[6]

Novice though he was, he could get by singing with other amateurs, learning music by ear. This was about as far as his contribution to the music life of Dublin might have gone, but for a chance occurrence. It was while practising at Ivor McDonnell's house that Williams went from his normal baritone voice into the alto range, impressing his friend with the quality and the ease with which he could sing in the high register.

Contrary to what is sometimes thought, the male alto is not a freak. Any male, be he tenor, baritone or bass, has the potential to sing in the falsetto range. Indeed the virtuoso French *basso cantante*, Pol Plançon (1854–1914) was said to have been able, as a party piece, to sing roulades, runs and trills in falsetto fit to rival the warblings of any female coloratura.

Williams gives no credit to Master Johnny for his facility to sing in falsetto but it is hard to see how his alto voice could have sprung into being ready-made without practice and lots of it. When he refers to Master Johnny singing in a 'piping voice', clearly he was singing in falsetto.

It took little time for word to get around that here was a new alto in the offing. The upshot was that Billy Murphy, assistant organist at St Patrick's Cathedral, gave Alexander another voice trial, as an alto this time, and 'told me that the quality of my voice was uncommonly good and that there was money in it'. As a light baritone (the most common male voice), it was pointed out to him, if he was not already aware of the fact, he was unlikely to progress much further. But Williams had reservations:

> It took me some time to make up my mind to take his advice, as a baritone I was unnoticed sitting comfortably at the far end of the Choir singing and getting support from others of the same voice. If I consented to change to an alto, I would have to take my place alone at the other end of the choir in full view of the congregation, sing a difficult inner part in a strange voice, and be obliged to depend entirely on my own ability for success. I had taken up the study of music so late in life that I felt great difficulty in progressing. I hardly knew one note from another and for a long time I was fearful of making mistakes.[7]

Not without regret he gave up what he described as 'the manly baritone' in favour of singing as a piping alto. He got coaching from Billy Murphy and had the support of a seasoned chorister during services. As it happened, the chorister in question was a son of the painter and academician, George Sharpe, RHA (1802–77), who, at the opening of Royal Hibernian Academy exhibitions, Williams recalled, 'was renowned for his terribly caustic remarks on the pictures of his fellow academicians. Walking up to a large seapiece he remarked very audibly on one occasion "The blessed Apostle Saint Peter wouldn't have the slightest difficulty in walking on that water."' But he was a man of courage. He had lost an arm and, nothing daunted, continued painting with the other, perforce in an entirely different style. Alexander acquired examples of both styles. As an exhibitor at the RHA himself, it may have been diplomatic to do so.

Sharpe junior appears to have been more genial than his father and 'was of great assistance in giving me confidence in my musical studies', but:

I felt like a traveller coming to two roads, and not knowing which to give most of my energies and application to. Music and painting appealed to me almost equally, but at one period of my musical career, I was on the point of flinging it to the winds and devoting myself entirely to painting, but I allowed myself to be persuaded that at no very distant date I would be able to command a certain income as a Cathedral singer.[8]

In the event, his first paid musical appointment was as an alto with the choir of the Chapel Royal, Dublin Castle, in 1874. The appointment was in the remit of Dean Dickenson, a man prepared to take a gamble: 'He knew quite well that I had very little experience, but with great good nature and belief in my sincerity and hard work, placed me in the position.' While there is unfortunately no record as to how much he was earning as a taxidermist, Alexander recorded that his salary at the Chapel Royal was £30 per annum, his duties light: one Sunday service at 11 a.m. and an evensong when the Lord Lieutenant was in residence, with the bonus of long summer holidays.

Oddly, there is no evidence that he ever went back to Dame Street to paint backdrops or dress cases, as an obvious way of supplementing his income on a casual basis. He mentions only that he began concentrating on subjects he most enjoyed, landscapes close to hand and maritime scenes from up and down the River Liffey and along the Irish coast; going further afield during holidays. For a brief period he had time on his hands to do exactly what he wanted.

However, making the change to alto brought Williams to the attention of Grattan Kelly (1832–97) who sang bass at Christ Church and St Patrick's Cathedrals. He was a singer all his life, starting as a boy chorister at the latter. Thomas Grattan Kelly was one of three brothers who all had cathedral appointments. His brother Charles Kelly, also a bass, was known as 'Young Handel' for his ability to sing florid music, and had a substantial reputation for his appearances in oratorio and in recital in England as well as Ireland. The impression is that Charles Kelly and perhaps Grattan too, among other vicars choral, had the vocal endowment to pursue a full-time career on the international circuit, had they so chosen. Alexander in time would sing with both of them. When William Murphy was found wanting, it was Grattan Kelly who was entrusted in 1876 with training the Amateur Choir. Kelly auditioned Williams, who recalled him saying 'there was one thing there was no mistaking, "I sang thoroughly in tune."' Not much of a compliment perhaps, but Kelly evidently thought enough of Williams to invite him to join in a new venture.

Grattan Kelly was intent on reviving a quartet known as the Dublin Glee and Madrigal Union (DG&MU). Unaccompanied part singing, now almost never heard in public, was then the height of fashion. Kelly invited Williams to join as the alto member. According to Williams, the former quartet had consisted of 'artists of the first water' who 'had brought the art of unaccompanied glee singing to a pitch of perfection hitherto unapproached in Dublin'. There was little chance of Williams ever being the equal of the outgoing alto, John Hemsley (1839–93), who hailed originally from Lichfield Cathedral and whose work in Dublin is commemorated by a brass memorial in St Patrick's Cathedral. As experienced a musician as Sir Robert Prescott Stewart described Hemsley as 'about the best cathedral alto I ever heard'.[9] Williams remembered him as having 'possessed an unusually fine pure alto voice of even quality with much power in the upper notes'. It was no doubt flattering to be asked to take over from Hemsley. The tenor too, Edward Peel, was English, originally from York Minster, reflecting the close connections the Irish cathedrals then had with their English counterparts. Many vicars choral at the time came from across the water, attracted not alone by the significantly higher pay offered by the Irish cathedrals but by the prospect of being paid for singing in both.

The two lower voices in the original Dublin Glee and Madrigal Union consisted of Grattan Kelly himself and baritone Richard Smith, who was remaining with the quartet. Cathedral singers all, which was typical of the times, choral singers regularly joined forces to sing both religious and secular music outside the cathedral precincts, in the public and private concerts. There were no females in the cathedral choirs in those days, so when the quartet became on occasion a quintet, they had to look outside their own ranks. The old union had the services of a fine mezzo soprano (also described in some newspaper accounts as a contralto), Mrs Scott Fennell. When in years to come Williams came to organise musical afternoons for his one-man art exhibitions, of which there were to be a good many, Mrs Scott Fennell with her 'rich and full' voice, albeit no longer in the first flush of youth, would feature among them. The new Dublin Glee and Madrigal Union acquired soprano Miss Bessie Craig, 'owner of a voice,' declared Williams, 'of delicious richness and sweetness and also distinguished for her great personal charms'. The press agreed. Unfortunately her career was to be tragically short.

Kelly did well to get as his tenor, if only briefly, Barton McGuckin. Williams described him, even in these early days of his career, as having 'star quality' and although 'fresh from being a chorister in Armagh Cathedral where his childish treble should have failed at the accustomed age, he seemed instead of losing his voice to have gone on singing "alto" and then tenor and it was now of delightful quality and he simply revelled in top notes.' With such a bountiful gift, McGuckin soon swapped cathedral choirs for the operatic stages of England and America, becoming the leading tenor of the Carl Rosa Company and, among other triumphs, is remembered for being the first tenor to sing the title role of Verdi's *Otello* in English.

Each member, Williams remembered, had their own little mannerisms and characteristics. McGuckin had a nose of more than average dimensions which apparently was the subject of frequent banter among his partners which he took in good part. Dick Smith had the habit of keeping a handkerchief partly rolled up in his left hand, even sometimes on stage, which Williams attributed to nerves. Bessie Craig had a habit of moistening her lips conspicuously before singing, and rolling her 'big dark eyes' to left and right to inform her partners when she was ready to sing and then set herself up by taking a deep breath. 'Her temperament was intensely emotional and nervous system highly strung,' Williams recalled, which might account for how she moved audiences when she sang sad and sentimental Victorian ballads. But her nerves were as apparent off stage as on: 'The rest of the Troupe used to be immensely amused at one phase of it, that was when she attempted to cross a London street when traffic was heavy. She would hesitate on the foot way, making feints at starting for a time, and at last would make a move, and when she got as far as the middle of the road would come to a dead stop, get confused, turn back, and as likely as not, become mixed up with a horse's head, and giving a quick little scream would become hopelessly bewildered. Even taking her by the hand did not always prevent her from losing her head.'[10] Bessie Craig's end was sad: 'Her raven black hair has changed to snowy white and as I write (1911) she is at present and has been for many years secluded from the world in one of our large asylums for the mentally afflicted.' One wonders if such incarceration was of benefit to her then and if it would be regarded as at all necessary now.

Williams now came in contact with luminaries of the Irish musical scene, conductors, composers and organists whose arrangements the singers often used. The union benefited most perhaps from its association with Sir Robert Prescott Stewart (1825–94), whose statue stands on Leinster Lawn. Stewart, who had attended Christ Church Cathedral school, became the cathedral's organist at the tender age of nineteen. He not only arranged and harmonised music for the Glee and Madrigal Union but 'very kindly attended some of our rehearsals and took great pains to tell us how he wished the music sung and helped us in every way'.[11]

The new Dublin Glee and Madrigal Union was formed at the end of 1874 with Kelly having concerts planned for early in the new year. Not too much of a challenge for seasoned singers perhaps, but an extraordinarily short period of time for Williams to familiarise himself with part singing, unaccompanied at that. The 'Colonel', as Kelly was known, came forward with a proposition. He would provide his new alto with private tuition, with payment deferred until he was receiving fees from the concerts. This time Williams did not hesitate: 'An offer like this, coming at a time when I had hardly decided yet whether I would follow art or music, bowled me over, and I at once agreed to his terms, and the very next morning walked across from the north side of the city and had my first lesson. The time was short . . . I was very much in earnest and worked exceedingly hard, studying for two hours with Grattan Kelly three and four mornings every week and then going to Dame St to business and painting work in my attic studio.' Little wonder that he had to sever his connections with the family business.

He was certainly serious in his musical intentions. He left the family home in Bayview Avenue, North Strand, and took up lodgings with Grattan Kelly at 102, Lower Mount Street, the better to fill every available minute with both singing and painting. In place of his studio in the family home, a small room at the back of Kelly's house was pressed into service. Apart from the convenience of this arrangement there were social advantages to living in the city at a time when many middle class families did – Dublin then being more like an overgrown village, in social terms.

That he had had the courage to throw up the settled job did not mean he did not have moments of agonising doubt: 'I, a duffer, as I felt myself to be in music, often quailed as I toiled at my musical studies . . . and sometimes the haunting fear of failure tempted me to throw up the sponge and scuttle away.'

But he stuck with it, while Kelly worked his troupe hard:

> The piano was rarely touched and the great object we kept in view was to endeavour to get the different voices to blend in one harmonious whole. Each little trifle was considered, and nothing was too small to escape attention. Suggestions were often made by the older members . . . Time and again, the same musical phrases were gone over and elaborated until the desired effect was produced. Good humour and light hearted merriment nearly always attended our meetings, and whilst resting our voices, jokes and stories enlivened our serious work.[12]

Clearly there were two sides to Williams' temperament. Painting by its nature tends to be a solitary occupation pursued by those who enjoy solitude and their own company. In painting Williams spent most of a lifetime exploring wild places. Equally, he relished the camaraderie of the musical world he had entered. He was more extrovert than introvert; in art circles he had a reputation for being outgoing and easy-going, a raconteur with a fund of stories gleaned from constant travels. These were to be good days for him. The two worlds of his choice were now joined.

The reconstituted Dublin Glee and Madrigal Union had a trial outing at the Antient Concert Rooms on 12 January 1875, contributing three quartets to the entertainment at one of the monthly dinners hosted by the Hibernian Catch Club, a venerable institution founded about 1680, the oldest club of its kind and still thriving. (Members of both cathedral choirs receive automatic membership, so Williams' colleagues at this time would all have been members.) 'Catch singers' were then expected to be capable of singing any glee or catch at sight.[13] This was the standard at which Williams would have to aim.

He was soon surprised to find that his colleagues, despite being old hands at public performance, were at least as nervous as himself before a concert: '. . . as I watched McGuckin pacing back and forward in the artists' room before his songs . . . his excitement and agitation increasing each moment I had a vision that my lot would always be the same in the music profession.'[14] Nervous energy, Williams had come to realise, is what gives performance its edge.

Engagements took the troupe across the water, including the old Free Trade Hall in Manchester, singing in one of Edward de Yong's 'big concerts'. De Yong's band once exceeded the popularity of the better remembered Charles Hallé, in whose orchestra De

Pen & ink sketch, inscribed in pencil 'Barton McGuckin and Miss Craig. Holyhead boat 1876. A Williams'.
The boat journey in fact took place the previous year. Inserted into the artist's 'Chronicles & Memoirs'

Yong had once played and of which he had been a founder member. It seems extraordinary now that there was a ready audience prepared to stand for an evening in the seatless pit of the old Free Trade Hall for orchestral 'pops' and a vocal troupe from Dublin, but such was the case. McGuckin did well by this concert, advancing his solo career by getting a three-year contract from De Yong. The troupe were introduced by De Yong to the German composer Edward Hecht (1832–87), who composed for and dedicated to the union a 'dashing composition' on the fashionable theme of: 'The Charge of the Light Brigade'. He must have admired how the troupe handled it, for he subsequently composed 'At Night When All is Still Around' for the DG&MU, which they featured at the Antient Concert Rooms on 11 March 1875.

The union's next engagement was a Royal Command performance, an invitation to sing at a *soirée musicale* for the Lord Lieutenant. On 9 February the singers duly presented themselves at the Castle and found themselves 'in the presence of the princely looking Viceroy', as Williams described him, 'the Duke of Abercorn KG and the Irish Court'. All went well until a request came forth from the viceregal party to hear Stephen Foster's 'Come where my love lies dreaming'. Singers are rarely short of *amour propre* and Foster apparently fell well short of what the troupe felt was music worthy of their talents. Alexander viewed the song with disdain, dismissing it as nothing better than a 'Christy minstrel', a view fully shared by his colleagues. There was, however, no question of refusing the Royal request:

EXHIBITION PALACE.

ON MONDAY EVENING, MARCH 15th, 1875,

Under the Patronage of

HIS EXCELLENCY THE LORD LIEUTENANT

And her Grace the DUCHESS OF ABERCORN,

The Right Honourable THE LORD MAYOR AND LADY MAYORESS,

SIR ARTHUR AND LADY OLAVE GUINNESS, and the Nobility and Gentry,

WHEN WILL BE PERFORMED

PROFESSOR GLOVER'S

GRAND NATIONAL ORATORIO,

ST. PATRICK AT TARA!

The introduction of Christianity into Ireland in the Fifth Century being the subject of this Cantata, the incidents are confined to the most remarkable event of that period—the visit of St. Patrick with a few Christian followers to the then classic regions of Tara, the residence of the Kings of Ireland—and the immediate conversion to Christianity of the people on that occasion.

WITH FULL ORCHESTRA AND CHORUS OF 500 PERFORMERS.

Principal Characters :—

St. Patrick	... ...	...	Mr. RICHARD SMITH
King of Tara	... ...	...	Mr. B. M'GUCKIN
King's Daughters ...	{ Ethnea and Fethelema }	...	Miss CRAIG Miss TAYLOR
Dufa	... ...	...	Mr. WILLIAMS
A Bard	... ...	...	Mr. GRATTAN KELLY

Harp ...	Mrs. MACKEY	Leader	...	Mr. LEVEY
Principal Violincello	Herr ELSNER	Organ	...	Mr. HORAN

Advertisement for the *St Patrick at Tara* oratorio

. . . to the intense disgust of McGuckin he was obliged to sing the solo, whilst the rest of the talented performers of the Union took part in the chorus in the most approved 'burnt cork' style. Grattan Kelly . . . was desperately angry that night at what he considered the indignity that had been put upon the Union in commanding them to sing such rubbish, and his resentment was only forgotten when at the close of the performance, we were taken in tow by the Chamberlain and conducted to a private apartment where a delicious supper had been prepared for us and his Excellency's powdered and pampered menials in profusion waited on us and magnum bonums of choicest champagne adorned the table.[15]

Oratorio was also in the sights of the 'Colonel' and the following month, on 15 March the members of the DG&MU were the principals in what was advertised as a grand national oratorio, *St Patrick at Tara*, by Dublin-born composer, John William Glover (1815–99), performed at the Exhibition Palace (now the National Concert Hall on Earlsfort Terrace). The performance was repeated five months later for the O'Connell Centenary celebrations. Dick Smith sang the role of St Patrick, Williams that of Dufa, a Christian follower of the saint. This was oratorio in the grand style with full orchestra and organ, a choir of 500, and the Band of the 6th Inniskilling Dragoons in a rousing performance of the 'Grand March of Tara'.

But it was the intimate venue of the Antient Concert Rooms that best suited the relatively small and nuanced sounds of the quintet. In the 1870s there was a ready audience for glees and part songs, to the extent that the union could give a series of subscription concerts in the Antient Concert Rooms, four concerts in as many months. 'Their delightful part singing is a musical feature of which Dublin may be proud,' ran one review after their third appearance. 'It is simply perfection. Such exquisite light and shade, such individual finish, such complete appreciation on the part of each member of what is required for the joint effect – all these characteristics are combined in such a degree in the singing of the members of the Union that it is no wonder their concerts should be in the highest degree attractive.' In the same concert Alexander was singled out by virtue of his 'pure and rich alto' which 'told with good effect'. They were in demand. They sang for 'The Sick and the Poor' at the Exhibition Palace and again at the Antient Concert Rooms in May, and the same month the union performed at a Philharmonic Society Concert, Alexander again being mentioned for having sung with 'great purity of quality and good expression'. He appears to have settled as an accomplished member of the union and was no longer the 'weak link'. 'We were now fairly in the running in the musical world,' he commented, 'and the likeliest musical combination to secure engagements.'

Secure them they did and Alexander found himself in houses that he would otherwise never have visited. Among them was an invitation to sing for the Dowager Lady Gort at No. 1 Portman Square, London at an afternoon concert. These were grand and elegant days, with few grander than a concert at Emo Park, Portarlington, when Prince Arthur of Connaught was the guest of the Earl of Portarlington. The union was extraordinarily well paid for its efforts, with each member receiving £10 on top of expenses, which was fully a third of what Williams was receiving for his appearances at the Chapel Royal in the year. He recorded nothing about their singing that night, being entranced by everything else:

The chief gentry in the county and elsewhere were invited by the old Earl to meet the Prince and the gentlemen appeared in hunting coats and knee breeches. After the concert there was a dance and a beautifully polished dark oak floor reflected the lovely dresses and the scarlet coats of the gentlemen whilst lights, shaded toward the onlookers, threw a radiance on each of the magnificent pictures on the walls. I picked up a most heavily embroidered lace handkerchief which I placed on the head of [a] couch where the owner recovered it. In the dancing one couple came hopelessly to grief on the slippery floor in the most undignified manner and the Prince in knightly fashion stepped forward and gracefully arranged the ladies [sic] clothes until she was helped to rise.[16]

Closer to home they trundled up the Dublin Mountains in treacherous conditions to sing at St Columba's College, a public school for boys. A quick jaunt in a car today, by horse and carriage it was something else: 'We started from Dublin after a heavy snow storm in a big carriage provided with foot warmers, and the incidents of that excursion, our slow progress on the mountain roads, had no effect on our jubilant spirits.' The occasion was the opening of a new schoolroom. At four o'clock the union did their party pieces and 'everything went off in flying colours', Williams adding that 'the return to town was even jollier.'[17] With such evident camaraderie and the fun of performance itself, little wonder if he was well pleased in having swapped singing for the tedium and long hours of taxidermy.

He even made one appearance in opera at the Theatre Royal, Dublin, when *Guy Mannering* was mounted on 12 May 1877. Bessie Craig, who had made her operatic debut in the same theatre only in January, stepped in to sing the role of Julia Mannering for the indisposed Mrs M. Gunn. It was not the soprano, however, whom the audience came to hear, but the most celebrated English tenor of the day, Sims Reeves (1818– 1900)[18] in the role of Henry Bertram. Reeves was as famous a recitalist as an opera singer, and *Guy Mannering* appears to have been mounted as much as an excuse for giving Reeves full rein to interpolate ballads of his own choosing as for the opera. Reeves was idolised by an adoring public despite a notorious reputation for cancelling at the last moment.[19] At the dress rehearsal Williams recalled:

> . . . there was the usual apprehension amongst the performers as to whether the great tenor would really sing or not. At the last rehearsal in the middle of the day, Sims Reeves sent down his wife, who got a chair placed for her a couple of yards in front of R. M. Levy, the conductor, and whilst the band and chorus went through the work, she whistled Reeves's part, stopping the band and saying Mr Reeves would do so and so here, and giving the most minute details.[20]

Mrs Reeves' whistling apparently provided the conductor and orchestra with all they needed to know about her husband's singing. No mishaps were recorded. For good measure glees appear to have been inserted along with the ballads. This was where Alexander had his chance: 'Sitting at a table in front of the stage, an amateur Dollard with a big bass voice, Aldred Manning son of Alderman Manning, and myself in appropriate costumes with tankards in our hands sang the part song "The winds whistle cold", a trio in parts accompanied by the chorus. Everything went off well and the performance was successful.'

Making up ad hoc combinations of singers such as was required for *Guy Mannering* were commonplace, and Williams records many events where he was called upon to participate with other singers at short notice. He also mentions an occasion at the Hibernian Catch Club when he was the only alto present and was required to take participate in every part song all evening long, a fair reflection of how far he had progressed as a musician. Even the names of groups could be flexible: when the same four members of the DG&MU performed for a Masonic dinner all of a sudden the same personnel became the 'Masonic Glee'. Membership of the Masonic Order was yet another 'wheel within wheels' where the opportunity to network was clearly to the benefit of his painting career.

The usual thing was for the Union was to have supporting musicians, as often as not the cellist Wilhelm Elsner and his pianist daughter Mlle Pauline Elsner, popular and accomplished figures in musical Dublin. There is no suggestion that Williams was ever attracted to Pauline Elsner in an amorous way, but her father evidently thought otherwise. It was after a concert . . .

> . . . where Herr Elsner and his daughter were playing that he 'accused' me of serenading his daughter. And nothing that I could say altered his opinion that a gentleman who was singing the night before in his garden under his daughter's window with a high voice was none other than the Alto of the 'Glee and Madrigal Union'.[21]

Sadly, beyond scattered reviews and Williams' own comments, there is no way of telling how the Dublin Glee and Madrigal Union actually sounded. Edison's talking machine was not invented until the end of 1877 and sound recording did not become commercially viable until the 1890s. Strange to say, however, Alexander did participate in the making of a recording, without, in all probability, knowing he was doing so. He was in the habit of paying annual visits to London and attended the Crystal Palace over several years for the great Handel festivals, when he would combine concert going with painting. In 1888, he was an official Irish representative for the Handel Festival, being chosen or volunteering from among the cathedral singers. The festival in question consisted of a general rehearsal on 22 June, followed by performances over three days. At this time Colonel George E. Gouraud, Thomas Edison's representative, was in England recording the great and the good in order to advertise 'the wonder of the age', Edison's newly perfected cylinder phonograph. Florence Nightingale, Gladstone and Tennyson all obliged by recording messages, which were played back to astonished crowds. Of course the phonograph would not only talk back to you but could deliver recorded music too, albeit in a raucous manner. On the last day of the festival, 29 June, Colonel George Gouraud set up his amazing, if cumbersome, hand-cranked phonograph in the Crystal Palace, taking up a position about 100 yards from the choir of 4,000 massed voices. The distance was no doubt necessary to prevent the volume of sound causing the stylus to 'blast' in the helical groove. As Gouraud furiously cranked the handle of the phonograph a vertical sound track was cut in the soft yellow paraffin wax medium. To all this the Irish representative was probably oblivious and of course through the cacophony of sound from that primitive cylinder the altos are barely discernible. Nevertheless, Alexander Williams was a participant in that historic live recording, the earliest of its kind extant.[22]

Barton McGuckin, the one singer in the quintet to achieve celebrity status, did make commercial recordings late in his career and may even have made much earlier recordings too. For the Zonophone label in 1905 he recorded at least two Irish songs, 'Avenging and Bright' and 'Savourneen Deelish', which are much prized by record collectors although they do not give much indication of what his voice may have been like in his prime.

Williams' connection with the Dublin Glee and Madrigal Union lasted only a couple of years and the union itself not much longer. Quartets seemed to be formed and disbanded with some frequency. But the reputation of the union lived on. In 1882,

The Irish Times, in reviewing a concert at the Antient Concert Rooms by the Dublin Glee Choir, remarked that the choir performed 'in the presence of a larger audience than has ever been seen at any similar entertainment since the regretted days of the old Glee and Madrigal Union'. A throwaway remark in the same piece provides an interesting sidelight on the behaviour of Victorian audiences: 'There was none of the half-suppressed conversation which has often been unpleasantly obtrusive in our concert rooms.'[23] Evidently Victorians did not always live up to the decorum that we attribute to them. Quite why the union, which had such a reputation, should have disbanded is unknown. Bessie Craig's own career appears to have been short-lived. She is mentioned as going to Cork in January 1881 'to sing in Mr Paul McSwiney's new opera "Ameriga"';[24] and may have retired shortly thereafter. Perhaps the financial returns did not justify keeping the DG&MU going. 'Music in Dublin is at a desperately low ebb at present. All the societies are tottering for want of support, and I know one or two that will be pretty certain to close after this year is out. Want of funds is the prevailing cry in all quarters.' So wrote the critic for *Irish Life*,[25] admittedly in 1891, but problems of finance tend to be a perennial issue. Interestingly, although Williams was to sing in other quartets, his obituary forty years up the road mentions only his association with the Dublin Glee and Madrigal Union. It appears to have occupied a special place in the affection of Dubliners.

If he had expected to get an early appointment in one or other of the Dublin cathedrals he was to be disappointed. He fluffed his chance in 1876, noting briefly in his 'Chronicles & Memoirs': 'March 9th Voice trial in St Patrick's Cathedral. I sang "He was despised" and "O Thou that tellest". Very much disgusted with myself.' It would be another two years before he finally succeeded at the voice trials held on 12 April 1878, when he and another alto were taken on at Christ Church Cathedral at £75 per annum, along with the basses Albert McGuckin (a brother of Barton McGuckin) and Edmond Oldham. His Sundays could be busy. For Sunday 5 May, he mentions that he sang in Trinity College Chapel at 10 a.m. at the Chapel Royal at 11.30 a.m. and at Christ Church at 3.30 p.m. This kind of rotation was a common practice. Choirmen required to go from one place of worship to the next with little time to spare would often slip out before the end of one service to arrive at the next. That same Sunday he sang his first anthem at Christ Church, 'I looked and lo', underlining the event in his 'Chronicles' to show what it meant to him. On 11 June he was elected a musical member of the Hibernian Catch Club at a dinner held at the Salthill Hotel in Dun Laoghaire.

Seemingly there was no let-up in his musical activities during his years as a choirman. There was always a pool of singers from the two cathedrals on call for engagements for those who wanted them. Alexander took what came his way and his 'Chronicles' are peppered with musical engagements. It could be strenuous work. He was one of the party who travelled to Dungannon, County Tyrone, to sing at a Masonic dinner, getting a fee of 5 guineas, but had to travel back on the night mail presumably because of cathedral commitments on the following day. Music provided an entrée to all kinds of events and was required for all sorts and conditions of men, including the members of the Irish Rifle Association:

> I made the acquaintance of Major Arthur Bougham Leech [actually Blennerhassett Leech],[26] Captain of the Irish Rifle Association, who used to often visit my studio at 32 Lower Abbey Street, a few doors from the Royal Hibernian Academy building. He was most anxious that I should take up rifle shooting but I could not find time for it without neglecting either my painting or music. I was invited as a musical guest to a very fine banquet given in the Gresham Hotel by the members of the Irish Rifle Association and the menu cards were printed in silver and were replicas of the Elcho Challenge Shield.[27]

Williams makes no mention as to how the stout riflemen responded to his piping falsetto. He certainly had enough in his life without taking up rifle shooting.

Riflemen or literati, he mixed with all and sang for all, dining with the Dublin Literary Club in D'Olier Street on 28 March when presumably he was expected to sing for his supper. A proud and unusual moment for both father and son was when William Williams read a paper on the great Irish elk (deer), the result of long years of study and research in the field, before the British Association on 19 August 1878, and Alexander was engaged to sing at the association's *conversazione*. As quartets formed and re-formed through these years, he became at one time a member of the Dublin Vocal Union, at another the Dublin Quartet Union (also written up in the press as Quartette Union) which featured Charles Kelly, perhaps the most celebrated bass among the vicars choral. If the Quartet Union never achieved quite the status of the old Dublin Glee and Madrigal Union, it certainly received comparable reviews: 'The singing of the Quartet Union . . . was, as usual, first rate', commented the *Freeman's Journal* when the quartet appeared at the third of Mr Sullivan's Ballad Concerts at the Antient Concert Rooms.[28] 'More than ever successful,' echoed *The Irish Times*, 'their singing of "When thro' life" was certainly the best performance we have heard by them yet.'[29]

In October 1880 Williams was finally appointed 'solo singer in the morning choir of St Patrick's Cathedral at a salary of £50'. In fact there is no such title as 'morning choir'; he must have meant he had been engaged to sing solos at morning services rather than at evensong. On the strength of this appointment he resigned from the Chapel Royal where he had been singing continuously for seven years. He provides an idea of his cathedral routines. 'Attending regularly at Christ Church Cathedral morning and evening on Mondays, Thursdays and Saturdays. Sunday morning at St Patrick's, evening at Christ Church Cathd', he writes for 1879. This seems to have remained the pattern over the coming years except that the weekly routine was increased to singing twice daily after he becomes a soloist at St Patrick's. He had more free time than a conventional desk job or taxidermy would have allowed, and he played nip and tuck between singing and painting: 'Tuesday, Wednesday and Friday afternoons sketching from nature on these mornings when possible, about Dublin.'[30] His energy never seemed to flag. With the lengthening days of spring he was well capable of topping and tailing the day with painting: 'Started rising early and making sketches of sunrises about Clontarf in oil also evening effects', runs an entry for March.[31] His cathedral duties curtailed him only in so far as he was limited by the distances he could travel. During holidays he travelled further of course.

Williams' career as a choral singer lasted until 1897 when he finally retired. Low voices wear better than high ones; but few voices remain as good after the age of fifty as before, and the alto voice is particularly prone to the ageing process. He was now fifty-one. His last service as a soloist in the choir of St Patrick's cathedral was on 19 December 1897. He looked back on his career with satisfaction. If not all his performances were to the standard he would have liked, he could nevertheless write: 'However I flatter myself that after an active musical career of over a quarter of a century I can only recall a couple of occasions that I came to grief.'[32] He had no regrets about retiring from singing. The strain had increased rather than diminished with the years, which was only to be expected if the voice was becoming less reliable. 'A delightful happy Christmas Day,' he wrote, boxing the sentence all around for emphasis, adding 'free from all musical worry, I did enjoy it.' He kept up his musical associations after his retirement by becoming a member of the board of governors of the Royal Irish Academy of Music.

While music had provided him with a secure income well into middle age, it was not for money alone that he sang. He clearly had a vocation for singing as he had for painting. From a purely financial point of view, he could in fact have survived on painting alone during his cathedral years. Instead he chose parallel lives. The same years as he had immersed himself in music were also, as we shall see, among the most productive for him as an artist.

PART IV

THE PAINTER

A study in contrast. Rare sketch of a turf or sod cabin, inscribed 'Mrs McLeen's Bochan foad' [sic]. A bocan fód was the last resort of the destitute. Note the fine house on the distant hill. Turf cabins were still in evidence when the artist arrived on Achill in 1873 when he did this sketch. 4 x 7 in. (10 x 17.78 cm).

Watercolour signed and inscribed in pencil: 'Kew' (London). These fashionable houses on the Thames, with their own moorings, can still be seen below Kew Bridge, minus the oast house. 9.5 x 6.5 in. (24.1 x 16.5 cm). Originally the property of Lady Aberdeen.

An Irish cabin, signed. 6.7 x 13.4 in. (17 x 34 cm). Note the decrepitude of the building. Williams illustrated, better than many of his contemporaries, the actual state of buildings on Achill and in the west.

CHAPTER 7

Foundations

A scudding yacht. oil on canvas. Signed. 9¼ x 14¾ in. (23.5 x 37.5 cm).

For all that the burgeoning family taxidermy business promised in the 1860s, it was not the life that Alexander wanted. While he knew he wanted to get involved in art, he had no idea how to go about it. The artist William Brocas, as we saw, had been no help at all and Williams was to look back upon his formative years with some regret:

> Alas there was no person at this time to whom I could turn to [sic] for advice or encouragement, and with the exception of a couple of courses of drawing instruction in the night classes of the Royal Dublin Society I blundered along in my yearnings after art and must ever deplore that I missed a proper art education. How different with me it might have been, had I been taken in hand, and had gone through proper courses of art study and my footsteps placed in the right course.[1]

It was not all loss. Although he initially flailed around, painting all manner of subjects with no clear direction, there is much to be said for experiencing as wide a range of subjects as possible when young. It gave him a taste for experimentation which he never lost and his work through much of his life showed a remarkable receptiveness for trying new things. There always remained, however, limitations to his draughtsmanship, evident in his pencil sketches and paintings both of the human form and of animals, which the early formal training he so much missed might have remedied. To judge from the number of pencil studies of faces to be found among his sketchbooks, he may have hankered after the idea of doing portraits, but never developed the necessary skills. Almost all his sketches opt for direct side-on views, with only occasional attempts at diagonal or face-on studies.

While he was floundering, he got a measure of encouragement from no less a figure than Tom Connolly of Castletown House in Celbridge, County Kildare, who had an interest in taxidermy and paid periodic visits to Dame Street. He saw some of Williams' early sketches and took it upon himself to buy some, studies of butterflies and the like, paying him five shillings per picture. It was a start. An unlikely friendship developed between the pair, and in 1870 Connolly invited his young friend to stay at Castletown. The largest Palladian mansion in Ireland, it then contained a substantial collection of pictures and opulent furnishings. Tom Connolly's friendship was a valuable introduction to the kind of patrons he might expect to have in the future. (The famous Castletown ghost did not put in an appearance, but the butler, a somnambulist, did as well by terrifying Williams in the middle of the night when he entered his room with a lighted candle.)

They got on well, old Tom Connolly and the aspiring painter. Connolly took Williams to his house in Duleek, County Fermanagh: 'Cliff House', 'a fine residence beautifully situated on a rocky bluff overlooking the Erne river, I saw it in the autumn time with the yellow foaming river rolling amongst the beautifully coloured foliage of the trees. I thought it a scene hard to be beaten in beautiful Ireland. The Hostess had a very pretty lady's maid of good family and gallant old Tom delicately hinted to me that I should pay

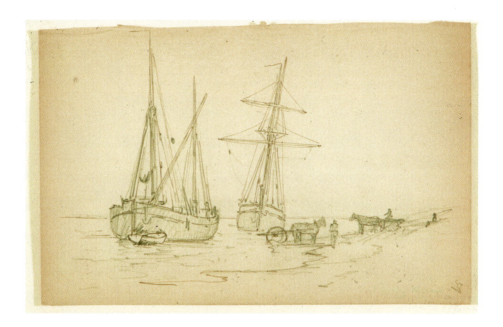

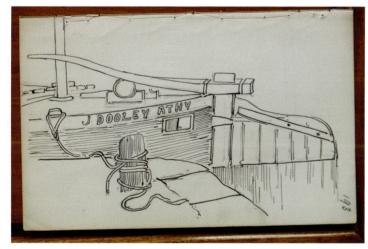

Above: Pencil sketch inscribed 'Bray River'. 4½ x 7 in. (11.4 x 17.8 cm).

Left: Pencil sketch of canal boat . 4.5 x 7 in. (11.4 x 17.8 cm).

her a little attention as she was a very desirable person.'[2] Williams gave no indication that he made any attempt to act on his patron's advice but the Erne and the rolling countryside gave him opportunities to paint and he would return to paint there again. Yet another country house to which Connolly took his young friend was Castle Caldwell on Lough Erne: 'a perfect treasure house', Williams recalled, 'majestically timbered'. The house is now a ruin but the woodland, a conservation area, remains. The return trip was rather more eventful than might have been expected: 'We went down Lough Erne by steamer to Castle Caldwell and on our return passed the residence of the eccentric D'Arcy Irvine where the vessel was held up for some time until he finished some rifle firing across our bows.'[3]

Monochrome sketch of a wreck, a favourite subject for the artist 4.5 x 7 in. (11.4 x 17.8 cm).

Pencil sketch inscribed 'Old gun on Kingstown Pier'. 4.5 x 7 in. (11.4 x 17.8 cm).

Encouraging as Connolly had been, Williams still had his craft to learn. For want of anyone else he turned to a photographer and painter by the name of Forster, of Forster & Scott, who had a studio just a few doors down from the hat shop, at 30 Westmoreland Street, and whom William Williams engaged from time to time to paint tempera backgrounds for taxidermy cases. This proved to be a turning point of sorts. Forster showed Williams some of his own oils of the rocky coast of Howth and 'they fixed my ambition to attempt something of the kind. So I asked him to tell me what was the very first thing I should do to commence to paint from nature. His reply was concise and to the point and I never forgot it. "Sit down in the first ditch you come to and try and paint what you see!"'

Study of a broken gate, one of many such small studies found in the artist's sketchbooks.

I did my level best to try and carry out his instructions. I gave up the pleasures of the chase, and put aside my gun, and instead of roving the country for something to kill, in the early mornings I sallied out with my sketch box under my arm, and looked into many ditches, and sat down in several, but usually did nothing, I felt completely bewildered with the variety of forms and the tangles of vegetation about me. At last wandering along the railway line beyond where Clontarf Station now stands one fine summer morning, I came across a ditch with a little running stream at the bottom, some stones had dammed the current and made a little pool, under the stones the water was reddish in colour, with reflections, and some tall weeds formed a background. This did not seem to be so despairing a subject to try, so I sat down and made about a two hours' study working rapidly as I had to be home at 8 o'clock. I still preserve this, my first attempt to paint in the open air. The colours were in tubes, but the white lead I used was the same as used by housepainters in their work and instead of canvas which was too expensive for my means I used thick whitepaper which had received two coats of stiff starch (a tip I got from old Forster) to prevent the colours from sinking too much. After knocking about for nearly 40 years this sketch is very little changed, and has never been cracked. I would strongly advise young students from nature to carefully treasure their efforts at painting in the open, for future reference, no matter how trivial or old they may become, there is always something to be learned from them, some happy touches may be discerned that cannot be produced inside the four walls of a room.[4]

Once he put his mind to it, he made rapid progress: 'The advice of the old photographer set me going in a safe direction.' He spent time around the River Tolka and a broad lagoon between Annesley Bridge and Fairview, dashing out in the early mornings to do a quick study of what caught his eye. 'I painted a good many subjects, and studies of broadleaved water plants introducing sometime butterflies with outspread wings resting on the upper leaves, and soon found myself strong enough to leave the ditches and try "my prentice hand" on groups of weeds, chiefly thistles and dockweed.' None of these early studies is known to have survived. His approach to learning to handle paint was to make studies of small things first, foreground subjects, and then as his technique improved expand to take in more, the mouth of the River Liffey and its fleet of trawlers and varied craft being a particular magnet to him, as the River Boyne and its busy cargo boats and steamers had been before:

So far I had been attempting only humble foreground subjects, but I thirsted for the time when I would be able to master landscape, sea and sky. The sea was always an absorbing feature, and I was continually sketching boats and ships and [I was] very fond of steamers. Before taking to landscape I was often found prowling along the quays and making pencil drawings of the old steamers and curious old wooden sailing vessels long since passed away from the Liffey. There was a huge fleet of about 60

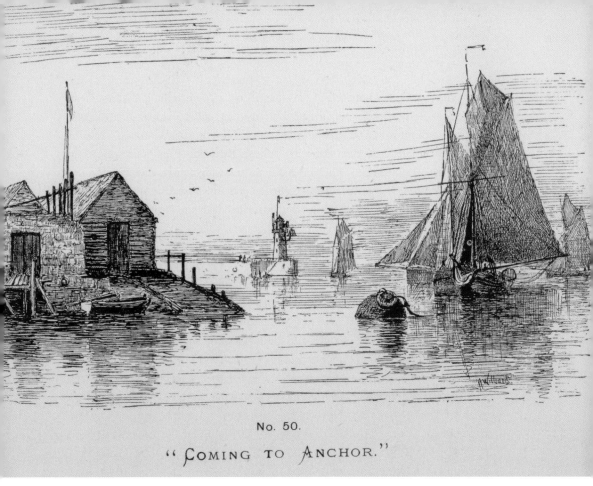

No. 50.

"COMING TO ANCHOR."

'Coming to Anchor', Dublin Bay, a print from the catalogue of the artist's 5th Exhibition, 1892.

sailing trawlers always at Ringsend, and they looked most picturesque, riding at anchor at evening with their red sails hanging motionless and reflected in the water, or at other times when leaving the river on a breezy day, when with their bulging sails they tore away rapidly out to sea.[5]

His efforts were rewarded by having an oil painting entitled *Hard Times*, a winter scene with birds from nature, accepted by the Royal Hibernian Academy for its annual exhibition in 1870. The picture was a study of a magpie and several sparrows crowding around some food scattered for them on snowy ground. It was just the thing Victorians would have appreciated for its charm and poignancy, even though bird pictures never rivalled the popularity of cased taxidermy specimens. *Hard Times* carried the not inconsiderable price tag of 6 guineas. Even though the picture did not sell, from this year, for want of a more significant date, Williams' professional art career may be said to have begun. He was twenty-four years old.

Thus encouraged, the following year he submitted no fewer than eight pictures,[6] a mixture of landscapes, a study of leaves from nature, and a type of picture with which he would show a particular affinity – an easterly gale off the Poolbeg Light, in this instance the subject of the picture being the Dublin and Glasgow SS *Lord Gough* caught

in the storm and running for port. He was less ambitious with his pricing this time, with
the most expensive of the pictures being no more than £3, and he had his first success,
selling from the exhibition *A Study from Nature on the Three Rock Mountain, Dublin* for
£1. Surprisingly perhaps, a number of these pictures had possibly been done some years
earlier, including, certainly, this one which Williams said he had painted in the spring of
1866, five years before. The sale of it had a particular poignancy for him. While his father
had given up on him so far as painting was concerned after the Brocas incident, his
mother had not, and this picture he associated with her, as he recalled forty years after
he had painted it:

> One incident which took place a few months before my Mother's untimely decease
> was a source of keen pleasure to both of us, and memory goes away back over the
> flight of years and lovingly dwells on the doings of one particular day when I
> persuaded her to accompany me on my first sketching day from nature, an excursion
> we made to the Three Rock mountain beyond Dundrum, where, on the mountain
> slope I endeavoured for the first time to make a sketch in oil of an old thatched cottage
> with a hilly background. My materials were of the most inexpensive nature, a sheet
> of stout cardboard which had received two coats of thick starch, and one of white
> lead ground in oil served instead of canvas which was altogether too expensive on
> which to make experiments. A few tubes of oil colours, a small quantity of
> housepainters white lead, turpentine and a couple of hog hair brushes, a present from
> my Mother, all contained in a small mustard box, a present from our grocer and which
> I had converted into a 'Sketch Box' formed my outfit. To these I added some
> assurance and a little confidence in my ability to produce something that should be
> like nature, and so we journeyed along the road and spent the best part of the day on
> the slope of the mountain enjoying the balmy spring air and 'the glory of the gorse'
> emblazoning the hillsides around us.
>   Had my mother lived it would have been a proud moment for her to have seen the
> little sketch (at the production of which she had so well assisted) hung in the front
> room no 340 at the Exhibition of the Royal Hibernian Academy of Arts Lower Abbey
> St Dublin 1871 . . . In due course I received from the Academy one sovereign free of
> commission and the possession of that gold piece gave me more intense enjoyment
> and satisfaction than any I have received since. My delight was clouded by the
> thought that she who above all others would have shared my feelings and rejoiced
> with me was gone, alas to that 'bourne from whence no traveller returns'.[7]

No sooner had he sold one picture at the RHA than he sold another. 'So that from the very
start my work found favour with the public,' he could say with minimal exaggeration,
only overlooking the fact that this was his second attempt at the RHA. His marine picture
*The Poolbeg Light, Easterly Gale, the Dublin & Glasgow SS Lord Gough Running for
Dublin* was a fortunate choice of subject for the artist as it 'attracted the notice of a bluff

Above: Oil on board 'River Liffey Dublin' with Howth in the background. Signed and dated 1878. 9 x 12 in. (22.9 x 30 cm). With preparatory watercolour sketch (left).

sea captain and he was heard to burst out "why that's my boat, I shall have that!" and he promptly got the red wafer placed on it', paying £3 for it. This was an early lesson for Williams to paint pictures that members of the public would want. It seems an obvious lesson but many an artist has the notion – or notions about himself – that it is demeaning to paint except for oneself. It was of course just luck that the bluff sea captain and the picture of the SS *Lord Gough* had met, but when it came to mounting his own exhibitions Williams would make a point of including pictures that were of specific interest to, even tailor-made for, his patrons.

Anyone who has tried self-employment will know only too well that there are two sides to the equation – producing the goods on one side, marketing and selling them on the other. Williams was never short of paintings to sell, indeed posterity might think he overdid it. On the other side of the equation, he was outgoing and extrovert and worked hard at getting himself known and then remaining in the public eye. Early on, he took himself along to the gilders and carvers along the quays; he mentions the names of Burke and Bennett who had small shops in close proximity to each other on Wellington Quay[8]

Oil on canvas of a cutter off the Baily Lighthouse, Howth Head. Signed. 12 x 18 in. (30.5 x 45.7 cm). In the artist's early style.

and they became among the first outlets for his work. Sensibly, given their location, he provided them with pictures chiefly of yachts and fishing boats, which they sold at prices from £1 to £2 a piece.

Hitherto I had been working altogether from memory and composing sea pieces chiefly of yachts and fishing boats but as I have stated I had a special fancy for the old lumbering paddle wheel steamers of the Liverpool Line, and the carvers and gilders on Wellington Quay were able to dispose of them. I find in the year 1871 that I got as much as four pounds for one painting, and a masterpiece of that time was a picture of the 'old SS St Patrick' which I sold for £3 . . . That year the Dublin Exhibition of Arts, Industries, and Manufactures, was opened by his Royal Highness the Duke of Edinburgh and on his departure in the 'Galatea' I made sketches from which I composed a picture representing the vessel leaving Dublin Bay and the war vessels firing a salute. This was a masterpiece for me and I took it down to Cranfield who had a splendid art gallery at 115 Grafton St and showed it to him. He had it on exhibition only a few days when one of the Captains of the Mail Steamers bought it for £15. This was a wonderful windfall, a great stroke of luck, and it gave me immense encouragement, opening up a vision of all the beautiful new brushes, colours, and canvases I would be able to purchase to carry on my painting work.

From the retail price of £15.0.0 that Thomas Cranfield got for the 'Galatea', a considerable amount of money, Williams received £12.5.0, meaning he paid a commission in round figures of 18 per cent, a fraction of what a gallery would charge an artist today. It was a stroke of luck to be taken up by Cranfield, a leading dealer who 'did a splendid business'. 'A very genial good natured old gentleman' was how Williams remembered him. Cranfield took Williams seriously as an artist, commissioning eight small oils from him, but Williams wondered if his confidence might be misplaced: 'I was told by a friend that he was quite disgusted at my taking up music and giving so much time to it as he feared I should neglect the art of painting.'[9]

When the family taxidermy business moved next door to No. 2 Dame Street in 1871, Williams set up a studio for himself right at the top, suitably lit by a skylight. It is the classic bind for anyone who wants to pursue a line of work which may remain unprofitable for a number of years. A steady full-time job pays the bills but may not allow much time to do much else. Typically, Williams would have worked at least a five and a half day week. Jobs that provide both secure employment and sufficient time to pursue an outside activity in earnest are few and far between. Neither the hat trade, had it survived, nor taxidermy, had he continued with it, would have left him with much time to spare. But this was precisely what music did have to offer, along with an income that was a living in its own right. It was not an opportunity easily passed up, whatever reservations Cranfield might have had and for twenty-three years Alexander pursued his two separate careers.

He had established himself at the RHA and had not found much difficulty in selling his work around about. He knew the coastal scenery around Dublin very well and Connolly had brought him as far as County Fermanagh. Eventually Williams would work his way around the whole of Ireland. Meantime a pivotal point in his artistic life was due to his friend A. J. More (1830–95) of the Dublin Museum of Science and Art who 'excited my curiosity immensely by telling me about the beauties of Achill Island, away on the wild west coast of Ireland and he strongly advised me to try and pay a visit to its magnificent scenery'.[10] So, having saved up a little money, in September 1873 Williams set off to visit the island and discovered an affinity with its wild landscape that was to continually draw him back.

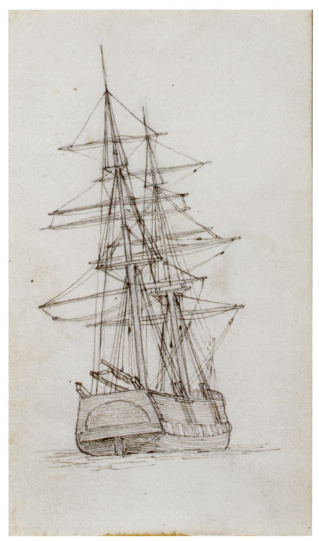

Ink sketch of tall ship, probably Dublin Bay. 4 x 7 in. (10 x 17.8 cm).

The Road to Achill, 1873

Inscribed 'Achill Island', a study of peasant costumes. The artist often added pencilled notes to his sketches, as in this instance.

Pencil sketch inscribed 'Achill Sound' showing the newly erected Michael Davitt Bridge. 4.5 x 7 in. (11.4 x 17.8 cm).

Achill Island is part of County Mayo and lies off the west coast of Ireland, separated from the mainland by a narrow sound which abounds with powerful currents. With a land mass of 57 sq km, 24 km from east to west and 18 km from north to south, it is the largest island off the Irish coast. It is Europe's most westerly island, being 10 degrees west, 54 degrees north, and contains some of the continent's highest and most spectacular cliffs, with the westerly Croaghaun-Slievemore range reaching to 672 m (2,204 feet) in height. Achill (which includes Achill Beg and Inishbiggle), is partially encompassed by Clew Bay to the south and Blacksod Bay to the north. The climate is typically wet, mild and windy. Two-thirds of the island is covered in peat bog. Trees and shelter are notably absent in what for farming is a desolate and intractable landscape. There was no wheeled transport on the island before the 1830s; no bridge across the sound until the Michael Davitt Bridge was opened in 1887; no railway until the line to Westport was extended to Achill Sound in 1894. The Midland Great Western Railway (subsumed under the Great Southern Railway (GSR) in 1925) to Achill ran for only a little more than forty years. Competition from improving road transport resulted in the line being closed in 1937.[1] The railway track has since been taken up, but embankments and bridges and most notably the fine cut stone viaduct over the Black Oak River at Newport remain as testimony to the fine workmanship and endeavour of days gone by.

Achill has been inhabited, probably continuously, for 5,000 years, since at least Neolithic times. Prehistoric stone monuments are to be found on Achill and surrounding islands; Williams left sketches of a number of them. Evidence of early agricultural endeavour is apparent by the lines of mounds, lazy beds, a means of allowing excess water to run off, a method used for growing crops for millennia, long before the introduction of the potato.

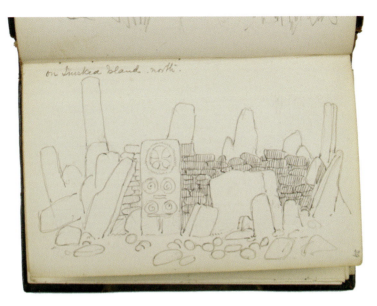

Pencil study of ancient stones, inscribed: 'On Iniskea Island. North.' 4.5 x 7 in. (11.4 x 17.8 cm).

Skipping forward to the seventeenth century, the population of Achill received a sudden increase in its population, from people forced west across the Shannon on account of Cromwell's policy of land clearance. Whether any of those who journeyed west and who now attempted to scratch a living from the peaty soil of Achill once farmed on the genial lands of Grove and Lappan, where John Williams, the Welsh feltmaker, had settled is unknown. The dispossessed left few records.

The small Achill communities or *clachans*, usually of interrelated families, were once entirely self-sufficient, supporting themselves as best they could from the land and the sea. In time, potatoes became the primary crop, as the one which thrived best in poor acid, moist soils; yielding acre for acre as much as four times that of wheat.

The population on Achill in 1841 was about 4,900. Ten years later, on account of the Great Famine, that figure was not much above 4,000. The Famine made for a radical change in the way of life of the Achill Islanders. From time immemorial, booleying or *buaile* had been an important aspect of the economy on the island, as elsewhere. On a seasonal basis, part of the population of each *clachan* would move with the cattle to fresh pastures, allowing the open or inadequately fenced land around the permanent settlement to be cultivated without the problem of the cattle destroying the crops. Booleying, after the Famine, was gradually abandoned, with whole communities moving to permanent coastal settlements.

In the latter half of the nineteenth century the British government was under increasing pressure to do something about the plight of tenant farmers. On wretchedly small holdings, many too small to be truly viable, the peasant had to try to eke out a living for himself and his family, while paying taxes to the landowner. For instance,

on top of paying a rent on land to William Pike of Glendarary, the largest landowner, he had what were known as 'duty days' on which the tenants were required to work for him. There were charges for grazing rights too.[2] Even collecting sea wrack on Achill for use as a fertiliser was subject to tax.

In 1891 the Congested Districts Board (CDB) was formed which enabled tenant farmers first to lease land at much reduced rates and then, in the following century, to gain ownership. It is a common misconception, however, that once tenant farmers got possession of the land they achieved a measure of prosperity. Many holdings were too small to be viable and the process of enlargement was a slow one. What ownership did mean for the small farmers was freedom from the threat of eviction; although emigration remained an ever present threat. It was reckoned at this time that to survive a family of six needed about £33.0.0 per year.

Oil on canvas. Transporting hay, presumed to be Achill Sound. Note the ghostly *pentimento* of a sailing ship in centre left. Signed. 8 x 14 in. (20 x 35.6 cm). *Provenance: Williams family collection.*

Cabins of stone and sod were of one or two rooms. Families of five and ten were common. Although stone was plentiful, the idea of having separate accommodation for animals was resisted. The CDB's inspector had found that the cattle and sheep were 'of the most inferior description that can be imagined'. Hens, however thrived in the conditions available to them. There were no inland fisheries and although sea fish were abundant around the coast, only the seasonal fishing for salmon between April and August provided an export market of any size. Trade was done with and through Westport by sail. No steamships normally plied the route.

This then was the impoverished state of Achill Island at the end of the nineteenth century. But to the young Alexander eager to explore new places the prospect was

Boat builder's cottage, a good example of the artist's 'photographic' style. Print taken from his illustrated catalogue 'Something about Achill', 1897.

wildly exciting. He knew little about the island and he was not alone in this. Just how little was generally known about Achill may be judged from a small illustrated booklet, *Something about Achill*, which the artist produced nearly twenty-five years after his first visit. The text opens with the question: 'Achill Island – where is it?' and goes on: 'Is it far off the coast? Is there a bridge over to it? And is it easy to get there? These are queries often asked, although repeated efforts are being made to bring its scenery into notice . . . In the year 1840 it was possible to reach it from Dublin in three days!' He recalled his own experience of making 'an aquatic excursion in the crossing of Achill Sound, no easy matter on a dark evening with a south-west wind, some cattle in the ferry boat, and a heavy sea on'.[3] This was written in 1897 and would have been aimed at a mainly Dublin audience. It is hard to conceive now just how remote Achill would have appeared from the capital in 1873, being socially and economically, as well as physically, disconnected from the rest of Ireland.

He has left us a very precise description of what it required for him to get to Achill in 1873. He had first to take the night mail with the Midland Great Western Railway, leaving Broadstone Station in Dublin at 8.20 p.m. and making Westport at 4 a.m. the following morning. He then had two hours to spend strolling around the town until the mail car left the post office in Westport at 6 a.m. Newport was reached about 7.30 a.m., where there was another stop and time for breakfast, before the journey continued at 8.30 a.m. At this point things began to get exciting: 'The scenery all along seen for the first time was entrancing. Mountains clustered in groups showed on the right, and Croaghpatrick across Clew Bay towered above the morning mists, whilst the early sun glittered on the waters amongst the numerous islands . . .' Williams was smitten with the west of Ireland from the start. At Mulranny, the horses were changed for fresh ones and they then 'rattled along under the shadow of Polranny Hill till the Sound of Achill was reached about 12.15'.[4] The journey had taken sixteen hours. He still had to find lodgings and left the crossing of the sound to the island until the following day.

Sepia wash over pencil inscribed 'Curraune Hill from Achill Sound' with hooker in foreground. From the artist's first Achill sketchbook, 1873.

He had warmed to his driver, Michael Ginelly, so 'I told him my business and asked him to recommend a quiet lodging'. Michael had no trouble doing so. 'He gravely stopped at the door of a very clean little cottage near the Rectory and told me he knew the woman who owned it was a "very desirable person".' What he failed to tell Williams was that he was recommending his own mother. Not until Michael returned to the cottage the same evening did Williams make the connection; but he had no reason to complain, finding himself 'installed in a nice clean, well kept, boarded bedroom, pretty little curtains in a small window, and a clean tablecloth on the little table in the centre of the room, and I enjoyed delicious home made bread, really new laid eggs and splendid tea'. Williams could not resist a little mischief of his own with his ventriloquism, first by confusing his landlady by carrying on a conversation with an imaginary visitor in his bedroom. Then over a roaring turf fire in the company of his landlady and her family, he imitated the cheeping of a clutch of young turkeys kept in a hamper by the fire. 'When I had continued it some time Mrs Ginelly came over and lifted the lid of the hamper to see if the birds were all right and having examined them went back to her seat. After a while I commenced again, and she again got up and lifted the lid. The third time when she lifted the lid, she exclaimed "What on earth is the matter with them birds, I never heard them going on like that before."' Michael was not so readily fooled and after Williams had tried 'other strange things, put me down as the author'. Then Michael came up with an idea: 'There was a poor woman who had lately buried her son and he said to me "Begorrah Sir! If you went outside of her window some night and made as if he was there ye'd have the divil's fun!" I was rather flabbergasted at the proposal,' Williams commented, as well he might, and there he drew the line at his ventriloquism.

But Williams liked to express his impish, not to say juvenile, sense of humour where and when he could and the Ginellys, by all accounts, were but one among many families whom he amused or bemused. 'He is a keen humorist and has a marked talent for ventriloquism,' commented the writer of 'Around the Social Clock'. 'He sometimes exercises the last-mentioned faculty when sketching lonely districts of the South and West, and there are islanders at Achill who are firm in the conviction that sheep and goats have spoken to them, that donkeys have complained of unfair loading, and that roadside fowls have promised to lay eggs in winter if provided with feather beds.'[5]

Victorians rarely travelled without useful introductions to be used at their destinations. A. G. More had not only set Williams on the road to Achill, but had provided him with an introduction to the 'chief man' of the island, as Williams put it, William Pike no less:

> Mr Pike was exceedingly kind, took me out in his trap, and brought me to where he considered the best views were to be had, and another time got the coastguards to take out their whaler through the narrow entrance at the Atlantic side of the Blind sound where the boat rose and fell in the big ground swell and huge rocks rose out of the water on each side as we went through; getting clear of the breakers we entered caves where rushes of blue wings were seen as the rock doves shot out and up the cliffs, and awkward cormorants stuck out their snaky black necks eyeing us from the weather worn points of the rocks, all to me so new and inexpressibly wild and romantic.[6]

In addition to the dramatic views, the trip through the Blind Sound offered the opportunity of shooting cormorants and rock doves, a popular pastime, which Pike's sons from time to time apparently enjoyed too. There is no mention of the shooting of seals in Williams' memoirs but this also was once a popular sport with tourists. Photographs from the Lawrence collection show well-dressed Victorian gentlemen accompanied by their womenfolk, and local boatmen, on seal hunting excursions. It was not, however, a sport which concurred with the sensibilities of islanders, among whom was the belief that seals embodied the souls of men. Reincarnation and transmigration of souls do not form part of mainstream Christian beliefs; but to look into the plaintive eyes of a seal suggests how such an idea might arise.

The contrast between the 'great house' and the rest of the island was stark. It did not take Williams long to discover the conditions under which many of the islanders lived and he never forgot it:

> Some of the dwellings of the inhabitants at that time were of the rudest description, and their sanitary arrangements simply appalling. One particular dwelling close to the shore was constructed by digging a square or oblong piece out of the sloping bank blocking the end up with turf sods freshly cut and roofing it over with 'scraws', or long ribands of sod having shortgrass on it. These 'scraws' were ingeniously cut about 2 feet wide and 6 feet long, rolled up and placed over rough branches, driftwood etc and then thatched over with rye grass. A hole was left for the smoke to find its way out, but most of it escaped through the doorway, and there was no window. An abode of this kind often contained a couple of cows, a pony, calves, as well as geese and fowls, the owner, and his wife and family. The animal 'that pays the Rint' had a little

sod house to himself 'convaynent'. I made a set of sketches in oil in the vicinity of the sound which I have kept ever since . . . 38 years have sped and very great changes have been made in the habits of the people and their dwellings vastly improved owing to the efforts that have been made to separate their cattle from the dwelling houses and it would be difficult now to discover any of the habitations I have described.[7]

What he never mentioned, although he could hardly have been unaware of it, was that the most wretched of the dwellings made in a hollow of a bank were surely the last resort of those unfortunate enough to have been evicted. Evicted even when snow lay on the ground, it was claimed by author Fr P. J. Joyce, when Pike was establishing his estate at Glendarary, Joyce noting that 'the evicted scattered themselves to other parts of the Pyke [*sic*] estate, Breanaskil or Sraheens, some to the Valley, and some across the Sound to Belfarsad . . .'[8] If Alexander knew of the displacement of islanders by William Pike he kept silent on the matter.

The artist's original sketchbook from his first Achill visit survives intact and shows both inside and outside the simplicity, not to say primitive contents, of a single-room stone cottage; many more such sketches and pictures would follow. He did not flinch from showing these primitive homesteads as they were, not with perfect whitewash, but peeling, damp and imperfect, the walls often cracked and subsiding, with spreading green algae; roofs are broken, thatch drips and weeds have got a hold. The air of subsistence living and the grind of life is unmistakable and all about.

Ink sketch of a barefoot woman carrying turf, a typical island image of the period. 4.5 x 7 in. (11.4 x 17.8 cm).

Watercolour, inscription obscure: 'Red Owen's House[?]', stone built, precariously located on a small spit of land. From the artist's first Achill sketchbook, 1873. 4 x 7 in (10 x 17.8 cm).

Pencil sketch of washerwoman. The fowl seems well fed. 4.5 x 7in. (11.4 x 17.8 cm)

Watercolour, inscribed 'Interior Ginellys House'. Basic, but better than a cabin made of sods.
From the artist's first Achill sketchbook, 1873. 4 x 7 in. (10 x 17.8 cm).

Pencil sketch inscribed 'Wool dyer Bullsmouth'. 4.5 x 7in. (11.4 x 17.8 cm).

Watercolour signed and inscribed 'A Washing Day in Achill Island.' 9 x 15½ in. (23 x 39.4 cm).

The scene was brightened by the clothing of the islanders, the women in particular; and immediately caught the artist's attention: 'The dresses of the natives took my fancy, they were very picturesque owing to varieties of red of all shades used for colouring and seen on the hillsides in bright sunshine they were remarkably picturesque.' He showed the Achill people going about their daily lives, not in contrived poses, but barefoot in the water collecting kelp, or with a creel or woven basket bent under the load, or handling a boat, catch laid out on the shore, maybe a tope or two, perhaps a conger eel – these were favourite subjects. But no more than the buildings, he made no attempt to romanticise the islanders, presenting them as he found them.

It would not have taken an ornithologist to be struck by the bird life on Achill in the 1870s. For any visitor there was the thrilling spectacle of finding that

. . . both the sea eagle and the golden eagle regularly bred in the sea cliffs of Achill Island and it was not an uncommon sight to watch them in their splendid flight soaring aloft. I was greatly interested in seeing for the first time numbers of the chough or red legged crow in their wild state. In the summer they inhabit the cliffs where they nest, but in autumn are chiefly found frequenting the cornfields of the inhabitants.[9]

Golden eagles have not inhabited, certainly not bred on, the island since before the First World War and the larger white-tailed eagle long before that, both species having been shot, trapped and poisoned to extinction. Perhaps with the re-introduction of both species to Ireland in recent years, coupled with closely watched breeding programmes, their great wheeling, soaring flights may yet again be seen over the cliffs of Achill.

Williams got closer to one particular eagle than he might ever have expected to, not by clambering down some vertiginous cliff face as obsessive collectors of eggs and chicks once did (and may illegally still do), but by finding that William Pike kept a golden eagle in a cage on the lawn at Glendarary. For company, the eagle was provided with a goose.[10] One wonders what the goose thought of that. The eagle had been taken from a nest as a chick and is said to have lived in captivity for twenty-six years.[11] It was not the first eagle to be kept in captivity on Achill. Isabella Adams, the wife of the doctor at the mission settlement, in a letter made a reference to a pet eagle which was kept at the mission and which had rather more company than a goose: 'I asked the other morning if two sorrowful looking sheep which I saw at the door had been in the garden all night? I was answered: No, Ma'am they were in Mr Baylee's parlour. Where is the old grey mare kept? In Mr Baylee's parlour. And the pet eagle? In Mr Baylee's parlour. Where is the Sunday school heard? In Mr Baylee's parlour.'[12]

Williams had one other introduction to make on that first trip of 1873, that was to John Sheridan at the Slievemore Hotel. If his attachment to Achill needed sealing, it came with his journey across the length of the island to Dugort:

> In this drive the ever changing views of the blue hills of Ballycroy, the endless windings of Blacksod Bay, and the great stretches of bogland broken into by glistening threads of silver water, was a sight not easily to be forgotten; and when the highest point of the road was reached, a scene of great grandeur was spread out. Looking westward the other side of the island came into view with the broad Atlantic in the distance. The island of Inishgalloon stands off the coast, and in the great hollow sandy plain lay the Strand of Keel, and the wide expanse of water, Keel Lake. A couple of miles off in the blue misty distance nestles the village of Dukinelly. Miles off across the valley Croughan Mountain and Achill Head rear their storm-riven heads, and on all sides we see rich brown boggy land. Dugort is an oasis in the wild wilderness of Achill.

Sheridan was to prove a good friend and a useful one. The two men had much in common, an interest in wildlife and in gardening. Sheridan even took up painting at one stage (taking lessons from both Alexander and from Paul Henry), and his wall-size paintings are still to be seen on Achill.[13] Williams would spend time at the Slievemore Hotel and Sheridan and his family would visit the Williamses at the sound. On his first visit Williams was curious to be introduced to the dubious pleasures of illicit Irish whiskey or 'potheen' (pronounced 'potch-een') and Sheridan was the man to do it.

Watercolour inscribed 'Menaan [*sic*] Cliffs Keel Strand Achill Island'. From the artist's first Achill sketchbook, 1873.
4 x 7 in. (10 x 17.8 cm).

Interestingly, when the inspector for the CDB calculated household expenditure among the tenant farmers, he reckoned that nearly a quarter might go on buying tobacco, an astonishingly high amount. No mention is made of what may have been spent on 'potheen', but it

> . . . was manufactured at that time in great abundance and quantities were smuggled over in canoes from the chief manufacturers on the wild distant island of Iniskea, about 12 miles from Achill on the Atlantic side of the Mullet, now the site of the great whaling station. I asked my friend Sheridan where I could procure a quart of the precious liquor and next day we paid a visit to the cabin of an old woman living at old Dugort. The old party was extremely cautious when told the purpose of our visit and evaded the subject, saying Don't ye know Mr Sheridan that I never keep a drop of it now, it's too dangerous a business altogether! And your friend here might be an excise man for all I can tell! After a close confab between them in a low voice in Irish at last she said, taking up a spade, 'Will yes come out and look at my praties I want to dig some for me dinner?' In her little garden were some young potatoes much too early to dig, but she removed a couple of plants, carefully laying them [to] one side, stalks and all, and as she put the spade again in the sandy soil it struck against something hard which proved to be a nice little 2 gallon keg. Even then she tried to keep up a deception and pretended to be surprised, and remarked that 'it was a quare place to put such a thing there, but whatever is in it, yer welcome to help yerself.' We managed to get at the bung and when she brought a quart bottle from the cabin we soon filled it, and then she replaced the barrel covering it with sand & taking the

Kildownet (*Gráinne Ní Mháille's castle*), Achill Sound, looking across to the to the mainland. From a print in the artist's illustrated catalogue 'Something about Achill', 1897.

potato plants carefully up she replaced them in the ground, smoothed the sand and left the surface as it was before.

That quart of 'potheen' lasted me for 20 years, and anybody who took a glass of it at night generally suffered from 'tight hat' the next morning.[14]

From which it might be judged Williams was not a toper. Sheridan did more than give him a hangover. In time to come his hotel became an outlet for the artist's pictures.

On that first visit Williams set down in his sketchbooks all that he could:

I spent days exploring and sketching the splendid scenery, visiting the Minaun Cliffs, Keel Strand, the extraordinary village and valley of Dooagh, Keem Bay with its marvellously beautiful strand, where one can view from a height the great shoals of fish seen moving over the silver sandy shallows, and away east in the opposite direction lies the Valley Strand and various sandy bays and loughs until the quiet waters of the Sound are met with. Ever since then, up to the present Achill Island has had for me an ineffaceable charm, and my friends tell me that I paint it as if I thoroughly loved it.[15]

The visit to Achill was a turning point in Williams' life. Writing back home to his father, he said: 'I had found a part of Ireland where there was an immense field for the activities of an artist, and that I intended to make it peculiarly my own, and devote myself to making its wonderful scenery known.'[16]

The following year, three of the six pictures he exhibited at the Royal Hibernian Academy annual exhibition of 1874 were of Achill subjects; two were dramatic scenes: 'The Rising Gale – Dugort Strand'; 'Picking up Wreck, Menaan Cliffs'; and the third also a sea scene: 'Hookers and Yawl, Achill Sound.' He would continue painting the scenery of Achill, its coastlines and interiors, its dwellings and its people, for the rest of his life.

Pen and ink sketch inscribed (top) 'Dooega, Achill Island Sept 4 1894'. Bottom: 'Clare Island from Dooega, Achill Island.' 4½ x 7 in. (11.4 x 17.8 cm)

The Dublin Sketching Club

Dublin Sketching Club medal, 1874.

I f 1873 was notable for Williams in being the year he first visited Achill, 1874 was no less important for him. He got his first singing appointment at the Chapel Royal and became a founder member of the Dublin Sketching Club, which flourishes to this day (it was renamed the Dublin Painting and Sketching Club in 2000 but is referred to by its original name here). While artists may be drawn to art because of its essentially solitary nature, most people from any walk of life value the reassurance of mixing with their own from time to time. Despite a much expressed need for some kind of art society, nobody got around to doing anything about it until a dentist stepped forward:

> Some attempts had been made by gentlemen inviting some artists to their houses where music and art were indulged in, but it remained for one very enthusiastic Dublin Dentist Mr Wm Booth Pearsall to organise a special meeting at his place in Westland Row to form a society where good artistic work might be done on a special evening in the week set aside for the purpose. It was on Tuesday evening the 20th of October 1874 that the following gentlemen having received invitations met together at 22 Westland Row.[1]

Twelve attended the inaugural meeting, quite a mix of professional and amateur painters, including two medal makers, a civil servant who was an aspiring writer rather than a painter, and three others from the medical profession apart from William Booth Pearsall. The attendees, exactly as Williams listed them in his memoirs, were:

J Todhunter MD	G. Pim jnr
John Woodhouse ARHA	Bram Stoker
Edward Purdon Jun	Alexander Williams
Chichester Alex Bell	Wm Booth Pearsall
Thomas Urry Young	Alfred Grey [not in fact present]
Charles Edward Fitzgerald MD	John Leech
William Stokes MD	

William Booth Pearsall, although he modestly referred to himself as an amateur painter, was rather more than the term might suggest. He had begun exhibiting at the RHA in 1872, two years before the formation of the Sketching Club, and would continue to do so until 1912. He was made an honorary member of the RHA in 1891. A good number of the founders had already exhibited at the RHA: Thomas Urry Young as long ago as 1841; John Woodhouse, ARHA, a medal maker, had exhibited from 1860, and Alfred Grey, RHA exhibited first in 1864 and was to continue over a span of some sixty years, much the same as Williams. Another medal maker, E. B. Purdon, exhibited at the RHA just once in 1872. So there was quite an amount of experience between them all as well as a diversity of painting styles, albeit of a generally conservative nature. It is interesting too to note how many of the artists lived in the centre of Dublin, all more or less within walking distance of each other. For example, Booth Pearsall had addresses in Merrion Street and Westland Row; Alfred Grey had an address on Lower Gardiner Street and John Woodhouse at Kildare Place. Williams always retained an inner city address, at Grantham Street, Harcourt Street and Hatch Street, even when he came into property in Rathgar. It is unlikely that so many artists will again live in such close proximity in Dublin city. Just one founding member of the club would become world famous, but not as a painter. This was Abraham Stoker, or Bram for short, whose Gothic novel, *Dracula*, published in 1897, would, in time, sweep the world. At this stage of his life Stoker was working in the civil service in Dublin Castle; writing he had taken up to supplement his income.

Dr Todhunter took the chair at the inaugural meeting and John Woodhouse, seconded by Bram Stoker, proposed the name the Dublin Sketching Club, which was passed unanimously; as was W. Booth Pearsall and J. Woodhouse's proposal that *in absentia* Alfred Grey be elected President and Augustus Burke Vice-President. Burke had also exhibited at the RHA, for the first time in 1870. Edward Purdon and William Stokes proposed the following members should form the committee for the working arrangements of the club: John Todhunter; John Woodhouse; Thomas U. Young and Bram Stoker, again passed unanimously. Oddly, at no point does Williams ever mention in his memoirs having been elected an Honorary Secretary of the club, yet another activity to fit into his already overcrowded life; it was a post he kept until 1928, becoming the club's longest-serving Secretary. That in itself bespeaks his ability to weather storms and offer the hand of friendship among artists, a group among which prickly temperaments are hardly unknown.

The Sketching Club got off to an encouraging start, immediately attracting a wider following. Williams recorded that:

There was much satisfaction expressed in artistic circles during the following week at the starting of a club being an accomplished fact and all were looking forward to the first working meeting which took place at the same address on October 26th. Present: Robert Mannix, John Woodhouse, W Thornley Stoker MD, Capt. WD Horan, JE Rogers, Edward Purdon, Alex Williams, TU Young, TA Jones PRHA [President of the Royal Hibernian Academy], Stephen Catterson Smith RHA, John Malcomson, John Leech and Henry O'Neill. A long table down the centre of the room was prepared for sketching purposes round which the members sat and for two hours worked to illustrate the two subjects chosen for illustration, 'Sunset' and 'Rejection'. Messrs JE Rogers, Alex Williams, T.U. Young and WB Pearsall contributed sketches of 'Sunset'. Messrs TA Jones, J. Leech and S Gatterson Smith 'Rejection' and Robert Mannix a pencil head of the hard working secretary. E. Purdon modelled in clay. J. Woodhouse in wax. Time was called by the Hon Sec. at 10.15, and each member placed his work on a screen where it was criticised by those present. A light supper of cheese and bread washed down with ale followed and the President of the Royal

Hibernian Academy of Arts took the chair for an animated discussion as to the best way of working the club.[2]

It was agreed that what the club most needed, if it was to operate successfully, was it own room, centrally located, from where events of various kinds could be organised. Clearly the society was intended not only for artistic but social gatherings as well: 'The first premises occupied by the club were situated at 212 Gt Brunswick St and many most enjoyable working evenings were spent there. The Club also gave *conversaziones* and smoking concerts, and the works of the members were exhibited on screens, attracting much notice.' Works done within the prescribed time limit of two hours were provided with their own exhibition space which was dubbed the 'hurrygraph'. It became common for musically inclined members, Williams included, to provide ditties and snatches during working hours.

As Williams put it: 'The success of the society was so pronounced that most of the active members of the Royal Hibernian Academy of Arts became members.' Such luminaries as Thomas Drew and the President, Sir T. A. Jones, Bartholomew Colles Watkins, Edwin Hayes, and P. U. Duffy all joined the Sketching Club. Overseas members included Rear Admiral Beechy from Plymouth and marine painters were well represented in the club. So Williams had several like-minded painters with whom to share his own interest in things maritime. He once painted Edwin Hayes in a maritime scene, suggesting more than a passing friendship. Among other painters who were to join were John Butler Yeats, Walter Osborne, Nathaniel Hone, Richard Orpen, older brother William, Percy French and Sarah Purser.

But it was not confined to painters. As it had started so it continued, with members coming from all walks of life. Alexander knew a number through activities quite unrelated to painting: Dr R. F. Scharff through the Museum of Science and Art was one, and Edmond Oldham, through quartet singing, was another. We find tenor Melfort D'Alton and Williams' own brother, Willie, serving on the Art Union committee of the Sketching Club. Membership was indeed spread widely.

The club did not stay long in Great Brunwick Street, moving for its second season to the Royal Irish Academy of Music, 36 Westland Row. The same year the club held its first public exhibition, in January 1876, at the Leinster Lecture Hall, 35 Molesworth Street, when 'The members presented their sketches for the benefit of the Artists' Benevolent Fund and they were disposed of on the Art Union plan', resulting in 'a very handsome donation'. Art Union schemes were once plentiful. They were adapted from continental models originating in Switzerland about the 1830s. The primary idea was to disseminate art among the less well off by means of subscriptions and the production of prints, with distribution by lot. In Ireland the formation of the Royal Irish Art Union (RIAU) was motivated less on the high-minded notion of bringing art to the masses than of trying to drum up interest in art among a middle class who showed a remarkable indifference to buying art of any kind.[3] Sales at the RHA exhibitions held between 1835 and 1838 amounted to the princely sum of £1.10.0. It was not a good time to be trying to make a living as an artist, but times were changing. By 1866 it is said there were no fewer than forty-eight Art Unions in Britain and Ireland. Williams recalled that Thomas Cranfield in Grafton Street 'was publisher of the Art Union prints which were in great vogue at the time of their introduction and even now at auctions they sometimes turn up splendidly framed in the old rosewood & maple and bearing the seal and stamp of the [Royal] Irish Art Union'.[4] Williams was a beneficiary of a variety of Art Union schemes, notably through the Dublin Sketching Club and also the Royal Hibernian Academy, where his work was chosen by the selection committee on at least three occasions.

In fact, enterprising young man that he was, he even held what he called his own Art Union scheme in 1878. This was six years before he mounted a solo exhibition and suggests that by the late 1870s he must already have had a fair following. Basically his Art Union scheme was simply a raffle for some of his pictures. He wrote:

It was about this time that I conceived a plan for raising some money by an art union. The tickets were 5/- each and I netted £30. There were a great many prizes consisting of sketches of my own, many of which were very small. One sarcastic winner returned his prize, about the size of a modern postcard; it was a sketch of a fishing boat in pen and ink. He had drawn a large flag from the top of the mast – on which he had inscribed in large letters 'THE GULL of ABBEY ST' and sent it through the post. However, it was conveyed to me after, that the great majority of the winners were well pleased.[5]

In May 1876 the Dublin Sketching Club held its first exhibition on behalf of its members. Some 435 works were exhibited, of which Williams contributed eleven. To his own astonishment and delight (and possibly the astonishment of his friends too) he sold every one. He made a pointed comparison between his singing and his painting careers, writing: 'If I found singing so difficult, I was well rewarded by my success in art.'[6] 'Greatly congratulated by my friends,' he noted with satisfaction. The club exhibited at other venues too, among them Messrs Cranfield County's Gallery, 115 Grafton Street, when 'Sketches and Studies' were held in the 1878–80 season. Williams had not yet forsaken bird studies. He exhibited *Spring, Dead Corncrake*; and what was a new and shortlived departure for him, under a section devoted to 'Pottery', he showed five paintings on china plaques.

There were many convivial and productive evenings when members both worked and socialised. However, there was a great deal of publicity over a row in 1884 when the controversial American painter James McNeill Whistler (1834–1903), who was based in England, exhibited his work. Whistler was very famous, and to have him associated with the society was regarded as a major coup. Moreover, in agreeing to provide twenty-six pictures, Whistler said it was the largest collection he had ever lent in the United Kingdom, outside of London. This did not go down well with some members, who took exception to the publicity and promotion Whistler received, which they felt was at the expense of their own work. In the event a motion of censure against the hanging committee was defeated, while a motion that Whistler should be made an honorary member of the club was passed.

Long before this row broke out, however, there was a potentially more damaging, if less public, row in November 1877 which led to much bitterness and to the resignation of a number of the club's most important members and not a few others. Williams did not dwell on the problem – and perhaps more significantly did not appear to take sides – recording only that: 'We had a great rumpus in the Dublin Sketching Club over the election of the Committee. A few names of members of the Royal Hibernian Academy were struck off and I was the recipient of several letters from those who felt aggrieved at this treatment.'[7] He transcribed two of the letters he received, and their tone certainly leaves no doubt as to what the writers felt. As the originals do not appear to have survived, they are given here as Williams transcribed them:

8 Stephen's Green Dublin (copy) November 13 1877

Dear Sir,

Whilst absent from home at the time the first General Meeting of the Dublin Sketching Club was held, I happened to hear that I was not elected on the Committee this year. This I regarded as it should be as I have always expressed a wish to be an independent member of the Club in preference and so attached no significance to the fact one way or another.

On making enquiries however on my return, I learn that a meeting consisting of 12 members of the Club, professing to elect officers and committee for the current year, has taken on itself to make a wholesale change, dismissing at least five gentlemen who served last year. I have to inform you by the way that this action being in express contravention of Bye Law IV which provides that 'two members shall retire annually' is wholly irregular and illegal and of no force if anyone thought it worth while to question it, which I doubt – and the so called President and Committee do not in point of fact hold office at all. However as regards the intention of the meeting there can be no hesitation in accepting it as a censure upon the Committee of last year, why and for what purpose I am utterly at a loss to divine. I take the liberty of speaking my mind when I say that I regard this proceeding as one of the most wanton and uncalled for affronts to four of the most distinguished and useful members of the Club that could be conceived, in fact an almost incredible impertinence on the part of the 'Club' to men of their rank and position. There may be a difference of opinion as to this and I do not presume to question the right of others to one differing from mine, but I take leave to express my own plainly in offering my resignation of membership which I do herewith.

Yours faithfully,

Thomas Drew RHA

[To] The acting secretary
Kylemore House
Kylemore
County Galway
Nov 27th 1877

My dear Williams,
I regret I was unable when up in town on the 18th October to attend the annual meeting of the Sketching Club, but it happened to occur on the day of the meeting of the Royal Hibernian Academy which completely occupied me. I have since learned to my great surprise that the few members of the Sketching Club present, twelve, I am told, took upon themselves to remove several members of the Committee.

I really cannot imagine what could have led to this line of action. The financial affairs are satisfactory – for after paying a considerable balance due when Mr Pearsall resigned the Secretaryship, sending to the Artists' Benevolent Fund a handsome donation which had been announced as the result and *raison d'être* of the Raffle, they carried over a larger sum than the Club ever had to begin the year with. One would think this deserved a vote of thanks.

However I do not care to seek further into the matter, let others do so if they choose; as Bye Laws have been thrown over board I look upon the Club as not legally in being – at least on its old footing – and have come to the conclusion of ceasing my connection with it, and will ask if you would kindly tender my resignation at the next meeting.

Believe me my dear Williams
Yours very truly,
B. Colles Watkins RHA

Alex Williams Esq
Secretary Dublin Sketching Club

To this Williams added: 'Misfortunes seldom occur singly and in addition to the above names, the President of the Royal Hibernian Academy Sir Thomas Jones and Augustus Burke RHA also resigned membership.' The inference from this little saga may be that some members bore a personal animus against some committee members, maybe resenting their status, and perhaps regarded the RHA as over-represented on the committee; and so targeted them for removal by fair means or foul. The records for the year appear to be lost. But the fallout following the resignations may be judged from Williams' single comment on the next meeting held on 21 November: 'A great rumpus and mix up in the Dublin Sketching Club.'

But where did Williams stand in all of this? He was known for his genial temperament and could have been relied on to have been a peacemaker rather than a warmonger on any committee. He does not say, perhaps because he would have regarded it as self-evident, but he would surely have been opposed to what had taken place or at the very least would want to remain neutral. It would not have made sense to him personally to have done otherwise, having nothing to gain by the removal of academicians and much to lose if he was entertaining hopes of becoming a member of the RHA himself.

There is plenty of evidence that he was on good terms with the academicians. He had visited Augustus Burke's studio in March, and Burke had bought a picture of his, *Limehouse*, as recently as November. Just a few months earlier, in August, he had been 'greatly complimented' by Colles Watkins who had bought two of his watercolours, *St Paul's* and *Near Windsor*. He had no reason to offend such people. The most important figure to resign, Sir Thomas Jones, President of the RHA, clearly held no resentment against Williams; as there is plenty of evidence that after his resignation he went out of his way to encourage and support him.

Strained and fractious relations continued to take their toll from time to time. No fewer than thirteen members sent in a letter of resignation to the Secretary on 2 March 1886, each one signing the letter, which survives among the club's records. The names included a number with whom Alexander had close friendships, such as G. B. Thompson and Bingham McGuinness; and even the founding father of the club, W. B. Pearsall, found reason to give up his membership. The thirteen signatories were: P. C. Trench; J. Hogg; T. B. Middleton; W. B. McGuiness; W. Rigby; G. B. Thompson; J. Hodges; G. Drury; W. Osborne; C. E. Fitzgerald; H. C. W. Tisdall; S. C. Smith and W. B. Pearsall. Curiously, the signatories gave no clear reason as to why they had taken their decision, demanding only that they be given copies of the financial accounts. As Secretary, Williams replied on 11 March, stating that Oldham would be forwarding copies of the accounts, and on the payment of approximately 6/- from each member, to cover the cost of the deficit of last year's exhibition, their resignations would be accepted. The Annual Report for 1886–7, written up by Williams, provides some hints as to what was behind the mass resignation, but perhaps does not tell all:

> . . . as the session advanced it was evident that a considerable discontent existed in a special quarter amongst some of the members, some blackballing of candidates for membership seemed to have added to this feeling and several members expressed themselves to the effect that the standard of work should be still further raised and that the club should attempt higher aims.[8]

In the same report Whistler is alluded to, but not mentioned by name. In what was described as a 'period of depression', but one in which the Dublin Sketching Club, it was noted, was suffering no worse than any other club, 'the expense of the previous year in bringing over a large number of pictures, the work of one individual, was greatly lessened [this year].' Other comments are of interest: 'The experiment of engaging workmen to hang the pictures has been found to add considerably to the exhibition expenses', in connection with which, it is worth noting that for his solo exhibitions Williams was always 'his own hanging committee'.

There is a sense of relief in a comment by Dr M. A. Boyd in the minutes of the following year, 1887, when he speaks of 'the utmost harmony prevailing in the conduct of the club business',[9] a remark pointing back to the fact that harmony was not always in evidence. The problems that arose were perhaps an inevitable component of a club that showed great vitality from the start and blossomed in all sorts of directions. It was reported that for the 1884–5 season membership more than doubled from thirty-four to seventy-six. In the 1887 season several different categories of membership were introduced to replace the simple distinction between honorary and working members. Membership was now extended to include working members; non-working members or associates; corresponding members and honorary members. Women – lady artists – had been admitted as members two years earlier, although not as full members: 'They shall have the privilege of sending works to the Exhibition, but shall have no voice in the management of the Club and no power to attend a meeting', according to the minutes of the AGM for 1885. Nor were they admitted to the life classes; the only female present, and you could hardly exclude her, was the model herself. Initially, life classes were popular. For one such session, ten members were reported as having turned up and it sounds like it was an enjoyable affair with live music laid on. 'A model was posed and several studies were made, diversified by music and a song by Mr Sterling "Do not forget".'[10] Life classes eventually petered out for want of support, it being reported that:

During the winter session of 1897/98, the attendance was meagre. We had models of a very high character. We gradually undressed them, trusting that as the figure grew barer the room would get fuller, but not so. The lady we exhibited was young, beautiful and well-proportioned, a trained and experienced sitter, but, to the shame of the members, be it stated, your Hon. Treasurer and one other enthusiast were left alone to worship at her feet.

It is unlikely that Williams ever attended any of the life classes, even in the early years, as he had little skill in anatomical drawing; and while his surviving sketchbooks show some animal anatomical studies, there are no human ones.

Early on the club began hosting festivities of various kinds. There were club dinners at 5/- a head; concerts at 2/- while *conversaziones* were 1/6d. 'Open Night' consisted of an exhibition followed by refreshments and music. Revelries might go on late into the night. There were plenty of adept musicians among the club members to keep the fun going. At one such event George Prescott is recorded as having played on a cello of *his own construction*, Alec Colles played the piano, there was a flute solo by the

Vice-President S. Adams, and Williams shared in the glees and part songs performed not only by members of the Sketching Club but by the Hibernian Catch Club and the Strollers as well.[11] The society members knew how to enjoy themselves.

As an easier alternative to organising singers and instrumentalists, responsibility for which would have been with Alexander, the band of the Royal Irish Constabulary was booked for a smoking concert but proved to be an unhappy experiment: 'Their playing was so vigorous that conversation was rendered almost impossible. It is hoped that at our next smoking concert the music provided will be of a more soothing nature.'

The club was quite innovative too in making efforts to reach out to the community at large. For example, pupils from the 'industrial schools', the Masonic and Artane Boys' Schools among them, were invited to attend the club's exhibitions; and when making a field trip out to Carrickmines, students from the School of Art had the opportunity to participate.

The club had a variety of locations including 27 Molesworth Street (the Institute of Porcelain Painting) and No. 9 Merrion Row, which became the official venue for the club and remained so for many years. This and the Mills' Hall next door (No. 8) were both popular exhibition venues used by Williams and many others. Clubs from across the water were invited in 1886 to exhibit in the Leinster Hall, Molesworth Street, under the aegis of the Dublin Sketching Club. These included the Bewick Club in Newcastle-on-Tyne, the Manchester Athenaeum Graphic Club and the Langham Sketching Club, London. Dr M. A. Boyd in his presidential address at the annual dinner that year praised Williams, whose work on behalf of the club, he said, was the main reason for its success. The Honorary Treasurer, Eldred Oldham, deserved credit too; 1886 had been a particularly difficult year, with the breakaway group intent on forming another club. It was recalled at the club's jubilee celebrations in 1924 that it was Oldham who got the English clubs over and 'saved that year's exhibition'.[12]

Clay modelling was an activity that was introduced in the 1883–4 season, by which time the club could celebrate its tenth anniversary. On 19 December the occasion was marked with 'good cheer' and the President, P. C. Trench, gratefully presented Alexander with a silver-mounted palette and a box of colours with an engraved silver plate for all his service. The presidency was taken by rotation a year or so at a time, while the workings of the society were underpinned by the efforts of the Honorary Secretary and treasurer.

A photographic wing was established and an early exhibition showed a prevailing penchant for trees in winter, with no fewer than eleven frosty examples on show.[13] Surprisingly perhaps, there does not appear to have been any sense of rivalry between the artists and the photographers. This was probably because, among artists at least, photography was not regarded as an art form. Sentiments to that effect are to be found among the club's records. Photographers and painters would share the same excursions, and some artists carried cameras; the photos could serve as an *aide memoire*. More disconcertingly, at least one member was armed with a pistol on the boat trip to Ireland's Eye:

Oil on board the 'Stacks' on Ireland's Eye painted from the mainland. Lambay Island in the background. 10 x 16.25 in. (25.4 x 41.3 cm).

> Running out of Howth Harbour with a pleasant breeze, she [the boat] carried them round the island, affording views of the cliffs that face the open sea, and that cannot be seen except from a boat. The birds sheltering in the crags from the blazing rays of the noonday sun, startled by the pistol shots discharged to awaken the echoes, shrieked their discordant indignation.[14]

One might wonder if there might not have been expressions of indignation from among the members too.

Lectures became a popular feature of the early club, and could involve the most esoteric of subjects as when Professor Thornley Stoker delivered his lecture on 'Some Characters of the Cranium' in 1886. But most lectures were more *à propos*, covering such subjects as 'The Constituents of Pigments from an Artistic Point of View' by Walter Noel Hentley FRS which was given at the Royal College of Surgeons, and there were lectures on specific historic painters, Irish and otherwise. What were called lantern exhibitions – of glass slides – became an early feature of the society too. Such things were a considerable novelty and remained so for many years. The artist's nephew, Robert D. Williams, recalled of a much later exhibition, that when a *coloured* slide was shown the audience burst into spontaneous applause.

Painting and sketching trips around Dublin and further afield proved immensely popular with members. Here is how the virtues of Howth were extolled back in the 1880s: 'Howth, so far from town life, so great a contrast to the dust and turmoil of the streets, has always been a favourite spot with the members of the club. The sea air freshness, the peace and quiet of the country, reached us almost before the greetings of the friends who joined us had ceased to echo in our hearts.'[15] If Alexander did not write that, he would

Photograph of the *Iris*.

certainly have concurred with its sentiments. *The Irish Times* claimed that: 'With the coming of the bicycle, however, men went off individually and got further afield, but the evening reunions were maintained for many years.'[16] Popular and useful as the bicycle may have been – more especially after the introduction of the pneumatic tyre around the turn of the century – it did not in fact preclude group excursions.

Boats were as useful to members as bicycles. What sounds like a particularly memorable excursion took place on 30 July 1887: 'At two o'clock the *Iris*, decked in her choicest bunting, lay moored off the coastguard station, Pigeon House Road', so noted an unprovenanced news clip kept by the club. W. Sterling provided further details in the club's minutes: 'The members of the club were invited by Mr Geo Prescott to have a happy day on the river . . . Arriving at the Coast guard station opposite which Mr Prescott's boat was moored the party was taken on board and afterward punted across to suitable sketching spots along the river working from about 3 p.m. to 6 p.m. when they were picked up again & went on board to partake of Mr Prescott's hospitality and to do ample and audible justice to his fare. After drinking their host's health amidst three times three and three cheers more the party broke up . . . a thoroughly successful and jolly day had been passed.'[17] Williams in his report for the year added his comment on George Prescott's onboard hospitality: 'Severe injury was done to the eatables and liquids.'

On both land and sea, Williams spent a great deal of time around Dublin Port. One of his largest watercolours was *Dublin Bay – Sunset* in 1890. It is an evocative and historical scene, full of interest for the variety of boats it shows and for the timber lighthouse. Marine historian Cormac Lowth wrote of this picture:

Everything about it tells me that this is Dublin Port, looking upriver with Ringsend on the left and ships berthed on Sir John Rogerson's Quay further up, except for the wooden 'lighthouse'. It looks like a floating structure on some sort of pontoons, and the position of it would place it east of Alexandra Basin. In 1890 this area was still unreclaimed and that was virtually open water in an area that is known as the 'North Bank' . . . There is a lighthouse on legs today on the North Bank and perhaps this was a wooden one that preceded it. The baulks of timber would seem to signify work going on.

Watercolour of Dublin Bay, signed and dated 1890. 30 x 48 in. (76.2 x 120 cm).

Thumbnail preparatory sketch for Dublin Bay picture. The caption in part reads 'Design for a picture sketched at Collissons Popular Concert, Dec 1889. Painted a picture from it in watercolor. Sold at the exhibition of the Watercolor Society of Ireland for £35. Purchased by Mr M McCorquedale Edinburgh. 1904 brought back to Dublin now property of Mrs Hume Dugdeon Blackrock'.

Watercolour 'A Calm Evening on the Thames at Greenwich'. Signed and dated '86. 19.5 x 28.7 in. (49.5 x 73 cm).

The fishing boats are certainly the Ringsend fleet. The paddle wheeler is a tug towing the sailing ship which is a 'full rigged ship' as distinct from a 'barque'. This is defined by the square sails on all three masts. The smaller sailing vessel heading upriver is a 'barquentine' i.e. square sails on the foremast, and fore and aft sail on the mizzen.[18]

A ship being towed by a paddle tug is a recurring theme in many of Williams' pictures and sketches of the Port and Bay.

For a period in the latter half of the 1880s the painter took to producing very large watercolours, featuring not only Dublin Bay but the Thames, for example, such as *A Calm Evening on the Thames at Greenwich*, signed and dated 1886 and now in the Hugh Lane Gallery, Dublin. Another on a similar scale he introduced at the RHA annual exhibition of 1887, *The Irish Times* declaring that it was 'the largest and best water colour that he has yet produced',[19] and later in the year he showed the same picture at the Dublin Sketching Club and at his solo exhibition in Leinster Hall.[20] The picture itself bears no title but can be identified in the RHA catalogue as No. 215, *Summer Evening on the Beach at Skerries, County Dublin – Trawlers – Landing Fish*. The picture is notable for

Watercolour exhibited at the RHA 1887 as 'Summer Evening on the Beach at Skerries, County Dublin – Trawlers – Landing Fish'. 28 x 48 in. (73 x 120 cm). Signed and dated 1887.

its misty, still atmosphere. The sea is completely calm and despite there not being a breath of wind it is notable that all the boats have their sails fully out. Williams had a particular penchant for painting the fleet of Dublin Bay fishing 'smacks'. There are comparatively few similar studies and the picture tells quite a story, as Cormac Lowth relates:

> In the early years of the nineteenth century a fishing company was started in Dublin . . . to take advantage of what were, at the time, virtually unexploited fishing grounds off the east coast. Irish boats were small and trawling was practically unheard of. The type of boats illustrated were in use in Devon at the time and owners and their crews and families were encouraged to come to Dublin. The company was based at Pigeon House Harbour and the boats moored in Ringsend opposite Alexandra Basin in the area now taken up by the Poolbeg Yacht Club Moorings. This was known as the Trawlers Pond or Pool. Many of the crews intermarried with the locals and settled in the Ringsend area. The boats remained virtually unchanged for almost a century. They were known as 'smacks' and they used beam trawls as distinct from the modern otter trawls. The larger smacks were about 70 feet long.

No. 80.

"THE BUSY THAMES."

Ink drawing 'The Busy Thames' from the artist's exhibition catalogue for his fifth solo exhibition, 1892

Alexander Williams clearly had a liking for these fishing boats . . . Many of the early smacks were built in Devon and in the fishing boat registers you will find that many of the boats owned in Ringsend retained their Devon registration numbers, usually Dartmouth (DH) in addition to those registered in Dublin (D). As the century wore on, many of the smacks were also built in Ringsend, in some of the many boatyards that once occupied the banks of the Dodder.

A feature that defines the Ringsend smacks is the distinctive topsail that you can see in this picture. These had a small gaff at the top of the sail and this feature seemed to continue in use in Ringsend long after it fell out of use in Devon. The jolly boats that were used by smack fishermen were also distinctive. They were deep chunky boats that would have been capable of perhaps taking a good proportion of the catch ashore. Also there was a tradition of sculling with one oar over the stern in Ringsend as depicted in the painting.

I think the smacks in the painting are all at anchor and not under sail. Apparently it was a common practice to dry the sails this way while at anchor.[21]

It was during the 1870s that Williams developed his draughtsmanship to its furthest point. He produced pen and ink sketches at this time with considerable attention to detail, firmly representational and literal, which would have found him a ready audience at the Dublin Sketching Club and elsewhere. The club was quick to include illustrations in its catalogues. The exhibition for 1886 for instance contains an illustration by Williams of the River Thames, and his own early one-man shows contain finely detailed ink drawings (see illustration on facing page). The same conscious care is apparent in his paintings at this time, when he favoured lightly washed watercolours, and also in his oils, the paint being lightly and economically applied, his use of impasto yet to come. Here is youth relishing new-found powers. As is typical of most painters, with age his style tended to loosen up and he came to rely more on broader brush strokes and, although not invariably, less minutiae of detail. Until his death he exhibited annually at the club, missing only three years and showing a total of 861 pictures.

His popularity ran parallel with the development of his skills. Sir Thomas Jones as President of the RHA was a useful ally and Williams certainly had reason to remember him, for 'during Sir Thomas's presidency I was deeply indebted to him for the manner in which he gave me encouragement by having my pictures placed in good positions, I am afraid rather to the disgust of some of the Academicians at these exhibitions'. It might be going too far to say that it was the position in which his pictures were hung in the annual RHA exhibition in June 1877 that produced for him sales of £50.5.6, but it must surely have helped. Williams declared himself 'greatly delighted', as well he might. This sum, garnered from a single exhibition, was considerably more than what he was getting from the Chapel Royal in twelve months.

For most of the year his painting had to be centred on the environs around Dublin and adjacent counties. During his holidays from his cathedral work he made the most of the opportunity to travel further afield, which suited a restless disposition. Apart from trips that took him all over Ireland, he regularly went to London, and made occasional trips to the English south coast and midlands. He twice visited Scotland. He never travelled on the continent, however, and never expressed any yearning to do so. He might have done so with his friend Bingham McGuinness, with whom he sometimes went on local trips around Dublin. It is unlikely that the economics of travel put him off; he generally spent freely. The answer is more likely that he simply did not want to, finding all he needed in the Irish light and scenery. His pictures, often with dolorous clouds, do not suggest he would have had much affinity with the light of the Mediterranean.

Following on from his trip to Achill in 1873, Williams headed north to the Antrim coast in 1875 and made a record of his trip in a diary. Similarly, he made a diary of what he evidently regarded as a chance of a lifetime, a yachting cruise to the Scottish isles in 1876. When the mood took him, he could do a good line in deprecating humour. He gives full vent to it in his Antrim journal and provides a gentle reminder for anyone who might think the life of a painter is one long idyll, that painting *en plein air* is not without its difficulties. Both journals are of interest today in providing vignettes of life that now seem impossibly remote from our own.

CHAPTER 10

Inveterate Traveller

Oil on canvas 'Silent Evening'. Signed and dated. 1895. 30 x 50 (76.2 x 127 cm).

On 6 September 1875, Alexander headed off for what he called 'A journey in search of the picturesque to the Antrim Coast', and wrote up the trip in his memoirs. He went via Belfast, staying with his first cousin Dr William Whitla, the younger brother of the babe with whom Williams was supposed to have got mixed up when they shared a cushion twenty-eight years earlier. He then made for Carrickfergus via Larne, where he was greeted by the rare and stirring sight of a man o' war, *The Gibraltar*, one of the few remaining 'old wooden walls of old England', then in use as a training vessel. 'She was a splendid sight, but her masts seemed very small for the size of her hull.' He stopped by the castle and painted a small watercolour but with no great enthusiasm: '. . . a very fine object spoiled by recent additions.' It pleased him better from a distance: 'Looking back, about a mile from the Castle I saw an exceedingly fine evening effect, the Castle a conspicuous object standing out against the sunset sky and the distant hills melting away in the warm air.'

He took a 'long car' for Glenarm and tried a sketch by the roadside.

A man with a horse and cart came up; he looked with much curiosity at my campstool, sketchbox and traps and bid me 'good mornin'. Then his face suddenly brightened up and he spoke, 'I say Siur, if I was to stand furmenst ye, with the mare and myself, will ye take me wid yer teleskop?' Ha! He takes me for a 'foggfier' [photographer]. On my declining, he moved off muttering something about it being 'too early in the morning'.

On 9 September he took the diligence to Ballycastle, which he had to himself until joined at Camlough by a sailor of 'diminutive proportions' whom he reckoned was about thirteen years old. 'He had been at sea six months and had just left his ship. He was going home for the winter, then would start again. Did he smoke? No. Or curse? No. Or chew tobacco? No. He was evidently a model youth.' Approaching Fair Head, Williams was fairly in his element at the sight of

. . . Cushendall, a small cosy little place, smothered in trees and the blue smoke from the houses curling upwards . . . All hands were busy getting the harvest saved, peasants with their wives, children and neighbours were cutting and binding the golden grain, and the scythe was very much in use. We passed a group of about a dozen gaily dressed girls sitting in the form of a square in a field by the roadside, they were busy making a quilt by sewing gay coloured patches together. Their blue and red gowns, white kerchiefs tied round their heads, in the brilliant sunshine made a stunning picture. I wondered why Erskine Nichol never had the luck to light on so stunning a subject. Kelp! Kelp! Everywhere kelp! On the roadside, by the margin of the sea, on bushes, stones, and round the houses, this gigantic seaweed was being prepared for burning; a few people not engaged at harvesting were busy at fireplaces composed of rough stones, burning it to be sold to Glasgow buyers.[1]

He was advised that Fair Head was only two and a half miles off and that he could get a fine view of it from sea level. So he alighted from the diligence and sent his baggage on to Ballycastle. Predictably 'it proved the longest two and a half miles I ever covered and I thought my informant must have meant the distance to be as the crow flies.' He still had to trek into Ballycastle, and in fact his day's work had hardly begun. He took note for further reference of the 'splendid sandy beach at Ballycastle sweeping in a curve for miles round to near Fair Head, sandhills above high water, and dark green breakers rolling in most majestically'. The sea in his descriptions is nearly always green rather than blue. At sundown 'I tried a small water colour effect of sunset, a purple sky with the top of Fair Head tinged with golden fire'.

Despite the trials of the previous day, he was up at 6.40 the following morning and 'did a little water colour dabbling' before breakfast. He then set off at 9 a.m., returning to Fair Head. Going by the mine workings in the cliff face he was struck by the appearance of the 'pale faced and hollow cheeked' miners. However long the trek, if he was intent on painting from nature he had all his heavy gear to carry. Carrying watercolours would have involved lighter equipment but he would often lug his full equipment of oils and brushes and turpentine along with him. It is not clear when he preferred to use one medium rather than the other. It was not a simple issue of size, as at one time, as we have seen, he painted quite large watercolours, more usually the preserve of oils. Generally it might be said his oils contain more of his darker and bolder effects. 'I made an oil sketch of Fair Head in the distance, with masses of dark red rocks; on the right a path round the base, and dark rocks in the sea on the left with sea breaking over them. The different effects of light and shadow on the rugged headland were very marked.'[2]

Wherever he went, with his outsized umbrella and pots and paints he was sure to gather an inquisitive group of locals, the attention of which seemed to amuse rather than irritate him. Kelp gatherers 'stood staring at me arranging my traps for some time, then they sat down the better to study me. I must have been a thorough puzzle to them, but finally they resumed work, and occasionally gratified their curiosity by taking a steady stare at me.'[3] Women would never have thought of approaching him to enquire as to what he was about and there was a marked difference in the attitude between town and country folk:

On my way back I lighted on a lot of lobster pots that formed a good foreground for a picture with the banks of a river behind them. Intense curiosity was shown by the natives. 'What is he doin'?' 'Bedad I don't know.' In Dublin the answer would be contemptuously 'sketchin' but here it was a case of blank bewilderment. They gave it up, couldn't make it out. One old lassie whose curiosity was dreadfully excited leaned half out of a cottage window, and failing to make it out, sent a juvenile rustic with vermillion hair, who moved slowly in large circles round me, as the hunters of the ostrich are said to do, gradually reducing the distance until he sat down beside me. Then after a careful examination he hurried back with his report. [4]

Oil on canvas. The lobster pots are believed to be made of heather. Signed. 9½ x 12½ in. (24 x 31.8 cm).

Despite all the gear he had to carry, Williams constantly sought out-of-the-way places, sometimes finding himself in precarious spots:

> I scrambled along amongst the boulders on the shore and at other times wound round the face of the cliffs in sheep tracks amongst the heather and loose rocks, halfway to the top. A false step here and bits of clothing, brushes and painting materials might be collected at the bottom. After a time I came to a very large bend in the coast and decided to make a sketch there for I could see nothing grander and better. Bengore Head stood out magnificently, rising out of the grey sea misty atmosphere.[5]

Other than the insistent guides which he found hovering around the Giant's Causeway, not much appeared to get him down and he was in jocular mood when he included a section in his journal with the heading 'The trials of the Landscape Painter'. It is a caricature of course and is intended as such, but it points up the problems of painting outdoors and shows the lighthearted manner in which he dealt with them. On Saturday 11 September:

> I started off in heavy marching order, which means sketchbox for oil and light waterproof coat strapped to it, small bag over shoulder, campstool, and my invaluable old six foot Gingham umbrella without which trusty friend and companion life would be miserable. A shelter from the burning sun as well as a defence from the refreshing deluges we sometimes meet in company. A sketch of Ballycastle Bay. Pitched my campstool on the sandy dry beach, the heat I would calculate at over 100° [38 °C] in the sun and stretched out the anatomy of friend 'Gingham' and set resolutely to work.

Oil on canvas: Northern Ireland coastal view. Signed. 14 x 24 in. (36 x 61.5 cm). The lighting and brushwork are suggestive of impressionist influence.

A short interval of profound repose, broken only by the gentle rippling of the incoming tide, the landscape bathed in exquisitely brilliant sunshine and not a breath of wind stirring, alas how sweet and how short an interval, for I was surrounded by numbers of virulent Irish mosquitoes, nothing short of mosquitoes could sting so desperately. Sitting on my campstool one leg of which would insist on sinking into the sand, I had my box on my knees and the stick of the umbrella resting on one side, palette in one hand and brush in the other, endeavouring to keep everything in position when I received a severe bite on the left cheek, drop goes the palette and with my right hand I squast [*sic*] the insect, a slight interval and I go through the same performance on the other cheek.

Hello! What's this on the palette? Dark insects crossing and recrossing where my flake white is spread out. I find they are beetles of various sizes that have been on the wing; one large specimen was wending its way deviously and indiscriminately through Raw Sienna, Light Red, Umber and Black and amalgamating the Blue and Yellow – not quite to my taste – add to these flies and gnats, some on the palette and some on the oil sketch to which they adhere tenaciously like fly paper, and a faint idea may be formed of the disheartening conditions of affairs. But my motto must be 'Excelsior'! Nothing is easy, nothing is difficult, and the true artist despises difficulties! Ahem! But misfortunes seldom come singly and whilst consoling myself, down came a ruthless shower of sand, like a desert storm. I was sitting close to a high sand bank unconscious that a portion of the top was covered with sweet herbage which a cow in endeavouring to obtain displaced this fresh cause of torment. We may gain some consolation in our trials. I felt if the animal had fallen on me I should have been 'cowed' indeed. After quite a lot of lesser annoyances, not forgetting the upsetting of a bottle of drying oil which I upset in frantic endeavours to squash a

Oil on board: Carlingford Lough, looking northwestwards. Signed. 10 x 17¾ in. (25.4 x 45 cm).

wasp and oleaginous fluid got mixed up with the handles of my brushes and flowed through a crack into another compartment and got well spread over a sketch I had in retirement.[6]

He packed up and made haste to retire from the scene. Sand was a constant problem. But all was not quite lost; the story ends with him reporting that once the oil paint had dried and hardened he was able to scrape the sand off it. Would it be possible to spot tiny grains of Ballycastle Bay sand in his painting today?

Clothing and equipment were another source of wry amusement to him:

Friday 17th I held a full dress parade and inspection of clothing accoutrements and kit. My 'tunic' is becoming much worse, it was quite fresh on leaving town, but now shows a wound on the left shoulder, the effect of the strap from which I sling my sketch box, my hat has quite lost its black lustre and exposure to the strong rays of the sun has given it a greenish hue, and 'old sol' has softened it and put it out of shape. Left boot is leaking, and 'Repeal of the Union' is going on in the other. My sketch box has a few of the angles at the corners pretty well rubbed down, the lid and bottom are split across, result of a fall. My campstool is the only part of my kit that does not show signs of the terrible wear and tear. Alas my faithful Gingham left town at short notice, minus one rib, using and abusing it as a walking stick, and as an assistant in climbing cliffs has taken about an inch off the point, alas how changed is its colour. I think I can see it now in all its pristine freshness as it looked the day I removed it from a shop in Grafton St.[7]

The nearly tropical heat continued while Williams sketched about Port Ballantrae, the Bush River and Dunluce Castle of course. Dunluce Castle proved to be among his most popular pictures as prints of it still circulate today. Early on the Monday the weather broke with a tremendous thunderstorm after which the temperature dropped markedly and fresh winds coming in along the coast made painting increasingly difficult. Back at

Oil on canvas, inscribed 'The Black Rocks Ballantrae', signed and dated 1876. 18 x 36 in. (45.7 x 91.4 cm).

Portrush he faced a 'piercingly cold wind' from which it was nearly impossible to get shelter. He returned to Dublin on 25 September. There is always, of course, a certain amount of luck as to how much work can be done outdoors. On this occasion he had got the best of it.

On 1 October he moved into Grattan Kelly's house, 102 Lower Mount Street, to combine painting with singing, in what initially seemed to him like an ideal set up: 'The light for painting work was so good that I made arrangements with him to board in the house and occupy the back drawing room as a Studio.' So it was that 'The year 1876 found me strenuously endeavouring to serve two masters, art and music, often twin sisters'. He was exhibiting at the RHA for the seventh year in succession and might fairly regard himself as an established exhibitor. But he confessed he had become dissatisfied with his work. The pictures he showed that year were *Noontide Portmarnock*; *Port Ballantrae Antrim Coast*; *Stormy – Dunluce Castle; When the Wind Bloweth in from the Sea* (a bay on the Antrim coast); and *Outward Bound, off the Poolbeg*. 'Most of them showed the effect that my northern tour had in enlarging and expanding my method of painting but I was disappointed with my endeavours, for my pictures showed a dirtiness of tone and quality when hung in the well-lighted rooms of the Academy House. I thought at the time this was due to the lighting of the new studio I had moved into in Mount St where instead of a top light, the illumination was from an ordinary window darkened half way up.'[8] It is not entirely clear what he meant. *The Black Rocks Ballantrae* is an evocative scene of sundown on a lonely cove with the wind whipping up the waves. A good portion of the cliff face is extremely dark, giving the scene a touch of menace, the kind of thing the Victorians rather liked, although critics sometimes commented on so much blackness as too much of a good thing, an easy option. Rosa Mulholland, for instance, in reviewing the RHA exhibition of 1889 for the *Irish Monthly* commented acidly: 'too many brushes seemed to have learned a trick of moderating the hues of the prism with an infusion of soot.' She would surely have disapproved of so dark a cliff face in the picture in question, but dark as it is, the artist has picked out details on the cliff and the colouring of the picture overall is well controlled. The bright gleam of fading light adds a touch of drama while the lone heron on the beach facing into the sea accentuates the loneliness of the scene. The rock elements, always a strong feature with the artist, are well defined and forbidding. Compared with his work in old age when his colours too often became drab, the tones appear fresh and vibrant. Whatever he had in mind, 'dirtiness of tone' would preoccupy him for some time.

His comment that he blamed, at least partly, the poor lighting in his studio suggests that what he had exhibited at the RHA, even if started on location, was substantially completed in the studio. This is of some interest as he was often praised for 'painting from nature' by knowing critics believing they could tell the difference between working direct from the subject and pictures from the studio. It is a fair guess that a good many of what were thought to be the former were very probably the latter and vice versa. While he would spend the long days of summer travelling in all directions throughout Ireland, the winter months were largely spent at home.

Whatever about the effect of the lighting of his studio, he did not stay long boarding with Grattan Kelly, moving after only eight months, on 1 June 1876, to 32 Lower Abbey Street. There he seems to have had a stream of convivial visitors, including his friend F. J. Power, special war correspondent of the *Daily Telegraph* and member of the Dublin Sketching Club. Serious as Williams may have been in his chosen vocation, that did not preclude him sharing an adolescent sense of fun with visitors. 'I had a cord from the ceiling with a brass ring at the end and our great amusement was to strike this ring in giving a high kick with the point of the toe. I used it to open the door downstairs to visitors, and as we became expert at the exercise we had to raise the ring a bit higher. Every visitor I invited to have a go at it, and some used to fall on their back when they first tried.'[9]

Williams stayed in this two-room studio a little over a year before 'removing to the next storey at a reduced rent of £10 less per annum' on 5 August. He does not say whether the move was up a storey or down (nor whether he brought the cord and brass ring with him), more likely he was upward bound if the rent was lower, so perhaps after all he did have a period as a garret painter of popular imagination.

In the heat of summer, his studio might have been oppressive but it was an easy matter to escape from the city centre. His love of the sea and ships, forged during his schooldays in Drogheda, with summer idylls at the coast, was enduring and he frequently left Abbey Street for the countryside and the sea. He painted all along the coast stretching north and sometimes south of Dublin. Howth was a particular favourite spot and Candlestick Bay a scene he painted often, but he would go further too, taking in such spots as Portmarnock and Skerries. His storm scenes – and he loved storms – sometimes resemble those of Edwin Hayes, whose virtuosic work may well have influenced him. Storm scenes regularly featured in his exhibitions.

He indulged his love of boating by having small boats around the Bull in Dublin and later a punt on Achill Island, where he was to build a jetty in the shelter of Bleanaskill

Watercolour sketch of Kingstown from the sea, c. 1873. 4 x 7 in. (10 x 17.8 cm).

Bay on the sound. There were plenty of opportunities to sail on larger craft owned by friends, enabling him to paint the shoreline from out at sea as well as islands around the coast. His earliest surviving sketchbook (1873) contains a watercolour of Dalkey Island, clearly painted from a boat, and likewise a watercolour panorama of Kingstown, now Dun Laoghaire.

A prominent member of the Dublin Sketching Club and a friend of Williams' was George Prescott (1847–1942). He was a man of quite extraordinary inventiveness and versatility. He had an electrical and optical business at 9 Merrion Row and at one time lived in what was the last house on the Merrion Strand Road, No. 20, known as 'The Hermitage'. Alexander painted it from the strand. The picture shows not only the paucity of houses along that now crowded stretch, but outside 'The Hermitage' is what appears to be a windmill, presumed to be a wind dynamo or possibly a pump and no doubt of the owner's own devising.

George Prescott's boat, the *Iris*, as might be expected of an owner of such individuality, was an unusual one. She was 60 feet long, had a beam of 12 feet 6 inches but a draught of only 3 feet 6 inches. The keel was fitted with what are known as 'legs'. The boat had two great advantages over conventional craft. It could negotiate bays much shallower than most boats of her size and the 'legs' meant it would remain steady in shallow water. Where the sea bottom was not amenable to the legs, stability was achieved by two deep bilge pieces, 10 feet long, and bolted to broad stringers about the timbers, the stringers extending out beyond the bilge pieces by 5 feet. A complicated arrangement it might sound and certainly unconventional, but for painting or having a placid dinner the arrangement was admirable. Up and down the coast the *Iris* would sail under Prescott's guidance with everyone on board required to man the vessel, no small part of

Original sketch for The Badminton Library of Sports and Pastimes. 6¼ x 10 in. (16 x 25.5cm)

the fun. The *Iris* was ideal for artists who wanted to paint along the coast and to island hop with visits to the likes of Lambay Island and Ireland's Eye, and was much in demand. In fact the boat was something of a celebrity in its own right and featured in *The Badminton Library of Sports and Pastimes* in a section entitled '"Graphic Cruisers" of Dublin Bay'. George Prescott wrote the text while most of the black and white sketches in the yachting section of the book are by Williams.

In 1876, Williams readily seized an invitation to participate in a yachting cruise to Scotland, sailing on the *Hinda*, a racing cutter of 20 tons. His host, to whom he refers as the Commodore, was George Black Thompson, a wealthy wine merchant and amateur artist living at 13 Fitzwilliam Place.

The *Hinda* travelled up the west coast of Scotland, visiting harbours and sea lochs en route, up as far north as the Clyde, the two men painting all the way. On reaching the Clyde they took what Williams described as a holiday, that is to say one day off, when they paid a visit to Glasgow by train. The docks might not be the first thing a visitor to the city would choose to comment on, but Williams, ever one for wandering docks and

Oil on canvas, signed and inscribed 'Old Merrion', showing George Prescott's house, The Hermitage, 20 Strand Road, and the Martello tower, Sandymount. 5.5 x 9.3 in. (14 x 23.5 cm).

wharves, sketchbook in hand, declared himself delighted with them: 'Glasgow black, dirty, and smoky seemed a wonderful hive of industry and shipbuilding yards all along the banks of the Clyde were a wonderful sight.' On visiting the Renfrew Street Gallery, he had nothing to say about the exhibit of modern art, commenting instead on the fact that 'the only visitors beside ourselves were two barefooted factory hands carefully examining the paintings.'[10]

Williams wrote up the cruise in a diary of more than 10,000 words, which he entered in his memoirs and had another, similar version typed and bound, perhaps for lending to family and friends. His descriptions of the Scottish scenery coming from a painter's eye and there is again more than a whiff of *Boy's Own* in his excitement at going to sea:

> People may talk of the pleasures of riding, bicycling, or motoring, but to my mind there's nothing like a freshening breeze when the wind pipes merrily through the rigging, the sun shines brightly on the white sails and the clean deck, the lee rail is under water, and the boat pumps and hisses through the green waves, leaving a long creamy trail of foam behind. Then it is that you feel a sense of exhilarating freedom, and as the salt spray is blown on your bronzed cheek, you wish there was never a smoky city, and you wonder will it be possible to become again a house dweller.[11]

The party had two days of brilliant sunshine in which to explore and sketch around Rothesay. To Williams' surprise the spectacular weather was the signal for the whole population 'to take to the water in little cockleshells of boats, many were fitted with

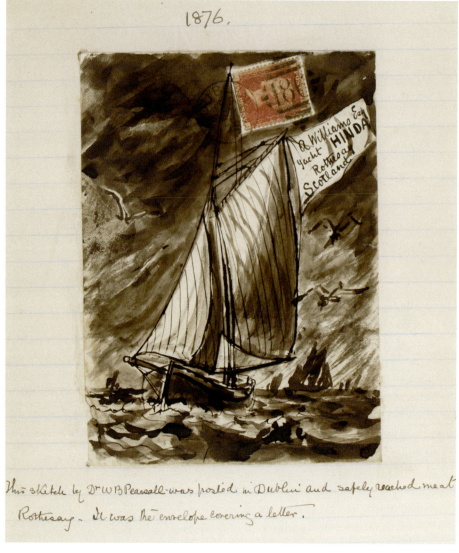

Envelope painted and addressed by W. B. Pearsall to: 'A. Williams HINDA Rothesay Scotland'. It got there.

circular wicker sterns like fancy chairs, and during the calm evening and late into the night the water for a distance of three or four miles in Rothesay Bay was covered with boating parties . . . A pleasant scene except for the exuberance of those 'who made night hideous, the occupants of several boats trying to sing or rather howl down their neighbours'. The flotilla had the added problem that 'Our crew were obliged to keep a constant look out for reckless oarsmen who would persist in rubbing alongside, damaging the copper sheathing. I fear a good deal of unparliamentary language was indulged in and freely exchanged on these occasions.' Not everyone found the singing as distasteful as the pernickety chorister and in fact Williams had to give praise to the haunting sound of a female voice carrying across the water: 'A boatful of fellows singing Christy Minstrels put our crew into a state of excitement, and they could with difficulty restrain themselves from dancing cellar flaps or breakdowns on the deck. Each evening, one highly favoured craft bore a lady with a very high soprano voice, who treated us to 'Ye banks and braes o' bonnie Doon', and other choice selections from the national melodies. When darkness set in, the town was a blaze of light, the water glittered and sparkled from the reflections of the rows of gas lamps, the windows, and the riding lights of the various yachts, and when the moon rose, the sight was positively enchanting and from the Band on the Pier bursts of melody and soft tender cadences floated out to us on the still night air.' From there, they headed for Brodick Bay on Arran where they lolled about in broiling heat, and from there went to Loch Strivan. After dinner they walked along the road bordering the loch and took stock of the area: 'Loch Strivan is not much visited . . .' Williams noted, 'but we found it to be very beautiful. We came to several spots that would delight an Aaron Penley,[12] nice foregrounds of rough stones and seaweeds of bright colours, with the road winding in and out along the shore, birch trees of graceful foliage close to the water, and the distant soft grey coloured mountains reflected in the smooth bosom of the loch.' It was entirely characteristic of Williams to find and paint less trodden ways.

Williams dubbed the Commodore the 'Admiral of the Blue' for what he regarded as his overuse of this one colour. Maybe he had a particular 'thing' about blue. In a playful letter, Olive Ardilaun once wrote to the artist: '. . . & I doubt not am using much too much "Tickety blue" which you have often complained of in my sketches!!'

On making a foray back to Rothesay to pick up post and provisions, there was a letter addressed to Williams from his friend from the Dublin Sketching Club, Dr W. B. Pearsall, who had inventively decorated the envelope with a sketch of the *Hinda* which Williams kept.

Then it was on up the East Kyle of Bute and Colintrave where 'the hills were clothed from top to bottom in purple'. Delving into woodland, a waterfall and rustic bridge caught their fancy; further on they had a view of Loch Ormidale, where the commodore tried a sketch in watercolour, while Williams again 'endeavoured to carry away an impression in oil'. The crew too were busy catching mackerel, and had 'seven dozen beauties on boar'. Freshly caught fish was a staple of their diet and in preference to salting or smoking fish, what now seems scarcely credible, the crew also had a method of eating piecemeal a fish while keeping it alive, until the Commodore put a stop to the practice:

He went forward to examine the anchor tackle in the forecastle and noticed a fishing line over the side and something attached to it moving to and fro under the boat. He hauled the line when a very fine ray came to the surface with a hook made fast through a fin which caused it to swim in circles. To his astonishment he noticed that a considerable portion of the fish had been cut away! Calling up the skipper to explain, he told us that is was a common practice in the South of England to take what they required of the fish, and keep it alive until it was again required. Needless

Pencil sketch of Luss Memorial Kirk, subsequently burnt down and rebuilt. 4.5 x 7in. (11.4 x 17.8 cm).

to say the Commodore was furious at such inhumanity and the skipper apologising explained "that as long as you did not injure a vital part it was considered at home that the fish did not mind".

From Colintrave in the Kyles of Bute they took a steamer and a 'floating palace' called the *Dona*, travelling through Loch Fyne as far as Ardrishaig in Loch Gilip, but apart from the castle at East Tarbet found nothing to warrant bringing the *Hinda* up. Moored off Tighnabruaich, Williams felt in closer contact with the Scottish landscape than anywhere else:

> The various headlands, the woods, and the surrounding mountains were all faithfully reproduced in the tranquil water. The absolute stillness, and the lovely succession of changing lights and shadows on the hills as evening approached struck a sympathetic chord through one's being, just like the effect on the mind of listening to exquisite music being played. The perfume of the heather and wild flowers stealing over the water from the adjacent shore, as the cool mists appear over the low lying land with the sinking behind the purple hills, makes one feel at perfect peace with the world.[13]

They moved on up north towards their final destination; exploring Loch Long 'we had to be exceedingly careful in sailing up these narrow passages as ugly squalls often rush down from the mountains'. The adjacent Loch Goil was also on their itinerary, where they sketched Carrick Castle. Williams noticed the heather was now turning a deeper purple and 'along the boulder strewn shore of the Loch' heather and 'many coloured bracken were mixed in wild abundance'. Bracken had a particular appeal for him, and a hallmark of his many lakeside paintings is the use he made of russet, autumnal foliage at the water's edge. Finally they moored opposite Helensburgh, the most northerly point of their trip, to spend their day's 'holiday' in Glasgow.

On the return journey, on 13 September, the morning rose bright and calm. Thompson and Williams painted their last pictures and headed for home:

> After a lovely run along the Irish coast we rounded the Baily Light Howth Head, crossed Dublin Bay, glided into Kingstown Harbour and threw our mud hook overboard at 3 p.m. after a smart passage of 25 hours and an absence of 37 days.[14]

He was well satisfied with his trip: 'I brought home what was to me a very interesting collection of sketches chiefly in water colour and they furnished me with material for many subsequent pictures in both mediums.' A comment again which indicates how much of his work was done in his own studio.

Among the eight pictures he chose for the RHA exhibition the following year, 1877, were *Scotch Herring Boats in a Squall, near the Burnt Isles*, *Kyles of Bute* and *Herring Boats, Brodick Bay, Scotland*. Two other pictures he showed that year were *Stormy – Achill Island, West Coast of Ireland* and *Thunder Clouds, Howth*. Scenes in and close to Dublin made up as much as half of his exhibits (the location for one picture, *Twilight*, is not known), reflecting the fact that much of his painting was still being done locally.

He does not appear to have returned to Scotland until fourteen years later, when in September 1890 he was joined on a painting trip by friends from the Dublin Sketching Club, of which he mentions two, Dr M. A. Boyd and Major Samuel Adams. The trip was centred on Luss, Loch Lomond. His more frequent visits to the south of England provided him with somewhat more. Scottish and English pictures were a leavening among his Irish work.

Having moved into 32 Lower Abbey Street to avail of a more genial light, he seemed well satisfied and stayed put for five years. What prompted his next move was the prospect of marriage. The young lady to whom he became engaged in 1879 was the girl who had so impressed him when he performed at a children's party with his ventriloquial dummy. Catherine, Kitty or Kate was no more than a child when they first met. She was now about eighteen and Williams thirty-two when they became engaged. We know that she sang (press cuttings attest to her concert appearances) but she possibly cut more of a social figure in musical circles than as a singer. There is little reason to doubt that Catherine or Kitty was regarded as something of a beauty, although extant photographs suggest little animation.[15] Of a matching pair of pastel portraits of the pair done in advanced age by E. R. Rogers, unfortunately only the one of Alexander has survived. It was said that even in advanced age Kitty retained much of her beauty.[16]

Williams was marrying very much into his own kind. He probably knew Kitty's father before he really got to know his daughter, as Williams and George Gray were both singing at St Patrick's Cathedral. Williams wrote of him with evident admiration that he was 'the embodiment of Longfellow's lines "a grey old man who sang in a cathedral vast and dim" . . . His clear affectionate grey eyes beamed out good naturedly from under a benevolent forehead, but he possessed a fearless iron will, and woe to the person he suspected or discovered engaged in any underhand plotting or intriguing.'[17]

It is unlikely that Williams fell foul of him. Of his courtship of Kitty Gray, or even when the romance began to blossom, Williams wrote almost nothing. He was not that sort of writer and his memoirs were not that sort of book. But we may be confident that the courtship was conducted with full Victorian propriety. We know that Miss Gray headed off to England for three months on 14 April 1879, presumably to stay with relatives. Was Williams fearful that he might lose her to a beau across the water? He himself took the boat to Holyhead to escort her gallantly back to Dublin. Would she have been 'Miss Gray' to him and 'Mr Williams' to her until they were married or at least until they were engaged? Williams certainly gives that impression: it was 'Miss Gray' who headed off to England and 'Miss Gray' whom he accompanied back. If heading off to England had anything to do with uncertainty on her part, she was no more decided when she returned. It would be nearly seven months before Williams was in the position to approach George Gray for his daughter's hand in marriage. This should not have been too much of an ordeal given how well the two men knew each other. On 22 November 1879 Williams was able to write, underlining it for emphasis, that he had 'obtained Mr Geo Gray's consent to engagement with his daughter Katie'. Here at last he feels at liberty to refer to her first name, and in a shortened version to boot.

How did the affianced couple amuse themselves? By skating, for one thing. Dublin experienced at the turn of the decade some of the severest winters of the century. There was skating to be had from early December 1879 until near the end of January, with only a brief thaw.[18] Williams had taken up skating the previous winter at Ballsbridge, learning the hard way: '. . . got 14 falls in 15 minutes'. He and Kitty now, rather than Katie, amused themselves skating in places as far apart as the Phoenix Park and at Blackburn's Demesne in Rathfarnham. All Dublin was iced over with 'good skating' to be had on the canal and in the Royal Zoological Gardens where one shilling was being charged to avail of skating there. It seems a lot of money but people were not put off. Williams records there were 500 people skating at the Zoo on 23 December and a staggering 1,000 on 11 January. The winters of 1880 and 1881 were almost as severe. Ever the early riser, he records skating before breakfast over the Clontarf Estuary on 20 January 1881. The same month he was out house hunting around the city. Eventually on 1 March he took No. 7 Grantham Street for three years at a rent of £45.00 per annum.

Alexander Williams and Catherine Gray were married at St Peter's Church, Aungier Street, on 4 April 1881. They left Amiens Street Station (now Connolly Station) at 2 p.m. and reached Sangster's Hotel, Rostrevor, County Down, at 6.15 p.m. where they stayed until 29 April. Honeymoon or not, there was no question of putting his pencil and paintbrush aside. How Kitty amused herself we do not know, but Williams spent 'most of a month' sketching about Rostrevor. Back in Dublin, he lost no time in building a studio for himself in the back garden, and mindful perhaps of his new financial responsibilities, he started giving painting lessons. This was not an entirely new venture in that he had taken on his first pupil, a Miss A. Sibthorpe of 36 Upper Leeson Street, the previous November. Most of his pupils appear to have been women – or ladies is perhaps the word – keen to improve on what was essentially a genteel pastime and for whom a little socialising did not go amiss. Teaching extended to occasional sketching trips to the local River Dodder and the seaside. Olive Ardilaun was possibly an occasional pupil or at least took his advice; Sir John Dillon was another, and these were surely useful connections. Williams also mentions a Captain Irwin of the 59th Regiment. Perhaps the captain was setting off for India or some distant frontier of empire and wanted to make a record of his travels in sketchbooks, as many Victorians did. Photography had yet to come into its own.

Marriage is a milestone and fatherhood another. Both of Alexander and Kitty's children were born in Grantham Street: George in 1882 and his sister Alice in 1884. Alice was exceptionally tall and rather ungainly. She was to remain at home as many spinster daughters did while her parents were alive. Alice was heading for fifty before she had to make her own way in life. George was a frail child and was to die young.

But this tragedy was well in the future. In the 1880s there were few clouds on Williams' horizon. He was married, he was a father and he had established himself as both a painter and singer with an income that could be described as comfortable. He recorded precisely what he earned in 1883, presumably because this was higher than in any previous year:

Salary at the Cathedrals	£125.00.00
All other sources	£158.12.09
Total	£283.12.09[19]

How well off was Alexander at this period of his life? An idea of what £283-odd was worth can be made by looking at what people in other walks of life were earning. The difference between the working class, better described as an underclass, and the next lot up was stark. For instance, the railwaymen who were to build the railway to Achill which would enhance Williams' own income by bringing in tourists were being paid at the rate of 12s a week for labourers, 16s for gangers.[20] To put that in context, in rough terms a labourer out in all weathers all week was being paid much the same, and a ganger hardly more, than Williams got for putting in one hour's singing at the Chapel Royal on Sundays, with extensive holiday time off. The stonecutters who did the beautiful bevelled stonework for the National Museum were getting 60d a day in 1886. In the period 1895 to 1903 Guinness labourers received 40d a day, which was the minimum wage in the building trade until 1910.[21]

Among the middle class, the chief of the Dublin fire brigade service was paid about £300.[22] In St Patrick's Cathedral at the point of Disestablishment the remuneration for vicars choral had ranged from £170 to £245 and the recipients, certainly at the upper end, considered themselves well paid. Williams was earning more than his father-in-law, who was at the top end of that scale. This, of course, is without taking into account Williams' outgoings, which included considerable travel and of course his painting materials. The Dean of St Patrick's, the Very Rev. John West, was on another level altogether, being paid a handsome £1,451 at Disestablishment.[23] The Church looked after its own. So did Dublin Castle; Williams' friend Bram Stoker ended his career in the civil service in what was a new post, that of clerk of inspection ranking next to the senior clerk, as such one of the higher grades, at a starting salary of £250 per annum with expenses (the job, with annual increments of £10, carried a maximum salary of £400, probably more than Williams ever earned per annum in his career). If one was to attempt a comparison with today, it would not be with the Church of Ireland which does not have the riches it once had, nor with the top jobs in the modern civil service; a better comparison would be with the private sector and business. An audit clerk with the Dublin & Belfast Junction Railway Company was on £100 and an assistant cashier (an outdated term akin to a comptroller today) was earning upwards of £175 per annum.[24] It would probably be fair to say Alexander was earning what a well-paid manager in the private sector might earn.

He still had some way to go and ambitions to fulfil. Being well established is not the same as being an Establishment figure. This would be his next step.

CHAPTER
11

The Academician:
Going Solo

Photograph of the artist in academic and court dress. Note the hilt of his sword under his left arm.
From an advertising booklet among his papers.

When Williams was elected an associate of the Royal Hibernian Academy of Arts (ARHA) in the spring of 1884, he decided, against all advice, that this was the time for him to mount a solo exhibition in Dublin. His friends were certain he would make a loss on it. In fact the results exceeded all expectations, astonishing not only his friends but most likely himself as well. His friend Bingham McGuinness already had one solo exhibition to his credit from the year before and was planning a second. No doubt this influenced Alexander, but solo exhibitions 'out of season' were still something of an innovation:

> Within the last couple of years Dublin artists have manifested a disposition to follow the example of their London brethren in one most important particular. Before the commencement of the art season proper they have thrown open their studios to their patrons and friends . . . This time Mr Alexander Williams is first in the field.[1]

Being first in the field may well have had something to do with the success of the exhibition; the energy of art viewers is not, after all, inexhaustible. The novelty of a first showing would also have been in Williams' favour as he was depending upon friends and acquaintances to support him. McGuinness had used Bartholomew Colles Watkins' studio at 6 St Stephen's Green (where McGuinness also had a studio). Even though this was his first effort, Alexander showed himself to be more ambitious in taking the Leinster Hall, 35 Molesworth Street for 18 and 19 November 1884. Viewing was by invitation only. In a thoughtful review *The Irish Times* pondered the virtues of this venue:

> Let it be remembered that only in very exceptional instances can the private studio afford sufficient accommodation, and we are forced to the conclusion, after a review of all other possible art galleries in Dublin, that this one only is suited to such a purpose. We are badly off in our city for good art accommodation . . . the artist seeks something more than mere space. If justice is to be done to his talent he must have a good light . . . even here the harsh tone of the walls forbids the best effect. But in this instance that difficulty has been almost wholly overcome. Mr Williams is, happily, his own 'hanging committee' . . . He has found means to mitigate the harsh prevailing tint of the walls, and by judiciously attaching a deep-toned strip of paper above his pictures, has contrived to mitigate, if not altogether remove, an otherwise severe and most trying glare.[2]

Faded sepia photographs taken in the Leinster Hall show how the artist hung his pictures nearly all on one line, with the heavy ornate gilded frames typical of the time, and a broad band of paper visible behind them. Thirty-five oils were hung on one side of the room and fifteen watercolours and sketches on the other. The catalogue came in for comment as the inclusion of illustrations was then far from usual. The cover Alexander had designed himself, while the back was 'tastefully illustrated with a sketch by the

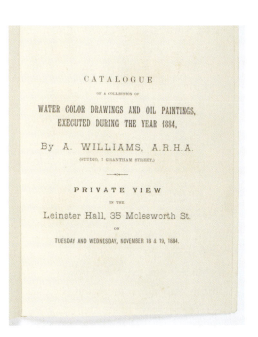

The artist's first exhibition catalogue, 1884, for which he designed the cover.

Rare sepia photograph from Leinster Hall exhibition, 1884.

artist reproduced by photo-lithography'. This was of Yarmouth, a windmill being the dominant feature. The medium of pen and ink came up well in the printing process.

What astonished the press was the sheer number of pictures on view. 'Fifty pictures a year!' exclaimed one reviewer in surprise, little guessing that the same artist in a few short years would be producing twice and thrice that number. By comparison, McGuinness in his second show had twenty. In the opinion of this reviewer, Bartholomew Colles Watkins (1833–91) was the benchmark by which landscape painting was to be judged. He now chided his hero: 'Mr Watkins, awake, and open your eyes. Two pictures in the Academy's Exhibition will never again suffice to represent your skill, while your newly-selected associate can turn out fifty.' Watkins needed defending against this newcomer: 'Not that Mr Williams' work is comparable with yours for minuteness of detail, fine finish and truth.' Still, the reviewer was prepared to add that he 'has proved what remarkable results may be accomplished by industry and aptitude, combined with technical knowledge and power of observation . . . He is, in a word, an artist of real ability.' Any newcomer would be pleased with comments of that sort.

The reviewer of the *Daily Express* was equally astonished by the number of pictures on show but while admiring his industry cautioned, not surprisingly, that some of the pictures rather showed the speed at which they had been painted. Most of the watercolours represented scenes in the vicinity of Dublin, many of which have passed into history: *Old Canal Boats at Dolphin's Barn*; *Tedcastle's Wharf – Winter Morning* (on the Liffey) and *The 9.30 Holyhead Boat, North Wall* among them. The *Daily Express* concluded that 'there were several very high finished works in pure water colours, being free from the tempting use of what is commonly called "body colour" . . . all cleanly and purely painted, and show clever execution of the most difficult style of this charming art'; economy of means, in other words.

The Irish Times, on the other hand, said nothing about hasty work, finding instead 'a distinguished advance upon the painter's previous art', which now 'frequently exhibited traces of dramatic and technical excellence which promised for the artist such future excellence as would bring him into the front rank of Irish painters'. The collection, the paper thought, showed him best as a painter of the sea and it also commended him, possibly the first to do so, for finding scenes of interest so close to home: 'Mr Williams shows that there is plenty of inspiration for the poet-painter right at hand. No Irish artist need travel to Betwys-y-Caed or the Leor [Loire] Valley for sources of imagination, or the Thames, while we have Howth and Achill, and Skerries, and the Liffey, with their rugged cliffs and placid bays, or dashing billows; and, again, their golden cornfields, or green dells and leafy groves, and deep pools overhung with a wealth of rich native verdure, to turn to.'

In fact his exhibition did contain pictures from across the water. There was a picture of Mortlake on the Thames and another near Kew Bridge, and even further afield, the Norfolk Broads. However, the paper was correct in pointing out that his versatility was amply demonstrated by the pictures of Ireland on which he had concentrated. The 'rich native verdure' supplied the artist, oddly perhaps, with a couple of pictures which the press described accurately enough as studies of weeds; in the catalogue one is called *Weeds in a Watercourse* – hardly the most attractive of titles – and the other simply as *Water Plants*, both oils. Weeds would turn up in later catalogues too.

If *The Irish Times* produced the most thoughtful review, it also produced a paragraph which pulls us up sharp. Williams had made a study of the interior of the hovel of an Achill peasant by the name of Paddy Barrett. The whereabouts of the painting is unknown, but there is no reason to think it would have differed in essence from other studies he made of primitive cabins. The Georgian cartoonists had regularly depicted the Irish peasantry as simian in appearance, almost a hybrid species, and this view of rural Ireland and its impoverished inhabitants was an enduring one that continued well into the nineteenth century. Alexander did not paint portraits of the poor but his work in the west was never intended to make fun of them. That, however, did not prevent *The Irish Times* from picking up on the title *Paddy Barrett's Interior* in order to make a joke out of it. 'Here we have not an anatomical study as might have first been supposed,' quipped the paper, 'but the furnishing of the full poor cell of an Irish peasant on Achill. The details are uncompleted as yet, but still they are full of humour.' The paper could apparently rely on its readers finding the peasantry an automatic source of humour. What would have been found humorous, as a *grotesquerie*, was the earthen floor, the paucity and primitiveness of the furniture, the damp, uncomfortable, even unsanitary conditions. The comment neatly if dismally displays the chasm across which the affluent of Dublin viewed the rural peasantry.

Williams was never explicitly political in intent, nor indeed was he politically minded, but he painted many desolate pictures of the west in which the subsistence living conditions of the rural poor was implicit. In this period of land agitation and turmoil, genre painting usually only alluded to social conditions, often in a sentimental and thus rather benign fashion. This was hardly surprising given that those who bought pictures would not have been in sympathy with the underlying social unrest in the country. When Lady Butler exhibited at the annual RHA exhibition of 1892 a picture entitled *An Irish Eviction,* 'a person, presumably of culture, was heard to express the opinion that the artist "had fallen very low" for condescending to portray a scene of the kind.'[3] The kind of paintings Williams was engaged in were often as much as audiences saw of living conditions in the west. It seems hardly credible now, but even as late as the early 1900s it was surmised by one reviewer at one of Williams' solo exhibitions that this might be the first introduction to some of the attendees as to how things were out west.

No picture in his exhibition of 1884 was priced at less than £4 or 4 guineas and there were several at £20. It might be expected that as an artist became better known, so he would put up his prices. Alexander did become better known but he did the opposite, making a point of including pictures often at £2 and even lower. He was nothing if not democratic in his approach. He mixed high prices with low and there was always something for everyone's pocket. We will return to this marketing policy later.

He boxed in his report of his first exhibition in his 'Chronicles', evidence of his delight as to how things had turned out:

November 18th. Opened a two days 'Private View' of my pictures at the Leinster Hall 35 Molesworth St. Room very crowded. Lady Ardilaun and Sir Thos Jones PRHA walked round and made a friendly criticism of my work. The second day's show was even better attended and I received numerous congratulations. I sold 9 pictures. 5 oils and 4 water colours. Total £80 to the amazement of many people who ridiculed the idea of my holding such an Exhibition . . .[4]

If his own figures for the individual pictures given below are correct, then sales amounted not to £80 but to £70.8.0. The subjects sold convey the variety of his work, yet they all appear to have featured water:

Water Colour Trawlers	£8.0.0
Water Colour Clonskeagh	5.0.0
Water Colour Off Sir John's Quay	10.0.0
The London & NW Steamers	6.0.0
Atlantic Surf, Dugort Bay	15.0.0
Evening, Skerries	10.0.0
Dugort Strand, Morning	4.4.0
Near Kew, London	4.4.0
Mortlake, London	4.4.0[5]

It was a productive year for Williams, 1884. He was out sketching in Malahide and Portmarnock in March, and the same month, at the opening of the Irish Fine Art Society exhibition, he sold three pictures: *Stormy Weather*, a watercolour which made 5 guineas; and what would now be thought less typical of his art, *Old Houses, Coombe* and *Below London Bridge*, for 4 and 3 guineas respectively. At the end of the month he was sketching north of Dublin again, at Balbriggan and Gormanstown. He preferred the northside, drawn to the rugged coastline more than the scenic beauties of Wicklow, which were, in any case, less accessible. He was always on the move. On 3 June he headed off to his beloved Achill with his taxidermist brother Willie: 'He shot and I painted during our stay.' Then it was back to the coast beyond Dublin again, heading off to Skerries this time. He makes it sound idyllic: 'July 14. Went down to Skerries with family and sister Eliza. Rented small cottage from Mrs Balfe, nice little garden full of roses. A bathing box on the strand at end of garden. Sept 15. Returned from Skerries after 9 weeks residence. Painted 23 canvasses and a number of smaller sketches and drawings.'[6]

He was back at the Leinster Hall the following year, with a marginally smaller collection of forty-six pictures, 'first in the field' again, noted *The Irish Times*. There was no sign of Lady Ardilaun putting in an appearance this year, but Williams bagged a

Oil on canvas laid on board. Skerries harbour. Signed. 13 x 25.6 in. (33 x 65 cm).

Preparatory sketch for Skerries harbour.

Oil on board. River Liffey at Blessington. Signed. 1889. 9.6 x 17.7 in. (24.4 x 45 cm).

few titles just the same with the Countess Lussi and Lord James W. Butler heading the list of those who 'honoured the private view with their presence'. *The Irish Times* and *Daily Express* on 20 November both printed lists of visitors without commenting on the pictures. Thus the doings of the great and the good could be followed by that part of the public eager to hear what such exalted people were doing, but without the tiresome inconvenience of having to wade through art critiques.

However, for those with an interest in art *The Irish Times* published a separate review, remarking that whereas Williams' reputation had previously been made on seascapes, his landscapes were now 'equally meritorious'. Howth, its cliffs and harbour, in particular featured prominently among the forty-six pictures he exhibited this year: 'We find a series of piquant sketches from that exquisitely picturesque locality, unhappily so little frequented by Irish artists.' Even less frequented by artists both then and since was the River Dodder, a subject which apparently appealed to Williams, in part perhaps because of the bird life along its watercourse and perhaps more because of the many quaint remains of mills and water races. Milltown, only a few miles from the city centre, had open countryside around it and Templeogue, further out but now as much part of suburbia, was well outside the city. From the west, Annakeen Castle on Lough Corrib was singled out. *The Irish Times* ended its review with a note of caution: 'Mr Williams is a hard worker, perhaps too hard sometimes. But he shows no bad work, and it is no indifferent merit that Nature is its first source and inspiration.'[7] By working too hard the paper meant he was producing too much too fast. No advice to the contrary would change him.

In February 1885 he exhibited with the Amateur and Artists Society, the same month in which his daughter, Alice, was born; and for the next few months, perhaps being a solicitous husband and father, he did not stray far from Dublin: 'Feb to June. Sketching

Pencil study inscribed 'Miss G[ore?] Dalkey Aug 1889', perhaps sketched during a painting excursion for his pupils. 4½ x 7in. (11.4 x 17.8cm).

at Carrickmines, Glencullen River, Dollymount, Grand Canal, Bray Strand, Carrickmines Cottage, 1st Lock Grand Canal, Rush County Dublin, Howth,' he recorded in his 'Chronicles & Memoirs'. Then at the end of June he took off for London, returning to Dublin on 29 July, having 'sketched at Limehouse, Greenwich and about London', he noted, and indeed further afield. He sketched on the River Lea, getting a 'good sketch opposite the Tottenham Sewage Works' (did the sewage works appear in the picture?) and tried his hand at the somewhat more exalted subject of the Abbey at St Albans. Landscape painter though he was, buildings always appealed to him. He noted that Ryehouse, Broxbourne, contained 'a little cluster of russet roofs topped by a quite coloured grey tower, nestling softly amongst the trees', and he recorded feelingly of Ware: 'A quaint looking little place. The oddest of little old fashioned houses crowd each bank of the river down to the water's edge and blossom out into all manner of bow windows and irregular bits of tiled roofs and patches of woodwork. The chimneys stuck about in original positions that might fill your modern architects with despair.' The same tumbledown, ad hoc appearance of medieval and old Dublin held a similar attraction for him and would become an important part of his work.

Watercolour, signed and inscribed 'Upper Lake Glendalough Co. Wicklow.' An example of the artist's heightened realism. 13 x 22.4 in. (33 x 57 cm.)

He was in Howth again on 18 July for 'high tea' given by Lord Justice Fitzgibbon for members of the Dublin Sketching Club. On two days in August he recorded giving sketching classes, at Salthill and Milltown on the River Dodder. These must have been pleasant social events in which amateur painters got to meet one another and pick up a few tips. He lists some of his pupils: Miss Handy, Miss Magee, Miss Gore and Miss Davis – no first names mentioned. He did a dainty sketch of an elegant young woman on a beach, well turned out in Victorian costume, and wrote underneath it 'Miss G'. It might be supposed it was his fiancée, Kitty Gray, but they were married by this date. Was it perhaps Miss Gore? There is no way of telling. The formal proprieties of Victorian etiquette were no doubt observed to the letter on all such occasions. He mentions also two gentlemen pursuing the art of sketching, a Mr Tresilian and a Mr O'Neill. None, so far as it is known, went on to make a living from their efforts. The artist himself had no compunction about exhibiting among amateurs. He recorded for September that he sold a picture, without naming it, at the Portrush Amateur Artists' Society and received 10 guineas for his trouble.

In 1886 Alexander recorded that he and the family headed off for Tramore, County Waterford, 'where I commenced a hard two months serious painting in oils' between 19 July and 18 September. It meant forgoing some of his earnings at the cathedrals. He seemed content to bring over all the way from Magdalen College Chapel, as his deputy, a Mr Joseph Samuel Churms and pay him £10 for a month's duty at the two cathedrals. Alexander exhibited fifty-five pictures at his solo exhibition that year, choosing this time the Dublin Sketching Club's venue at 9 Merrion Row. Scenes in and around Tramore and County Waterford made up about half the exhibition.

Untypically, he appears not to have travelled at all during 1887, perhaps retrenching with two young children to support and the prospect of moving into a new house. In fact in every way this year was untypical of him. He cut down the number of pictures he exhibited at his solo exhibition to thirty-seven, concentrating on scenes of or close to Dublin, most being watercolours with only a handful of oil paintings among them. *The Daily Express* approved this parochial approach, commenting: 'We have more than once called attention to the tendency of Irish artists to ignore the beautiful which is so easily to be found in this country, and Mr Williams certainly has taken the hint, and, so far as can be seen, has no reason to regret that he did not make longer tours in search of the picturesque.'[8] *The Irish Times* thought the collection 'not of uniform merit' but conceded that 'Mr Williams is as successful in painting the summer landscape as the more dramatic scenes which are to be found upon the rough sea coast and the contrast cannot fail at once to strike the eye of the observer.' The paper picked out studies of the River Dodder as 'full of the poetry of colour', adding that 'for such teaching as this [the subject] might miss the passing eye'. The same paper drew a comparison between his treatment of the Dodder and the Cathedral Rocks, Achill Island, as a measure of his range, noting, of what was one of his favourite subjects that 'There is a noble impression conveyed of these stupendous cliffs, beneath which the waves surge wildly. Mr Williams never fails as a painter of the sea, and this is a characteristic specimen of his ability.'[9] A picture from near the city centre, *First Lock, Grand Canal*, also a favourite subject at least at this time, was regarded as among the best of the larger works. He had tramped north and south of Dublin for his exhibition, his study *At Raheny* being 'a bold and very admirable sketch', while *At Loughlinstown* was an autumn study in which 'the tints are rich and mellow, and the colouring is harmonised with rare perfection.' It was in oil in which Williams generally depicted the darker emotions of land and sea, and it was perhaps in such that he was most expressive. The *Daily Express* picked out *Sketch after a Gale* as 'being the most noteworthy, the long, lonesome beach in the dying day showing the artist at his best'.[10]

For each of the four exhibitions he held between 1884 and 1887, two at the Leinster Hall and the two at 9 Merrion Row, the format was the same, with invitations being sent out for a private view over two days. In a handsome book with blue covers and ornate tooling in gold are preserved his visitors' signatures, and guest books for two further exhibitions have also survived, those of 1893 and 1895. The names therein recorded are of interest; some names are still very familiar, others long since departed from the Irish scene. Bewleys, Findlaters, Sibthorpes, Goodbodys, names remembered yet, and more besides, Coghill, Storey, Fetherstonehaugh and Pennyfeather, Barton, Overend, Gaisford and Trevelyan all turned out in numbers for 'one of their own'. Other names, familiar once perhaps, now sound strange and even foreign. Such signatures as Atthill and Hatchill, Bedat and Bease, Cogger, Elrington, Pentland and Norbett, Wentworth and Trebor remind us of how the social fabric of Ireland rapidly changed with the First World War and more especially after 1922. There was a fair smattering of the titled, a few military men, and some drawn from the hunting and fishing fraternity, clients of Dame Street no doubt. The museum supplied A. G. More and Dr and Mrs Scarff, and among the fraternity of ornithologists Richard M. Barrington provided loyal support. From the RHA and the Dublin Sketching Club came Sir Thomas Jones, PRHA, always supportive, and Thomas Drew; and among others Alexander Colles, Henry Doyle, Walter Osborne, S. Catterson Smith, and W. Booth Pearsall. Bingham McGuinness was a faithful attendee, his signature appearing for all the exhibitions. Sarah Purser's signature appears in broad letters, John Butler Yeats appears to have written his signature in a tiny self-effacing spiky hand at the bottom of one page. Bram Stoker was in England by this time, but his brother Thornley Stoker and his wife both added their names to the guest lists. From the church came clerics aplenty and members of the vicars choral. Rank might then be counted more important than a man's name. 'Dean of St Patrick's' was all that the Very Rev. John West saw fit to write. R. M. Hill added to his name, for those who wished to know, 'Adjutant RIC Depot'. The names of the Elsners are there, along with Mrs Scott Fennell and other members of the quartets, Grattan and Charles Kelly, and tenor Walter Bapty's signature writ large. (He joined the Dublin Glee & Madrigal Union, after Barton McGuckin had departed). Also from the world of music came Mme Esposito, T. R. G. Lozé and a colleague of Kitty's, Dr Annie Patterson, founder of the *Feis Ceoil*. (In the same month as his own exhibition of 1895 Alexander attended Annie Patterson's public meeting at the Mansion House to promote a *feis ceoil* on the lines of the ancient festival of Bealtaine at Tara.[11]) There were boating-cum-painting colleagues who could be counted on too, with the names of George Prescott of *Iris* fame and G. B. Thompson, commodore of the *Hinda* appearing among the guests. Some 180 visitors turned up on the first day of his first exhibition and more on the second. Many of the same names reappear over the four years while new ones are added, suggesting that the artist both retained and extended his base of support.

For all that, Alexander gave up his solo exhibitions for some years after 1887. The beginner's luck he had had in 1884 may not have been repeated or not with the same largesse, although this is speculative as accounts for only two of the exhibitions have survived. In 1884 he had grossed, as mentioned, £70.8.0 on the sale of nine pictures. In 1886 the figure was only £50.14.6. Maybe his takings for the following year were smaller again, given that the show was mainly of Dublin and local scenes. Besides there is a limit to how often an artist, no matter how personally popular, can make calls on the generosity of friends and acquaintances. In 1889 he had managed to get £34.13.0 on the sale of five pictures at the Water Colour Society of Ireland exhibition, this without all the effort and cost involved in mounting a one-man show.

What was to become a critical factor in the future success of his solo exhibitions was the link that he would forge with Dublin Castle, ensuring the continuous patronage of the Lord Lieutenant or his wife and their entourage, year after year. When he started his solo exhibitions again he had an altogether more ambitious plan.

CHAPTER 12

The Castle Set

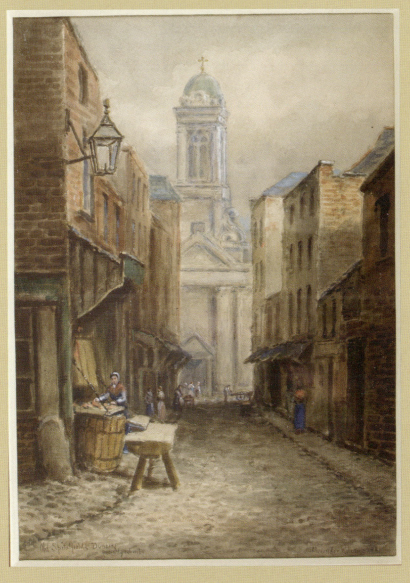

Watercolour signed and inscribed 'Old Spitalfields Dublin recently rebuilt'. Signed. 10 x 14 in. (25.4 x 35.6 cm).
c. 1892. The church is St Nicholas of Myra in the parish of Francis Street.

The arbiters and setters of fashion in Williams' day were the Ascendancy, the Anglo-Irish. If 'society' adopted a fashion, patronised a painter, then lesser mortals were certain to follow the lead. Today it might be footballers' wives or so-called 'celebrities' who set the trends but the marketing principle of association remains as it ever was. Alexander well understood the importance of patronage, and the simple truth that the more elevated the personages the more valuable the patronage.

At the top of the social scale in Victorian Ireland was the so-called Castle set, and at the very pinnacle was the Lord Lieutenant. There was no higher office in the land; the Lord Lieutenant was the Queen's representative after all; he was treated as royalty, and his activities and those of his circle and events at the Castle were provided with breathless and admiring, even reverential, press coverage. The aura that at one time surrounded the Lord Lieutenant and his entourage has no equivalent today, for it was unique to the times.

There is nothing quite like the pomp and ceremony of a court and its entourage. Dubliners, en masse, certainly thought so and made the utmost of whatever entertainments were on offer, be it as participants or bystanders. Percy Fitzgerald (1830–1925), a sculptor and writer who enjoyed the entertainments as much as anyone else, nevertheless was well aware of the element of fantasy that attends royalty. Sensibly writing anonymously as 'A Native', he left this memorable and mischievous description of a bygone era:

> The chief 'make-believe', however, was the Viceregal Court, or 'Coort', that strange, theatrical installation, whose tawdry influence affected everything in the place down to the commonest little tradesman, or to the 'Castle waiter', whose service it was a great comfort to secure, even at a higher fee.
>
> As I look back across this long stretch of years, to what were really very jocund days, one scene arises before me which seems highly significant, and which furnishes a sort of keynote for the various things that I am about to recall. It was at a concert in Dublin – at 'Th' Ancient Concert Rooms'. An English friend was staying with us, and, not without pride, we promised to take him to a Philharmonic concert, supposed to be highly fashionable and exclusive because 'his Excellency' and his Court was to attend. 'Th' Ancient Concert Rooms' was a rather shabby tenement in Brunswick Street, about the size and proportions of a moderate Dissenting chapel; but it justly boasted that it was the 'finest thing of the kind in Ireland', or 'Daublin', as the genteeler ones strove to sound it . . . We had scarce seated ourselves in 'the reserved seats' (little is worth having in this city unless it be reserved *for* you and *not for* others), when suddenly there came a bustle and a fluster. Every one rose to his feet; there were agitated cries of 'Here he is! He's coming!' and half a dozen men, carrying white wands, appeared, struggling their way along a very narrow gangway. A dapper-looking, clerk-like man came last, wearing a star, following the stewards. This was THE LORD LIEUTENANT, or the Lord '*Lift*nant', as he was usually spoken of by the crowd. He came along bowing and smiling, and trying to be as gracious as he could.

Following him were the aides-de-camp, or 'edukongs', supercilious young men, with blue silk facings to their coats – sure and certain seal of their office, the blue being reverenced, even to all but prostration, by the society of Dublin – behind whom glided a number of limp, faded dames, some veterans, attired in garments as faded as their persons – the 'Ladies of the Household' – wives of the secretaries, or ancients who were passed on from Government to Government, and who grew more firmly fixed as years went on. It was entertaining to see how the suite behaved, with what an air of pride, and at the same time of assumed affability, they moved on in the train, two and two. In the admiring crowds which lined the avenues they would recognise a friend or acquaintance, and were not too proud to nod.

Well to return to my Englishman. I noticed that he was gazing through his monocle with unfeigned astonishment and amusement at the show. 'Dear me!' he said at last, 'this is most astonishing. Think of that man in London! Why, no-one would turn their head to look at him. It's most singular!' And so it was. But it was the same everywhere, and on every occasion. Did his carriage stop at a house, a crowd gathered, eager almost to *feel* the horse, supposed with the vehicle to be hired from a London job-master . . .

The little scene I have been describing is significant, for the same unmeaning adoration permeated every class of society. This theatrical make-believe of a Court leavened everything. Everybody played at this sham Royalty, and, I am convinced, firmly believed in it, or fancied they did. The 'Kestle' was the cynosure. To be asked to the 'Kestle', to know people at the 'Kestle', or even to know people who knew people at the 'Kestle', was Elysium itself![1]

A parody no doubt, but Fitzgerald perfectly points up how Dublin society took its cue from the Castle. For decorativeness the imperial era has had no equal since. Like it or loathe it – or poke fun at its pretensions – Williams liked it, indeed admired it and saw the Irish court as a means to his own advancement. Bram Stoker liked it as well. On 14 January 1877, the pair of friends had a celebratory dinner at Bram's house at 7 St Stephen's Green to mark the entry into Dublin of the latest Lord Lieutenant, in this instance His Grace the Duke of Marlborough. The establishment politics of the pair is hardly remarkable given their background, although it does seem surprising that they might have been so stirred by the arrival of Marlborough as to celebrate the event. But it would be surprising, even at this early stage in his career, if Williams was not mulling over the idea of gaining castle patronage. He was not a complete outsider; he had connections both peripheral and not so peripheral. His friend Bram was a civil servant employed by the Castle. Fishing and shooting were traditional Castle activities and Williams of Dame Street a natural port of call. He had sung at the Castle, by royal command, on at least one occasion; and as President of the Dublin Sketching Club in 1880 he got a trial run, so to speak, in being the man to receive the Lord Lieutenant, Lord Cowper, at the club's annual exhibition when it was held that year in Cranfield's in

Royal Hibernian Academy of Arts.

Lower Abbey Street

Dublin July 24th 1891

Sir,

I am directed by the President and Members of the Royal Hibernian Academy to inform you, that at a general meeting held on Saturday the 18th inst. you were elected a Constituent Member of the Academy, which election has received the approval of their Excellencies the Lords Justices

I am
Sir
Your obedient Servant

B.J. Mushratters
Secretary

Alexander Williams Esqre R.H.A.

I HAVE pleasure in presenting this week a portrait of Mr Alexander Williams, R.H.A., one of our most successful Irish painters. Mr. Williams has devoted his talents chiefly to the production of marine subjects, and by means of these has achieved a very enviable reputation. At the outset of his career his pictures for the most part represented still-life studies, and, although beautifully conceived and finished, might have been considered somewhat cold, or at any rate lacking in "movement." Finding the fact occasionally noticed by critics, the artist, with admirable sense and acumen, subscribed to the ancient adage that what everybody said must be true, and by and by admirers of his always fascinating pictures noted with pleasure the introduction of occasional figures, human and animal, with of course concomitant advantages of colour, movement, and general enlistment of interest. Sometimes it might be a hardy fisherman; again, a cockle gatherer, a woman looking out westward for the flutter of a coming sail, a harvester, a shepherd's dog—according to the scheme of the painting; but all in turn gave life and enlisted attention, and ere long it was noticed that at most of our local exhibitions Mr. Williams's pictures soon bore the coveted red star. Then the artist struck out a bolder line, and exhibited annually in a distinctive way as well as in company with others. The movement, at first tentative and modest, gradually assumed quite dignified proportions, and was not only patronised by Viceroyalty and others, of high position, but was noticed exhaustively by the press, and proved in every way most gratifyingly successful. Our present Lord Lieutenant evinced interest in Mr. Williams' work from the very first year of his Viceroyalty, and has not wavered in kindly patronage and encouraging notice of the marine painter's exhibits ever since. Emboldened by fair fortune at home the popular artist ventured further afield, and last year took his collection of West of Ireland pictures to Liverpool, where the talent shown in them and the beauty and novelty of the subjects, soon found favour among English critics,—and, indeed, among English buyers, too, because a large number of the paintings then exhibited remained in the Land of the Rose. This year Manchester is the artist's fancy, and I know that he was over last week, making arrangements for the opening of a little gallery there. With his collection to be despatched to the busy centre referred to, will probably go a remarkably well-executed painting of the Queen's arrival at Kingstown—or disembarkation, rather—on the 4th of April. The artist has caught the moment at which the royal cortège is just prepared to start from the effectively decorated landing-stage on the opening section of the lengthy road journey to the Capital; and the pose of the figures in the carriages, and even the likeness of the Sovereign herself, strike an onlooker as being conspicuously faithful to life. The scene is most happily depicted, and shows an abundance of life, as well as what might perhaps be considered a superfluity of colouring, were it not for the remembrance (still pleasantly lingering) of the actual splendour and many-hued surroundings of a tableau that can never be forgotten. In the background are shown the gaily-decorated flagship and splendid vessels of the Fleet, flying their abundant bunting; nearer we have the Royal yacht most accurately portrayed and nearer still the pavilioned landing-stage, with the royal carriages drawn up in front; the splendidly-mounted escort, the brazen helmets and tossing plumes of the Life Guards, the fine body of Bluejackets, the Duke of Connaught on horseback beside the Queen's carriage, and, on the right of the canvas, the serried crowd of eager on-lookers, shown cleverly in back view by the limner. Every detail of the interesting picture commands attention, because of absolute fidelity; and although the artist's work was incomplete when viewed by his Excellency the Lord Lieutenant, the promise of it was recognised and complimented by the noble critic, to whose kindly friendliness and encouragement the subject of my remarks owes so very much. There is very little patronage extended to Art in Dublin, I am sorry to say; in fact, both retrospect and outlook are depressingly discouraging and gloomy; but when Mr. Williams takes his attractive wares across the water, it happens, as has already been said, that he is fortunate enough to leave a good many of them behind when he starts on his journey home. I have only just to add that my versatile "portrait" is extremely musical as well as artistic, and is married to a beautiful woman who shares his tastes, and moulds, as it were, all the best refinements of his nature into visible excellence by the influence of her plastic hands.

MR. ALEXANDER WILLIAMS, R.H.A.

Above left: Letter informing the artist of his acceptance as a constituent member of the RHA. While the letter is dated 24 July 1891, the decision to elect him had been made more than six months earlier, on 18 January.

Above right: In court dress, posed this time with hand on sword, for the *Irish Letter*. An artist not only patronised by the Lord Lieutenant, commented the writer of the article, but 'noticed exhaustively by the press'. Williams was adept at getting press coverage.

Grafton Street.[2] A closer connection was his friendship with Dean Dickenson, for the dean, as chaplain to the Lord Lieutenant, would certainly have had the ear of his lordship as well as his court and would have known how things were run. These connections, however, still left him at some remove from obtaining patronage for himself. He bided his time.

On 10 January 1891 Williams was elected a full constituent member of the Royal Hibernian Academy of Arts. There was a gap of almost seven years between his election as an associate member in 1884 and his election as a constituent member. Such a delay was not unprecedented, although a year or two was more typical. Had Sir Thomas Jones' singling out of Williams' paintings for preferential placement at the RHA's annual exhibitions caused lasting resentment in high places? No records remain as to how votes were cast or what opinions were expressed at the meetings of the RHA.

Williams himself merely records his election in his 'Chronicles', expressing neither impatience nor delight, but being a full RHA member was an exponential leap forward from being an associate. It was at this point that he resumed his solo exhibitions, but on an extended basis, and he had every intention of defraying if not entirely covering his expenses by charging an entrance fee. He drew up a set of what he called, rather grandly, regulations:

EXHIBITION REGULATIONS[3]

Each person <u>paying one shilling</u> entrance to receive <u>a plain catalogue.</u>

Holders of invitation cards and all others to pay three pence for <u>plain catalogue</u>.

Holders of Art Union Tickets to be admitted every day during the week <u>free</u>.

Members of the Dublin Sketching Club Free.

Purchasers of pictures Free during the week.

Special Illustrated Catalogue <u>Six Pence</u>.

On the face of it this looked like a high-risk strategy, applying charges for an exhibition mounted expressly to sell pictures. The press made no comment on the matter and he continued the practice thereafter. We can deduce, however, that by this time he had assembled, indeed stockpiled, a huge number of paintings. There is no other way of explaining the fact that when he decided to return to mounting solo exhibitions, he would put on show 148 pictures. This could not have been the work of a single season, no matter how industrious he had been.

In passing, one wonders what the inside of his house at 7 Grantham Street or 58 Harcourt Street or 4 Hatch Street, to which he finally moved in June 1892, looked like. True he had an art studio at Harcourt Street (which he kept for ten years after he had moved to Hatch Street where he had another). But his houses must have been cluttered, to say the least; the maids must have been kept busy with their dusters, what with his collection of birds' skins and mounted specimens, and pictures floating around, finished and half finished, framed and unframed, packed and half packed ready for dispatch to patrons, and, besides, the inevitable paraphernalia of a busy travelling artist. The Victorians liked a sense of opulence, and if he was not rich enough for that, clutter was perhaps the next best thing, a measure of worldly effort and worth.

There is no doubt Williams liked living in some style. Hatch Street Lower was a fashionable address. At one time there were at least nine barristers living along the street which featured only thirty-two houses.[4] He must have had some wealthy neighbours; a successful barrister might then have earned £1,000 or more. Located on the corner of a short terrace, No. 4 Hatch Street was a sizeable Georgian townhouse, since converted into offices. It consists of four storeys over a basement, making a total area of about 3,000 square feet (278 sq m). The period features are now gone, the fireplaces removed and whatever Georgian or Victorian plasterwork there was has given way to plain ceilings. A hint of the house's grander days may still be discerned by the impressive archway between the two largest rooms, one being the dining room, the other the drawing room. The spacious garden has been built over. The place had been built for gracious living.

This time he chose to mount his exhibition not at the beginning of the so-called season in November or December, as he had done before with success, but in the heart of it, in the middle of February 1892. Returning to his favourite venue, the Leinster Hall in Molesworth Street, he invested no small effort and indeed money in this exhibition. As he had started so he was to continue, providing the rather bleak hall, by the addition of draperies and friezes, potted palms and ornamental plants, with 'the aspect of a drawing room', as *The Irish Times* commented. The pictures, the *Irish Society* noted, 'are displayed on a ground work of pink terracotta. Above is a frieze of green drapery, attached by immense square-headed gold nails, and below is a dado of the same tone of green mingled with cream.'[5]

Again the illustrated catalogue came in for praise, described as 'very novel and dainty . . . The design of the cover is original and striking, and there is a series of seven reproductions of the artist's works in the finest style of the process of photographic printing on choice paper.' (This proved too expensive as he only occasionally illustrated his catalogues thereafter.) Maybe in principle it was a good idea to shift the exhibition from November or December. But what could not be controlled was the weather and, as luck would have it, the artist could hardly have chosen a worse week. The author of 'Our Irish Letter' reported that:

> While I write we have a foot of snow on the ground here, and a torrent of it in process of descent. All art lovers and supporters are seriously sorry for Mr Alexander Williams, RHA, who opened a pretty exhibition of his painting on Monday afternoon at the Leinster Lecture Hall, Molesworth-street, in frightful weather, and kept it open all the week – with, of course, small encouragement from a shivering, influenza-fearing, and home-keeping public. To the opening of the show on Monday, Mr and Mrs Williams had invited a large number of private friends, and had prepared a charming reception room . . . but the battle that raged all day long between two great powers – Boreas and Pluvius – kept the great bulk of the company absent and, of course, spoilt the *éclat* of the artistic meeting.

The author evidently expected readers to have remembered sufficient of their Latin to know that *Boreas* was the Greek god of the North Wind – but not so much that they could tell that *pluvius* is not a noun but an adjective and that the Latin for rain is *pluvia*. Never mind, pluvia or not, visitors turned out in numbers just the same, for Williams had a card to trump even the weather and that was the presence of the wife of the Lord Lieutenant. Better again, she and her entourage bought pictures. Alexander was good with the press and kept in close touch with newspaper men. The social side of the exhibition was well reported: 'Her Excellency the Countess of Zetland honoured with a visit yesterday afternoon Mr Williams's exhibition of sketches from nature . . . accompanied by a large and distinguished party from the Castle . . .' ran one newspaper report, not forgetting to list the distinguished party from the Castle. The report continued: 'Lady Zetland bought picture No. 11 *Close of Day* for 2 guineas while Lady Langford with an address at the State Steward's House, Castle Yard, bought No. 37 *Toilers of the Sea*. Who bought pictures mattered if they had titles, and so too did their address apparently if it was in the

Oil on board. An incident at the Poolbeg Light. Signed. 13 x 15 in. (33 x 38.1 cm).

precincts of the Castle. In addition, Lady Ardilaun braved the weather and added three more pictures to her collection. On the financial side some forty pictures, a third of those on view, were sold, realising £168.5.0.

The *Irish Times* not surprisingly seemed fazed at the sheer size of the exhibition: 'The fact that he is able, unaided and single-handed, to put together a collection of pictures numbering about 140, none of which can truly be described as worthless, while many of them are excellent, and not a few are perfect gems in their way, speaks volumes alike for his talent and for his industry.'[6] Praise of sorts which the *National Press* was not prepared to give – 'well-drawn and nicely coloured and finished' – but concluding that 'there is not much in the small landscapes in style or tone to distinguish one from the other.'[7] The *Irish Society* concluded that while 'Mostly, the pictures and sketches show a consummate master of his art . . . There are also occasional signs of the artisan, as distinct from the artist as too palpable blackness of shadow is a short cut to hidden effects.'

The *Irish Daily Independent* had no such reservations; homing in on his reputation as a painter of the sea, the paper asserted that: 'Mr Williams occupies a prominent position amongst the marinescape painters of the Three Kingdoms, while he unquestionably takes the lead in that department amongst the painters of his own country.'[8] The paper picked out for special mention 'the most ambitious' painting in the exhibition, a large oil entitled *The Golden Eventide* in which on a beach foreground 'an older salt than he who stands at the water's edge is seated in a dismasted "trawler", which has been partially keeled in the sand . . . the scene depicted is natural in every detail.' At £30 the picture, however, went unsold. The paper went on to suggest that 'it is not in sunlight effects that Mr Williams shows at his best. A gloomy sky, a dark crag, a surf-covered sea, and a vessel or two scudding before the wind . . .' All the newspapers singled out picture No. 40, *An Incident at the Poolbeg Light during the Gale of October 5th, 1891*, representing 'The *Iris* rising on the crest of a wave just inside the Poolbeg while the artist himself is seen on board sketching the tugging-in of a large three-master by a very small tug.' Nothing appealed more to the artist than a storm, even, it would seem, to the point of being embroiled in it.

The fortnight he had spent at Altamont in County Carlow was rewarded by praise for his studies of *The Lake, Garden, Summer House* and a *Curious Old Entrance Gate*, the *Daily Express* regarding them all as 'very carefully executed'. No sign of haste here; meticulous representational work still held its appeal and he could do it well. Despite the praise, he did not exhibit any comparable studies of gardens again. He had yet to forsake the painting of birds. He included pictures in this exhibition: *A Study of Sparrow and Apple Blossom*, a rather more congenial combination than bullfinch with hedge-sparrow's nest and eggs, it might be thought, but *A Study of a Kingfisher and Ring Dotterel* seems utterly anomalous; these two birds would never be seen together, occupying entirely different habitats. More unusual was the inclusion of a study of a *Dogfish*. Fish were never his line, other than when painting Achill Islanders when he might include their catch as part of the scene.

A new departure, also given a separate section in his catalogue, were sketches of 'Bits of Old Dublin' which drew praise from all quarters. According to the *Irish Society*: 'Most of these latter drawings were sketched by the artist at four or five o'clock a.m. on summer mornings, when immunity from street traffic and idle watchers could be securely counted upon.' They included such bygone scenes as Skipper's Alley, St Patrick's Close, a Georgian doorway in Malpas Street (look at the architectural degradation of this street today) and a corner of Nicholas Street. He chose the scenes because he knew they were about to disappear: *A Site of a Ruined Industry*, seemingly an unidentified tannery, drew special praise from *The Irish Times*, noting first that it was quite different from the other scenes: 'The dilapidated condition of the premises is presented with wonderful effect. The decaying roof, the broken windows, and the general aspect of desolation which are so vividly presented, indicate the work of a master hand.'[9] The inner city Dublin scenes he painted were dilapidated too, if not so ruinous as the tannery; they were slums full of the poor and indigent. The narrow streets and lanes, the medieval layout, the topsy-turvy buildings with a bit added here, another bit there, ad hoc fashion, charm by the sense of their human scale, the intimacy of small spaces, and the effects of light obscured at one point, emphasized at another: a buckled roof picked out in sunshine, the shadowy alley below, an appealing pool of light in the street beyond that draws the eye through – these chiaroscuro effects suggest a well-lit stage set. Whatever the squalor within these houses, in these pictures a strong sense of community seems to emanate from them. Williams' studies of buildings showed a strong sympathy for architectural forms too. Although hardly recognised as such, some are perhaps at least the equal of his sea pictures and landscapes. Where others perhaps did not, the *Daily Express* recognised the importance of what he was doing: '"Bits of Old Dublin" are highly interesting little pictures, and as some of them relate to such localities as Hanover lane, Nicholas street, and Old Wood street – unsavoury relics of bygone times, which have recently been effaced by the Public Health Department – they may serve a useful historic purpose hereafter.'

It might have been thought that an exhibition on this scale would have been enough for any artist in a year, but no sooner was it over than Alexander was gearing up for an exhibition in July to coincide with the tercentenary celebrations of Dublin University, choosing for the first and last time the new hall of the Civil Engineers at 35 Dawson Street, 'a fine lightsome chamber'. The exhibition was to all intents and purposes a re-run of the one in February, except that to the bulk of what he had already shown the artist added about another thirty pictures, making what can only be described as a gargantuan display of around 182 pictures. He used the same catalogue too, simply pasting in a new title page and adding additional pages at the back. This raises the question: what about the forty pictures that had already been sold? Their titles all appear for a second time and the accounts for both exhibitions show that four pictures with the same titles and numbers, namely 35, 40, 48 and 69, were sold at both exhibitions; he must have used duplicates to suit the same titles.

He was probably banking on the nostalgic appeal of his pictures to those returning from abroad, and the small size of many of the pictures meant they could be readily taken back home overseas. However, he had no 'names' in attendance and he got scant coverage in the press. Over the four days there were just fifty-five paying visitors, who bought twenty-three catalogues. He might have taken comfort in the *Daily Express*'s comment that 'he has the true artist's faculty of finding some hidden beauty in all things . . .'[10] It was just a pity that there were not more buyers who felt the same. Just a dozen pictures were sold, to make a total of about £77, a very poor return for such a large exhibition. Moreover, what the overall figure conceals is that half the takings were accounted for by only two pictures valued at just over forty pounds. *The Golden Eventide* was at last sold at its asking price of £30 and *On the Shore at Tarbet* fetched its price of 10 guineas. Without the sale of these two pictures the exhibition would have been an abject failure.

A long, hot summer this year provided him with congenial opportunities in the west and southwest, with Killarney now becoming a centre of his activities comparable with the west and Achill. He was back yet again for what was his third solo exhibition of the year, at his old haunt of 35 Molesworth Street, for four days, 19–22 December 1893. This time he had no snow to contend with, while he did have a visit from the Lord Lieutenant himself, the Earl of Zetland, and upwards of 200 turned up for the private view. He sold twenty-four pictures, fifteen before the exhibition was thrown open to the

Oil on canvas. Upper Lake Killarney. Signed. 18 x 30 in. (46 x 77 cm).

public, indicating the importance of having a private showing of invited guests. He realised £159.11.0, slightly down on his last exhibition but a larger return relative to the number of pictures on show, a more modest sixty-four this time;[11] and he got enthusiastic reviews. This time round *The Irish Times* in a long review commended him on 'an expansion of style and treatment that demonstrates his grasp of artistic impressions, and a power of reproducing them without restriction or sameness of manner'.[12] This must have pleased the artist because at the tercentenary exhibition and elsewhere his work was sometimes regarded as monotonous. From the sales list it is interesting to note that the pictures bought reflected the mix of work, without a cluster in any one section, suggesting the painter understood his market.

The happy hunting ground of Killarney, as *The Irish Times* had put it, was to continue as one of his most fruitful areas of work. Few landscape painters since the eighteenth century, visitors and Irish alike, have not included Killarney on the itinerary. It has been suggested by Carla Briggs that Williams was the most prolific painter of Killarney of his time.[13] The *Irish Daily Independent* thought his Killarney miniatures as 'perfect specimens of what such little pictures should be'. He did many large-scale canvases of Killarney too. On account of his friendship with the Hilliard family, who owned the Lake Hotel, Williams spent many happy summer days painting from its precincts; evidence of which remains both in his memoirs and on the walls of the Lake Hotel itself. A letter survives from 1905 from Jack Hilliard to the artist:

I have laid your offer before my brother. And he agrees with me to offer you £100.0.0 one hundred pounds for the pictures in the Coffee Room. I would not like to see the walls stripped. The room in my eyes would look awful the contrast would be so great. I hope you will see your way to accept this, and that it will be of service to you. If any one asked me to spend the amount for any other purpose I would say I could not afford it. I will as soon as I can work Mrs B for the other two with kind regards.[14]

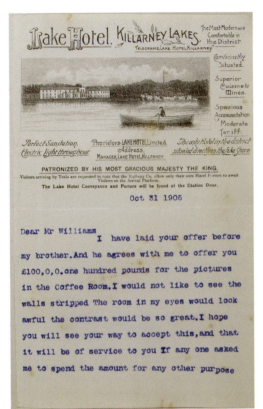

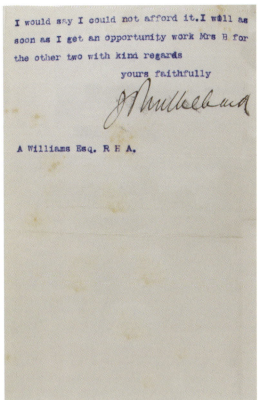

Lake Hotel. KILLARNEY LAKES. The Most Modern and Comfortable in the District.
TELEGRAMS.LAKE HOTEL.KILLARNEY
Conveniently Situated.
Superior Cuisine & Wines.
Spacious Accommodation Moderate Tariff.
Perfect Sanitation. Proprietors-LAKE HOTEL Limited. The only Hotel in the district
Electric light throughout Address, situated direct on the Lake Shore
MANAGER,LAKE HOTEL,KILLARNEY
PATRONIZED BY HIS MOST GRACIOUS MAJESTY THE KING.
Visitors arriving by Train are requested to note that the Railway Co. allow only their own Hotel Porters to await Visitors on the Arrival Platform.
The Lake Hotel Conveyance and Porters will be found at the Station Door.

Oct 31 1905

Dear Mr Williams
       I have laid your offer before
my brother.And he agrees with me to offer you
£100,0,0.one hundred pounds for the pictures
in the Coffee Room.I would not like to see the
walls stripped The room in my eyes would look
awful the contrast would be so great.I hope
you will see your way to accept this,and that
it will be of service to you If any one asked
me to spend the amount for any other purpose

I would say I could not afford it.I will as
soon as I get an opportunity work Mrs B for
the other two with kind regards
                              yours faithfully

A Williams Esq. R H A.

Letter to the artist from J. Hilliard, Lake Hotel, Killarney, dated 31 October 1905.

Further pictures were apparently added later, and the collection of seven oils and two watercolours, a century later, still hang in the Lake Hotel, making it the largest collection of the artist's work on public view.

While Alexander Williams painted the well-known beauty spots of Killarney, Glendalough and elsewhere, he was very much regarded as a pioneer in opening up scenes of faraway and unknown places. It is hard to appreciate today just how unfamiliar so much of Ireland would have been, and not only to visitors across the sea. Travel was opening up but it was still limited by modern standards; and because photographs were generally monochrome and limited to the better-known beauty spots (uncoloured in any case, unless by hand), painting was the thing, often a revelation of places unseen. Alexander knew how to exploit this aspect of painting. For example, a new road had just been constructed near Clew Bay. Few of the readers of *The Irish Times* would have travelled on it even if they were aware of its existence. The artist made it his business both to travel the road and to paint scenes from it. Here was a subject that was not only of artistic interest, it was newsworthy too. This is how *The Irish Times* reported it:

The Clew Bay group, from Nos 9 to 16, open up fresh ground. No. 11, for instance, a splendid work, and No. 9 have been painted from points on the new road, which, if we are not mistaken, tourists of the future in the wilds of the West will prefer to take to the old route. These pictures, and others that hang in their neighbourhood, will serve to draw attention from the beaten track, and they suggest to the lover of the

Oil on canvas, 'Muckross Abbey.' Signed. 23½ x 41¼ in. (59.7 x 104.8 cm).

Oil on canvas. 'Dingle Bay from Ventry Cliffs.' Signed. 23¼ x 41 in. (59.1 x 104.1 cm). *The Irish Times* commended the artist on 'the softness of his paintings capturing the moisture-laden atmosphere of Ireland'.

Oil on canvas, 'At Muckross House, Middle Lake.' Signed. 23 x 41 in. (58.4 x 104 cm).

Oil on canvas, 'Colleen Bawn Rock, Middle Lake.' Signed. 24 x 41½ in. (60 x 105.4 cm).

Irish scenery that there are unexplored regions about the skirts of Croaghpatrick, in the neighbourhood of the Killeries, and on the road to Doo Lough, which heretofore have escaped the traveller's vision, and which the artist now reveals.[15]

The paper went further; these pictures were not simply interesting representations of unknown places, but the artist had managed to capture the evanescent changes of the western day: 'No. 16, a scene near Murrisk Abbey, is a typical Irish landscape of mountain swept by drifting clouds, of bog, of bright patches of water, and wide moorland and glinting sun-shift. Those who are familiar with the changeful scenery of the West will recognise these cunning touches, and of this group as a whole it may be said that a finer or more skilful [collection] has never been brought home by an artist from the heart of so exquisite a country.'

Ten years had now passed since he had first ventured into going solo, and his exhibitions had evolved into annual events of some social standing and a fixture on the calendar of events in Dublin. It is a moot point which side of the equation mattered more to the press and public, the pictures or the society figures who attended the exhibitions. The writer for the *Lady's Pictorial*, in a piece of tittle-tattle, made no attempt to suggest that the pictures were anything like so important as the visitors: 'My jottings at Mr Alex Williams's picture exhibition on Monday afternoon were, that his Ex. [cellency] seemed really pleased with the artistic little show, and that his observant but always blamelessly discreet eye speedily singled out, and dwelt upon, the prettiest pictures in the gallery – pictures in the flesh I mean: not on canvas – including Mrs de Willis, and the exhibitor's classically fair wife. Mrs Charles Allen was the best dressed woman present, and the little white fox terrier in blue pilot coat, the most undisguisedly admired.' Even dogs gained admittance, presumably free. That pictures were necessary for the social event goes without saying, but the fashionable status of the events was what sold them.

There was never any mention of wine or alcohol being available. Rather it was tea, presided over by the artist's wife, which would be served in the library adjacent to the exhibition hall. Here is the contributor to the *Lady's Pictorial*, in her element, describing the scene: 'The company numbered upwards of two hundred, and included representatives of all the arts . . . as well as a large number of the best known and most popular "society" people. Mrs Williams, handsomely costumed in lavender silk, trimmed with jet lace, and veiled with striped gauze, received her guests with graceful cordiality, and was unremitting in her efforts to promote enjoyment and dispense appreciated hospitality.' For middle-aged chic, Kitty could probably hold her own with the best of them and the press liked reporting on what she wore: 'brown tweed, black velvet toque, trimmed with violets' her costume for the exhibition of 1895. Achill had become topical this year because the railway was about to be extended from Westport to Achill Sound. It was reported that after His Excellency, Lord Houghton, was received by the artist, he was 'conducted round the gallery, where a considerable time was passed in closely examining the pictures, especially those from Achill Island. His Excellency was pleased to select a water-colour drawing, *Owen Kilban's Cottage and Boatyard, Shraheens, Achill Sound*, and before leaving complimented the artist on his successful endeavours to make the scenery of Ireland better known.'

Always thinking of ways to promote his exhibitions, Williams took to including something new and novel each year as a talking point. Some ideas were more felicitous than others. He included a musical recital for the first time at his exhibition of 1893. This proved so popular that when he extended his exhibitions to four weeks, there was a well-advertised musical recital held every Friday afternoon at 4 p.m. for about an hour. (Originally the recitals were held on Saturdays.) Plenty of people seemed to be free on a Friday afternoon, with audiences of 150 and more in attendance. The music was typical popular Victorian fare, occasional opera solos, for singers who could manage such things, more often sentimental songs performed by local worthies, accompanied by local pianists, teachers from the academies, or the wife of a friend from the cathedrals might play, adding a piano solo here and there, and perhaps a violinist might do the same. The artist's wife, Kitty, was not averse to singing a song or two, and likewise their daughter, Alice, would occasionally sing a solo or a duet with her mother. What impression they made on the eye and the ear can only be conjectured. The press were consistently kind. To the eye they must have made an unlikely pair: Kitty elegant by all accounts and with the poise of a woman who knew she could rely on her looks and natural elegance; Alice presenting a rather less feminine image, being toweringly tall and clumsy with it. Such floral treats as 'The Message of the Violet' (*Prince of Pilsen*) and 'The Passion Flower' were part of their repertoire, with mother and daughter having a soft spot for singing together Boscovitz's 'Bella Napoli'. Some of the singers, such as the 'society' tenor Melfort D'Alton, soprano Agnes Treacy, who had the soubriquet 'the Irish nightingale', and the handsome baritone J. C. Doyle, 'a matinee idol' according to his recording label Pathé, were all well-known names in Dublin. Many singers occupied a position

somewhere between full-time professional and amateur. One imagines Madame Nora
Borel was something of a *grande dame*. When she writes with her list of songs she adds
'I have no objection to my name being in the paper,' meaning, one suspects, that she
would be absolutely delighted to see her name in print. Williams had presumably asked
her if he could use her name in an advertisement. Madame would have been gratified to
read the 'rave' review by *The Irish Times* that she was 'the bright particular star. For her
exquisite rendering of "She wandered down the mountain side" the encore was inevitable.
Later in the programme she gave a delightful interpretation of "Down in the forest",
which was also encored, and "Daddy's darling" was given; being still further recalled she
sang beautifully "Mifanwy".'[16] Sung no doubt with the sweet sentimentality such fare
required. More appropriate, it might be thought, than Mr Arthur Murnaghan's offering,
'If I were a sunbeam'. There is no accounting for Victorian ideas of what was appropriate:
in singing – as in painting: think of canaries and cabbages, bullfinches and hedge-
sparrows' eggs. Letters that survive contain the typical preoccupation of singers with the
condition, real or imagined, of their throats and the minutiae of performance details.
Frank Sellers from Sutton says he hopes 'to be able to sing for you the songs on the other
side', presumably referring to a now lost sheet of paper rather than that he would be
singing in another world; and he adds rather ominously: 'I am in very bad form but I
daresay I shall get thro'.' Not what someone trying to draw up a programme wants to
receive. One way or another Alexander never seems to have been short of participants.

Viewed as a microcosm of Dublin life, his exhibitions point up the incongruity of the
well-to-do of the city entertaining themselves with pictures of those living at subsistence
level on the western seaboard. Here is what was said of one of the artist's later solo
exhibition by the *Irish Society and Social Review*: 'An opportunity was given, to some
perhaps for the first time, of seeing a vivid picture of life among the poor peasants of the
West of Ireland, and no doubt such scenes awakened a deep sympathy for those toilers
of the sea and marsh.'[17] This was written as late as 1906. Clearly, Williams' pictures
were, to a point, art as reportage, more especially, if, as the *Irish Society and Social
Review* suggested, the images came as something new and perhaps even startling to those
attending the exhibition. They would not, however, have startled the Lord Lieutenant's
wife, Lady Aberdeen, because she had taken the trouble to visit the west and Achill to see
things for herself, as had Lady Dudley. The *Irish Society* continued: 'It is significant of
the kindly heart of Her Excellency that when purchasing two pictures from the collection
she choose [*sic*] as one *A Poor Village in Achill*, which represented in all its intensity the
grey misery of our Western shore.' The Aberdeens and the Dudleys before them, among
those who occupied Dublin Castle, did show concern for Irish affairs and were noted for
their good works. They pointed the way; the choice of *A Poor Village in Achill* may have
been made with that in mind. Lady Aberdeen knew it would be reported. Pictures may
not often change minds, still less bridge the gap between the viewer and the viewed.
Alexander was not, in any purposeful sense, a didactic artist. But it is possible that some
pictures in some of his exhibitions did give visitors pause for thought.

Viewed purely as a social activity, his exhibitions sound beguilingly civilised: carriages turning up at Molesworth Street to decant elegantly clad guests into a pleasantly decorated hall (*heated*, the press observed); there was an opportunity to while away a Friday afternoon looking at pictures, recalling perhaps your own visit to Wicklow or Howth, Killarney or the west; a chance to meet up with friends – so many lived close by – and meet the convivial artist himself as you walked about, perhaps catching one of his humorous anecdotes that the press spoke of; then a cup of tea and if you were inclined and had the time, not in short supply in those more leisurely days or so we now suppose, stay on for the musical recital. And if your visit happened to coincide with the arrival of the Lord Lieutenant and his entourage, maybe you would even be introduced to him – once the artist had shown him around the exhibition of course; that would be something to remember. Caught up in the pleasure of it all, you might even come away with a picture. What more could be asked of an afternoon in Dublin?

CHAPTER
13

Into the New Century

a very old cabin built without a window. Road to Falcarragh

Rare sketch inscribed 'a very old cabin built without a window. Road to Falcarragh.' 7 x 4¼ in. (17.8 x 10.8 cm). This windowless cottage so struck the artist that he made two studies of it in his Donegal sketchbook of 1908.

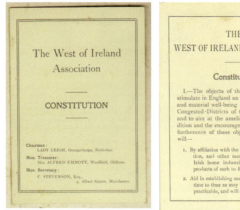

Booklet of the *Constitution of the West of Ireland Association*.

The time had to come when Williams would depend entirely on painting for his income. He retired from the choirs of the cathedrals in 1897 and would go into the new century as a painter and nothing else. Around this time he put together a curious book containing mainly printed and typed testimonials. The 'Red Book', for want of a better term, was impressively bound between bright red covers. It is the kind of thing one might associate more with the purveyor of patent medicines than a painter. It would have been largely redundant in Ireland as the names of his patrons appeared at the front of the catalogues for his exhibition. So what was the point of it?

The book itself provides some clues. Pasted inside the front cover is a little booklet, the *Constitution of the West of Ireland Association*, the first article of which makes plain that 'The objects of the Association are to stimulate in England an interest in the social and material well-being of the people in the Congested Districts of the West of Ireland and to aim at the amelioration of their condition and the encouragement of self help.' The rest of the document continues in the same vein: '. . . to encourage Irish home industries . . . and introduce the products of such to English purchasers . . . establish and support district nurses in necessitous parts . . .' and to 'publish information as to fishing, shooting, and hotel accommodation in, and railway facilities to, the West of Ireland, and stimulate in other ways the flow of visitors from England to these parts'. These were aims which Williams actively supported, taking an interest in the West of Ireland Association, the work of the Congested Districts Board, the Countess of Dudley Fund and writing to the press and even the Lord Lieutenant about Achill affairs.

On 11 April 1899 the artist wrote to Charles Stevenson, the Secretary of the West of Ireland Association in Manchester, receiving a reply by return: 'Do you show the products of Irish Industries or is it a lecture with views you propose to give? I shall be glad to hear your idea as to terms & to have some references.' It would seem that the Red Book was intended to be used for promoting his own work alongside exhibits and products of the association. While no deal appears to have taken place, a few years later

Williams did for the Congested Districts Board what he appears to have been aiming to do for the West of Ireland Association. He exhibited some forty-four oil paintings, representing various areas of the west, as part of the Congested Districts Board exhibits at the Irish Industrial Exhibition at the St Louis World Fair in 1904. Hugh Lane was then an Honorary Director for the Department of Agriculture and Technical Instruction for Ireland. He championed the idea of exhibiting Irish paintings at the Louisiana Exposition as 'the first real opportunity we have had of proving to the world the artistic talent that Irishmen possess, and which has led them with very little encouragement to produce great works'.[1] In the event all that the government could manage to send to St Louis were black and white photographs of pictures from the National Gallery. The pictures assembled by Lane for St Louis went instead to an Exhibition of Irish Art at the Guildhall Art Galleries, London; Williams was represented by *View in the Isle of Achill*. In passing it is interesting to note that his brothers were represented too at the Louisiana World Fair. Exhibit No. 138 was a 'Collection of Irish Sea Birds' from Williams & Sons (sic), 2 Dame St, Dublin, the only taxidermy exhibit from Ireland. None of the brothers attended the exhibition. Later, Williams exhibited elsewhere in the States, in O'Leary's Gallery in Detroit for example in September 1916, although he never visited North America in person.

Aside from the testimonials, the Red Book shows the artist's reach and throws up some surprises. One correspondent, an A. B. Wynne, who signed himself as an 'Ind. Civil Ser. (Ret.)' but with an address at Villa Rolli, Veytaux, Montreux in Switzerland, wrote to congratulate the artist 'on the collection of Irish sketches which I have seen at Mons. Schlessinger's gallery at Territet'. A news clip from the *Evening Globe*, New Brunswick, Canada reported that Messrs Maculay Bros & Co were showing *The Colleen Bawn Rock, Middle Lake, Killarney*. Exhibitions in Canada would follow.

The very last letter in the Red Book was from the Dublin City Treasurer, Edmund W. Eyre, stating that he was 'directed by the Finance and Leases Committee to ask that you will be so good as to inspect the pictures in the Council Chamber, City Hall, and report to them as to their condition, detailing the weak points (if any) of each picture, and stating what in your opinion is necessary to be done for its restoration.'[2] The artist had already overseen the restoration of the collection in the Mansion House, his report to Dublin Corporation being regarded as 'eminently satisfying'.[3]

As if to prove that his energy was undimmed at the close of the century, the artist ventured across the water with two exhibitions in England in 1899: 'Wildest West of Ireland', held at 4 Exchange Street, Manchester, in June and the second at the Studio 9 Temple, Dale Street, Liverpool, in December. This amounted to three solo exhibitions in twelve months, since his annual exhibition, his twelfth, at the Leinster Hall Molesworth Street preceded both, the first sale from which, Williams made a note, was to Lord Powerscourt. He was still in fashion. There had been a change of Lord Lieutenant in 1895, and it was the Countess Cadogan and her entourage who patronised this exhibition, the Countess buying a picture of *Mornington* for £2.10.0 and *Toilers of the Sea* for 3 guineas. The press reported that, after viewing the exhibition, 'Her Excellency and her guests subsequently drove to the Earlsfort terrace Skating Rink,' not to skate but to present the prizes at the Ambulance Competition, the proceeds of which were to be given to the funds of the Children's Clothing Mission. Such were the duties of the Castle.

A Beehive Cabin, Keel Strand, Achill was singled out for its historic interest: '. . . a faithful picture of the last of these curious domed dwellings of the past', noted the *Daily Express*. The same paper also picked out *Toilers of the Sea* in which 'we get a glimpse of what the fisherman's life is like in Achill Island, the effects of sea, sky, and shore on a tempestuous day being rendered with marvellous fidelity, while life is given to a charming picture by the introduction of figures and the canvas boat of the fishermen.'⁴ In the context of a tempestuous day, the use of the word 'charming' might be regarded as indicating the gulf between the perceptions of a land-based writer and those of the fishermen in the picture whose very lives depended upon their currachs.

Another sea picture that caught the attention of the press was a 'large water colour, *The Port of Dublin*, which was exhibited at the World's Fair Exhibition, Chicago [1893], and which ought to find a permanent resting place in the city ere long'. If this was the same picture exhibited at Chicago, and not another picture on the same subject, then the title had been changed; it was originally called *Sweet Dublin Bay*. It had the enormous price tag of £100 for a sale in which the next highest price was £30 and most of the pictures were on offer for just a few guineas. The picture went unsold. The *Irish Daily Independent* claimed that the picture had also been exhibited in California 'and other places', but evidence is lacking that the picture did go as far as the west coast.

Keeping to his policy of introducing a novelty to his exhibition, this year he displayed a large spray of the Irish heath *Erica erigena*, which is native to the west of Ireland and obligingly flowers in winter. Sure enough the heath proved a talking point, and to emphasise the motif of the west, the artist featured the heath in a picture entitled *At Mallaranny* which the *Daily Express* thought 'a lovely bit of work, and is remarkable from the fact that it was painted direct from a collection of Mallaranny heather, sent up by the Midland Great Western Railway Company. Visitors to the exhibition will be able to inspect this remarkable heather, which is in full bloom all the winter, and the stems of which reach a height of nearly five feet.' In addition to his study of the Irish heath, attention was called to 'a fine study of Hawthorns in the Phoenix Park. The Viceregal Lodge stands in the centre background, and the prevailing grey tone is cleverly utilised.' (None of his plant studies has been located.)

He now set his sights on London, not a prospect of which Williams' aged father approved. Perhaps he had a wiser head when it came to business. In what was probably the last letter the old man, now eighty-eight, ever wrote to his son, he cautioned him:

> Dear Alex, I was glad you did not forget to write it has relieved my mind from a load, you have been laying out too much in expenses but I hope you are sowing the seed, and feeling your way so that it may be a foundation for future operations. London is a hungry place and your landlord should be satisfied with his rent without commission.⁵

There was also advice from Lord Mayo, writing from Palmerston, Straffan, County Kildare: 'Put your prices in London not much higher than in Dublin and you will most likely have a good sale.'[6] Mayo's advice was probably unnecessary while it was too late for Williams to heed his father. He had already done a deal with Edward Freeman of the Modern Gallery, 175 Bond Street, London W1 to exhibit 144 pictures (three more than listed in the catalogue), with the all-encompassing title 'Picturesque Ireland.' The exhibition ran for the month of April and then again in June 1901. By modern standards the fees Freeman was charging – they varied as we will see – were modest. This, however, took no account of overheads. A gripe common among artists is of receiving inadequate press coverage and advertising. Freeman certainly could not be faulted on this score; however, he was not paying for the advertising out of his percentage, the artist was and the advertising did not come cheap. A circular announcing the exhibition was widely distributed and taken up by numerous papers. The *Court Journal* of 23 March 1901 dutifully set the scene, announcing the exhibition as being 'under the immediate patronage of the Lord Lieutenant of Ireland and the Countess of Cadogan, the Duke and Duchess of Abercorn, the Marquis and Marchioness of Zetland . . .' and so forth, giving out a list of about twenty names of the nobility and titled. Freeman knew his job; nearly thirty papers took up the call and provided notices. Every notice was valuable, as competition among exhibitions was considerable. To give an idea as to how considerable, on the day Alexander held his private view, Sunday 31 March, *The Sunday Times* published a list of thirty or more artists, all offering 'Studio At Homes' around the capital.

His reviews were generally favourable, his oils being preferred to the watercolours. The *Morning Advertiser* prefaced its review by stating that: 'In his larger examples Mr Williams affects the smooth style of painting,' while coming down strongly in favour of the smaller pictures which made up the greater part of the exhibition: 'He is infinitely to be preferred in his smaller works, in which he obtains strong and vigorous effects of light and shade by adopting a sterner method of impasto. Some of his open air studies have a freshness and a vitality, so to speak, which are absent in the easel work in the studio.' It might be mentioned again that it is questionable if all the smaller works were necessarily done on the spot, or even started outdoors. His copious notebooks suggest otherwise. The use of impasto was a new development for the artist. What was consistently agreed down the years by reviewers in Ireland was that he always stood out as a maritime painter and the English critics thought the same. The *Sheffield Daily Telegraph* took up the theme of figures in the landscape: 'But Mr Williams has not stopped at scenery. He has painted the cabins of the peasants inland and by the seashore. He has painted the peasants toiling in their boats or fields, but always with a compassionate eye for their poverty, and a keen eye for the picturesqueness of their surroundings.' Whatever about the 'smiling landscapes' of Killarney and the 'pleasant verdure of the Phoenix Park' over which the *Northern Whig* enthused, the *Art Record* took the view that 'Mr Williams seems most at home in the minor key, those aspects of nature which partake of the melancholy,'[7] a view generally shared.

The Irish Times summed up the value of the exhibition in this way: 'This unique display has been the means of increasing interest across the Channel in the scenery of Ireland, and it is of special importance as occurring at the opening of the tourist season,' concluding that 'Ireland could have no better advertisement as a tourist resort, and much is owing to the industry and enterprise that Mr Williams has shown.'[8] A commentary that was a running theme through the artist's career.

A study of the arrival in Ireland of Queen Victoria, an unusual study for the artist, garnered a lot of publicity. For what was to be her final visit to Ireland, the aged Queen on board the yacht *Victoria and Albert* arrived at Kingstown Harbour (now Dun Laoghaire) on 4 April 1900. Alexander was down at the port, his vantage point the balcony of the railway station, from where he had a panoramic view of the Victoria jetty, the royal yacht alongside, and battleships in the bay firing a salute. The Queen's death the following year enhanced the historical interest in the painting. Williams made the most of the picture, hanging it for the first time at his first London exhibition and frequently thereafter. It was always taken notice of by the press. 'The carriage drawn by four horses followed by its brilliant escort is just starting from the jetty. Crowds of people are awaiting its arrival. In the harbour every ship is gay with flags, and a cloudy sky is casting shadows on the distant hill of Howth. This is a most interesting memento of a visit which will ever be remembered in the annals of the distressful country.'[9] While a good many of the preparatory sketches survive, sadly the whereabouts of the finished picture have not been traced.

People are more secretive about their earnings than almost anything else. By good fortune, the accounts for Williams' first Bond Street exhibition, 'Picturesque Ireland' 1901, and some subsequent ones, handwritten and signed by Edward Freeman for submitting to the artist, were preserved. Interesting reading they make, in showing how the gallery's dealings with the artist affected the outcome for both sides.

The April part of the Bond Street exhibition netted the painter £179.13.2 on sales of fifty-two paintings. The agreed commission with Freeman was 10 per cent on sales, with the addition of what Williams' father had taken exception to, rent of £63.0.0. A 10 per cent commission is small beer compared with today, when gallery owners regularly charge a commission of 40 to 50 per cent. But Freeman's deductions did not end with commission and rent. There were sundry other expenses to be accounted for, including £12.17.0 for advertising, £4.17.0 for postage (invitations to the private view), while refreshments for the press came to £5.8.10. Money well spent perhaps, but it is unlikely that the artist would have had much say over how the money was used. That said, Freeman's total deductions of £127.16.10 for the April exhibition amounted to 41.6 per cent of sales, which meant Alexander received the balance of 58.4 per cent. He might not have had reason to complain. The problem was that no subsequent solo exhibition at the Bond Street Gallery netted anything like as much.

Turning to the summer exhibition, the figures look completely different. This time only fourteen pictures were sold, realising £72.8.0. The rental of the gallery was agreed at less than a third of what it had been in the spring, £20.0.0, presumably on account of the summer months being traditionally much leaner, and there was no charge for lighting or gas this time around. But Freeman's commission had now risen to 15 per cent, which, with rental and sundry charges added in, brought his deductions to £56.12.5, or 78 per cent of what the pictures had made. Alexander ended up with a mere £15.15.7, less than 22 per cent of sales.

This sort of arrangement meant that if sales were good the artist did reasonably well, but if sales were poor then the artist came off far worse than the gallery. The artist was taking a disproportionate burden of the risk. Did he think back to the warning in his father's letter? Seemingly not, or maybe it was a case that beggars cannot be choosers, Freeman having the whip hand, being the gallery proprietor. Williams exhibited in Bond Street at least five times in the eight years from 1901 to 1909, both for solo exhibitions and two in combination with other artists (see Appendices II and III).

Whatever about the provinces which probably produced only a small return, it was clearly much more profitable for him to exhibit in Dublin than London. Sundry receipts provide an idea of what his outlay was costing him in Dublin. The Leinster Hall in Molesworth Street cost him about £1 a day, seemingly reduced in later years. He could sometimes recoup the cost of hiring the hall by subletting it when his pictures and floral decor were wanted for an evening 'at home'. A plain catalogue would cost something over £1 to produce, an illustrated one more, but he could also recoup at least some of this cost by selling a proportion of them. He employed B. McGlade, 'bill poster, poster writer and street advertiser', who provided two posters at 5/- and a sandwich man at 1/6d per day for 9 days, total bill of 18/6d.[10] In addition he had press advertising; thirteen insertions in the *Daily Express* in 1905 for example came to £1.80,[11] one of several papers he used. In 1899, he records having 556 visitors over eleven days which brought in £9.18.0, to which he could add £1.0.0 for hiring the hall to a Miss Little. As his rental was £12.0.0 plus 10/- to illuminate the annexe and have a coal fire, the hall was only costing him £1.12.0. As visitor numbers rose he may well have covered his advertising and miscellaneous expenses as well, even perhaps making a profit before selling a single picture.

His next London exhibition took place in the spring of 1903 and had the title of 'The Land of the Shamrock', which presumably did not have quite the same clichéd connotations the title would have today. Williams went over on 29 March for the hanging of the pictures, returning to Dublin on 6 April. On 20 April Freeman wrote in bullish mood: 'The *Morning Post* has come out well as I fully expected & has mentioned what I said about your Dublin show. I have sold Nos 9, 34, 104, & 124 (£14/14/) today & hope we may keep the "stars" a going.' But his optimism did not last long. He wrote again on 5 May: 'The total sales amount to £185.11 including the Dublin exhibition sketch you sent direct to Mrs Sloane. I need hardly say I am very sorry for both our sakes that we have fallen short of last time. Very few of the 1901 buyers have turned up for this show.

The pictures will go off tomorrow (Wednesday) for certain to Grundy & Smith & I hope they may have better luck for you – so that Ireland may see no more your works included in this lot.'[12] Naturally enough, Alexander did not want the expense of transporting his pictures back home. It would be interesting to know if he had negotiated a better deal for himself on this occasion, but the accounts have not survived. What is clear, however, from the catalogue sales records is that one picture alone made up a disproportionate amount of total sales, in this instance *The Horses Glen, Mangerton Mountain, Killarney*, which was listed at 50 guineas. If the 1901 buyers had not returned as expected it may have been because they had had a surfeit of Irish pictures by this time. Percy French had got in just before him, in 1903, showing in the same gallery.

In 1904, Alexander participated in a group exhibition at the Bond Street gallery, sharing the event with five others: Joseph W. Carey, Miss Jessie O. Douglas, Percy French, C. MacIver Grierson RI, and G. Wakeman; but as there is not a single reference among his papers to this exhibition we have no idea how he fared. Well enough presumably, as he returned to the Modern Gallery, 61 New Bond Street, for his fourth exhibition, 'The Green Isle of Erin', for the month of May 1906.[13]

By this time the artist was making strenuous representations to entice the British royal family to patronise his work. Ishbel Aberdeen replies to him from the Vice Regal Lodge on 10 May 1906: 'I shall be glad to do what I can in the direction you indicate if I have an opportunity, but I would suggest your also writing to the Countess of Dudley, as she will be in London and would therefore probably be better able to draw the attention of Their Majesties and other members of the Royal family to your exhibition.' Lady Arran was another useful ally in this regard, as she evidently understood the labyrinthine ways of communicating with royal courtiers, although a letter to her from a contact in Marlborough House, Pall Mall, did not sound encouraging: 'Dear Lady Arran, The Princess much fears that it will not be possible for her to find time to visit the Exhibition of Mr Williams' paintings as her time is so short and so taken up until her departure for Spain. Should she have a moment she will gladly look in, but she really does not see her way to it. Yrs sincerely Katherine [Illegible].'

After much speculation as to whether she would or would not put in an appearance, Freeman was eventually able to relate the glad tidings to the artist in a telegram on 12 May: 'Princess of Wales [later Queen Mary] visited Exhibition today purchased number 25 Freeman.' Given his genial reputation in his dealings with his patrons, it was perhaps unfortunate that Williams was not there to receive her as it might have led on to further things.

The following year, 1907, Williams participated in two group exhibitions held in the Modern Gallery. The catalogue of the first exhibition listed 223 works by thirty-five artists, including Percy French, Joseph Poole Addey and Samuel Adams. Williams put in sixty pictures. Here he was competing very much on his own patch, with Adams featuring *The Way to Slievemore, Achill Island* and *Baldoyle Flats, near Dublin*. Around the corner, so to speak, Williams also tried some watercolours with Waring & Gillow's Gallery in

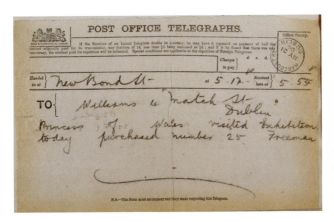

Telegram from Freeman to artist to tell him the Princess of Wales (future Queen Mary) has bought a picture. Dated 12 May 1906.

Oxford Street, but recorded that he sold none. In October 1907 the Modern Gallery featured an exhibition of watercolours by five artists. There was no shortage of variety: Augustus O. Lamplough specialised in scenes from the Nile; Sophia Beale scenes from North Africa and Italy as well as English scenes; and Alice B. Ellis with her selection of English scenes had one with the intriguing title 'Why Don't They Open the Door?' Williams was the only painter of Irish scenery, so no problem about rivalry this time. In his own handwritten accounts the two exhibitions are run together. He sold just eight pictures at £67.15.0,[14] of which a watercolour, *The Approach to the Gap of Dunloe*, one of his favourite subjects, was the highest priced at £26.5.0. Freeman's deductions amounted to £19.8.0, just 26.6 per cent of pictures sold. This represented more or less a reversal of the percentages taken by the gallery and artist for a solo exhibition. Thus the artist's profit as a percentage of sales were higher and the risk lower in a group exhibition, but with a correspondingly smaller number of pictures on which to make a profit.

Whatever Williams may have felt about his arrangements with the gallery, Freeman evidently felt himself under pressure. The artist may have been badgering him for money owed at this time. There is a testiness about a letter from Freeman to the artist written at the end of the year:

> No. 10 Sold is the oil that has been with me for ever so long & I let it go including the copyright for £10 – for the Colonies. Nos 180 & 221 are also old ones – I think this should make all 'as clear as daylight' to you, & I enclose statement of a/c right up to date – so that now I have no pictures at all of yours, or your three friends [Adams, Addey and Percy French] . . . P.S. You can send a couple of those 'nerve testers' & I will put them in the show case if they won't break the glass by the shock![15]

Whoever's nerves were to be tested, Freeman's appear to have been become increasingly taut. Williams may have been surprised to get this ambiguously worded letter from him six weeks later:

IN DUNFANAGHY BAY
IRELAND.

Watercolour print of Dunfanaghy Bay, Donegal. Signed. 10 x 15 in. (25.4 x 38.1 cm). Indicative of the artist's popularity is the number of prints that were made of his work, of which this is an example.

My dear Williams

Yes – 'Times is awful' & I never had such a <u>doing</u> before. I have had to 'meet' so much already this year that I am 'stumped' for ready money. Could you get a 'Bill' discounted and then let me have cash, taking 'a bit' of it for the credit of the balance of a/c I owe you? This would help both of us. If you can do so let me know for how much as of course your 'bit' would depend upon the total of bill you could get discounted. I have another show following the present ones of which I am sending catalogues but am at present blank in most of March but have three months let after in large Gallery.

Everybody wants money now & no-one seems to have any ready cash – On a/c of £6/6/0 due <u>2 years ago</u> I cannot even get paid! Hope things are improving in Ireland but this weak Government is very bad for all.

I will send Addey's little cheque next week I hope.

Kind regards from self & Percy,

Yours very faithfully

Edward Freeman[16]

Contempt for governments, chasing people for money, being stumped for cash, nothing dated about that trio of sentiments. To what extent, if at all, Williams obliged Freeman is not known. At any rate, the artist was to return to Bond Street for one more solo exhibition. In 1908 Williams had concentrated his travels in Donegal. A surviving sketchbook from that trip includes two sketches of a windowless cottage which evidently attracted his attention, even in that day a rarity. 'Ould Donegal, was the title for this exhibition, held in London the following year. 'On the whole, Mr Williams' work shows industry and careful study, but it lacks imagination and feeling,' wrote the reviewer for the *Standard*.[17] Twenty-eight pictures realised £183.11.6 and with Freeman's deductions amounting to £124.17.6, the artist received a paltry £58.14.0 or 32 per cent of gross sales. Maybe the Bond Street gallery had struggled during these years, but by any standards Alexander cannot be said to have done well by Freeman.

Back home we get an idea of the painter's popularity by *The Irish Times* reporting of his annual exhibition for 1901 that 'the attendance of visitors since the opening day has been considerably over 1,000 persons.'[18] By this time his solo exhibitions marked him as an 'Irish' painter in that he did not travel 'abroad', and as the painter most closely associated with the west. *The Irish Times* was emphatic on these points:

> Mr Williams has devoted his life to depicting the beauties of Irish scenery of every phase, from the rugged coasts of the West to the quiet rural scenes nearer home. In this he has done the nation service. He has helped stimulate public taste in the appreciation of native scenery. Many who knew nothing of the enchantments of Achill Island have been led to find them from first seeing the Cliffs of Meenaun or the Valley Strand upon the walls of the Leinster Hall. His devotion to Ireland in his art is worthy of all praise.[19]

A window on the times and the ways of the world are revealed throughout the many letters he kept over the years. Some things never change. Of Oscar Wilde's brother, Williams made a note: 'Willie Wild[e] bought a sketch. 3 guineas <u>and paid for it</u>!'[20] Willie Wilde was notorious for his debts.

It is a great pity that Williams' response to this letter has not survived:

Spring Gardens
Naas
County Kildare
Feb. 20 [no year]

Dear Mr Williams
I am taking the liberty of writing you rather an unusual & perhaps presumptuous letter. But I can only ask you to forgive me. I have long been a very great admirer of your beautiful pictures, & for many years have written an account of appreciation of

all your exhibitions in 'The Queen' newspaper for which I am Irish Correspondent. I have no doubt you have seen them (including the one in the present week's issue – page 322) & perhaps you wondered who wrote them.

As a memento of the many appreciative little pars. [paragraphs] I have written about your pictures I should prize more than I could say a tiny water colour of Killarney or Parknasilla done by yourself, & so I venture to write & ask if you would very kindly gratify my wish. It would be one of my greatest treasures, especially as I have very dear associations both with Killarney & Parknasilla. Forgive me for asking so great a favour – I am sure you will & Believe me yours very truly (Mrs) L. Webb.[21]

Supposing the artist did not fulfil her request, could she be expected to continue to write the 'many appreciative little pars.' as she called them?

There are one or two letters where the artist is asked to make some alterations or additions to a picture, and he seems always to have agreed to do so. Most artists have probably been the recipient of the picture-does-not-suit-the-wallpaper rejection. It is good to see, however, that a Mary Ross from Dalkey put it the other way around. Inviting the artist to see the pictures she has bought, she adds: 'We shall soon want to re-decorate the dining room to provide a proper background.'[22] As she had paid 15 guineas for pictures, the cost of a decorator would have added only a fraction to that figure. On the other hand, the only apparent concern of M. Ross Graham, writing from Ontario, was size:

> The pictures have all arrived safely and are really fine. I still have a couple of wall spaces to fill. Will you let me know if any of your catalogued pictures are unsold & the different sizes of them?[23]

How quickly was his work dispersed across the globe. It was reported of two Killarney pictures that they were 'both going out to the Fiji islands as specimens of Irish scenery'.[24] The ultimate owner of these pictures remains unknown, but the initial purchaser was the Rev. Dr John Pentland Mahaffy, an admirer of the artist, who wrote to Williams from the senior lecturer's office at Trinity College Dublin to say he would send on the address to which the pictures should be sent. Kathleen Corry Hodgson writes to the artist from 3 Belgrave Terrace, Monkstown: 'Thank you very much for making the little alterations, & I hope the two pictures will arrive safely at the end of their 11,500 miles journey to Valparaiso, Chile, where my husband is the British Chaplain.'[25] *Up Trawl and Away*, bought as a wedding present by Sir Charles Cameron, ended up in the Gold Coast where its recipient, Sir Philip Smyly, was Chief Justice.

It comes as no surprise that late payment was a perennial problem, just as now, with the Castle frequently accompanying a cheque with a letter of apology for being tardy. One patron stands out for never failing to look for – or take – something off the marked price. 'Dear Sir, I received the four pictures today & have pleasure to enclose cheque for

Oil on canvas 'Up Trawl & Away'. Signed. 10 x 13½ in. (25.4 x 34.3 cm). Exhibited at RHA 1905.

£13.13.0. I am sorry I cannot see my way to make it £14 as requested,' he writes in one letter, among several in the same vein, 'but I had fully made up my mind that I would not exceed the first named sum.'[26] Take it or leave it. No doubt Williams took it; a bit off here, a bit off there is a hazard of the sole trader marketing his own wares. Another of his letters runs '. . . the catalogue prices are too much for me. Please state lowest price – and I shall write you in reply "yes" or "no".'[27] To be fair he provides a list of five pictures.

At the other end of the scale, Amelia Kennedy from Monkstown was a regular attendee at his exhibitions and a generous patron. She was a wealthy widow who sent her coachman around to pick up a picture on one occasion and one might wonder if she did not have a *grá* for the artist as well as his paintings. Certainly she was warmly appreciative of his work and doubtless an hospitable host. 'I think the *Dublin Trawlers* a little gem,' she writes in one of many letters to the artist, 'the colouring is heartfelt and it is quite unlike any of the others I have of yours.'[28] Without demur, she spent a small fortune on building up a collection of the artist's pictures. 'I will be very glad to see you on Sunday afternoon and if Mrs Williams will come with you I will be very pleased,' she writes, enclosing with the letter a cheque for £40.4.0,[29] while with yet another comes a cheque for £35.2.0.[30] Her interest was sustained; five years later she is still writing to him: 'I congratulate you on your good luck this year. Indeed the pictures were lovely. Of course I think I have got the <u>cream</u>,'[31] enclosing her cheque for £24.4.0. He may have thought he had got the cream too. What Amelia Kennedy spent annually made up a sizeable proportion of what he earned in a year.

Alexander had the good fortune that his social life was all of a piece with his work, an indication doubtless of his own sociability and the modes and manners of the time. Clients buy pictures and invite him around to view the pictures *in situ*, or to view the garden, afternoon tea always on offer. 'When the days are a little longer,' writes Gertrude Hamilton from Killiney Castle, 'we hope you will all come here & spend a long aftn.'[32] In another she suggests he gets the 2.45 from Amiens Street which arrives at Dalkey half an hour later: '. . . we shall have time to go round the Hill before tea.' He had many such invitations.

Train and bus could provide transport even for unaccompanied pictures. Mrs P. Neville of Enniskerry, County Wicklow, had great confidence in the tender care of the transport companies. She writes in connection with one of her purchases: 'I think that there is no glass over that picture and if simply packed in paper it might be sent by Tram to Bray Station if "<u>To be forwarded per Bus to Enniskerry</u> could be put on label – I will send addressed label to your secretary if this would be any help.'[33] It was particularly useful to have friends and patrons to offer hospitality when away from home and on his painting excursions; among them was J. J. Fuller, whose warmth and sense of humour come through vividly in his letters. From 179 Brunswick Street, he writes: 'Dear Mr Williams, I send you the filthy lucre. I'm sorry I didn't stick you for a frame or mount – It can't be helped now. Yours, J. J. Fuller.' He was not quibbling and the amount was paid in full. Fuller must have been a delightful patron, always writing tongue-in-cheek. Here he is again:

My dear Williams

Cash is very hard to get these times – However I am goin for the little bit of Dunloe at £3.3.0

Arrange to pay me a visit in Kerry for a fortnight in June July or August and you'll be able to get some nice Kerry bits.

Leave your claw hammer coat behind you in Dublin and you can resume the 'proprieties' when you get back.

The tail-coat does not fit in with the sublime scenery of my native Country.

We had Bingham McGuinness last year so it is your turn now. He said he'd come to Kerry again. If he does there will be room for [you] both, and if you fight it will be all the better sport for.

Yours

J.J. Fuller[34]

Williams' visit to Altamont House, a fine country house with extensive well-kept gardens in County Carlow, evokes leisurely summer days before the First World War. The owner, Dawson Borrer, and his wife were themselves both painters and Dawson's brother William an ornithologist, hence the evident connections with the artist and the invitation. 'At Altamont, the Borrers generally lived the Victorian idyll,' noted Anne O'Dea, 'photographs from the time show them and their guests relaxing in the splendid gardens, boating, playing archery on the lawn, shooting and fishing.'[35]

It would seem to have been a full and varied period of his life. But nothing is ever perfect and there were years which were overshadowed by constant concern for his son, George, who contracted rheumatic fever in 1897. On 4 January 1904 he died, having caught a chill three weeks earlier. He was twenty-one. His father simply noted his death in his *Chronicles*, boxing it all around as he did with most of the major events in his life. He made no further comment in his writings either then or later. His grief he kept to himself, although his nephew said it ran deep.[36]

For those who lived in the sunshine of empire and not its shadows, the Edwardian era was a golden afternoon and it was in the years leading up to the First World War that Williams reached the height of his popularity and enjoyed the fruits of it too. If one exhibition stands out more than another as representing the Edwardian era, it was his silver jubilee exhibition of 1905 held at the Molesworth Hall. There was an appropriate fanfare of trumpets from the press and the exhibition was a triumph, the only shadow being a letter from the Lord Lieutenant's Secretary, Walter Callan, to the artist saying that: 'As you will [see] by tomorrow's papers H.E.[the Earl of Dudley] is ill & cannot leave his room for a couple of days at least.'[37] Never mind, everyone and everything else was in place, which is to say the Lord Lieutenant's wife, her entourage and high fashion. 'Lady Dudley looked very handsome in a brown plush velvet gown and sable tail, stole and hat of brown tulle, and sable tails finished with a brown lace veil . . .' and so on. The press, as usual, went to town in describing the style and fashion of it all. How easy it is to forget that there was no colour photography in newspapers at the time. Readers of the *Figaro and Irish Gentlewoman* were even informed that 'Mrs Vickers, who came in a bath chair . . . looked much stronger'. which was good to know. Evidently the journal could assume its readers would know who Mrs Vickers was – or those who mattered would – tantalising for those who did not. With record crowds attending the exhibition, Alexander, convivial by nature, was in his element, mingling with all and sundry. There may even have been something of a cachet in meeting the artist. A disappointed Sophia C. White of Glen Druid, Shankill wrote to him: 'I came to see your very interesting exhibition of pictures this afternoon, but as you were engaged in conversation with others most of the time, I did not like to interrupt you. I am sure you hardly recollect meeting me, but I remember the day you came to Charleville very well.'[38]

A particular talking point for this exhibition was a large oil entitled *Summer Time on Ireland's Eye, Dublin Bay* that Williams donated to the Countess of Dudley's fund for the establishment of district nurses in the poorest parts of Ireland. It was sold on the Art Union plan and realised the sum of £14. The subject, however, had less to do with the fund than another picture in the exhibition called *An Errand of Mercy*. The painting remains untraced and is known now only because it was chosen to illustrate an article on the Nurses' Fund in a long since vanished magazine called *Lady of the House*.[39] The print quality of the magazine was poor and the painting was reproduced in black and white. Nevertheless, the intentions of the artist are clear. The picture shows to the left a very dilapidated cottage close to a seashore, with a spur of land behind the cottage providing the suggestion of a bay on Achill Island. Two figures, both barefoot, stand near the entrance of the cottage and before them is the district nurse, readily identified by her uniform. To the right of the group, behind the nurse, there is a rowing boat, but it does not appear to have been the nurse's form of transport. It is pulled well up on the shore as if it is currently out of use. It might belong to the owner of the cottage, the implication being perhaps that it is he who is lying ill inside. *Lady of the House* reported in the article that a nurse might travel ten miles to see a patient, with four miles being undertaken by water. We are left to guess as to how the nurse made her journey, just possibly on foot, but it might be that the artist lacked the confidence to paint a horse at such close quarters. One way or another, the few uncluttered elements in the picture, along with the breadth of the beach and the spit of land suggest, unambiguously, the isolation of the place. Most striking about the picture is its simplicity and complete repudiation of anything smacking of sentimentality. In his matter-of-fact realism, Williams differed from what most of his contemporaries produced by way of genre paintings.

The silver jubilee exhibition was by far the most successful the artist ever held, or at least for which records survive, and there is no reason to think any other exceeded it. He had an attendance of 1,147 over the three weeks, and the sale of sixty-two pictures realised £261.14.0.

His pace did not slacken. He continued to tour Ireland – Killarney and Achill Island being his main ports of call – sometimes more than once in a year. He made several trips to London shortly before the war, perhaps as much for social reasons as for painting but he combined both. Ever the restless traveller, he chose to visit Wales in 1908, spending a fortnight there in lodgings at Prestatin. Landscape painter though he might be, to judge from a surviving sketchbook the buildings of north Wales appealed to him as much as its scenery. There was often a comfortable domesticity to his travelling in that Kitty and Alice frequently accompanied him. One wonders at the cost of it all.

He had little reason to worry during those palmy days before the First World War when his earnings from his solo exhibitions remained consistent, with the one exception of 1911 when sales took a precipitous dip to £81.9.0, down from £183.11.6 in 1909. Apart from spending less on advertising than in some other years, the 1911 exhibition differed in a number of ways: it contained a larger proportion of watercolours than usual and in place of louring clouds and storm-dashed coastlines, this time he treated nature in her 'kindlier moods'.

Oil on canvas laid on board of cottage scene. Signed. 14 x 20½ in. (35.6 x 52 cm). This cottage, with its red sandstone or red-brick chimney and roof of straw, is unlike any other cottage known to have been painted by the artist. The old lady in the scene is wearing a white bonnet, not a shawl. It is speculated that this is a cottage along an old toll road in England or Wales.

Double-spread sketch pen over pencil inscribed: 'Dyserth N Wales'. 7 x 9 in. (17.8 x 22.9 cm).

But the answer for the drop in sales this year may lie in what *The Irish Times* noted: 'fewer small pieces than usual'.[40] He probably had a niche market for small pictures, which it may be supposed appealed to the expanding Dublin middle class of the time who occupied the new, smaller suburban houses that were being built in quantity and which were now encircling the older inner city.

That he was extremely effective in generating publicity through most of his career there is no doubt, but his marketing strategy was a different matter. He never seemed to consider that scarcity drives up prices as well as prestige. In the absence of lower-priced items, a small number of high-priced pictures might easily have matched and exceeded as a total what he made from selling many lower-priced ones. Mounting large exhibitions in which the cheap and expensive were hung cheek by jowl may well have been counter-productive. Yet it was a strategy he stuck to throughout his career, using the same very broad pricing structure in all his solo exhibitions. 'I am convinced,' wrote fine art auctioneer John de Vere White, 'that a small number of paintings of quality given space and hung in optimum conditions achieve higher prices,' and he added the corollary: 'Works of lesser value have a better chance of selling well if they are not put in competition with the upper end of the market.'[41] Had he been taken in hand by a gallery or agent, as painters today tend to be, Williams might well have painted much fewer pictures at higher prices, and made more from them.

In 1911 Blackie & Son commissioned him to do a series of watercolour illustrations of Ireland covering the four provinces in their popular series of books entitled *Beautiful –*, which covered Britain and further afield. A sum of 100 guineas was agreed with the artist for the reproduction rights of forty-eight pictures, while he retained the pictures. Stephen Gwynn, a prolific writer with a reputation for travel books, was chosen to provide the brief text. *Beautiful Ireland* was published in separate volumes, each covering a province, and then as a single volume covering all four provinces.

Williams made the best of the publicity opportunity. The forty-eight pictures were duly featured in his one-man exhibition held for three weeks, 20 January–10 February, in his usual venue, 35 Molesworth Street under the same title of 'Beautiful Ireland'. Forty-eight pictures might have been thought sufficient for any artist but, true to form, Williams added almost as many again to produce a catalogue totalling ninety-two.

Blackie & Son were at the cutting edge of colour printing technology which was still in its infancy and attracted much comment. The *Freeman's Journal* was struck by the value of the books: 'At two shillings each the books are marvellous, and a few years ago would not have been possible. The introduction of three-colour process work has revolutionised the illustrating of books.'[42]

Photography was now beginning to rival painting, if not yet to oust it. To take just the province of Leinster, by the turn of the century there were 314 professional photographers in the province as against 222 artists.[43] *The Irish Times* felt compelled to come robustly to the defence of art, asserting that 'No photographic album, even in these days of artistic coloured camera-work, could give the same idea of the beauty of these

Left: Self-caricature: Raphael MacSwigger (alias James Abbot McNeil Whistler).
Right: In the presence of Lady Aberdeen.

scenes in all corners of Ireland. We refer, of course, to the selection of views; the merest sketcher has an advantage over the photographer in the choice of perspective, capturing a sublime little delicacy of effect where a camera would find only something commonplace or insignificant.' The paper continued: 'An artist like Mr Williams, of course, lifts the thing into a different plane. For his special quality is the realisation of that softness of atmosphere which gives tender and haunting glory to the aspect of the country in Ireland.'[44] The public were of the same opinion as the press and the exhibition realised £188.14.0 on the sale of forty-three pictures, one of his best results.

As with his writing, in his sketching too Alexander was willing to poke fun at himself. We have seen how he could write amusingly of his trials and tribulations during his excursion along the Antrim coast. Equally he enjoyed doing humorous doodles at his own expense, a number of which he saved. Perhaps of most interest is a caricature which he pasted into his exhibition book of 1911 but which is likely to have been done earlier. It depicts a dishevelled painter, round faced, scant of hair on the top of his head but thick around the sides, and with a floriferous moustache. The sketch is surely of himself as it matches his own appearance in all respects. If that much is obvious, the caption is a puzzle and requires explanation. It reads: 'Raphael MacSwigger (post-impressionist) and the source of his inspiration – constant good spirits'. Alexander was never known as Raphael, much less MacSwigger. If he ever had a nickname it was probably Miggs, at least this is the name he gives himself on another cartoon. So what sense can be made of him using the name Raphael MacSwigger? Brendan Rooney has persuasively suggested that the caption is a thinly disguised reference to the great American painter James McNeill Whistler:

> Significant in the context of Alexander Williams's little sketch . . . is the fact that Whistler was held up, lampooned and in some cases pilloried by sections of the more academic art fraternity as the epitome of the self-aggrandising avant-garde artist. One reading would be that Williams was lampooning Whistler, albeit retrospectively, but perhaps more importantly, cocking a snook at the avant-garde that Whistler was seen to represent . . . Alternatively, and more plausibly, one might consider the drawing to be mischievous and fanciful rather than malicious. Williams's caricature certainly looks more like its creator than it does like Whistler. I suspect that he was merely casting himself, impossibly, in the role of Whistler for comic effect.[45]

Certainly Williams had plenty of reason to have Whistler on his mind, if not in 1911 in the 1880s when there was all the brouhaha following Whistler exhibiting his work at the Dublin Sketching Club. Williams was in the thick of that exhibition and as Honorary Secretary of the club it was his function subsequently to write to Whistler and inform him that he had been elected an honorary member; 'with acclamation' he wrote, rather disingenuously, as there had been fierce resentment shown by a number of members. The name Raphael could be interpreted as a reference to the Pre-Raphaelites with whom Whistler had a connection through his friendship with Dante Gabriel Rossetti; and there were pictures of Whistler's which some critics regarded as showing characteristics of the Pre-Raphaelites. Significantly perhaps, the first exhibition of the so-called Impressionist painters was held in 1874, the same year as the founding of the sketching club. Whistler had been invited to participate with the Impressionists by no less a figure than Degas, but refused. This might be the reason for Williams putting 'Post-Impressionist' on his cartoon. In any case Whistler, even if he belonged to no school but his own, as he claimed, was nevertheless susceptible to modern trends. The reference to constant good spirits perhaps has less to do with alcohol as such, despite the picture on the easel and the scattered bottles, than simply the notion that Whistler was a *bon viveur*, as was Williams. In his cartoon he was surely also cocking a snook at the avant-garde, of which he was never a part. Ultimately, the cartoon tells us more about Williams than Whistler, showing that he had a delightful sense of the ridiculous, even to the point of sending himself up by making this far-fetched comparison.

Likewise, one would not have thought to associate Williams with either Impressionism or post-Impressionism, yet surprisingly the press occasionally made such a comparison, praising the artist precisely for *not* being an Impressionist. 'I confess that what pleased me best in Mr Williams' collection,' wrote the correspondent for the *Irish Society and Social Review* with evident feeling, 'is the entire absence of "impressionist" pictures. No more deleterious school was ever started or nourished than that of which we

Watercolour of beached craft in broiling sunshine, Signed. 5.9 x 13 in. (15 x 33 cm).

now happily see the shroud.'[46] *The Irish Times* took a similar line, even to the point of picking out two pictures both entitled *My Garden* and to remark of them: 'The artist seems to be poking some quiet fun at the impressionists.'[47] It seems, however, extremely unlikely that he had any such intention in mind. We cannot examine the pictures as they remained untraced, but it is more likely that he had simply produced work that was slap-dash. What the press seem to have been driving at was not Impressionism in any precise sense but simply having a 'dig' at the avant-garde and modernists in general, and using Williams, a straightforwardly representational artist, as representing what they admired. We know that Williams kept in touch with modern trends in art by the exhibitions he attended, but what he thought of them or of individual artists he left entirely unrecorded.

That said, the artist was not immune to changing fashions. It is not fanciful to see in the spangled iridescence of some of his later sea pictures the influence of Impressionism. Similarly, the broad brush technique he adopted in later life is so marked as to indicate that it was not simply the progression of age but a conscious response to changing fashions when a less rigid and formal style of representational art, aligned with a drive for greater spontaneity, was coming into vogue. He was much given to experimenting all his life and produced work in widely differing styles. Self-taught, he had no one role model but picked ideas from what he found around him.

Another cartoon shows him meekly listening with downcast eyes to 'Ishbel' who towers over him, while she says: 'I'd like something really nice Mr Williams – something about fifteen shillings.' Ishbel is of course Lady Aberdeen, one of his most generous patrons. Part of the joke here is the fact that he would never have dreamt of calling her so familiarly as by her first name and it is a fair bet she never laid eyes on the cartoon. The Aberdeens not only faithfully attended his exhibitions and bought his work, but on occasion provided what would now be called soundbites for the press. In one visitors' book, knowing full well it would be taken up by the press, Lady Aberdeen wrote: 'Very pleased to have the opportunity of a sight of the beautiful scenery of the West and South-West, in the midst of the Dublin Season, and much indebted to Mr Williams for reproducing it so faithfully. Ishbel Aberdeen.'[48]

'Dear Friend,' began a letter from a Nan Doyne living in London in response to an earlier exhibition, 'I was so glad to see such a fine notice of your pictures in the paper, & that Lady Aberdeen had been helping to make you a millionaire, more power to your elbow!'[49] He certainly never became a millionaire or anything like it. Nevertheless, he had made a living where others have failed, and he understood, as others understood, how much he had achieved through patronage. What he could not anticipate, no more than anyone else, was that the convulsion of a world war, the upheavals in Irish politics and concomitant changes in Irish art were about to sweep away his world and the living he made from it.

CHAPTER 14

The Achill Diary

Cliffs along the Atlantic Drive, Achill. Oil on board. Signed. 10¼ x 18¼ in. (26 x 46.4 cm).

All of a sudden in May 1899, at the age of fifty-five, not young for what he was about to embark on, the artist obtained a lease for sixty-five years on a ruined three-room cottage from Mrs Marion Pike.[1] It stood on 3 acres of land on the edge of Bleanaskill Bay (also called Breanaskill). Marion Pike was probably glad to get a tenant as the meadow, and even the cottage itself, was liable to flooding. It had been empty for years, previously occupied by a priest, Fr Michael Gallagher, to whom it had been given by William Pike in 1847.

By 1899 the cottage was quite uninhabitable and its surrounding acres had lain untouched for a decade or more. The place was a windswept wilderness when Williams took possession of it. Yet for all its drawbacks it is easy to see what attracted him. By any reckoning Bleanaskill Bay is a beautiful, even idyllic, spot. It is a curling, sheltered bay set in Achill Sound, protected from the worst excesses of the Atlantic weather by rising ground on the outer rim of the bay and beyond that by Curraune Hill on the mainland. On the island itself, behind the bay, is a long panorama of undulating hills that slope down to the water's edge. The bay is tidal, with extensive mudflats exposed at low tide; as the water recedes sea birds of many kinds arrive to feed, their myriad calls a recurring feature of the bay.

What possessed Williams to take on this challenge? He could just as well have continued staying at guest houses and hotels, as he had done on Achill for decades and which he continued to do around the rest of Ireland. He might have continued to concentrate solely on painting (to the likely advantage of his art). He had every opportunity to allow others to administer to his needs. He was the only man in a household of four women: his wife, his unemployed spinster daughter and two full-time maids.[2] A surfeit, it might be thought, when it came to meeting one man's needs. His brother Willie with a wife and two or three young children managed to get along with just one maid. How *did* the women, Kitty and Alice, occupy themselves? They cannot have been overburdened with household chores. So they amused themselves with endless rounds of tea parties – an 'At Home' book of Kitty's survives, giving the days of when her friends had their visiting days – calling on other ladies of suitable class, gentlefolk, and by engaging in 'good works' (certainly during the First World War); and with gardening.

On at least one occasion the three of them, Alexander, his wife and daughter, went to Achill unaccompanied and he recorded that '. . . as we brought no servant down it was a "squatter's simple life" and everybody worked for the general good.'[3] It sounds like it was quite a novelty for all concerned. On another occasion he records going down to Bleanaskill with one of the maids, '. . . where we set to work to tidy up the house, light fires, air beds etc.' in advance of his wife and daughter's arrival. Alexander might have passed for a model modern husband.

There is nothing, of course, quite like having a place of one's own. Bleanaskill Lodge when it was eventually completed was a big house by Achill standards, with five or six bedrooms, and all the rooms on both floors facing the bay; corridors on both levels ran the length of the house on the opposite side. Large as it was, it did not prove quite large

SKETCHING AT ROWARDENNAN, "LOCH LOMOND."

The artist with his trademark umbrella, a photograph he used in at least one of his exhibition catalogues.

enough. A room on the ground floor designated for the two maids was divided into two for their own privacy. Williams was immensely proud of what he had built and liked to give both addresses to the press – Bleanaskill Lodge, Achill Sound, and his Dublin address at 4 Hatch Street.[4] He evidently fed the press with enthusiastic descriptions of the place, and the press duly responded by waxing lyrical about his 'island home', clearly never having been near the place. Whatever he may have thought of it, by no stretch of the imagination could the house have been considered attractive. It was a barracks of a house, stolid, with small windows, presenting a plain facade. The magic lay not in the building but in its situation on the water's edge, where weather, tide, and the sea never seem quite the same two days running, with the weather moving, often within the hour, from one extreme to the other; dramatic, even exhilarating, storms giving way to the softest of days with glass reflections in the bay and the maturing woodland and ornamental garden providing the otherwise undistinguished building with its sense of peace and seclusion.

It is a two-storeyed house no longer but a much remodelled modern bungalow, the upper storey having been destroyed in a fire in 1983. Remarkably, against the odds, the garden survives, in a much developed form; the only garden surviving on Achill that was laid out before the First World War.

Williams was a popular figure on the island, easily identified at any distance by his giant outsize gingham umbrella, a versatile item. Apart from providing shelter when he was painting, it sometimes served as a makeshift sail when he went out boating. A photograph of the artist painting on a lake shore in Scotland, which he used on the back of an exhibition catalogue, gives an idea of the extent of the umbrella.

Group of islanders set against backdrop of Slievemore. Oil over pencil on board. 8 x 12¼ in. (20.3 x 31.1 cm). This size of board would have been typical of what the artist would have kept with his travelling box of colours. *Provenance: family collection.*

On Achill he was known as 'the sketcher', a term that islanders with long memories would recall if his name was mentioned, even as late as the 1970s. Old-timers could then still remember him and sometimes too their children, now elderly themselves, whose fathers had worked for him. Even today the term 'the sketcher' lingers in the conversation of local historian John O'Shea. To the islanders with their subsistence way of life, sketching appeared as a harmless if eccentric occupation. Alexander meant more to them by being a valued employer. When he missed out on going to Achill in 1908 (when he went to Donegal), and returned the following year, as he made his first walk from Achill Sound to Bleanaskill he was gratified to receive 'many hearty handshakes from the neighbours and people on my way, many welcoming me "home" after my absence'.[5]

Ever the diarist, just months after beginning his ornithological diary in 1907, Alexander started a separate notebook for what he called 'Achill Natural History Notes & Diary' which he kept going until 1913. It is unusual in being the memoir of an artist who both lived and worked with the islanders at the beginning of the twentieth century. It provides wildly contrasting vignettes of island life; quaint period snapshots of a small affluent community before the First World War, with visual descriptions of the island presented in an almost paradisiacal light, described against a backdrop of the stark, elemental world of the islanders with whom he worked.

The diary starts with that elemental world, with the artist arriving on the island in April 1907 and finding the 'people complaining of the delay, owing to the harsh weather, in planting their potatoes. The ridges are prepared and covered thickly and evenly with

Oil on board, cabin with Slievemore in the background. Signed. 7 x 14 in. (17.8 x 35.6 cm).

Sea Wrack for the reception of the tubers, giving the fields a curious autumn coloured appearance.'[6] Things hardly looked up thereafter: 'The summer of 1907 will be long remembered for its wretched bad weather and want of sunshine. Achill suffered greatly and at one time it was feared that there would be a bad failure of potatoes. There was a melancholy falling off in the number of visitors to the Island and all hotel keepers and drivers of vehicles for hire complained bitterly of the loss of business.'[7] Little wonder if the artist often showed in his pictures louring clouds and the prospect of rain descending on the landscape.

Emigration was waked as deaths were waked, there being so little expectation of emigrants ever returning. Even seasonal emigrations were waked, such was the sense of dislocation they caused. On the inside of the front cover of the diary, Alexander pasted a sheet in his own handwriting, a poem composed, he tells us, by a Miss Keppel from Glendarary, when she was leaving the island. 'Frequently sung at wakes by the Achill folk or when leaving for England or America,' he wrote beneath it.

Achill Island
Isle of the Eagle farewell to thy mountains
With all their bright blossom of purple and gold
No more shall I sit by thy murmuring fountains
Or from they bold heights the Atlantic behold.

The references to Achill being the isle of the eagle suggest the poem was quite old. Eagles were sufficiently scarce at the time of the diary for Williams to report hearsay that one had been spotted on the island.

As the railway line to Achill was now in full swing, Williams could make swift and regular trips to the island direct from Dublin. His spirits always rose in anticipation of

'Toilers of the Sea' exhibited at RHA, 1902. Signed. Oil on canvas. 14 x 24 in. (35.6 x 60 cm).

Oil on canvas. *Written on back in pencil in artist's hand*: 'On the beach at Dugort Achill Island Co. Mayo, A. Williams, 4 Hatch Street, Dublin'. 7 x 13.8 in. (17.8 x 35 cm). A frequent subject with the artist, he treated it in many ways.

returning to Achill. Getting up around 5 a.m. he would catch the 7 a.m. Limited Mail Train leaving Broadstone Station, arriving at Achill Sound by 1.15 p.m. – a rail journey that unfortunately cannot be made today, fast or slow.

Once on the island he travelled by foot largely by choice. He never learned how to drive, and there is no record of him ever using a bicycle, though a visitor who rode one was thought worthy of comment. While the lodge was being built he would put up at the sound, where Mrs Robins ran a B&B along with the post office. For preference he would walk from the post office at the sound to Bleanaskill, a distance of about two miles. He would then foot it back in the evening, after a day's work. It was less than the daily slog of Jimmy Masterson, the postman, who, Williams noted, had a six-mile walk daily from the post office at the sound to the office at Cloughmore. For Williams, walking and birdwatching were the pleasurable habits of a lifetime, which any faster form of locomotion would only have diminished. Only infrequently, when he had materials or visitors most usually, does he mention taking one of the local cars, meaning a horse-drawn conveyance. The impression is that his regular walk from and to the sound and Bleanaskill Bay was often made in fits and starts as he became absorbed in the antics first of one bird, then another: 'A Common [*syn.* Corn] Bunting was singing on the telegraph wire and was so ridiculously tame that I stood underneath and listened to his curious song. A Yellowhammer was so tame on the road that I passed him and could have touched him with a stick and outstretched arm.'[8] Elsewhere he mentions '12 common buntings about'.[9] Common once but now extinct over the whole of Ireland. Its song was as familiar on Achill as was once the call of the corncrake, a species for which Achill was once a stronghold.

Employing local labour on an ad hoc basis meant the building of the lodge was spread over many years. Labour could be scarce; even as late as the 1950s the ESB could record that: 'Once the migratory labour season started, neither quality nor quantity was available . . . farming conditions on Achill are almost non-existent and migratory labour, which originally arose from economic conditions, is now almost a hallowed tradition.' (In passing it is worth mentioning that the ESB once operated a 54-hour week.)

As men came and went, Alexander came to rely most on his neighbour Michael Corrigan: 'A most satisfactory and conscientious workman and gives splendid value for his wages. 2/6 per day and feeds himself!' But he had other calls on his time: 'Corrigan is away today and tomorrow road mending. He has a contract and the county surveyor is expected any day, so things must be in order for him.'[10] Another diversion, if a temporary one, for Michael was fishing, which appears to have been something of an experiment for him: 'He has been up and out fishing for three nights with poor luck. Half a hundred weight of herrings & mackerel was all they caught on Friday and 6 herrings on Saturday. So he is going to chuck the job and stick to his work.'

Williams records three days in a row when he had as many as six men working for him, probably as many as he employed at one time with most of the labour coming from just over the fields. 'The men do more work when they see me take a spade or shovel in hand and cheer them on.' He made a list of the men he had working for him in the summer of 1907: 'Old Tom Corrigan quarrying. Martin McGinty of Ashleam stone mason. Brien Masterson of Sharkeens. Tho. O'Donnell my neighbour over the river on the left. Young Cooney, one of my next door neighbours on right. Young Tom Corrigan, son of the Contractor, Breanaskill Bridge, and "Michael the Fool" a poor half clothed creature but a strong worker.'[11]

The primitive maternity care of those days, home births attended by a local woman, if a nurse was not available, and the problems associated with late pregnancies meant the likes of Michael the Fool, so called, were alas only too common. It is doubtful if Michael got a living wage out of his efforts. He would hardly have got more than 'Jimmy [Doogan] a curious ½ witted poor fellow who lives across the Bay of Breanaskill on the hill, I have engaged to help at 6d per day. It is astounding the size and weight of the creels of turf that this gaunt half starved creature will carry on his back from the mountain bogs on to the main road and then a mile and a half to where he lives without laying down his load. He is very useful when in the humour and can turn over a lot of ground with [a] spade.'[12]

Alexander employed children too, lots of them, no issues then with health and safety. Children worked at home and in the fields as a matter of course: '5 boys busy collecting stones off the beach to fill up a hollow ditch where water lodges. I gave them buckets of zinc and put handles to a box on each side and there was quite a competition amongst them to have the honour of carrying this hand barrow.'[13] He does not say how those without these hand barrows were expected to transport the stone, bundled in their arms perhaps, nor did he record what the boys were paid, as he did with adults: 'Martin McGinty is building up wall at entrance and Johnny McNeeley for half day is helping him. McGinty 3/- McNeeley 1/6.'[14] This would seem to have been the range for a day's work unless you were offering transport as well: 'Yesterday I had a young man and his cart and horse drawing stones all day from the quarry other side of the Bay. Paid 6/- . Today I had a stone mason building without mortar or cement a wall to widen the road opposite my entrance. I paid him 3/- for the day and another man who was not a stone mason but as good and a quicker worker 2/6. They are very clever at this kind of work, chipping off bits and thinning the stones with a heavy hammer and before night they had about 4½ feet built. Long stones were laid across from one side to the other, they called them "throughers" for binding the stones together.'[15]

What made Williams an unusual employer was that he was prepared to try everything himself. He had a high respect for physical work and those engaged in it. Here he is involved in a day's work at the end of summer:

Sunshine very hot & the landscape looking most beautiful in that glamour that seems peculiar to the island at times. Johnny McNeeley hard at work selecting and dressing stones for the railing piers. I tried my hand at it, but it's hard work the stonemason's heavy hammer tires the wrist. I did a good bit of stone building myself as I had to raise the ground about 2½ feet inside the wicket gate. I collected all the large stones I could lay my hands on and built them in tiers shovelling in earth and sods or scraws as they call them. The small bits of stone that the masons put into the interstices when building they call 'spawls', a word they use very frequently.[16]

There is no doubt Williams retained an astonishing amount of energy well into his later years. Here he is at the age of sixty-three buying a sizeable sheet of glass at Achill Sound and being quite prepared to transport it himself on foot, and this in a strong wind:

Morning fair but strong Westerly gale blowing. Went to Sweeney's Store at the Sound and got a large pane of glass 36X22 which I carried on foot in the teeth of the gale to Breanaskill where Corrigan and self put it in position in the corrugated roof as a skylight to lighten passage. Men lashing away all day at the big fence to the road. With Corrigan we prepared a stone foundation for a big concrete tank 7 feet by 4 to be nearly 6 feet high. I am determined that there shall be a good supply of pure rain water and this tank ought to hold about 600 gallons . . . Hanging doors, very busy all day.[17]

He then had the return journey at the end of the day to his B&B at the post office at the sound; a fagging walk, he admits, in muggy weather.

Items for the house came from wherever he could find them. From a sale held in the yard of Dublin Castle, Williams picked up the door of 'the "Chief Clerk" of some department there and I bought it and others at a sale in the Castle yard'. The chief clerk's door became the back door at Bleanaskill. He enjoyed doing joinery work in the house and likewise renovating second-hand furniture, picking stuff up at bargain prices. This entry from 1911 gives an impression of his life on the island in the round:

On the 31st of May when the Friends' Institute was clearing out of the premises their lease having expired, I bought a fine old Dresser for 5/- which I sent on to Achill Sound. I gave it a coat of priming on Monday and another today. I had it put in the open at the end of house in the sun and it was quite a treat to get at it with a pound oil brush and white paint. It was so different to sitting up in my studio in smoky Dublin painting pictures. After that was finished I broke loose with a large tin of paint and painted doors etc wherever required. The sun was glittering the surface of the incoming tide, Skylarks were singing in the clear air over my field, and bright clouds were sailing across a blue fleecy sky, and my neighbours might be seen weeding their potatoes alongside vivid green patches of young Rye. About 4 o'clock I put on a pair of old boots without stockings and took a trip down the Bay wading in the shallow streams on the look out for flat fish, but met with very few. Ringed Plover, 3 Herring Gulls, a party of Blackheaded Gulls also some Common Gulls were on the sandy flats.[18]

Mutton and fish were available locally, but not beef. The parcel post was so reliable that meat sent from Dublin could confidently be expected to arrive fresh. The diary often combined the practicalities of life with enthusiastic observations of the scenery around the bay, written with an artist's eye for colour:

> I met a cart full of splendid mackerel caught early that morning and I bought 3 for 3d.
> I was offered by Anthony Patten who owned them 16 for a shilling. We had a fine
> beefsteak pie for dinner all the way from Dublin, for we cannot get beef in Achill but
> Parcel Post is convenient. After we all sat in front of the house in the shade. The sky
> was cloudless and Currane Hill stood out in all its loveliness of greens, pinks and
> browns. Glencoe Point opposite was brilliantly lighted up, the roofs of the white
> cottages mellow brown, vivid green patches of cultivation, grey rocks and near the
> water line a band of reddish seaweed. Derreen Hill opposite showed the weather
> beaten rocks peeping out from the burnished green and brown undulations of its upper
> parts and the closely scattered cottages and grey stone walls dividing the cultivated
> parts are mapped out all the way down to the water. Green of every shade in the
> growing crops may be seen, and the whole hill is reflected in the little bay. In the
> immediate foreground is our foreshore and little boat and I am writing this in lovely
> perfume from the white clover spreading from my feet to the sea wall. Some day I
> must put up wire netting and make a lovely little tennis ground of it.[19]

He never did, of course; Bleanaskill was never that kind of garden. He had the greatest difficulty in securing what he had: 'It is a constant battle to keep out the wild animals cows, horses, donkeys, pigs, geese, they have had the run of this place for years and cannot understand why they are kept out. A pig, notwithstanding all our precautions, squeezed in early this morning and nosed up the sod in the drive.'[20]

A major part of the attraction of Bleanaskill was the opportunity to create a garden from scratch and he lovingly filled pages of the diary with his battles to do so. The windswept meadow was devoid of trees. Williams set about making windbreaks, native planting for wildlife and adding ornamental trees and shrubs to his taste. Coming from the vicinity of Clontarf he must have been very familiar with the cabbage palm (*Cordyline australis*),[21] which abounds there and indeed is a widespread introduction in Ireland. It has a long, thin, bare trunk, on top of which cluster its sword-shaped leaves. The palm Williams planted at Bleanaskill sometime before the First World War now stands at 11 m (36 feet) and its trunk has a circumference of 2.06 m, making it by far the largest specimen in County Mayo.[22]

The newcomer to gardening in the west, and on an island at that, soon finds what will survive and what thrives in the exposed conditions. The old Victorian reliable, the fast-growing Monterey cypress (*Cupressus macrocarpa*),[23] Williams successfully planted in a group in what became the lawn on the northwest side of the lodge, beyond which is a small ornamental pond. At one time the Montereys must have been the most dominant trees in the landscape, and though much ravaged by time, a number still remain as a feature of the garden. Another pond he made near the water's edge appears to have since been filled in. 'I want to hurry up a jungle round the artificial pond I am making in the sea corner of the field,' he wrote, 'where I hope to encourage birds to resort.' He had exactly the right idea: native species in abundance to provide both food and cover.

Gardeners are always interested to know what does well in other people's gardens. There are no surprises as to what Williams found would grow in the unpromising conditions with which he started. Top of the list was the common alder (*Alnus glutinosa*), as tough as an old boot, thriving in the wet, and when once established, tolerating dry conditions just as well. No species is more versatile. He had difficulty with getting sallies (*Salix*) established, most likely because they dried out in summer. Other species he could rely on: escallonia, euonymous, fuchsia, hydrangea, thorn and the far too invasive *Rhododendron ponticum* are what one would expect, all Achill stalwarts resistant to salt and storms. Some of the plants he chose for Bleanaskill were novelties to him, but few would probably surprise us today. He eulogises over plants that he has recently discovered, the Chilean fire bush for one, *Lobelia cardinalis* for another, exotics to him but species that would be familiar to almost any gardener in Ireland today.

What is most striking is that almost everything he planted was home grown, if not by himself then by somebody else. That was how things were done; like-minded owners swapped plants or simply gave them away as a mark of friendship, a common practice when garden centres were non-existent and nurseries far apart. When he had the chance to visit an estate, Williams would make a point of seeking out the head gardener and requesting material. He did much of his gardening the old fashioned, painstaking way: establishing nursery stock from cuttings, growing on small plants, garnering slips. He experimented and learned from his mistakes, as every gardener does. He found, as might be expected, that small plants and cuttings planted directly into prepared banks and ground around the perimeter were likely to fail. The tough conditions required plants to be well established before 'planting out'. His failure rate was enormous. Marauding animals, drought and the fact that he was often absent were all reasons for a high casualty rate.

It did not deter him. In among the observations on birds, he filled pages of his diary with plants he got from far and wide: 'I have planted 6 small plants of Arbutus from Killarney [probably from the Lake Hotel], and received a present of 6 rooted plants of the Chilean holly (*Desfontanea spinosa*) from General Clive's place Rock House, Ballycroy. Received a bale of plants from Maddens Nursery Ballymurray Roscommon. Common Bunting singing and a good many Song Thrushes are observed about the gardens.'[24] The following day he posts off two of the Chilean hollies to Geoffrey Trumbull at Beechwood, Malahide; and records planting the same day '30 Privet and 30 Laurels, also 4 Apple trees and 4 Currant bushes', adding at the end of this diary entry: 'An exquisite beautifully still moonlight night, the Bay like a calm lake full of reflection.'

Plants came and went by circuitous routes. 'I interviewed Moran the gardener at Glendarary and he promised me 50 wild Cherry trees. He also pointed out in the bog a large patch of Pernettya which a nurse brought from Scotland years ago and planted at this place where it had increased and spread all about. It has white flowers in spring and white berries in autumn.' The very next day he notes in his diary: 'I sent off by parcel post a lot of young Rhododendrons & Pernettya to my friend J. Perry living near Tintagel, Cornwall.' So Pernettya, taken from Scotland, planted on Achill, ends up in Cornwall. In return Perry sends over a parcel of plants (unspecified); and so it goes on, with the Glendarary estate providing the bulk of what Williams needed, and Sheridan down in Dugort helping out, even preparing nursery stock for him. Few are the occasions when Williams reports obtaining plants from commercial nurseries. This is remarkable considering that the number of trees and shrubs (even if only whips and nursery stock) that he planted ran into thousands. A rare instance was when he took delivery of 100 trees from Tully's nurseries at Hollymount, County Mayo, consisting of alder, ash, sycamore and what was a surprising and surely ill-judged choice, Lombardy poplar.[25]

Including the sea front, the perimeter of his property, in round figures, amounted to about 475 yards (435 metres), all of which had to be secured. Along one flank on the southwest side he built a tapering bulwark of stone and soil, sods on top of that and planted it off, adding stakes and barbed wire for good measure, no small undertaking: 'Walked out to Breanaskill in the teeth of a furious S.W. gale, heavy showers. The big sod fence along the road being so deep going down into my field, [it] is taking a great deal of labour to build. Men have been working hard at it all day. We are taking the sods out of my field and digging them between the old rusty furrows. I amused the men by telling them that the sods with the "Whiskers" were best! They are the tufts of rushes and stick out when placed in position just like whiskers. I helped the men taking my spade and digging sods or between the handles of the hand barrow taking the load up to the sod builder Michael who is quite an artist in his way. Weather cleared in afternoon.' And he gives an idea of the size of it: 'All hands then were transferred to the shore where the intended big fence over 100 yards long, 4 feet broad at base, 5 feet high from outside and 18 inches at top is to be constructed at the road, cutting off I hope all access of wild animals, principally sheep from the field outside. The men work with a will cutting huge sods and placing the grassy side out, finishing off the top with a broad grassy "Scraw" saddle shape over 2 feet long. Some of them with plenty of "Whiskers".'

The scale of planting the 'fence' is indicated in an entry for Friday 21 October 1910: 'Lovely weather again. Exquisite reflections in the waters of the Sound from the surrounding mountains. Corrigan with horse and cart gravelling the walks. I have them now nearly completed. I have had a terribly hard day's work planting 500 Thorn Quicks on top of fence all round the house on the land side, 800 strong Fuchsia cuttings, 300 Escallonias, and a lot of cuttings of Hydrangeas.'

What might have been considered a sensitive task for Williams was informing the islanders that he intended closing off a right of way that ran through his property to the

Study of figures at an Achill Fair Day

bay, proposing to provide an alternative route parallel to it. He seems to have handled the matter sensitively and no resentment was shown:

> There has been a right of way to the shore for over 20 years down the path past my house. I have had a talk with the people who use it, drawing seaweed by cart from the boats at the mouth of the little river in winter and I have told them that I mean to close it up but will make a new road for them giving a passage by the river outside my grounds. They seem satisfied and I am doing my best to give the new passage a gentle slope all the way up to the road.[26]

He could be well satisfied with their reaction: 'The passing country people are astonished as the right of way is being closed up but they cordially greet us with "God speed the work".'[27]

To an extent that seems astonishing now, in building and gardening, items were used and re-used, and constantly and painstakingly repaired rather than discarded. From the local Rector, the Rev. Thomas Boland, Williams receives 'a present of an old wheelbarrow without a wheel'. Some present, one might think, but Williams tarts the thing up by making new legs for it and fitting a wheel that his sister 'Liz brought from Dublin'. Repairing wheelbarrows was a running theme: 'The wheelbarrow I borrowed from Tom Corrigan came to grief, one leg breaking off short near the top and I had to set about repairing it. I got a bent piece off the old stem of a Rhododendron which I bored with a bit and brace for a bolt. A rusty nut on the old barrow gave me trouble, and not until I put a square thin plate of iron under it and lighted a little fire of sticks on the nut, and then poured a little lamp oil on it, was I able to knock it off. I got the old bolt through the new leg and tightened it up with a wrench, making a sound job of it.' When all else failed he was prepared on at least one occasion to make a wheelbarrow from scratch. He would turn his hand to anything that required doing, even, as he records in the same entry, taking on 'another kind of art work for the Contractor Tom Corrigan by painting the [newly installed] Post Office Letterbox at my gate a regulation coat of Red Lead according to contract'. Surely the only instance on record of an artist painting a public letterbox.

For all the reluctance Williams showed in not discarding or wasting things, he had little sense of conservation as we would understand the term. Gravel for making concrete for the house Williams got locally from the bay and he even mentions going out in his boat to collect gravel from Bleanaskill Bridge – activities not likely to enhance the environment, and if doing so was not illegal then, it would be so now. Taking advantage of a high tide, on one occasion he sent two men off in a yawl 'away round the opposite point [from Bleanaskill] and then round the farther one and quarried out of the face of the rocks a fine boat load of stone. They were roundly abused by 2 viragos who have houses close by, who told them they had no business to be taking away the stones.'[28] It would be hard to disagree with the ladies.

While lime for the plastering of the house was burnt locally by Tom Corrigan, supplies sometimes were delivered directly into the bay: 'This evening I saw a white sailed yawl beating up from Achill Sound heaving laden as the tide was near the full. She was single manned and steered into a cove between Cooney's & my house. She had a cargo of sharp sand ordered by Corrigan for plastering and came all the way across from Currane Hill although [the wind was] blowing very hard.'[29] A white sail, as opposed to pink or red, was thought worthy of mention.

After his spring visit in 1907, Williams returned to Achill in the first week of August, the lodge having remained undisturbed in the interval: 'On entering the house I found that a pair of swallows had built a nest in a corner of the bay window and it contained 5 eggs as well'.[32] The opportunity to observe the nest at such close quarters became a running saga incorporated in his bird notes for several weeks. By 10 August the eggs had hatched. Williams had no compunction about disturbing the nest: 'On putting my finger into the Swallows' nest I found a number of warm fluffy little youngsters.' Little by little the adult birds got used to Williams' presence. They learned to come in by the window he left open for them, although 'if I show myself she make[s] a single loud note of warning exactly as one hears the Swallow make at sight of a hawk and instantly her brood leave off twittering and become perfectly silent'.

On 26 August, he notes: 'The warm sunny weather brought a fine supply of flies, and I noticed that one of the parents was very particular in giving each its share of food, not feeding the big yellow mouths indiscriminately but starting at one end fed each in succession.' Even though the young were now almost fledged the success of the brood was far from being a foregone conclusion:

Aug 28
This has been a terrible day for the poor Swallows owing to the storm. Although the parents did their best, there were very long intervals between the feeding of the young

and the supply of insect food was very short . . . Doesn't it seem incredible at this date August 28th that these tender little fledglings in a few weeks' time will join their kindred and set off on a voyage to the great unknown?'

It took twenty-two days from when Williams had found the eggs to the fledglings vacating the nest, an especially dangerous time for the youngsters.

Aug 30
Two youngsters remain rather neglected by the parents who are much too busy feeding the 3 outside to look after the weaklings. I got up to the nest to examine them when one flew straight out of the opening. The other tried to do it but fell short and struck the glass where I caught it and took it outside . . . A Rook happened to alight on a post quite close when both Swallows vigorously attacked him, pursuing him and making lunges to strike him. Each time the Swallow almost struck him, he jerked down in his flight to escape and gave a hoarse croak . . .

   Heard the first Whimbrel this evening.
Waders, Greenshanks 4, Redshanks, Dunlin, Curlew, Seapie, Ring Plovers, very numerous and bay quite lively every day a flock of nearly 200 Redshanks. 6 Hoody Crows.

We hear no more of the fate of the swallows hatched in the lodge. Perhaps some survived to make the arduous journey to Africa and back again – and perhaps their descendants are among the swallows that still come to our shores, albeit in much reduced numbers.

   Another creature to prompt his concern occurred when 'A greyhound caught a hare and ran along the strand with it. The squealing of the poor animal was heartrending to hear. I got a rake and dashed out in pursuit. The hound leaped over the stone wall at Cooney's and dropped the hare in a potato furrow where I found it dead and brought it home for hare soup.'[30] Williams was not anti-blood sports. He would take out his gun from time to time: 'Shot 2 Twites for my brother Willie in Dublin,' he records. On another occasion he 'got a shot at the Starlings this evening with my walking stick gun and charge of No. 10 shot, killed 9 all in very interesting plumage. Grey with the blackwhite [sic] spotted feathers moulting through.' He turned some or all of them 'into skins', the usual point of the exercise. Birds of prey were of particular interest to him. They were constantly hunted on Achill as elsewhere. An otter shot by Michael Corrigan Williams was turned into a muff. Such things were à la mode, as note the arrival of Madame Fanny Moody, of Moody–Manners Opera Company fame, at Williams' twenty-seventh picture exhibition in 1907 'wearing pale grey voile, with diamond-shaped discs of silk embroidery around the skirt, and a moleskin coat and muff',[31] the very height of fashion.

   But by this time Williams' interest in shooting had largely run its course, overtaken by gardening. He could hardly get enough of it. Had all his plants survived, he would have had an impenetrable jungle, not a woodland and garden. But the failure rate remained high. On his return to Bleanaskill in 1909, he recorded that he

> . . . was very much disappointed to see that my 'Nursery' in the field seemed bare and that my fine Fuschia hedge of which I was so proud had almost disappeared. Tom Corrigan put it down to the frost but the neighbours told me that the brute had been driving his cattle into the place in my absence and every thing had been nibbled close . . . Where things planted had the most protection from the South West Wind they flourished accordingly, and where exposed, showed signs of failure . . . Veronicas had all completely disappeared. Rhododendrons all sprouting and seeming to be accommodating themselves to perfectly exposed conditions. The trees that have succeeded best of all – and it is a lesson to me for planting in exposed places – are the Alders. But oh! The slowness of waiting for growth from cuttings nibbled by cattle. I cannot find any trace of the great quantity of cuttings of all kinds I put into the bare turfy fences all round.
>
> One great success. Tree Mallows some young plants I stuck in at Doogans shed are 6 feet high with stems nearly as thick as my wrist! Another success was the Escallonia, where not nibbled they have done well in the most trying and exposed places.[32]

When he returned in 1910 he found the opposite problem: 'My first sight of Breanaskill was a surprise because after the wet season and no cattle having trespassed, the whole place was smothered in tall rank grass and covered with flowering weeds.' Gardening with long absences can only be partially successful. But little by little he imposed some structure on the 3 acres, creating windbreaks and effective hedges, shrubberies and woodland, ponds and a vegetable garden; even a nursery bed for perennials and herbaceous stock tended by the ladies. He laid the basis for the transforming influences of future owners. To his own delight he had succeeded in what was one of his primary aims, attracting birds to Bleanaskill. Returning to the lodge in the spring of 1911:

> I was agreeably surprised to find a pair of Reed Buntings evidently nesting inside the fence near the house. The male perched on top of a post was repeating incessantly its curious, abrupt and restricted ditty. At my backdoor 2 Common Sandpipers were behaving in a most excited manner. Skimming quite close to the grass and bushes all round, and alighting on the top of a fencing stake they both squealed out their very musical call of 'Weet, Weet! Weet!' . . . A pair of Ringed Plover were close to my seawall a few yards off behaving exactly as if they were nesting and giving same breeding cry. Whilst from the meadows came the voice of the Corncrake and the whistle of a Curlew. Pipits are in the enclosed space behind the house, and the Skylark hovers and sings there too. Young Wheatears are about the fence along the sea side. I heard Wagtails and a mother Wren greatly excited over her young brood among the Fuchsia hedge. A couple of Twites pass overhead. The Wagtail is heard and a couple

of Rock Doves are in the next field. When the tide was full a Common Gull behaved in a singular way; flying a few feet over the water it repeatedly dived head first as a Tern would but not folding its wings, the water only covered them to the elbow; head neck and breast were covered, it repeatedly dived in this way.[33]

For all the years he had spent birdwatching, he could still be taken by surprise:

I was much deceived today. I thought I heard the breeding note of a Ring Plover in the corner of my field where we had potatoes last year. I noticed it several times during the day and at last walked up to make sure, as I thought it was hardly possible that the birds I heard on shore would come into the rushy field to nest. My surprise was great when I saw that the bird making the sound was a splendid old male Wheatear. It flew over the ditch and then out to a loose stone wall where it most successfully imitated the notes of the Meadow Pipit, Wagtail and Sparrow. They were most accurately reproduced and I then recollected that whilst planting trees during the day I had heard the same notes but thought they proceeded from the different birds so beautifully imitated. I have for years closely watched the Wheatears in various places and know their snatching song given very often on the wing, but I never gave the bird credit for being so excellent a mimic.[34]

For 17 September 1910 Alexander was able to record in bold capitals: 'THIS IS A RED LETTER DAY in the history of Bleanaskill Lodge, for today, after years of waiting and many disappointments we occupy our house for the first time.' One should not imagine that conditions inside the house were luxurious. Fortunately on hand, before he headed off to China as an engineer, was Frank Pike, who proved a useful ally in dealing with Williams' recalcitrant 'force pump'. This was intended to draw water up manually from an adjacent stream to the homemade concrete tank to provide water for the kitchen. The proud boast of the Lake Hotel, Killarney, in 1905 that it had 'perfect sanitation' may not have applied to any dwelling on Achill. Few would have tried, and Bleanaskill, so far as may be judged, had nothing better than a dry pit. (As a matter of record, the Valley Hotel on Achill, even as late as the 1940s and 1950s, drew water from the local lake but without any great regularity, often leaving patrons high and dry, so to speak.[35]) Williams' force pump proved no replacement for the services of a boy to collect, daily, spring drinking water.

Rain water was a different matter. 'Day too bad for the workmen. I tarred part of my skylight where there was a leakage. It seems impossible to perfectly staunch an Achill house. The rain is blown in far amongst the slates and comes dripping in.'[36] If he had two ambitions it was to keep the rain out of the house and the sea out of his fields. 'Some one has declared that no house in Achill Island is secure from the weather. I shall do my best to disprove it.'[37] Disprove it he did, at least to his own satisfaction: 'Tom Corrigan having arrived the shutters were removed and daylight let in for the first time in 9 months.

I found the house remarkably dry. In fact some matches I found on the floor I ignited by friction which is a very satisfactory test for such a length of time.'[38] There was no electricity at the lodge until the 1950s, well after Alec's time. The post was the lifeline to the outside world, that and the telegraph at the post office.

His diary suggests that there were times when he was doing as many and indeed more pictures of Killarney and Donegal on Achill than he did of the island itself, depending no doubt on his copious sketchbooks. The conclusion is inescapable that he often dashed off at speed pictures for the tourist trade. He says as much himself: 'Monday July 15th. Rain early morning. Clouds low down on hills. Painted a water colour. Dr Arthur Croly, Vi Croly and Miss Dobbs came to dinner . . . Dashed in a 15 x 8 W.C. of Slievemore and one 15 x 8 of Dooagh.' He put himself under pressure from the many chores he undertook but evidently enjoyed.

The lodge had been ten years in the making and Alexander would have just ten more years in which to enjoy it. Throughout he records a stream of visitors to the island. Achill was a popular destination for scientists, both on its own account and because of its proximity to Clare Island. Regarded as one of the most important projects of its kind ever undertaken, a multidisciplinary scientific survey of Clare Island and surrounding districts was carried out over a period of three years from 1909 to 1911 and the results published by the Royal Irish Academy in 1915. Alexander was consulted on the birds of Achill, corresponding with R. J. Ussher, who contributed to his survey paper on birds to the Clare Island project shortly before his sudden death in 1913. The records of Williams & Son were made available to the academy for the purposes of the project, as Ussher acknowledged. Two other members of the project with whom Williams was in constant touch were Professor C. J. Patten and R. M. Barrington. Ussher and the lepidopterist William Francis de Vismes Kane both came to Achill in July 1911 'bound for Clare Island the next day' and briefly met up with the artist. There was the inevitable afternoon tea at the lodge, Ussher, his man John (Ussher must have travelled in some comfort) and a Herr Lindner from Saxony making the trip to Bleanaskill: 'I showed them the Reed Bunting's nest and Ussher was interested about my Redshank notes, and also hearing the Whimbrel.'

Patten made frequent and often extended visits to Ireland from Sheffield. He was on Achill in September 1907 for about seventeen days, putting up at the new Atlantic Hotel but 'boarding' according to Williams with his family, meaning that they fed him – but perhaps not too luxuriously. 'Kitty and Alice boiled potatoes and made tea for our lunch,' Williams noted with no further comment. If the meal was no more extensive than spuds and tea no mention was made of the additions.

Patten had with him a new wonder of the age: a telephoto lens to go with his plate camera. This was pioneering stuff. Lens and camera would most likely have required separate tripods: 'Patten very enthusiastic . . . getting the camera to work in the window.' He used the lodge as a hide for a day or two, setting up his apparatus facing the bay, anxious to obtain a picture of a greenshank and expressing himself pleased with the outcome. He must have taken the results on faith as it is unlikely that he developed the

Menaun Cliffs, Achill. Oil on canvas. Signed. 14 x 24 in. (35.6 x 60.9 cm). This atmospheric sketch shows the so-called 'Cathedral Rocks' which had vaulting arches, accessible at low tide. Violent storms have since altered this feature of the cliffs.

cumbersome plates then and there. Kitty, was busy too, when not boiling potatoes: '. . . with her a basket of plants she got from the Sampeys at Ballinlough . . . she started and made the first flower bed at the Lodge under the shelter of the sea wall, together we planted a good many things.' The next day while Williams painted a picture of Bleanaskill Bay, the professor worked 'all day' with his camera, but sadly not a single original negative or photograph of that Achill trip is known to have survived. Yet Patten's photographic collection of Achill and elsewhere at one time must have been extensive. Perhaps in some dusty archive or private attic it lies hidden, waiting to be rediscovered.

As both men were experienced walkers, Patten's presence was an occasion to put all else aside and tramp over the wild terrain of Achill: 'Patten and self started about 11, walked through Breanaskill to Glencoe, Derreen, Kildownet, Cloughmore to the Blind Sound where we bathed. Too misty to see Clare Island or the great panorama stretching all across the South. We walked along the cliffs where we saw Herring Gulls and Turnstones and some splendid rocks to Bounafaghy and then up the incline to the top of the road overlooking Ashleam Bay along the zig-zag road past Ashleam Village, past Breanaskill and home to Post Office at 7 p.m., a tramp of 16 miles or more.'[39] This however was probably a less taxing walk than going over the Menaun Cliffs with its reward of a panoramic view of the whole island, and which included the descent to Keel Strand where 'we stripped and bathed in icy cold water where the foamy breakers were majestically rolling in.'[40]

If they swam right under the Menaun Cliffs they had chosen an exceedingly dangerous spot as the current, at particular times, can all too readily sweep unsuspecting bathers away from the shore, with fatal results.[41] Williams appears to have been unaware of the danger but reported no difficulties.

They spent a few days, Williams and Patten, down at Dugort, too far for a single day's run with exploration on the agenda. The weather was 'very fine and scorching hot at last'. They took the mail car, lunched at the Slievemore Hotel, walked to what Williams calls Pat McGrail's Rock, meeting the man himself, presumably a local living close to

Watercolour over pencil. Signed. 'Cabins on the beach at Dugort Bay, Achill Island' inscribed on back.
10 x 17 in. (25 x 44 cm).

the cliffs. Williams then writes that 'Patten got some shots at groups of Shag Cormorants on the rocks with white foam curling round the base.' Did Williams mean by 'some shots' that Patten photographed the cormorants with his telephoto lens? Along the coast they found John Sheridan with 'Walker from London' trying their hand painting 'big marine pictures'. Some of Sheridan's work, and large pictures they are, can be seen to this day in McDowell's Guest House in Dugort. Then it was time for the professor and himself to bathe in what Williams calls 'Williams' Cove', no doubt a favourite bathing spot which can no longer be identified, 'where I found the marinums[42] in great profusion'. How easily did Williams' interest in painting, birdwatching, gardening, walking and swimming intermingle. He does not leave Dugort without visiting Sheridan's garden where he gets 'a big bundle of splendid strong rough growing Euonymus cuttings with "heels", also purple Plum twigs'. Then it is back to the sound by long car: 'After lunch at Robin's I got a lovely 18X10 sketch on the roadside near Stauntons. Exquisite effects on land and water all day.' The weather is in everyone's favour. So it goes on during Patten's stay, walking, painting and visiting: 'After lunch all went to Glendarary where I got another 18X10. Evening with a hazy effect on the trees and shore at Bleanaskill. The Professor and self enjoyed a most glorious bathe at the ladies bathing place. No ladies but plenty of midges.'

In 1911 he entertained his brother Willie at Bleanaskill and recorded a day – one of those days of high summer and perfection on Achill – when along with an extended boating trip, shooting, sketching, swimming and a garden visit were all combined:

When the tide was about half ebb with Willie we rowed off in the Punt for a whole day excursion . . . We noted a Hooded Crow on a stone near the water and stealing in shore my brother fired at it and must have hit it in the head as it flew off and returned to the same locality when my brother fired again making a blind miss. It then flew away down the Sound and we marked it on some loose stones near the road. We followed it up and my brother getting out of the boat fired a third shot which dispatched it. I think the Hooded Crow is a rascally bird, which should be shot at

Oil on canvas, signed and inscribed 'Pass of Kylemore.' 24 x 36 in. (61 x 91.4 cm).

sight owing to the merciless way in which it destroys the eggs and young birds of other species in the nesting season. Where the Sound broadens opposite Kildownet Castle Willie obtained an immature specimen beautifully marked and speckled all over the grey marking. We rowed across to the lovely sand bank covered with rich green verdure, landed and walked about. It was now nearing low water and the scene spread before us in the glorious intense sunlight was delightful. There was not a breath of wind and the surface of the water of the Blind Sound was serenely tranquil where we stood on the shore was part of a long rich yellow strand and we both stripped and had a very satisfactory and luxurious swim in the pellucid water, so strong and buoyant. Having enjoyed our bath, we got into the punt again and allowed ourselves to be swiftly carried on the surface of the Sound which divides Curraune from Achillbeg Island out into Clew Bay and turning to the right side we rowed into a beautiful perfectly smooth sandy Bay which leads to a ravine that almost divides the Island of Achillbeg. Here was a village and a group of boys resting, who soon came running down at the sight of strangers landing from a gaily painted boat. Whilst Willie remained on board I made my way up the rocks and sand and made pencil sketches . . . and passing Darby's Point we made for Curraune shore again, where we moored the boat and started off to visit Curraune House, Mr Dicken's beautiful garden. The gardener Mr Gosden, a clever Englishman, kindly took us over the grounds where on the bare cliff a wonderful collection of rare plants are growing behind wind screens and protecting walls. We returned to the boat and after a pleasant row reached Bleanaskill Lodge at 6.45. Thermometer registered today Sun 112° Shade 92°.[43]

Needless to say plants from Curraune House found their way to Bleanaskill. Not all introductions, however, were felicitous. *Gunnera tinctoria*, an invasive species resembling a giant rhubarb with prickly coarse leaves, which has colonised Achill, Clare Island and parts of the mainland, is believed to have originated at Curraune House.

Oil on board. Sketch signed and inscribed: 'Bleanaskill Bridge Achill Island.' 9¾ x 17½ in. (25 x 44.5 cm). The picture is noteworthy for the absence of *Gunnera* spp. (a rhubarb-like plant, although a different genus) which now abounds on Achill. The rowing boat may be the artist's own. From among the artist's effects and probably a late work.

The arrival of a 'motor' was still regarded as something of an event, duly recorded in the diary, and Williams had prepared for the eventuality by having 'engaged McNulty to finish the building of the wall at entrance and to leave a space alongside the gate pier for the wicket gate, so that the big heavy iron gates need not be used except on state occasions when visitors with cars or motor cars honour us with their presence'. They were duly honoured when 'Mr & Mrs Joseph Tatlow on their honeymoon arrived from Malranny. I joined them, and we drove to Darby's Point and round by the Blind Sound. It was their first sight of the West Coast of Achill and both were delighted with the scenery though Mrs T was visibly nervous of motoring and elected to walk down the Corkscrew Road at Ashleam Bay.' Better to be a live widow than a dead bride, she had sensibly concluded.

The artist would return reluctantly to Dublin in late autumn when he was required to organise the annual exhibition of the Dublin Sketching Club, his feelings at leaving intensified by having started his Achill project relatively late in life: 'Deeply sorry to come away from a spot that has given me untold delight for nearly six months and where I have spent the "Indian Summer of my life". It would be impossible to attempt to describe the intense pleasure it has been to me to walk round and round my three acres during that time and carry out all my schemes of improvement.'[44] Williams at least had the advantage of months in which to assemble a portfolio and could accommodate non-painting days. When Alex Rolles, Treasurer of the Dublin Sketching Club, put in a brief appearance, Williams took him along the Atlantic Drive, from where, John Sheridan later quipped, Rolles viewed the mist and missed the view. Interestingly, for a man who responded to both heavy clouds and bright weather, Williams suggests he did not care for the effects of heat haze, however atmospheric, not when it came to painting: 'I walked up the Ashleam Road and was disappointed by the hazy landscape. I came back to O'Donnell's bog near Breanaskill and got an 18X10 looking down the valley and across the Bay to Currane Hill but didn't like the mist.' For all that, he was praised for 'sketches . . . characterised by breadth, a fine sense of colour and atmosphere and misty effects'.[45]

For the most part Williams' social life on the island revolved around constant visits to and from the Pikes at Glendarary, the Rev. Canon Thomas Boland and his wife in the Rectory at the sound, and excursions to the Sheridans at the far end of the island. Meals may have been laid on, but the visits recorded were more usually the inevitable, ritualistic, afternoon tea. If you were intent on bringing a gift, and few would not, then plants, or probably for preference, if you were local, vegetables were always welcome. Everyone grew their own. Visits more than a few miles away needed to be arranged in advance, usually by horse-drawn transport. Usefully, the horse-drawn mail car daily crossed the island and provided transport for those who needed it. Given the distance of Dugort from the sound, Williams and Kitty would stay overnight in the Slievemore Hotel. In the absence of other amusements they made their own, with an evening of song around the piano. If not making music, then the two men had painting to discuss – Williams gave his friend lessons, as later did Paul Henry – and if not painting then their conversation would range over plants, birds, wildlife and taxidermy, of which the hotel had an abundance. The crest of the Slievemore Hotel featured a golden eagle, an irony given that Sheridan is reputed to have shot the last one on the island.[46]

The pastoral pressures on the local rector were apparently none too severe. He made a habit of calling at Bleanaskill and took a keen interest in the progress being made at the lodge and the 3 acres of wilderness. Williams' passion for trees evidently made an impression on his reverence: 'Went to supper at Rectory 7 p.m. Mr Boland regrets he did not take up the subject of tree planting years ago, a great deal could have been done to beautify the Rectory grounds.' Evening visits could be hazardous in a way one now forgets, with glimmering oil lamps the best on offer. 'It was pitch dark when we got to our car and before we reached the Rectory the worthy divine had to get a lantern and walk at the horse's head as we were in danger of landing in the ditch.'

There were unexpected hazards too. The annual Harvest Festival was an occasion for the local ladies to decorate the church and serve refreshments. The cohesion and size of the Protestant community in that day may be judged by the fact that the service was held midweek:

Worked till 3 p.m. at water colours. Thanksgiving service in Achill Sound Parish Church. Corrigan drove Kitty, Alice, Liz & Eleanor to the Rectory. I walked, arriving at 6 p.m. Met Revs Mervyn, O'Connell, Hayes, Boland . . . High tea and delicacies of all kinds. All adjourned to the Church where I sat with the Choir and helped them. Our car came at 9.30 and during the fierce gale returning Liz lost her umbrella, Alice her stick, Kitty a brooch, and a long hat pin.[47]

It must have been a rough journey indeed.

At one point it did not look as if there would be much of a harvest to celebrate with Williams quoting newspaper coverage in August: 'Rain and Floods. The crops seriously damaged. ROADS UNDER WATER. ANXIETY THROUGH COUNTRY',[48] adding that the month had not produced a single day with a temperature as high as 70 °F. He found solace in bird song, which was not apparently much affected by the weather: 'Did weeding in the middle garden. Robin and Wren have taken to singing again. Flock of 13 Pied Wagtails observed, 36 Oystercatchers on Glancoe Point. Choughs and Rock Pigeons in field near house. Gray Wagtail sings on the house top.'[49] It was not the only species. Earlier in the year he mentions hearing a whitethroat singing very often on one of the chimneys of the house.

In one of his London diaries Williams mentions, in passing, drinking beer in a pub. In his Achill diary there is not a single reference to entering a public house, which is not to say he never did, but clearly it was not a significant aspect of his social life. It is certain that Williams and the Northern Irish artist Paul Henry (1876–1958) would never have been drinking companions. For all that, it seems inconceivable that Williams and Henry, who arrived on the island in 1910 and made it his home for many years, never met. If they did, neither mentioned the fact. Henry would have had no inclination to acknowledge the work of his predecessor. As his biographer, S. J. Kennedy, has humourously remarked: Henry refers to himself in his autobiography as if he were the first white man to arrive on Achill.[50]

Henry could be morose and withdrawn, and went through bouts of heavy drinking. After one such bout, it is said locally on the island, Henry managed to get himself locked up by the local Garda sergeant 'for his own good'.[51] The contrast between the temperaments of the two men was marked. Henry, who had a difficult, suffocatingly puritanical Protestant upbringing in the North, found solace in Achill away from his roots, and produced work that could be sentimental and comforting – the winding road going over the brow of the hill dotted with pleasantly arranged cottages. Alexander, on the other hand, who had the happiest of childhoods, relishing his explorations of the Boyne and the woods around Drogheda, often produced work strongly marked by melancholy, leaving the viewer with no doubt as to one aspect of the nature of the west as he saw it.

Another artist to make Achill his home was the American painter Robert Henri (1865–1929). He did not arrive on Achill until 1914, the year after the diary had ended, and again there is no record as to whether Henri and Williams ever met. Henri, who lived at Corrymore House (better known for having been the notorious Captain Boycott's house) between 1924 and 1928, painted many notable portraits of Achill Islanders.

If you had been gazing across Achill Sound on a Sunday morning in the early 1900s you might have caught sight of Williams, Kitty and Alice all heading for church in their Sunday best, not walking but rowing. The tide was not always propitious and sometimes going there or back they had to dock part way and walk the rest. Under the best conditions when the right wind prevailed his capacious sketching umbrella did duty as a sail. Here he is with daughter Alice valiantly heading for church on a Sunday in August:

> . . . how entrancingly beautiful is a real fine morning in Achill Sound. Water as still as a mirror. Before 10 Alice and I started off to row to the Bridge at Achill Sound for church. A sudden change came on and the wind in our teeth gave us a hard row. The breeze was so bad and the sea so choppy that we put in to Father Colleran's moorings and pulled up the boat, walking on to church. After the service Frank and Dick [Pike] helped us to get the boat launched and we sailed down the Sound before a good wind by hoisting up my large sketching umbrella. 86 Redshanks, 30 Ringed Plover, 22 Common Gulls, 1 immature crying on rock, 4 Blk Headed Gulls.[52]

Whatever the subject, the birds usually got a mention. Religious zeal would hardly be sufficient reason to explain the fact that Williams would attend church not once but sometimes twice on a Sunday. The church was a social as well as a religious meeting place, and he made full use of the invitations to the Rectory or Glendarary House that came after the service.

As both the maids were Roman Catholics, they headed off in the opposite direction for their religious observances. This entry is for a Thursday, 29 June 1911, the feast day of Peter and Paul:

> Our two servants Kate & Eileen went to Kildownet Chapel for 11 o'clock mass this morning notwithstanding the rain and were greatly edified by the islanders' devotions. The men and women were divided and a barefooted boy prepared the sacred table. Many of the congregation yawned frequently and one woman rattling off her prayers in Irish made a marked impression on them.[53]

In another entry Williams comments when rowing to church that he 'did the trip easily within an hour', which suggests it often took longer, and that was one way. Occasionally the weather defeated even his efforts and he would tie up the boat and continue on foot for safety.

A major event on Achill which generated much excitement well beyond the confines of the island were the annual races and regatta held at the sound. 'Tickets at excursion fares will be issued day of sports from Ballina, Castlerea, and intermediate stations.' Variety there was in plenty. The regatta in 1912 had a rowing race for yawls, a race for square stern boats, another for canoes (currachs) and, with the highest prize money, a race for hookers, with £2.10.0 for the winner and 10/- for the runner-up. There were horse, donkey and bicycle races and athletic events of various kinds, including 'Climbing a greasy pole' and an 'Old Age Pensioners' Race' (qualifying age not specified in the programme). There was also a 'Hop-step-and-Jump' open to all comers. How far might a man travel by such means? According to Williams' pencilled notes on the back of a programme, Mr Timoney won first prize, hop, stepping and jumping 41 feet and 10 inches (12.75 m).

The horse races had prizes up to £4.0.0 while the athletic prizes ranged from ten shillings to £1.0.0. The exception was the competition for 'Catching and holding a pig' where the prize was the pig itself. For some reason competitors had to be fifty years of age or older to qualify. As an adjudicator for the horse races Williams would have been familiar with rule No. 4:

> All matters of dispute which may arise, to be referred to a Committee of appeal, consisting of the following stewards: Messrs R. N. Pike, Alex Williams, and Ed Sweeney JP, whose decision shall be irrevocable but in no instance shall there be recourse to a Court of Law.

There was a dispute to be settled. On the following Monday Williams 'walked to the Sound to attend a meeting of the Sports Committee in the Courthouse. Objections to the result of the 1st Horse Race was heard and the Committee and referees agreed to ask the competitors to run the race again on the last Saturday in August' when 'only 2 horses competed. I had to go out on the strand to the post where the horses turn to see that they properly rounded it, and got my feet well wet. The same winner again came in first.'

One further glimpse of island life of long ago comes from a news clip from *The Irish Times* for 21 August 1906, the year before the diary starts but pasted into it. It records 'a concert and theatricals' got up at Dugort for the Countess of Dudley District Nurses' Fund. This kind of thing was very popular before the First World War, events in which everyone could play a part, amateurish no doubt, but in the absence of other forms of entertainment they tended to be remarkably well attended. The second half was the real novelty, consisting of 'a short play, written for her daughters by Lady Clarinda, "Red Riding Hood" (up to date)' which featured a cast of about a dozen, including Sheridan's three daughters – little Mildred all of eight or nine as the grandmother. Williams played the woodsman and along with Mr Mowbray from Mountmellick, who played the wolf, was responsible for the stage fittings. Whatever the standard of it all, the idea of a homemade drawing-room play in which children and adults all participated in the far reaches of Achill suggests an enchantment with improvisatory pleasures that has since been lost.

If Williams were to return today he would surely be astonished and and profoundly moved to find how the lives of the islanders have been transformed, to a degree inconceivable in his own time. He would doubtless also be delighted to find his island home and its three recalcitrant acres developed to their current state. But in other respects he might have mixed views. On a personal level he would likely be saddened to find the social network that he enjoyed, and much which he took for granted, gone forever. The church on the sound, once a social cornerstone of island life to Williams, to which he and his family would row and sail back and forth, his giant painting umbrella held aloft, is a church no more. It was deconsecrated before the turn of the twenty-first century and sold off for conversion into a domestic dwelling. How quickly the little Church of Ireland community faded. Not a single wedding was celebrated in the church between 1921and 1936, the consequence of both emigration and what was known as 'mixed marriages', between Protestant and Roman Catholic and the *Ne Temere* decree.

Glendarary House, which Williams visited so often, lasted not much more than 100 years before being demolished, the stone used for road building. Something of its size may be judged from the immensely thick stone walls and arches of what is left of the basement, visible through the surrounding scrub, a broken reminder to some of Victorian opulence and gracious living, to others of an overbearing social inequality. The lawn on which the golden eagle shared its cage with a goose has long since returned to being a wild meadow. The woodland, in private hands and strictly private, extensive by Achill standards, is still preserved. Sadly the Slievemore Hotel is a hotel no longer. The facade remains but the building has since been converted into apartments. This is more than a sentimental loss; the hotel was once the heart and hub of Dugort. If the hotel is gone, many more holiday homes are spread across the landscape, not always with a mind to preserving the wild beauty of Achill, and great swathes of commonage where Williams and his friends once roamed freely have since been fenced off. There has been loss as well as gain.

To Williams' generation an accusing finger can be pointed as regards the fate of both the sea eagle (*syn.* white-tailed eagle) and the golden eagle. The white-tailed eagle was extinct from Achill even before Williams had started his diary, although he described it in the previous century in his memoirs. The golden eagle had become a rarity in the early 1900s; it was probably extinct from Achill, at least as a breeding species, by the time of the First World War. Other species have followed. The common bunting is not only extinct on Achill and throughout the mainland, but much reduced in numbers across the water, and its survival as a European species is in doubt. Modern agricultural practices have decimated the national population of the corncrake. It still has breeding populations in remote corners of Ireland, in Donegal for instance and some outlying islands, but seemingly not Achill, certainly not as a regular breeding species. The twite appears to be absent from the island now although still a breeding species on the mainland. The merlin makes periodic appearances on Achill but may no longer breed there. Williams seems to have been able to make a distinction, by their coloration, between merlins bred on the island and those on the mainland. The diary was never intended as an inclusive list of birds on Achill, but of the more than seventy species he mentions, other than the golden eagle, none he regarded as particularly rare at the time. Yet the loss of five species with which he was familiar represents an alarming reduction of about 6 per cent from his list, all in less than 100 years. Happily, the rarest of the crow family, the chough, with its characteristically 'fingered' wing tips, its red legs and beak and its acrobatic displays during its breeding season, is as familiar today on Achill as it was in the artist's time. Achill remains one of the strongholds for the comparatively sparse populations of this species, with populations of the chough greater in the west of Ireland than anywhere else in northern Europe.

After her mother, Kitty Williams, died in 1933, Alice kept the lodge for more than a decade, selling it in about 1948. She never lived in it herself and she was never to live in a house of her own, spending the remainder of her days, after her parents died, as a peripatetic lodger. She made at least one visit to the lodge after her parents died. The last tenants at this stage were the Scanlons, who had taken it over from a family called Kemple around 1935. Vera Scanlon, as a child, remembered Miss Williams as a stout lady who was entertained to tea on the lawn. Alice remarked on the black hair of another sister, Maureen, which showed streaks of white, suggesting to Mrs Scanlon that she include spinach in the child's diet to combat the white streaks. It is not known if the remedy was tried. Vera also retains an arresting memory of childhood which is given here for what it is worth. She was in the lodge alone when a man, a stranger to her, walked in and without saying a word continued on through. She remembered he was conspicuously bald and sported a heavy moustache, a description that answers Williams' appearance. Had he returned, in spirit, to cast one lingering look behind?

From time to time the political activist and writer Peadar O'Donnell (1893–1957) and artist Paul Henry came to stay with the Scanlons at Bleanaskill Lodge. Intriguingly, the children were under strict instructions to keep silent about these visits. Why it should have been thought important to keep Henry's occasional visits a secret is hard to fathom. It is more understandable why John Scanlon, a JP, might not want to draw attention to whatever connection he had with Peadar O'Donnell, who had IRA connections, and possibly there were occasions when O'Donnell did not want his presence known. In time the Scanlon family took the emigrant's boat as so many islanders did, making good in foreign cities located as far apart as England and Australia. But the island has not been forgotten. Among the abiding memories of Elizabeth Morgan JP, the fifth Scanlon child and born on Achill, is of the fine education she received there, of the courage and generosity of the islanders in the face of hardship. The island and Bleanaskill Lodge, she says, with emotion, remains to her and her siblings embedded in their memories as 'home'.[54]

By good fortune the lodge has had the attention of a number of successive owners interested in gardening and, as of writing, is the only garden on the island open to the public. Within the span of the author's memory: in or around 1970 Bleanaskill was bought by Sir Anthony and Lady (Noël) Bevir. Then retired, he had once been a private Secretary to Sir Winston Churchill. He was a studious, pipe-smoking Old Etonian with impeccable manners and English reticence, who was astonished to find himself referred to by a local workman by his first name, as if they were old buddies. He did no gardening, but Lady Bevir was a keen gardener and within the limitations of age and little assistance maintained the garden, adding her own touches, favouring plants that attracted wildlife. Noël was born in 1899 and raised in some style in an Anglo-Irish family at Breaffy House (now a hotel), Castlebar, County Mayo. In just how much style may be judged by

The lily pond, Bleanaskill Lodge.

her own recollections. Asked what life had been like before the First World War, she paused for a moment before telling this story. She remembered sitting in the drawing room as a child with her grandmother, who let the newspaper she had been reading slip off her lap. Noël rose to pick it up, but her grandmother admonished her and rang the bell for the butler, who duly entered the room and retrieved the newspaper from the floor.[55]

The Bevirs were followed by Roddy Heron, a retired bachelor farmer from County Wicklow (whose sister was the artist and sculptor Hilary Heron),[56] and he had something of Hilary's artistic flair. With remarkable energy he extended and improved the garden, adding flourishes of his own. A novel feature of his, which has been retained, is the thick rope edging for the main driveway and pathways. He had the loyal assistance of local lady Sheila McGinty. But he confessed, particularly as age took a grip on his mobility and his joints, that much as he enjoyed what the lodge had to offer, he had found it tough living alone.[57]

The present owners needed some toughness and resilience too. After the death of Roddy Heron in 1994 at the age of ninety, the lodge was bought by a Dutch pair, Willem

A view of the garden at Bleanaskill Lodge. Note the old macracarpa and woven fence on the left.

Van Goor and his wife, Doutsje Nauta. In what must have seemed like a giant leap of faith, they swapped life on a canal barge in their own densely populated (and, according to Willem, over-regulated) country for the rural freedom of Achill. They had the advantage of relative youth on their side; and with the continuing assistance of Sheila McGinty, single-mindedly transformed the somewhat inchoate layout into a series of interconnecting gardens, both formal and informal, one leading to the next, so the visitor may stroll through Bleanaskill in a spirit of exploration. They introduced wickerwork fencing, carefully woven from collected brushwood, and discreet sculptures in a variety of materials. In a way that Williams anticipated but never saw in its maturity, the canopy of trees and shrubs now provides ideal shelter and protection (see www.achill-art-garden.com). Through generations of cultivation, the once barren soil has been enriched by the time-honoured practice of mulching with seaweed, to which modern practices of composting and recycling contribute. In the moist and mild climate – and with the protection of the surrounding woodland – plants now grow at a prodigious rate as do weeds, the owners will tell you. Building on the work of those who went before them, they have assembled an enviable collection of native and exotic trees and shrubs. Among exotics are the Chilean fire bush (*Embrothium coccineum*), which Williams had so much admired when he first saw it at Rock House, Ballycroy; the Chinese euonymous (*Euonymus cornutus*) with flowers like jester's caps; the Chilean hazel (*Gevuina avella*), ideal for sheltered woodland; and the Chilean guava (*Ugni molinae*; syn. *Myrtus ugni*), a shrub with fragrant white to pink flowers and dark red berries. With 5,000 daffodil and other spring bulbs, there is nothing else quite like it on the island.

Gardens are vulnerable creations subject to time and circumstance. Williams, for all his enterprise, never quite succeeded with his wall along the shore of keeping out the highest tides and they are higher now. Between about 2000 and 2010, the sea level may have risen by as much as several centimetres. After a recent storm when Doutsje was asked if the sea had got through their defences, she smiled gently and replied quietly: 'You forget we are Dutch.' For the time being the garden is in safe hands.

Looking back again to the years when Alexander began it all, it is perhaps the variety of his activities and his engagement with Achill Island that stand out in the diary. The impression is of a man for whom boredom must have been a rare experience indeed. The diary ends in June 1913; perhaps at this point Williams felt he had written himself out. He valued what he had made on the island all the more because it had been done in the latter part of his life when time becomes increasingly precious. We leave the diary with this quotation from July 1911; a slightly self-conscious piece of purple prose perhaps, nevertheless it shows as well or better than any other entry the depth of what Achill and his 'island home' meant to him as both artist and naturalist:

The air is perfectly still and a dreamy silence prevails but as I sit sometimes with closed eyes voices of the children of the village opposite travel over the placid water. There is the occasional bark of a dog. The mooing of cattle. The voice of the Corncrake, and the following birds can be detected Curlew, Herring Gull, Black Headed Gull, Common Gull, Ringed Plover, Common Sandpiper, Blackbird singing, Common Bunting, Yellow Bunting, Sparrow, Twite, Pied Wagtail, Rook, Wren, Common Linnet, Skylark, Pipit. As the afternoon light of copper coloured sun slants over the Bay the hillside glows with a golden refulgent light and as the other birds become quiet the liquid notes of the Blackbird echo across the water. There are no

Watercolour study of Hooker, possibly in Bleanaskill Bay. Signed. 13¾ x 6 in. (34.9 x 15.2 cm).

trees nor even low bushes on the other side but the beautiful singer instead perches on the stone walls and fences. As the tide ebbs the Curlew are heard over head calling, and the quarrelsome cry of the Herring Gull is also heard . . .

. . . The shadows of evening approach; and only the upper part of the hill is lighted by the declining sun. The blue smoke from the cottages steals forward. The cattle are being driven by gaily coloured peasants, and the gulls that always arrive at the fall of the tide are busy at one particular part of the shore. The Blackbird has left off but the Robin now charms the ear. The sun's fiery light lingers about the hill summits but all in the valley is becoming dull and grey and soon the light of another beautiful Sabbath will fade.[58]

He captures well the inherent sense of the transience of all things.

CHAPTER 15

Changing Worlds

Pastel of the artist in old age, *c.* 1925, signed E[dward] J[ames] Rogers [1872–1938].

Williams could be upbeat in the years before the Great War, having no inkling that the political convulsions that were to overtake Ireland, even more than the war itself, would sweep away the *ancien régime* by which he had done so well. Even more to the point, politics was only part of what was taking place. Nationalist aspirations towards a new identity for Ireland were everywhere apparent, not only in politics, but in the arts. Alexander was well aware of the shifting ground.

The years leading up to the Great War had been good to him in a way that would not be repeated after it. He was well regarded, an established senior figure in his chosen profession, and among art enthusiasts and, even beyond that nucleus, a household name. He was sixty-eight in 1914, 'still going strong' he noted in his 'Chronicles & Memoirs' on 21 April, and, as if to prove the point, he remained as much involved in Dublin life as he had ever been. He held his annual solo exhibition albeit at the smaller venue of Mills' Hall, 8 Merrion Row in January; then it was the opening of the Water Colour Society of Ireland exhibition at 35 Dawson Street on 18 February in which he exhibited eleven pictures. Between the two he was at Jack Yeats' exhibition, 'Pictures of Life in the West of Ireland' at 8 Merrion Row on 23 February. 'His work has a distinctive Celtic atmosphere,' commented *The Irish Times*, 'in which peculiar mystic effects are produced. He observes, for instance, a boy seated on a donkey trotting through a village. Most artists would depict the incident as they see it, but Mr Yeats sees something more.'[1] Here was something new, even radical, and by its apparent disregard for careful handling of paint and form, daring. Williams kept abreast of the changing times, even if he was not part of them. In the previous spring while on a visit to London he visited the Irish Exhibition at the Whitechapel Gallery, an event also regarded as a landmark: 'The exhibition which represented almost every aspect of the fine and applied arts in Ireland and which included both historical and contemporary works, may be regarded as the authoritative statement on the subject at that time.'[2] He was represented by a work entitled *As Evening Grey Advances Slow*, a title suggesting the picture was characteristic of his work. While he was not a historical figure, neither was he now a contemporary one.

Indicative of a change in expectation that was now emerging regarding Irish art, the English press took a rather critical, not to say condescending, attitude to the exhibition. The *Athenaeum* came out with the blanket statement that 'the large collection of paintings by Irish artists does not show any distinctively native characteristics,'[3] There was much more in this vein. The *Morning Post* conceded that: 'In the Irish exhibition . . . there are plenty of native artists – indeed they abound remarkably – but a distinction must be made between Irishmen who paint and the Irish painters.'[4] While *The Observer* went so far as to contend that: 'Even these modern painters who devoted themselves to the pictorial interpretation of Irish life and scenery are, with few exceptions, under alien domination.'[5]

It is unlikely that Williams would ever have regarded himself as under alien domination, artistic or otherwise. To his generation of academicians such a dichotomy along the lines proposed would have been incomprehensible. If their style and approach differed little from painters from across the water and showed influence from further

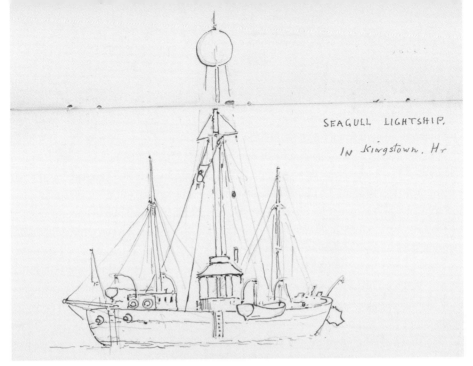

Pencil sketch of the *Seagull* lightship in Kingstown Harbour. 6.1 x 7 in. (15.5 x 17.8 cm)

afield, that would have had little relevance at the time. They regarded themselves as part of the mainstream of art in these islands. In that context Williams, like most of his contemporaries, regarded himself as an Irish painter, for how else could he regard himself?

It was the ferment of the years leading up to the creation of the new state and during its formative years that threw up searching questions of national identity and what it means to be Irish. The response by the press to the Whitechapel exhibition was indicative of what was to follow.

Meanwhile, the old world still continued. Before the end of February 1914 there was an 'At Home' held by Lady Rosse; and Varnishing Day at the RHA. Alexander exhibited seven pictures this year. On 18 April he headed off for his old haunt, the Lake Hotel, Killarney, where he stayed until 25 April.

In May 1914, he left Kingston for what was his final trip to London. He stayed with the Markels, as he had previously, at their fashionable address of 20 Queen's Gate Terrace, SW, and relished swanning around the city in their chauffeur-driven motor. It was a whirlwind tour, written up on sheets of paper and then pasted into his 'Chronicles'.

He took in the Royal Academy and 'revelled in the enjoyment of the pictures'; singling out a portrait of Mrs Stewart Clark by Sir James Jebusa Shannon[6] as giving him the 'most pleasure'. It is the only reference in his papers to an individual painting by another artist. Perhaps at heart he would have liked to have been a portrait painter. He paid a visit to 'Morrell of Great St Andrew Street to examine a frame mitering machine' costing £2.13.0, went into the workshop where 'an artisan explained the working, must surely get one of these as soon as possible'. Not the comment of a man contemplating retirement.

He knew how to make the best of a few days, mentioning cinema visits (three reels at a throw, silent of course); of being chauffeured with the Markels to the Aldwych

Theatre to see Chekhov's *Uncle Vanya* where he found 'a very Bohemian audience'. More bohemian was the Alhambra Theatre for a variety show. 'It was grand,' Williams commented, 'lots of lovely girls with little on.'

He had dinner with the sculptor Conrad Dressler (1856–1940) and they both attended a lecture at the Royal Society of Arts on firing pottery, by a friend of Dressler's, a Mr Burton from Lancashire. Williams thought it was 'badly given, full of stops etc as if the lecturer . . . was not up to his subject.' Dressler might have done better. Much influenced by the Arts and Crafts Movement, he had set up a tile factory and invented the tunnel kiln. He took the train as far as Windsor intending to get to Virginia Water, but 7/6d for a taxi was 'altogether too much to lay out' and he thought better of walking the five miles across Windsor Park. He would return, so he mused, to sketch in the vicinity some other time; but the circumstances of his personal life, as well as the Great War, would conspire against him ever returning.

He kept travelling through the year. Less than a month after his London visit he was down at the Parknasilla Hotel, Kenmare Bay, for a few days. Then it was back to Dublin before heading off with Kitty and Alice and the two maids to Bleanaskill Lodge, Achill on 26 June. Evidently he had yet to find a reason for cutting back on expenditure. He returned to town on 3 November when he had to arrange, as he did every year, the annual exhibition of the Dublin Sketching Club. He showed eleven pictures and rounded off the year by exhibiting with the 'Society of Black and White Artists' – a reference of course to the medium represented – at Mills Hall, 8 Merrion Row in December, alongside Jack Yeats; Sarah Purser; the two Orpens, Richard and William; Dermod O'Brien and Bingham McGuinness, among others. However, he did not wait in town for the exhibition, having already returned with his family to Achill before the end of November. He spent Christmas on the island, staying on into the New Year of 1915 before heading back to Dublin to prepare for his thirty-fifth exhibition which ran even longer than usual, from 12 February to 27 March. It overlapped with the opening of the annual exhibition of the Water Colour Society of Ireland, on 18 February. In April he recorded selling a watercolour for £30 at the RHA's annual exhibition. He could still sell pictures at high prices even though that sum of money was worth less than it had been just a few years earlier. On 17 February 1915 he had duly noted the departure of 'His Excellency John Campbell and Lady Aberdeen' and on 14 April the public entry of the new viceroy, Lord Wimborne. The new man lost no time in visiting the RHA exhibition and he would do the traditional rounds. Nevertheless, his arrival marked the point at which Williams' best days of patronage were over; the Aberdeens had been particularly supportive of him.

The outbreak of war in August 1914 had not done much to disturb the even tenor of the artist's life. For others it even looked like an opportunity. Conscription was never introduced in Ireland, it being regarded as too sensitive an issue. However, as unemployment was rife there was good reason to take the King's shilling, whatever one's political standpoint, and many did. It may not have been seen as such a big deal initially

– 'they'd be back by Christmas' was a common cry, young men out for a bit of adventure and a square meal. Being too old to fight did not prevent Alexander getting caught up in the patriotic fervour of it all. He joined the cheering throngs that accompanied troops as they left for war from the port of Dublin, walking all the way to the end of the North Wall. Neither he nor his brother Willie had a child of soldiering age. But like everyone else, Williams knew plenty who had. Among them was his old Achill friend, John Sheridan, who lost both his sons in France, officers in the Dublin Fusiliers. Williams could not have ignored the thought that had he lived, his own son, George, would have been of soldiering age.

In a window at Hatch Street he placed a doll, a caricature of the Kaiser. Was this his ventriloquist's dummy Master Johnny reincarnated? If he could not fight, Williams could show where his heart lay. Soon the wounded were coming back, showing the reality of war at the front and filling up the Dublin hospitals. Williams, Kitty and Alice all helped with charitable causes; there were the wounded from the Meath, Jervis Street and St Vincent's Hospitals to be entertained for tea at Hatch Street and ferried to church. 'Alice's soldiers', as Williams put it, had their own concert party, singing at the North Bull Recreation Hall. There were pictures he could donate to charities.

Alexander had done well by the Ascendancy and like many of his generation he would have taken for granted the union of Britain and Ireland as part of the natural order of things. He was not given to making political comments in his writings, but with the taking of the GPO in 1916 he made an exception: 'Easter Monday. Rebellion broke out at 12 o'clock in Dublin to the everlasting disgrace of Ireland at a time when England was fighting for her existence.'[7] His outrage was commonplace. The leaders of the Rising as they were led away after their surrender were greeted with hostility, even spat upon, by working-class, inner-city Dubliners, who at the time saw no virtue in their action. The owners of property in the city were appalled at the widespread destruction of buildings and the press roundly condemned the rebellion. It was as a result of the ferocity of the British reaction and in particular the execution of the leaders of the rebellion that attitudes swung the other way.

When news of the signing of the peace treaty at the end of the First World War reached Dublin early in July 1919 Union Jacks were flown from business premises around the city and from private houses. 'This evidence of rejoicing at the termination of the war was more marked in the suburbs than in the centre of the city, flags being hung from almost every house in some avenues and terraces. The display was not on such a large scale as when the Armistice was announced, probably in view of the request of the Government that there should be no celebrations until the day fixed, when there is to be a "chain of fire" throughout the whole Empire.'[8] The day fixed for the 'chain of fire', a public holiday, was Saturday, 19 July. It was to be the last great expression in Dublin of loyalty to the British Empire. Williams was there, in the 'Great Peace Day Celebration in College Green 10.45 a.m. Got a splendid position in the Band directly opposite to where General French took the salute. A grand sight.'[9]

Outside Trinity College when the peace treaty was announced things had been rather different.

> The soldiers were naturally elated over the consummation of the victory, in the bringing about of which many had bled, but they confined themselves to singing songs, most of the music hall description. The first of a series of ugly incidents occurred . . . members of the crowd snatched small Union Jacks from those who were wearing them, and set them on fire, to the accompaniment of cheers for the Irish Republic and its 'President'. 'The Soldier's Song' and 'The Red Flag' were also sung, these songs evidently being considered a fitting termination in the ceremony of burning Union Jacks.[10]

Multitudes had waved the boys off to war with unmitigated enthusiasm but not everyone greeted them on their return as heroes. Even before the Peace Day and the British Empire were being celebrated, the political unrest had erupted in the War of Independence from which the Irish Free State emerged. Doubtless Williams would have felt marginalised as the old political order crumbled about him. He would have enjoyed the anarchic antics of his young nephew, Teddy Williams, who had 'during the Troubles . . . painted the underside of a herring gull red, white and blue, which flew up and down over Nelson's Column in O'Connell Street'.[11]

There is some mystery surrounding the painter's last decade. On the face of it, he should have had sufficient money for his old age, not because he had saved during his good years but because he had accumulated considerable property. In 1917 his sister Eliza Anne died, to be followed less than twelve months later by Eleanor. The two sisters had lived as reclusive spinsters for some years at the family home, 19 Garville Road in Rathgar. Williams now came into possession of the house and the adjoining orchard. He had the house rented out before the end of the year. In addition to Garville Road, Eleanor left Alexander two adjoining houses on Longwood Avenue, which he appears to have disposed of.

Meanwhile the Great War had brought galloping inflation in its wake, which neither the prices Alexander could charge for his pictures nor his turnover could begin to match. In 1919 he put up for sale a number of pictures priced at £100 each. It is not known if they found buyers, but even if they did, most of his output was still valued at just a few guineas, representing only a fraction of what they would have been worth before the war. Moreover, given the long period over which he had been working and his large output, it would be surprising if his market had not reached a point of satiety. As he aged so of course did his patrons, those that were still living, and picture buyers tend to come from among those in late youth and middle age, not old age. His market was shrinking.

He looked for other sources of income. In May he let the cottage at Balscadden, Howth, where he had stayed during part of that spring. Just four days later he travelled to Achill with his friend the Rev. Boland and let Bleanaskill Lodge as well. Apart from the wrench this must have caused him, giving up his 'island home' was not, in the long run, an unqualified financial success. The island was still impoverished. One desperate tenant for want of turf to burn actually dismantled the staircase for firewood.[12]

He then took a more drastic step. At the back of 19 Garville Road, beyond the enclosed garden was open ground accessible only by the adjacent lane. It appears to have been here that the orchard was located, and where there was what Alexander described simply as 'a hut', a timber building probably built by himself, basic but apparently habitable.[13] In 1920 in his 'Chronicles' he noted that he 'Spent summer in orchard'. Then for 23 June 1923 he is somewhat more explicit: 'Moved from Hatch St to Orchard. Slept in hut and went into residence.' The comment is all boxed in, his way with writing something he regarded as a milestone, and there he stayed for the summer.

A bank overdraft, opened in 1898 against the title deeds of Hatch Street, was mounting up in the 1920s, as was the interest on it. By 1930 the facility stood at £347.13.9.[14] He could never have repaid this amount out of earnings, not even in his heyday. He had smaller personal borrowings too which were noted on the probate document. It is hard to think of any reason for vacating Hatch Street other than that he was intending to rent it, although there is no evidence that he did so. One possible scenario is that the old pair moved into the hut, leaving Alice to run Hatch Street as a boarding house, but this is no more than speculation. The 'Chronicles' offer no clues. The next entry is for 1926 when he records, again without a pronoun, spending Christmas Day in Hatch Street, as if he had just returned there. (He had not been forgotten on Achill over the festive season – the Corrigans sent up a goose.) It was an odd arrangement, moving to and forth, if this is what he did; maybe the hut was simply too cold to tolerate in winter, especially for a pair in old age. He comments on January 1926 as having been particularly cold.

There are no entries at all for 1924 or 1925 except the dates; perhaps his notebook was abandoned in Hatch Street. He was still busy, with 1924 being the year the Dublin Sketching Club celebrated its silver jubilee. The press noted that at seventy-eight Alexander was the only survivor among the original founder members who had attended the first meeting in 1874. (Alfred Grey, although elected as the club's first President, and still alive and painting, had not been present.) Fifty years later Alexander was still Honorary Secretary and would remain so until 1928. Standards had perhaps slipped at the club. *The Irish Times* was not entirely enamoured with the fifty-first exhibition of the club in 1925, going so far as to say that 'there are a number of pictures that hardly deserves their wall space', without mentioning any names. The paper did, however, single out a number of artists for praise, noting that 'Mr Williams's work is well up to his long fixed reputation as an interpreter of nature in her Connaught moods. A gallery of his Achill scenes translated into poster form would be the greatest value to the development of Ireland as a tourist resort.'[15] Evidently even at his advanced age of seventy-nine he could still please the press and he had the distinction of selling the first picture at the annual RHA exhibition of 1925, when his painting of the Gap of Dunloe was bought by

'When the boats come home, Skerries beach, evening,' oil on canvas. Signed. 1889. 24 x 36 in. (61 x 91.5 cm).

the Governor-General no less. The following year Alfred Grey died and Alexander replaced him as the most senior member of the RHA.[16]

There were some surprising outlets for his work in the latter part of his life. He records that G. A. Sterling in Canada sold 'many pictures' in 1919. The following year, in October, there was an exhibition of his watercolours in Hamilton, Ontario, which realised £45.0.0 and in November a B. A. Twiss in Saskatoon sold a number of his pictures to the value of £22.0.0. How he made these Canadian connections is not known. (*The Times*, in its obituary notice of the artist, was to say that he exhibited in Australia and South Africa but exhibitions in these countries have not been traced.) In February 1919 he got a commission worth £100.0.0 for three paintings for Mooney's new Gin Palace in Abbey Street. The largest was a very large oil of Killiney Bay. Its most striking feature to modern eyes, apart from the appealing faint pinkish tinge left after dawn and the calm sea, is the lack of houses and how rural it all seems. The picture remained in the Gin Palace until the 1960s, when it was removed during renovations and sold on. He was now described as the 'veteran artist', still receiving warm reviews, although it is difficult to take at face value the comment made at the RHA annual exhibition of 1928 that his 'work betrays no waning of skill'.[17] More might be understood from a comment on the three Achill pictures he contributed to the Water Colour Society of Ireland's exhibition the same year: 'smaller, but at the same time, more carefully composed, than most of his recent work'.[18]

One way or another, his staying power was remarkable. He had exhibited almost every year with the Dublin Sketching Club from its first exhibition in 1876 until the last year of his life, not missing a year during the 1920s (with the exception of 1922 when no exhibition was held) and was represented at the Water Colour Society of Ireland almost every year between 1892 and 1929. He mounted his last solo exhibition entitled 'Beautiful Ireland', at Mills Hall, 8 Merrion Row, in the spring of 1926 when he was in his eightieth year. 'He has sought his subjects in many parts of the island, from Harold's Cross to Achill, from Kenmare to Donaghadee,' wrote the critic for *The Irish Times*, 'an hour spent in this exhibition is like a tour of picturesque Ireland.' That was true too of his career as a whole. Given the way fashions in painting were moving, the paper went on to say: 'Mr Williams is a "straight painter" – one of the old school that is not ashamed to paint nature as she is, and as most ordinary people like to see her portrayed.'[19] He remained an exhibitor at the RHA until the end of his life, an unbroken period of sixty-one years. It is not the longest span over which an artist has shown at the RHA but it is the longest continuous period.

Ever conscious of the passage of time, Williams made a final tremulous entry in his 'Chronicles' to mark his eighty-fourth birthday on 21 April 1930, but without comment. Towards the end of the year he broke his hip in a fall. As he lay dying in Dr Steevens' Hospital he believed he was back on Achill, indicative perhaps of the depth of his attachment to the island.[20] His death took place on 16 November 1930. His estate was valued at £1,694, of which the contents of Hatch Street, including an unstated number of unsold and unfinished pictures, were assessed at £504. Willie undertook to pay his funeral expenses.[21] The funeral was a private one for family and a few friends, including the painter Alexander Colles and the singer Melfort D'Alton. He was buried in Mount Jerome Cemetery, Harold's Cross, in a grave he had originally bought for the interment of his wife's sister in 1902; and in which his son, George, was buried in 1904, twenty-six years before his father. Kitty, fourteen years younger than her husband, survived him by just over two years. She died, in Hatch Street, in 1933; their only remaining child, Alice, in 1955. There is no headstone on the family grave, only a bevelled concrete kerb on which the four family names are incised. On a whim, sometime in the 1960s or 1970s, the artist's nephew, Robert, collected a large stone from Achill and placed it at the head of the grave, where it still lies.

As an almost inevitable consequence of a long life, Alexander lived beyond his era. In the week of his death the Society of Dublin Painters exhibited fifty canvases at the Gallery, 7 St Stephen's Green. This society had been formed a decade earlier and showed where Irish art was going.

A particular criticism among the new blood was that the academicians portrayed nothing that was distinctively or idiomatically Irish, their work being, for the most part, indistinguishable from anything an English or continental painter of the past might have produced on Irish tours, precisely what had been said at the Whitechapel exhibition. Worse still, the Royal Hibernian Academy came to be seen as unamenable to fresh ideas.

It became a target of contempt for a number of young artists and they had no compunction about expressing their views. In January 1922 Paul Henry and the writer and critic Arthur Power, fired by the Irish Literary Revival and aiming to spur Ireland to a comparable revival in art, mounted an ambitious exhibition of continental and English contemporary art which they called 'Some Modern Pictures'. Their aim was to remove the complacency in Irish art by showing the freshness of what was taking place abroad. To drive their point home the exhibition was accompanied by leaflets with an almost missionary fervour: 'For your Nation's Sake – WAKE UP! . . . DEMAND MODERN WORK AND YOU WILL GET IT . . . HELP TO CREATE REVIVAL OF ART IN IRELAND' and much more in this vein.

In December of the same year the Irish Free State came into being, and the position of Lord Lieutenant was replaced by that of Governor-General. It was ironic, but not inappropriate, that the Castle, for so long a bastion of conservatism, should, in its last year of operation, send forth its last Lord Lieutenant, Edmund Fitzalan Howard, to open an exhibition with such radical aims. To provide a forum for modern Irish art the Society of Dublin Painters, limited to ten painters, had been formed in June 1920, with rooms at 7 St Stephen's Green. Paul and Grace Henry were primary movers in its founding, with Paul its first Secretary. The Society of Dublin Painters was united by a common purpose, rather than a common idiom or style, aiming to supplant the old with art that should be inimitably Irish. Its members were Jack B. Yeats, Letitia Hamilton, Mary Swanzy, Mainie Jellet, Charles Lamb (who replaced Harry Clarke) and of course Henry himself. Yeats and Henry, and later Seán Keating and Gerard Dillon among others, turned to the west as representing what Charles Lamb described as 'the national essence'. Art served as a conduit in the emergence of a new and dignified image of ourselves through what the west had to offer. In a young nation bent on forging its own identity, art played a role in providing a comfort zone of idealisation. Perhaps inevitably, in the process there were excesses. In the opinion of Aidan Dunne, writing of Keating and Lamb: 'The West and its inhabitants are mythologised in a way directly analogous to the Wild West and its denizens in the history of the United States. In fact, while the peasants and fishermen in their paintings are authentic enough, they are depicted with production values reminiscent of the efforts of Hollywood lighting cameramen.'[22] Even Henry, if for no other reason than financial exigencies, got drawn into producing poster pictures of perfectly whitewashed cottages neatly laid out in fairytale landscapes of the western seaboard which did not depict the harsh reality.

Williams was essentially a painter of the late nineteenth century, albeit that thirty years of his life were lived in the twentieth. His earliest pictures show something of residual, early nineteenth-century influences in the stately manner he painted reflections and the dappling, filigree technique that was used for the foliage of trees to add a sense of grace, and something of their striking, majestic depictions of sunsets, but generally he showed little in common with their Arcadian view of nature. In the latter part of his life, in respect of the rising generation of Irish artists bent on forging a new Irish identity, he

Watercolour of canal scene, signed and dated 1890. 17¼ x 29 in. (44 x 73 cm). The filigree painting of the trees and parkland effect are suggestive of early or mid-nineteenth-century painting.

remained an Irishman with nineteenth-century precepts. He was not, however, immune to the influence of changing styles, evident by an increasing spontaneity and informality in his work as he allowed broader brush strokes to do more. The work of his middle and later years frequently show a marked contrast to the more detailed 'photographic' realism of his early days. Set between the Romantic painters of the mid-nineteenth century and the Irish painters of the early twentieth century, Williams' approach to painting was direct and straightforward. The subject was the thing, not its transformation. He was largely, but not invariably, a realist in his approach, an intuitive artist without an overt agenda to idealise. Yet because he experimented freely, if not broadly, in both style and substance he produced work of considerable variety. As every painter imparts to his own work something of his own nature and vision, Williams demonstrated a particular affinity with minor keys, often painting with a restricted, sombre palette.

He was not a painter who confined himself to east or west coasts, on both of which he lived, but embraced almost the whole of Ireland. He sought out not only the set pieces, the beauty spots of Killarney and Glendalough, but the much less frequented midlands and he made a point of exploring the unknown and untrodden parts of Ireland. His prodigious output may thus be regarded, almost uniquely, as a record of the entire island. If he did not have the virtuosity of, among others, his near contemporary John Faulkner (1835–94), for that reason, if no other, his draughtsmanship does not draw attention to itself, and his paintings of the west have a compelling ruggedness that Faulkner's more careful, manicured depictions sometimes lack.

Williams' first love was the sea and it was perhaps with the sea and with boats that he showed most fluency, like a linguist who, however fluent in other languages, homes

Study of Dublin boat D408, artist's signature on stern of rowing boat. Oil on canvas. 12 x 9½ in. (30.5 x 24.1 cm).

in on what he has first learned. He had a self-professed delight in storms and painted plenty of them. Never a figurative draughtsman of proficiency, his storms show less of the human predicament and threatening human tragedy than Edwin Hayes could show with distraught quayside figures in the foreground while desperate sailors fight the elements outside the safe haven of the harbour. Nor did he always equal some of the powerful lighting effects and painstaking detail of which Hayes, when he had a mind to it, was capable. But his storms have the same forceful realism, more often on a smaller scale, and they lose nothing in being less melodramatic. He had the same sure touch with impending storms with boats running hard for port, ominous clouds behind them. He did not strive for effect, perspectives were not manipulated to make more of mighty waves against hapless small boats; he painted each scene as he found it, as an onlooker, with directness and spontaneity, not theatricality. He filled countless notebooks with boats, yachts, ships, barges and steamers from boyhood on and his sketches and marine paintings remain as a record of Irish boats and marine paraphernalia over a period of more than half a century. The wind-lashed coasts and inlets of north Dublin and Achill were among the most popular of his pictures. He enjoyed rivers and canals too, sketching barges wherever he came upon them. As he lived first in Clontarf and then in the city

Oil on canvas: Storm north Dublin coast. Signed. 23 x 41 in. (58.4 x 104 cm).

Oil on board: beached fishing smack. Signed. 7.1 x 10.6 in. (18 x 26.9 cm).

Watercolour signed and inscribed 'St Audeon's Gate a bit of the old city wall Dublin.'

centre, he spent much time around Poolbeg. He caught storms there, relished the busyness of the port and documented commercial and pleasure craft, and rarely passed up the chance to record warships of the British navy, and wrecks when he came upon them. The same historical interest attaches to many coastal scenes. Sometimes it is no more than bathing boxes along the shore, sometimes a few quaint old buildings, tumbledown and long since gone, or the curiosity of a turbine windmill on the otherwise undeveloped strand at Sandymount, Dublin, but all record a vanished moment. A similar, if smaller part of his output was devoted to the south of England. Again it is the historic interest that pertains to his work along the Thames, with Greenwich and Kew favoured spots, and the coastal resorts and harbours along the east coast that are of most interest. His Scottish pictures make up a smaller proportion again of his output.

More consciously, he sought to record the disappearing fabric of Dublin, particularly of the medieval city, and sketched buildings in other parts of Ireland, notably Cork and

Oil on canvas inscribed 'Pass of Delphi Killary Bay'. 24 x 36 in. (61 x 91.4 cm). *Provenance: family collection.*

Waterford. We may regret that he did not do more. His studies of buildings are among the least considered part of his output, despite their evident historical interest. St Audeon's Gate is among few medieval features still standing in Dublin. In seeking to preserve it, Dublin City Council have used the artist's close record of it. There is immense interest in the street scenes he painted, the narrow streets, sunshine and chiaroscuro effects, buildings topsy-turvy and timbered, awnings under which trades were plied and goods offered in the open air, all evoking a Dublin now utterly remote and otherwise forgotten save by such paintings as his.

It was, however, with landscape painting of Killarney, the west of Ireland and most especially of Achill that Williams was most associated during his lifetime. He was by no means the first painter into the west, of course; but his career coincided with the development of the railway, with an increasing access to, and interest in, the west and that most far flung of islands, Achill. Contemporary newspaper reviews we find, time and again, describing him as the painter who was making the west, and more particularly Achill Island, known to a wider public. All this before painters of the early twentieth century supplanted their predecessors in popular consciousness and by a neat elision came to be thought of as pioneers in the field. Williams, among others, was a generation and more ahead of them.

Remarkably, for a painter who provided such a stimulus for tourism, his art remained free of anything approaching the sentimental. Save for an occasional lurid sunset, sometimes overworked by modern tastes, his work offers no picture-postcard effects. He could be pedestrian, there is both wheat and chaff, but not the sense of a painter softening what he saw in order to appeal or to reassure. It is no less remarkable that his genteel audiences in Dublin apparently neither sought nor required such reassurance. The frisson created by viewing the bleakness of the western landscape and the hovels and cottages therein did not need toning down or refracting, for the very reason that between east and west there was, as yet, no national or cultural identification, either real or imagined.

Williams caught for us what we can hardly experience for ourselves, the west and Achill of his own experience before the First World War. He takes us back to the west when it was wilder and lonelier for being less travelled. Long shadows cast across the landscape, empty save for the barely perceived dwelling at the foot of a hill, is a sufficient and implicit reminder that here lives were lived at subsistence level. His sense of the remoteness of the island and its detachment is palpable. His work is robustly direct and unadorned, the images of workaday islanders on beaches, figures in the landscapes, in boats or in the fields or on the hills, are simply that, the record of an observer, in which we can share. The cottages he recorded as they were, not as he might have wished them to be. He showed their imperfections in detail, with window spaces moving out of line, patched thatch competing with weeds and green algae seeking out cracks and crevices along imperfect walls. He recorded too how cottages were so often composed in the landscape, in an ad hoc and irregular manner. The terrain, as he depicts it, is as rough and ready as the cottages themselves. He was in time to record the last of the beehive huts on Achill. He was an outdoors person by temperament and found stimulus in the rigours of the weather in the west. He once wrote: 'We had a nice grey sky all the time and some very beautiful effects passed over the hills.'[23] He does not flinch from showing the prevailing climate, its louring clouds, incipient rain, the damp. He was responsive to the changes of mood in landscape, to those exquisite still, calm days on Achill, capturing the early morning mist over the Menaun cliffs and the serene effect of slow, fading light on western hills and shores. He had a strong sense of the spirit of place and was at his most typical in evoking in his landscapes a pervasive, gentle melancholy portrayed in soft, muted colours and the autumnal tints that he favoured. He might fill the canvas right across but still there is the sense of empty space, of silence and solemnity. Another country he called it; he meant it and felt it.

To friends and in company Williams was known as a *bon viveur*, but his pictures suggest there was also a more reflective, even melancholic, side to his nature. His long involvement in Dublin society, through his attainments in ornithology, music and painting, made him a respected figure in widely differing, and – given the nature of Irish society at the time – often intertwining circles. He understood the importance of Dublin Castle, its regal court and all that that world had to offer him; yet as happily he spent ten years of his life, on and off, side by side, in manual labour with the men of Achill. We may salute a man of wholehearted enthusiasms, who grasped with equal wholeheartedness what life had to offer him and the opportunities he was able to make for himself. His surviving papers provide access to a life of unusual diversity and to aspects of Victorian Ireland hitherto overlooked or forgotten; and, hardly less diverse than his life, his paintings remain as a vivid legacy of the Ireland he loved.

APPENDICES

APPENDIX I: CHRONOLOGY

1846 On 21 April Williams is born at the home of his aunt, Anne Whitla, in the Diamond, Monaghan town. The Williams family of six live over their hat shop at the junction of St Peter's Street and Lawrence Street in the town centre.

Describes his boyhood as idyllic, shooting along the mudflats of the Boyne, sketching along the wharves of the river, learning the skills of birdwatching and the art of taxidermy from his father. The brothers paint backdrops for the cases of their stuffed specimens. The skills of local artist Bernard Tumalti become a source of wonder and inspiration for the young Alexander.

1860 His education at Drogheda Grammar School comes to an end when, at the age of fifteen, the family move to Dublin, living at 19 Bayview Avenue, North Strand. William Williams takes premises at 19 Westmoreland Street where he sets up his hat shop. Alexander begins a seven-year apprenticeship to his father as a hat-maker.

Alexander takes lessons in drawing at night at the RDS, the only formal art training he was ever to have.

1866 A disastrous fire destroys the hat shop and adjacent premises. William Williams, underinsured, moves to Bachelor's Walk. As a sideline Alexander and Edward set up a taxidermy business.

1867 Alice Williams dies in one of the periodic outbreaks of typhus fever. In a fine copperplate, Alexander begins his 'Ornithological Notes & Sporting Diary, 1867', the first known diary among several that he would write.

1870 The hat business is moved to No. 3 Dame Street around this time. Alexander exhibits his first picture at the Royal Hibernian Academy, *Hard Times*, a winter scene with birds painted from nature. He would continue exhibiting at the RHA without a break, for the next sixty years.

1871 The family business moves again around this time to No. 2 Dame Street where Alexander sets up a small studio for himself.

Has his first sale at the RHA, *A Study from Nature on the Three Rock Mountain, Dublin*, painted several years before. Traders on Wellington Quay agree to take his pictures for sale. Cranfield on Grafton Street sells his *Royal Salute* for £15. His art career is under way.

At the same time takes up singing, and appears in public as a ventriloquist, with a dummy of his own devising.

1872 William Williams gives up making hats around this time, and joins his sons in the taxidermy business, the new business remaining at No. 2 Dame Street.

1873 Alexander visits Achill Island for the first time.

1874 Appointed an alto singer at Her Majesty's Chapel Royal, Dublin Castle, at £30 per annum and gives notice that he is quitting the taxidermy business. The Dublin Sketching Club is formed. Alexander is a founder member and becomes Honorary Secretary, a post he keeps, except when he serves as President, until 1928.

1875 Invited by Grattan Kelly to become a member of the re-formed Dublin Glee and Madrigal Union and boards with Kelly at 102 Lower Mount Street where he sets up a studio. The union sing in Ireland, and in Manchester and London, with considerable success.

He makes a tour of the Antrim coast, writing up an amusing journal on the woes of painting *en plein air*.

1876 He leaves 102 Lower Mount Street and moves his studio to 32 Lower Abbey Street. He joins G. B. Thompson on board the cutter, the *Hinda*, for a 38-day sketching cruise along the west coast of Scotland and keeps a journal of the trip.

Exhibits at the first exhibition for members of the Dublin Sketching Club and remains a frequent exhibitor thereafter.

Fails at voice trials held at St Patrick's Cathedral.

1877 Celebrates the arrival of the new Lord Lieutenant, the Duke of Marlborough, with dinner with his friend Bram Stoker at Stoker's house, 7 St Stephen's Green.

He appears at the Theatre Royal in the opera *Guy Mannering* which is mounted for the celebrated English tenor, Sims Reeves.

Receives a cheque from the RHA this year for £50.5.6. Attends the Handel Festival in London and sketches around Windsor with his friend Bingham McGuinness.

Is 'greatly complimented' when B. Colles Watkins buys two of his watercolours, *St Paul's* and *Near Windsor*. 'Another compliment' when Augustus Burke 'honoured me by purchasing a water colour of Limehouse'.

1878 Sets up an art union of his own which nets him £29.5.0, selling 117 tickets at 5/-, but not every winner is satisfied with the prizes.

Succeeds at the cathedral voice trials and obtains a place as an alto in Christ Church Cathedral at a salary of £75 per annum.

Moves his studio to the 'next storey' in the same building, 32 Abbey Street. He concentrates on watercolours and sketches along the Liffey and the coast north of Dublin, mentioning Dollymount, Malahide and Howth.

William Williams reads a paper on the 'Irish Elk' before the British Association at the Royal College of Surgeons and Alexander sings at a *conversazione* held by the association.

1879 Sketches extensively in the west and attends porcelain painting sessions at the Queen's Institute.

As President of the Dublin Sketching Club this year he receives the Lord Lieutenant at the society's annual exhibition. One of the severest winters of the century. Alexander becomes engaged to Catherine Gray, daughter of a vicar choral, George Gray, and they amuse themselves ice skating in the Royal Zoological Gardens and elsewhere.

Starts giving painting lessons.

1881 Rents 7 Grantham Street for three years. Marries Catherine Gray at St Peter's Church on 4 April and spends his honeymoon, most of a month, sketching around Rostrevor, County Down. The Lord Lieutenant buys one of his sketches, *Decay*, at the Dublin Sketching Club annual exhibition.

1882 His son, George, is born in Grantham Street on 26 July.

With his brother Edward, Alexander tours Donegal, sketching while his brother collects bird specimens.

1883 Returns to London for the Handel Festival and sketches on the Thames. Makes a return trip to Rostrevor, County Down. Exhibits at the Cork Exhibition and sells *A Quiet Evening on Bonchurch Cove, Ventor* for £15.15.0. He builds a wooden studio at the back of 7 Grantham Street.

1884 Sells several pictures at the Irish Fine Art Society exhibition. Returns to Achill and follows this trip with nine weeks at Skerries. Paints along the Irish coast north of Dublin, including Balbriggan.

He is elected an associate member of the Royal Hibernian Academy and opens a two-day 'Private View' of his work at the Leinster Hall, Molesworth Street. The large attendance includes Lady Ardilaun and Sir Thos Jones, PRHA. He sells nine pictures 'to the amazement of many people who ridiculed the idea . . .'

1885 His daughter Alice is born at 7 Grantham Street on 12 February.

Sketches locally: Carrickmines, Glencullen River, the Grand Canal, Rush and Howth. Returns to London and sketches extensively around Limehouse, Greenwich and 'about London'. Takes on more pupils and they venture out to Milltown to sketch from nature. He repeats his private exhibition held over two days at the Leinster Hall.

1886 Chooses Waterford this year to sketch and paint over two months. Mounts solo exhibition at the smaller premises of the Dublin Sketching Club, 9 Merrion Row.

1887 Puts on a private view of his pictures again at the Dublin Sketching Club premises, 9 Merrion Row, realising £50.14.6.

1888 He is a member of the Dublin General Committee for the Irish Exhibition at Olympia, London, where he sells *Trawlers Becalmed* for £30. Participates in the Handel Festival at the Crystal Palace as an Irish representative. Now gives 58 Harcourt Street as his studio address.

1889 Appointed as alto singer at St Patrick's Cathedral at £100 per annum.

1890 Stays with Dawson Borrer at Altamont House, County Carlow, for twelve days; does studies of the garden and the county, mainly in watercolour.

Makes a sketching trip to Luss, Loch Lochmond, where he is joined by members of the Dublin Sketching Club.

1891 Elected a constituent member of the Royal Hibernian Academy of Arts.

1892 Moves from 58 Harcourt Street to 4 Hatch Street Lower.

Resumes his solo exhibitions with two shows at the Leinster Hall, the first in February, the second in December. In between he mounts an exhibition at 35 Dawson Street during the week of Dublin University Tercentenary celebrations which proves a failure. He will continue to hold solo exhibitions in Dublin, almost annually, for more than thirty years.

1893 He introduces weekly musical recitals as a feature of his solo exhibitions. These become increasingly popular, attracting audiences of 150 and more.

He exhibits a large picture, *Sweet Dublin Bay*, at the World Fair in Chicago.

1895 Extends his annual solo exhibition at the Leinster Hall to four days. His solo exhibitions will eventually last three and four weeks. Heavy snow does not prevent this one being a success. The Lord Lieutenant, Lord Houghton, buys a watercolour of an Achill boat-builder's cottage.

Visits Belfast for a fortnight's sketching in July, then spends six weeks touring Sligo and Galway in September and October.

1897

He is invited by Dublin Corporation to report on the renovation of the portraits in the Mansion House being undertaken by Nairn of Belfast.

His travels take him to Killarney in May, London in June, and Sutton during July and August. He twice visits Dugort, Achill Island, in the autumn. In October his son, George, contracts rheumatic fever.

On 19 December Alexander retires from his position as alto at St Patrick's Cathedral.

1899 At Bleanaskill Bay, Achill Island he takes a lease on 3 acres of land at £3 per annum.

For the first time he holds solo exhibitions across the water, mounting 'Wildest West of Ireland' at Grundy & Smith, 4 Exchange Street, Manchester during the summer, followed by an autumn exhibition at The Studio, 9 Temple Dale, Liverpool.

1900 Mounts solo exhibition at the Hannah More Hall, Park Street, Bristol in June for a fortnight.

1901 His first London exhibition, 'Picturesque Ireland', held at the Modern Gallery, 175 Bond Street, W1.

Travels to Achill with George in July and stays at Sheridan's Hotel, Dugort. Visits the Inishkea Islands. Rents a cottage in the west for nine weeks. Returns to Dugort for a fortnight in October.

William Williams dies on 10 December aged eighty-eight. Alexander returns to Achill at the end of the month with his friend George Prescott.

1902 In June he moves his studio, which he had retained at 58 Harcourt Street, to 4 Hatch Street. Buys 'lease of house for ever for £60.'

1903 He has his second solo exhibition in London, 'The Land of the Shamrock', at the Modern Gallery, 175 Bond Street. Travels to London on 29 March to hang the pictures himself. The exhibition then moves in May to Grundy & Smith, 4 Exchange Street, Manchester. Visits C. J. Patten in Sheffield, and the Markels in Bewsay, Warrington, sketching in the environs, returning to Manchester daily.

In June visits Cork on a sketching tour 'in scorching weather'. Attends the 'Great Gordon Bennett Motor Race' on 1 July.

He is back in Dublin for a royal levee at Dublin Castle on 22 July when he is presented to King Edward VII.

22 November: the Dublin Sketching Club annual exhibition opens. The Lord Lieutenant, Lord Dudley, buys a small sketch of Connemara by the artist.

1904 4 January: his only son dies at home, 4 Hatch Street Lower.

11 May: he sells a number of sketches of Old Dublin to Lord Iveagh for £54.

In connection with the Congested Districts Board he exhibits at the St Louis World Fair. Participates in a group exhibition at the Bond Street Gallery, London.

15 May: with Edward goes on an excursion to Woodenbridge and Vale of Avoca 'in search of summer migrants'.

11 June: visits Inny Junction, County Westmeath to collect butterflies. 'Caught numerous specimens [of] Greasy Fritillaries.' Preliminary sketches and a finished oil of the adjacent River Inny are extant.

Tours Kerry for two months during the summer, boards at Ventry and paints 'a large number of pictures in the vicinity'.

1905 Holds his diamond jubilee exhibition over three weeks at the Leinster Hall, Molesworth Street. It is attended by 1,147 visitors.

24 May: receives a station to station pass from the Great Northern Railway Company and spends the remainder of the month travelling along the line, sketching as he goes. In June he returns to Killarney, Aghadoe, Castleisland and Valentia, staying with friends en route.

3 December: makes a note in his chronicles that on this day the three brothers, Alexander, Edward and Willie, went for their last birdwatching excursion together. Edward dies unexpectedly on 15 December.

1906 He tours the south of Ireland and visits London in April and May for his 'Green Isle of Erin' exhibition at the Modern Gallery, now at 61 New Bond Street. (In his 'Chronicles & Memoirs' he mistakenly places this exhibition in 1905.)

His ornithological notes & news cuttings, in two volumes (with overlapping dates) are begun this year and continue until 1915. As neither volume bears a title it leaves open the possibility that they were preceded by others.

1907 Begins his 'Achill Natural History Notes & Diary', a daily account of his life on the island which he continues until 1913. Working in earnest on building Bleanaskill Lodge and making something of the grounds.

Participates in two group exhibitions at the Modern Gallery, London.

1908 Pays a visit to Prestatin in Wales with his family. In addition to landscape sketches he includes a surprising number of studies of Welsh houses in his sketchbook.

1909 In April the Modern Gallery puts on 'Ould Donegal' exhibition, his last in London.

1910 Goes to Killarney on 24 February where there are great floods, of which he gives an impression in a sketch of the Lake Hotel. Tries his hand once again at taxidermy, setting up a case in the lounge of the hotel containing artificial rockwork and no fewer than fifty birds. (The case has long since been dismantled, part of the contents of which were buried in the hotel grounds.)

In June he stays in Skerries in a house rented by his brother Willie, before returning to the Lake Hotel, then going to Youghal, County Cork. On 3 August he visits ornithologist R. J. Ussher at Cappagh House near Cappoquin, and writes up the event in his 'Chronicles'.

He returns to Achill on 31 August and stays at the post office. On 17 September he and his family and his two sisters occupy Bleanaskill Lodge for the first time.

1911 January: is commissioned by Messrs Blackie & Son to illustrate *Beautiful Ireland*, to be published in four volumes by province. Fee is 100 guineas for the copyright of forty-eight pictures with the artist retaining ownership.

In June visits Belfast, boards the *Titanic*, tours parts of the North, taking in the Red House, Strabane, and, on what he describes as a 'Red Letter day' visits the Duke and Duchess of Abercorn at Barons Court.

Starts his two volumes of 'Memoirs' which take his life only to 1876; but year-by-year entries, albeit with evident gaps and some years missing, in 'Chronicles & Memoirs', cover his entire life.

1913 He participates in the Irish Exhibition at the Whitechapel Gallery, London, contributing *As Evening Grey Advances Slow*.

1914 Visits London for the last time, staying with the Markels at Queen's Gate and enjoys being ferried around by their chauffeur. He pastes an account of the trip into his 'Chronicles & Memoirs'.

1915 He and his family involve themselves in war charities and entertaining the wounded from the local hospitals. His life in Dublin proceeds much as before, contributing paintings, as usual, to the RHA, Dublin Sketching Club and the Water Colour Society of Ireland, as well as holding his own annual exhibition with music recitals. Continues to spend time on Achill, his 'island home'.

1916 15 March: his sister Eliza dies.

On 21 April celebrates his seventieth birthday and declares: 'Still going strong no appearance whatever of senile decay.'

Exhibits at O'Leary's Gallery, Detroit but never visits North America in person.

The Rebellion at the GPO Dublin breaks out on Easter Monday, 24 April, 'to the everlasting disgrace of Ireland at a time when England was fighting for her existence'; this is the one and only political comment among his all his writings.

1917 6 March: his sister Eleanor dies and Alexander comes into the family property 19 Garville Road, Rathgar. Spends summer preparing the house for letting and clearing the adjacent orchard.

1919 Travels to Achill and lets Bleanaskill Lodge.

Attends the Great Peace Day Celebration in College Green: 'Got a splendid position in the Band directly opposite to where General French took the salute. A grand sight.'

'Many pictures sold in Canada during the year by G. A. Sterling.'

1920 Obtains a commission for £100 for three pictures for Messrs Mooneys' new Gin Palace in Abbey Street, which include a large canvas of Killiney Bay.

In October there is an exhibition of his watercolours in Hamilton, Ontario, Canada which realises £45. The following year B. A. Twiss of Saskatoon sells pictures to the value of £22.

This year he appears to have vacated, at least temporarily, 4 Hatch Street and goes to live in 'the hut' (probably of his own making) in the orchard behind 19 Garville Road.

1926 He is eighty years of age this year. He mounts his last solo exhibition, at Mill's Hall, 8 Merrion Row. Spends Christmas in 4 Hatch Street. 'A very cold wintry January up to the end. Intensely cold without frost.'

1928 Resigns as Honorary Secretary of the Dublin Sketching Club.

1929 Exhibits for the last time with the Dublin Sketching Club, contributing seven pictures.

1930 Now eighty-four, he exhibits for the last time at the RHA, where he has exhibited every year since 1870, and at the Water Colour Society of Ireland, at which he has exhibited most years since 1892.

Towards the end of the year falls and breaks his hip. He dies on 16 November and, after a private funeral, is buried in Mount Jerome Cemetery, Harold's Cross, Dublin.

APPENDIX 2:
CATALOGUES OF SOLO EXHIBITIONS, 1884–1915

Note: The following catalogues are those which have survived among the artist's papers, with the exception of the list of pictures exhibited at the St Louis Exposition, 1904, which has been taken from the official catalogue. In some instances both printed and handwritten catalogues have survived. Where the printed catalogue is available it has been used in preference to the handwritten. There are occasional small variations between the two. For the pictures the artist exhibited at the Royal Hibernian Academy see Royal Hibernian Academy of Arts Index of Exhibitors 1826–1979, Vol. III, *compiled by Ann M. Stewart. Similarly, for pictures the artist exhibited at the Dublin Sketching Club, the Irish Water Colour Society of Ireland and sundry other societies, see* Irish Art Societies and Sketching Clubs Index of Exhibitors 1870–1980, Vol. II *by Ann M. Stewart.*

CATALOGUE

OF A COLLECTION OF

**WATER COLOR DRAWINGS AND OIL PAINTINGS
EXECUTED DURING THE YEAR 1884**

**By A. WILLIAMS, RHA
(STUDIO, 7 GRANTHAM STREET, DUBLIN)**

**PRIVATE VIEW
IN THE
Leinster Hall, 35 Molesworth Street, Dublin
on
TUESDAY AND WEDNESDAY, NOVEMBER 18 & 19, 1884**

CATALOGUE

1	Sketch in a Cornfield – Twilight	£5
2	Weeds in a Watercourse	£7
3	Farm near Milverton	£10
4	Sketch of Sea, Achill Island	£10
5	Clay Cliffs at Sutton	£10
6	Shore near Skerries	£15
7	A Quiet Pool – the Red Island, Skerries	
8	Fishing Boat on the Beach	£10
9	In Candlestick Bay, Howth	£12
10	Rocks in the Bight of Barnageragh	
11	Evening Shadows	£12
12	Barley Field, Red Island, Skerries	£10
13	The Windmill, Skerries	£8
14	Evening near the Sea	£25
15	Low Water	£10
16	A Grey Day – Skerries, looking towards Balbriggan	£12

Sketches in Achill Island, Mayo

17	Paddy Barrett's Interior	£8
18	Keel Strand 'Peaceful in the vale extended lies the loveliest of all Strands –	£15
	Keel, whose azure waves are blended with a blaze of golden sands.'	
19	Keem Bay	£20
20	The Cathedral Rocks, Minaun Cliffs	£20
	'And the Minaun heights uplifted, fling their shades from pile to pile,	
	Down fantastic chasms rifted, like an old cathedral's aisle.'	
21	Dugort Sands – Morning	
22	Slievemore Mountain, from Valley Strand	£10
	'Now the giant Slievemore frowning intercepts my roving gaze,	
	O'er its slopes, the summit crowning, fleeing mist in gambol plays.'	
	A. H. KNAPP, M.A., *Hartford College, Oxford*.	
23	Atlantic Surf – Dugort Bay	
24	Sketch in a Watercourse	£10
25	Reapers – Sketch in a Cornfield	£5
26	Water Plants	£8
27	The Red Island, Skerries – Evening	£8

Water Colors

28	Early Morning on the Liffey – Lighting Furnaces,	£6
	Holyhead Boats	
29	Between Clonskeagh and Miltown	£10
30	Off Sir John's Quay – Grey Morning	£10
31	In Baldoyle Estuary	£8
32	A Gleam of Sunshine, Dollymount	£8
33	In the Ringsend Docks	£10
34	Canal Boats, Dolphin's Barn	£20
35	Entrance, Ringsend Docks	£10
36	Showery Weather, North Bull	£8
37	Tedcastle's Wharf, Winter Morning	£10
38	Templeogue	£8
39	Clonskeagh	£5
40	Trawlers at Anchor – a Calm	£8
41	The Tolka at Ballybough Bridge	£5
42	The 9.30 Holyhead Boat, North Wall	£6
43	A Sunset Sketch	£8
44	Barley Field, Skerries	£10
45	The Captain's Point, Skerries	£8
46	Corn Field – Sunset	£8
47	Rocky Shore	£8
48	Sketch in Corn Field – Evening	£8
49	The Brewery, Mortlake, Thames	£4
50	Near Kew Bridge	£4

Catalogue
of the
Pictures and Sketches
By
Alexander Williams, RHA

Exhibited at the Leinster Lecture Hall
35 Molesworth Street
Dublin

February 1892

1	Rocks, Ireland's Eye	£2.2.0
2	River at Wicklow	£2.10.0
3	Rocky Coast	£2.2.0
4	Study of Apple Blossom	£3.3.0
5	Low Water at Twickenham	£2.10.0
6	Evening, Ireland's Eye (Prize)	£2.2.0
7	Moonlight, Liffey	£2.2.0
8	Winter, Rathfarnham	£2.2.0
9	Boggy Ground, Raheny	£3.3.0
10	Thames at Kew	£2.2.0
11	Close of Day	£2.2.0
12	Bray River	£4.4.0
13	Near Dargle	£3.3.0
14	Road to Shore (Prize)	£4.4.0
15	The Holyhead Boat	£4.4.0
16	Howth from Kosh	£3.3.0
17	Old Bridge, Tramore	£4.4.0
18	Boats, Bray River	£5.5.0
19	Not for sale	
20	Rathfarnham Bridge	£2.2.0
21	On the Dodder, Milltown	£4.4.0
22	Old Milltown Bridge	£3.3.0
23	Wicklow Church	£2.2.0
24	Old Doorway, Malpas Street	£4.4.0
25	A Corner in Nicholas Street	£4.4.0
26	Hanover Lane	
27	Skipper's Alley	£2.2.0
28	Not for sale	
29	An Ancient Entrance	£3.3.0
29A	Site of a Ruined Industry	£6.6.0
30	A Boatyard, Greenwich	£4.4.0
31	The Haunted House	£4.4.0
32	Rough Weather	£2.10.0
33	A Comfortable Homestead, Skerries	£4.4.0
34	Early Spring, Rostrevor	£5.5.0
35	When the Wind Bloweth in from the Sea	£3.3.0
36	Bucky Boats, Howth	£3.3.0
37	Toilers of the Sea	£2.10.0

38	At Merrion Gates	£2.2.0
39	A Hazy Afternoon	£5.5.0
40	An Incident at the Poolbeg Light	£7.7.0
41	A Boatyard, Ringsend	£4.4.0
42	A Mountain Road	£4.4.0
43	A Fisherman's Home	£2.10.0
44	On the Liffey, Chapelizod	£3.3.0
45	Shore at Sutton	£3.3.0
46	Spring, The Dodder, Templeogue	£6.6.0
47	Near Baldoyle Station	£2.10.0
48	A Sunset Sketch	£4.4.0
49	Grand Canal Richmond	£4.4.0
50	Coming to Anchor (not for sale)	
50A	Collier Unloading	£3.3.0
51	Summer Day near Kew	£5.5.0
52	Rocks in Balscadden Bay	£3.3.0
53	On the Grand Canal near Baggot Street	£4.4.0
54	Morning Strand near Howth Harbour	£2.10.0
55	A Cottage at Tramore	£4.4.0
56	Dutch Boat at Limehouse	£4.4.0
57	A Sketch at Shankill	£4.4.0
58	Dog Fish	£2.2.0
59	Becalmed	£2.10.0
60	The Golden Eventide	£30
61	At Anchor	£2.2.0
62	Old Mill, Donnybrook	£3.3.0
63	Evening Sketch	£2.10.0
64	In the Dargle	£3.3.0
65	In Red Rock Bay	£7
66	Rowardennan, Loch Lomond	£10.10.0
67	Evening on the Thames, Greenwich	£20
68	A Calm Evening, Killiney (not for sale)	
69	On the Shore at Tarbet	£10.10.0
70	Squally Weather	£7.7.0
71	Skerries Sands	£4.4.0
72	Autumn, The Liffey	£5.5.0
73	Dunhill Castle	£6.6.0
74	Fitting Out, Ringsend	£2.10.0
75	In the Demesne, Rathfarnham	£3.3.0
76	Lifting an Anchor	£2.10.0
77	Rocky Shore, Killybegs	£3.3.0
78	Tranquillity (Prize)	£3.3.0
79	Summer in the Brides Glen	£2.10.0
80	The Busy Thames	£5.5.0
80A	In the Rocky Valley	£4.4.0
81	A Wet Morning, West Pier, Howth	£3.3.0
82	The Liffey at Chapelizod	£3.3.0
83	Return of the Trawlers	£2.10.0
84	Near New Ross	£5.5.0

85	The Grand Canal, James St Harbour	£3.3.0
86	Preparing to Sail	£2.2.0
87	Cottages near Mount Charles	£5.5.0
88	The Entrance Gate	£4.4.0
89	The House	£4.4.0
90	The Summer House	£4.4.0
91	The Lake	£4.4.0
92	The Garden	£4.4.0
93	From the Lake	£4.4.0
94	The Shore at Bray River	£3.3.0
95	Head of the Upper Lake, Glendalough	£4.4.0
96	View from Howth Demesne	£3.3.0
97	View from Rothesay	£3.3.0
98	Never Again	£3.3.0
99	Pier Head	£2.2.0
100	Carrick Castle	£3.3.0
101	On Ireland's Eye	£4.4.0
102	The River, Gloomy Glendalough	£4.4.0
103	In the Alexandra Basin	£2.10.0
104	Spring time on the Dodder at Templeogue	£5.5.0
105	A likely place for a Trout	£5.5.0
106	Gone to the Dogs, Halpin's Pool	£3.3.0
107	Winter at Dolphin's Barn	£4.4.0
108	Dunhill Castle	£3.3.0
109	First Lock, Grand Canal	£4.4.0
110	The Pond at Inchicore	£2.10.0
111	Killiney Strand	£3.3.0
112	The Dodder at Clonskeagh	£4.4.0
113	A Grey Day, Balbriggan Strand	£4.4.0
114	Boats at Dollymount	£2.10.0
115	Two Old Salts	£2.2.0
116	Summer Afternoon, Ireland's Eye	£5.5.0
117	Killybegs, Donegal	£4.4.0
118	September Gold	£2.10.0
119	Brighton Fishing Boats	£2.10.0
120	Brick Barges, Portobello	£2.10.0
121	The Remains of the Thrasher	£3.3.0
122	In the Dargle	£3.3.0
123	Retiring to Rest	£2.2.0
124	An Old Stile	£2.2.0
125	Low Water, Howth Harbour	£3.3.0
126	On Wicklow Head	£3.3.0
127	The Deerin [Derreen] River, Carlow	£4.4.0
128	At Putney	£2.10.0
129	Luss Straits (Prize)	£3.3.0
130	Of No Further Use	£3.3.0
131	Easterly Wind, North Bull	£2.10.0
132	Summertime, Grand Canal, Richmond	£2.10.0
133	A Sunny Day	£2.10.0

134	Breezy Weather	£2.10.0
135	At Malahide	£2.2.0
136	River Steamer, Thames	£23.2.0
137	Boats on the Beach	£2.10.0
138	Study of Sparrow and Apple Blossom	£3.3.0
139	In Baldoyle Estuary	£2.10.0
140	Aughanure Castle	£2.10.0
141	Two Sketches in Frame	£3.0.0.
142	Two Sketches in Frame	£3.0.0
143	Nothing recorded	
144	Study of Kingfisher and Ring Dotterel	£3.3.0
145	Rathfarnham	£2.2.0
146	On the North Bull, Dollymount	£2.2.0
147	Shore near Balbriggan Harbour	£2.2.0
148	When Daylight Dies	£2.10.0

New Gallery, 35 Dawson St.
July 4, 1892
Exhibition of Pictures by A. Williams, RHA

1	Rocks, Ireland's Eye	£2.2.0
2	River at Wicklow Town	£2.10.0
3	Rocky Coast, Holyhead	£2.2.0
4	Study of Apple Blossom and Sparrow	£3.3.0
5	Low Water at Twickenham	£2.10.0
6	Evening, Ireland's Eye	£2.2.0
7	-	
8	-	
9	Boggy Ground, Raheny	£3.3.0
10	The Thames at Kew	£2.2.0
11	Close of Day	£2.2.0
12	Bray River near Gas Works	£4.4.0
13	Near the Dargle River	£3.3.0
14	Road to the Shore, Portmarnock	£4.4.0
15	The Holyhead Boat	£4.4.0
16	Howth from Kosh Point	£3.3.0
17	Old Bridge, Tramore	£4.4.0
18	Boats, Bray River	£5.5.0
19	Sea Holly (not for sale)	-
20	Rathfarnham Bridge	£2.2.0
21	On the Dodder below Miltown	£4.4.0
22	Old Miltown Bridge	£3.3.0
23	Wicklow Church	£2.2.0
24	Old Doorway, Malpas Street	£4.4.0
25	A Corner in Nicholas Street	£4.4.0
26	Hanover Lane	-
27	Skipper's Alley	£2.2.0
28	Old Wood Street	£3.3.0

29	An Ancient Entrance	£3.3.0
29A	Site of a Ruined Industry	£6.6.0
30	A Boatyard, Greenwich	£4.4.0
31	The Haunted House, Donegal	£4.4.0
32	Rough Weather, Antrim	£2.10.0
33	A Comfortable Homestead	£4.4.0
34	Early Spring	£5.5.0
35	When the Wind Bloweth	£3.3.0
36	Bucky Boats	£3.3.0
37	Toilers of the Sea	£2.10.0
38	At Merrion Gates	£2.2.0
39	A Hazy Afternoon	£5.5.0
40	An Incident at the Poolbeg	£7.7.0
41	A Boatyard, Ringsend	£4.4.0
42	A Mountain Road	£4.4.0
43	A Fisherman's Home	£2.10.0
44	On the Liffey, Chapelizod	£3.3.0
45	Shore at Sutton	£3.3.0
46	Spring, The Dodder at Templeogue	£6.6.0
47	Near Baldoyle Station	£2.10.0
48	A Sunset Sketch	£4.4.0
49	Grand Canal	£4.4.0
50	Coming to Anchor (not for sale)	-
50A	Collier Unloading	£3.3.0
51	A Summer Day	£5.5.0
52	Rocks, Balscadden Bay	£3.3.0
53	On the Grand Canal	£4.4.0
54	Morning Strand, Howth	£2.10.0
55	A Cottage, Tramore	£4.4.0
56	Dutch Boat	£4.4.0
57	A Sketch at Shankill	£4.4.0
58	Dog Fish	
59	-	
60	The Golden Eventide	£30
61	At Anchor	£2.2.0
62	Old Mill	£3.3.0
63	Evening Sketch	£2.10.0
64	In the Dargle	£3.3.0
65	In Red Rock Bay	£7
66	-	
67	Evening on the Thames, Greenwich	
68	-	
69	On the Shore at Tarbet	£10.10.0
70	Squally Weather	£7.7.0
71	Skerries Sands	£4.4.0
72	Autumn	£5.5.0
73	Dunhill Castle	£6.6.0
74	Fitting out at Ringsend	£2.10.0
75	In the Demesne, Rathfarnham	£3.3.0

76	-	
77	Rocky Shore	£3.3.0
78	Tranquillity	£3.3.0
79	Summer in the Brides Glen	£2.10.0
80	The Busy Thames	£3.3.0
81	A Wet Morning, Howth	£3.3.0
82	The Liffey, Chapelizod	£3.3.0
83	Return of the Trawlers	£2.10.0
84	Near New Ross	£5.5.0
85	-	
86	Preparing to Sail	
87	Near Mount Charles	£5.5.0
88	The Entrance Gate	£4.4.0
89	The House	£4.4.0
90	The Summer House	£4.4.0
91	The Lake	£4.4.0
92	The Garden	£4.4.0
93	From the Lake	£4.4.0
94	The Shore at Bray	£3.3.0
95	Head of the Upper Lake, Glendalough	£4.4.0
96	View from Howth	£3.3.0
97	View from Rothesay	£3.3.0
98	Never Again	£3.3.0
99	Pier Heads	£2.2.0
100	Carrick Castle	£3.3.0
101	On Ireland's Eye	£4.4.0
102	The River, Glendalough	£4.4.0
103	Alexandra Basin	£2.10.0
104	Springtime on the Dodder	£5.5.0
105	A Likely Place for a Trout	£5.5.0
106	Gone to the Dogs	£3.3.0
107	Winter at Dolphin's Barn	£4.4.0
108	Dunhill Castle	£3.3.0
109	First Lock	£4.4.0
110	The Pond, Inchicore	£2.10.0
111	Killiney Strand	£3.3.0
112	The Dodder, Clonskeagh	£4.4.0
113	A Grey Day	£4.4.0
114	Boats at Dollymount	£2.10.0
115	Two Old Salts	£2.2.0
116	Summer Afternoon, Ireland's Eye	£5.5.0
117	Killybegs	£4.4.0
118	September Gold	£2.10.0
119	Brighton Fishing Boats	£2.10.0
120	Brick Barges	£2.10.0
121	The Remains of the Thrasher	£3.3.0
122	In the Dargle	£3.3.0
123	Retiring to Rest	£2.2.0
124	-	

125	Low Water	£3.3.0
126	On Wicklow Head	£3.3.0
127	The Deerin [Derreen] River	£4.4.0
128	At Putney	£2.10.0
129	Luss Straits	£3.30
130	Of No Further Use	£3.3.0
131	Easterly Wind	£2.10.0
132	Summer Time	£2.10.0
133	A Sunny Day	£2.10.0
134	-	
135	At Malahide	£2.2.0
136	River Steamer	£2.2.0
137	Boats on the Beach	£2.10.0
138	Study of Sparrow	£3.3.0
139	The Baldoyle Estuary	£2.10.0
140	Aughanure Castle	£2.10.0
141	Howth Harbour	£5.5.0
142	In Steephill Cove	£4.4.0
143	Shrimp Boats	£4.4.0
144	At Bray	£2.10.0
145	A Country Road	£8.8.0
146	On Inishanboe	£3.3.0
147	Stone Cabin	£3.3.0
148	Harbour, Grand Canal	£8.8.0
149	Donegal Harbour	£2.10.0
150	Heavy Weather, Killybegs	£25
151	At Carrickmines	£4.4.0
152	Low Water, Donegal	£2.10.0
153	A Landing Place	£2.10.0
154	After a Stormy Night	£6.6.0
155	The Sands of Fintra	£10
156	Hooker in Achill Sound	£3.3.0
157	A Bright Day	£5.5.0
158	In the Glen of the Downs	£3.3.0
159	Sunset in the Harbour of Dublin	£40
160	On the Kilbroney	
161	Salmon Weir	£10
162	Ben Lomond from Luss	£10
163	Under Repairs	£3.3.0
164	Dublin Bay from Vico [Road]	£5.5.0
165	When the Boats Come Home	£10.10.0
166	A Grey Day	£5.5.0
167	Stormy Weather	£8.8.0
168	A Spate on the Kilbroney	
169	Black Castle	£10.10.0
170	The Channel Fleet	£2.10.0
171	Rocks in Balscaddan Bay	£3.3.30
172	On the Back Strand	£5.5.0
173	When the Hoar Frost was Chill	£10

174	Showery Weather	£10
175	Wreck of the Susannah	£4.4.0
176	Muckross Bay	£3.3.0
177	Rocky Coast	£5.5.0
178	Hazy Weather, Loch Long	£8.8.0
179	Two Sketches	£3.3.0
180	Two Sketches	£3.3.0
181	The Islands of Keem	£5.5.0
182	Keem Bay	£10
183	Stormy Weather	£8.8.0
184	Skylarks	£2.10.0
185	Evening, Grand Canal	£10.10.0
186	Morning in the Harbour of Dublin	£35
187	The Pigeon House Fort	-
188	Repairing the Trawler	£6.6.0
189	Low Water in the Bay of Fintra	£10

EXHIBITION AT 35 DAWSON ST. JULY 4, 1892

Although this list appears in the artist's notebook, it is not in his hand

Monday the 4th between 10 & 3 o'clock

5 catalogues at 6d – 2/6d	7 visitors at 6d – 3/6d	£ 0.6.0	
After 3 o'clock			
4 catalogues 2/-	Visitors 6/-	£ 0.8.0	£0.14.0

Tuesday the 5th – 10 to 3 o'clock

3 catalogues at 6d – 1/6d	11 visitors 5/6d	£0.7.0	
After 3 o'clock			
1 catalogue at 3d	3 visitors 3/-	£0.3.3	£0.10.3

Wednesday the 6th from 10 to 3 o'clock

12 visitors at 6d – 6/-	4 catalogues 2/- 1 at 3d £0.8.3		
After 3 o'clock			
2 visitors 2/-	2 catalogues – 1/-	£0.3.0	£0.11.3

Thursday the 7th from 10 to 3 o'clock

12 visitors at 6d	2 catalogues at 6d 1 at 3d	£0.7.3
After 3 o'clock		
2 visitors 2/-	2 catalogues 1/-	£0.3.0 £0.10.3

CATALOGUE
OF THE
PICTURES AND SKETCHES,
BY
ALEXANDER WILLIAMS, RHA,
ON PRIVATE VIEW
AT THE LEINSTER HALL,
35 MOLESWORTH STREET, DUBLIN,
Tuesday 19th, Wednesday 20th, Thursday 21st,
December, 1893.

THE STUDIO, 4 HATCH STREET.

1	A Wet Sheet and Flowing Main	£2.10.0
2	Summer Evening off Kingstown	£4.0.0
3	Rattling Along	£2.10.0
4	Close of Autumn	£2.10.0
5	Showery Weather	
6	An April Day, Carrickmines	£8.8.0
7	Storm	£2.10.0
8	Calm	£2.10.0

SKETCHES AT CLEW BAY, CO. MAYO

9	Croagh Patrick from Boat Haven Strand	£12.12.0
10	Close of an Autumn Day, Boat Haven	£4.4.0
11	Old Head	£5.5.0
12	Closkeen, Road to Doo Lough	£12.12.0
13	Clare Island from Old Head, Evening	£5.5.0
14	Home Sweet Home	£4.4.0
15	Cottage at Old Head	£10.10.0
16	Bad Harvest Weather, Murrisk	£15
17	The Clear Cold Eve Declining	£3
18	A Bright Spring Morning, Carrickmines	£5.5.0
19	Over the Rolling Sea	£2.10.0
20	A Stilly Afternoon	£3
21	A Hazy Summer Day, Baldoyle	£4.4.0
22	Duncraggan, Brig o'Turk	£10
23	Portobello Bridge	£2.2.0
24	At Orkneyville, Drogheda	£2.2.0
25	Harold's Cross Bridge	£2.2.0
26	The Pond, Stephen's Green	£2.2.0
27	On the Boyne at Mornington	£2.2.0
28	The Dodder at Clonskeagh	£2.2.0
29	Ganavan Strand, Oban	£10
30	A Summer Day on Ireland's Eye	£4.4.0
31	A Cottage by the Sea	£2.10.0
32	Shipping in the River Liffey	£5.5.0
33	River Sketch, Mornington, Drogheda	£3.3.0
34	Halpin's Pool, Liffey, Sunset	£30

35	Sketch on Frosty Morning, Portobello, Grand Canal	£5.5.0
36	A Sandy Stretch at Portmarnock	£8.8.0
37	An Easterly Gale in Kingstown Harbour	£30
38	Dutchman's Creek, Limehouse, Thames	£3.3.0
39	On the Grand Canal, Dublin	£3.3.0
40	Clearing after Rain	£3.3.0
41	Newfoundland Bay, Long Range, Killarney	£10.10.0
42	Shades of Night	£2.10.0
43	Two Sketches, at Kew and Arklow River	£3.3.0
44	Under Torc Mountain, Middle Lake, Killarney	£10
45	After the Gale	£2.10.0
46	The Glare of Summer	£5.5.0
47	Morning Mists, Glena Mountain	£10
48	Early Morning	£3
49	A Spring Sketch, Templeogue	£3.3.0
50	A Dark Morning, Eagle Rock, Killarney	£15
51	Soft Evening's Light	£2.10.0
52	A Hot Spring Morning, Templeogue	£5.5.0
53	Cloudy Weather, Muckross Shore, Lower Lake, Killarney	£15
54	A Stirring Breeze	£5.5.0
55	Below Greenwich, Thames, Evening	£3.3.0
56	Brickeen Bridge, Killarney	£10
57	Off the Harbour's Mouth	£5.5.0
58	Near Carrickmines, Early Spring	£3.3.0
59	MacGillicuddy's Reeks, Killarney	£10
60	Autumn Winds	£2.10.0
61	Near the Gas Works, Bray	£4.4.0
62	At Rest	£3
63	In the Harbour of Dublin, Sunset	£30
64	Making for Port	£3

[12th Exhibition, Leinster Hall. January 26th to February 4th, 1899]

1	Colleen Bawn Caves	£3.3.0
2	Meeting of the Water	£3.3.0
3	Upper Lake, Glendalough	£3.3.0
4	Still Waters, Glendalough	£3.3.0
5	Passing Shadows	£3.3.0
6	A Quiet Day, Glendalough	£3.3.0
		£2.2.0
7	A Bye Way, London	£3.3.0
8	Near Greenwich Hospital	£3.3.0
9	Polinass [Pollanass Waterfall] Glendalough	£5.5.0
10	Spring, Templeogue	£4.4.0
11	Lough Annagle	£3.3.0
12	A Blue Haze	£3.3.0
13	Meeting of the Waters, Avoca	£4.4.0
14	View from the Cliffs	£20

15	Off to the Wreck	£3.3.0
16	Autumn Shore, Skerries	£6.6.0
		£5.5.0
17	Hawthorns Phoenix [Park]	£5.5.0
18	Beehive Cabin	£3.3.0
19	Canal, Leeson Street	£4.4.0
20	Kildownet Castle	£3.3.0
21	Dalkey Sound	£7.7.0
22	Lough Annagle	£3.3.0
23	Lake, Furry Glen, Phoenix [Park]	£4.4.0
24	Port of Dublin	£100
25	Toilers of the Sea	£3.3.0
26	Flowery Meadows	£5.5.0
27	Wooden Bridge, Avoca	£6.6.0
28	Rathfarnham Demesne	£2.10.0
29	Summer, Ireland's Eye	£10.10.0
30	Rocks in Balscadden Bay	£4.4.0
31	In an Hour of Softened Splendour	£25.0.0
32	At Mallaranny, Mayo	£5.5.0
33	Collier Unloading	£2.10.0
34	A Lone Widow's Cabin	£2.10.0
35	The Minaun Cliffs	£10.10.0
36	Sutton Howth	£4.4.0
37	Slievemore Mountain	£3.3.0
38	Sunset	£2.10.0
39	Tedcastle's Wharf	£3.3.0
40	Storm	
41	The Slaney, Carlow	£20.0.0
42	A Green Glade, Rathfarnham	£15.0.0.
43	Red Rock from Sutton	£43.0.0.
44	The Sun is Sinking Fast	£25.0.0
45	The Bay of Wicklow	£2.2.0
46	The Liffey, Chapelizod	£2.10.0
47	Sketch	£2.10.0
48	A Silver Strand	£5.5.0
49	The Minaun Cliffs	£3.3.0
50	Summer Cliffs, Dugort	£7.7.0
51	A Moorland Stream	£20.0.0
52	Spring Sketch, Carrickmines	£4.4.0
53	Sutton Howth Shadows	£10.0.0
54	The Thames at Putney	£2.10.0
55	Rain Squall, Glena	£5.5.0
56	Dublin Bay Trawlers	£3.3.0
57	Barges at Twickenham	£4.4.0
58	The Bailey Light from the Cliff	£10.10.0
		£8.10.0
59	Achill Sound	£3.3.0
60	A Corner in Lough Gill	£5.5.0
61	View from the Tennis Ground.	£5.5.0

62	After a Gale, Lough Gill	£5.5.0
63	A Most Distressful Country	£3.3.0
64	Spring Sketch	£5.5.0
65	Glena Mountain	£20.0.0
66	Dooega Beach	£3.3.0
67	A Grey Day, Mornington	£4.4.0
68	Dalkey Island Church	£5.5.0
69	Gloomy Weather	£4.4.0
70	Clouds Down Minaun	£3.3.0
71	Shore at the Battery	£5.5.0
72	Croaghaun from Dooagh	£3.3.0
73	A Wet Harvest Achill	£4.4.0
74	A North Wall Ferry	£4.4.0
75	Low Water, Greenwich	£2.10.0
76	McGillacuddy's Reeks	£3.3.0
77	Looking Down from the Upper Lake	£4.4.0
		£3.0.0
78	Castlelough Bay	£3.3.0
79	Bridge at Glendalough	£3.3.0
80	Brickeen Bridge	£3.3.0
		£2.5.0
		£4.4.0
81	Upper Lake, Glendalough	£3.3.0
82	Ireland's Eye	£2.10.0
83	Bay of Wicklow	£2.10.0
84	Mornington	£3.3.0
85	Portobello House	£2.2.0
86	Keem Bay, Achill	£3.3.0
		£2.15.0
87	An Irish Cabin	£3.3.0
88	Near Brickeen, Killarney	£4.4.0
89	Carrickfergus Castle	£5.5.0

WATERCOLOR ROOM

1	Portrush Strand	£1.10.0
2	Malahide	£2.2.0
3	Boatyard	£3.3.0
4	Kererra Sound	£10.0.0
5	Lough Goil	£1.10.0
6	Dugort Strand	£3.3.0
		£2.10.0
	Picture to be painted	£3.3.0
7	Glendalough	£2.10.0
8	Bray River	£2.2.0
9	Malahide	£1.10.0
10	Raheny	£2.2.0
11	Dugort, Achill	£3.3.0
12	By the Sea	£1.10.0
13	Afloat	£2.2.0

14	Clonskeagh	£3.3.0
15	Howth Demesne	£2.2.0
16	Killiney	£2.10.0
17	Kyles of Bute	£3.3.0
18	River Sketch	£1.1.0
19	Arklow	£1.1.0
20	Ringsend	£1.1.0
21	Fitting Out	£2.2.0
22	Dollymount Links	£3.3.0
23	Achill Hooker	£2.2.0
24	Old Ringsend	£2.2.0
25	Rothesay	£2.2.0
26	Boatyard, Ringsend	£4.4.0
27	Ashore	£1.1.0
28	Rosstrevor	£3.3.0
29	Rathmichael	£1.1.0
30	Kew	£3.3.0
31	First Lock, Grand Canal	£5.5.0
32	Mornington, Drogheda	£1.10.0
33	River Boyne, Drogheda	£1.10.0
34	Off to Fish	£2.2.0
35	Evening	£1.1.0
36	Dugort Strand	£2.10.0
37	Croaghpatrick	£2.10.0
38	Ashore	£1.10.0
39	Robbswall	£2.10.0
40	Killna Castle Demesne	£1.10.0
41	The Boyne River	£3.3.0
42	Dargle	£10.0.0
43	Baldoyle	£2.2.0
44	Old Boats	£2.10.0
45	Loughlinstown	£10.0.0
46	Balbriggan Coast	£4.4.0
47	Mornington	£2.10.0
48	Loch Lomond	£4.4.0
49	Breaking Up	£1.10.0
50	Killiney Beach	£3.3.0
51	Croaghpatrick	£1.10.0
52	Dalkey Island	£4.4.0
53	Newcastle, Wicklow	£4.4.0
54	Red Rock Bay, Howth	£7.7.0
55	Carrickmines	£10.0.0
56	Lough Goil	£10.00
57	Liberties, Dublin	£7.7.0
58	Lough Conn	£8.8.0
59	Chapelizod	£2.10.0
60	Baldoyle	£4.4.0

'Picturesque Ireland'

Exhibition of Pictures
Water-colour Drawings and
Sketches
of
Irish Landscapes, Home Life,
Sea Coast, Lake and River Scenery,
including the commemorative painting of
Queen Victoria's Last Visit to Ireland
by
Alexander Williams, RHA

The Modern Gallery
175, Bond Street, W 1   Edward Freeman, Secretary

Last Day 27th April

[April 1–27 1901]

Patrons.

UNDER THE IMMEDIATE PATRONAGE OF
THEIR EXCELLENCIES THE LORD LIEUTENANT, K.G. AND
THE COUNTESS CADOGAN.

THE DUKE AND DUCHESS OF ABERCORN.
THE MARCHIONESS OF WATERFORD.
THE MARCHIONESS OF HEADFORT.
THE MARQUESS AND MARCHIONESS OF DUFFERIN AND AVA.
THE MARQUESS AND MARCHIONESS OF ZETLAND.
THE EARL OF SHAFTESBURY.
THE COUTNESS OF FINGAL.
THE COUNTESS OF ARRAN.
THE EARL AND COUNTESS OF MAYO.
THE COUNTESS OF ANNESLEY.
THE COUNTESS OF ERNE.
VISCOUNT POWERSCOURT.
LORD AND LADY CLONBROCK.
LORD AND LADY ASHTOWN.
LORD AND LADY PLUNKET.
LORD AND LADY ARDILAUN.
MISS FARQUHARSON.

Catalogue.

Oil Paintings.

Queen Victoria's last visit to Ireland; scene from the Balcony of the Railway Station, Kingstown; Her Majesty Starting from the Royal Pavilion, Victoria Jetty, on her way to the City, April 4th, 1900. [Note that the artist here, as elsewhere, sometimes inadvertently used the same number twice, i.e. 13]

1	An Approaching Storm	4 gns.
2	The Haunt of the Eagle, Achill Island	4 gns.
3	Early Morn; 'When the hoar frost was chill'	15 gns.
4	Slievemore Mountain and Achill Coast	10 gns.
5	Lake in the Furry Glen, Phoenix Park	4 gns.
6	Upper Lake, Glendalough, County Wicklow	3 gns.
7	'Beautiful surroundings but nothing in the larder.'	3 gns.
8	In the Time of the Yellow Iris, Achill	5 gns.
9	River Liffey at Blessington	5 gns.
10	In Groomsport Harbour, County Down	6 gns.
11	A Rough Day on the Achill Coast	30 gns.
12	Falls on the River Moy at Foxford, Mayo	6 gns.
13	A Bright Clear Day	8 gns.
13	Glendarary, Achill Sound	15 gns.
14	The Valley of Tonaton, Achill	5 gns.
15	Flowery Meadows, Achill	5 gns.
16	No Place like Home	6 gns.
17	Roadside Cottage, County Carlow	4 gns.
18	Minaun Mountain, Achill	3 gns.
19	The Minaun Cliffs, Achill Island	4 gns.
20	'The Home of the Rock Dove'	10 gns.
21	A Hawthorn Glade, Phoenix Park	5 gns.
22	Trawlers Becalmed, Landing Fish on the Coast of Skerries, County Dublin	60 gns.
23	A Sunny Afternoon	5 gns.
24	'Return, oh Setting Sun'	5 gns.
25	Cabin at Oldhead, Clew Bay	6 gns.
26	Road to the Mines, Achill	7 gns.
27	Queen Victoria's Favourite Drive, Phoenix Park	5 gns.
28	Poor Achill Folk	8 gns.
29	Looking along Blacksod Bay	8 gns.
30	Clare Island from Dooega	4 gns.
31	Bright Harvest Weather	8 gns.
32	Glena Mountain, Lower Lake, Killarney	12 gns.
33	'Where women must work'	8 gns.
34	Eagle Mountain, Killarney (evening)	30 gns.
35	A Ballycroy Cottage	5 gns.
36	Morning, Achill	6 gns.
37	Mayo Cabins, Achill Sound	4 gns.
38	Tramore Bay, County Waterford	3 gns.
39	Castlelough Bay, Lower Lake, Killarney	12 gns.

40	'Atlantic Surges', Blacksod Bay	15 gns.
41	A Soft Southern Breeze	7 gns.
42	Gathering Sea Wrack, Clew Bay	8 gns.
43	Late Autumn	3 gns.
44	Poor Fisher Folk, Mayo Coast	4 gns.
45	'Where sea and river meet'	20 gns.
46	A Summer Day	8 gns.
47	'Silent Evening'	30 gns.
48	The Morning's Catch'	5 gns.
49	Achill Moorland	5 gns.
50	'When the wind bloweth in from the sea'	15 gns.
51	On the Slaney at Ballintemple, County Carlow	12 gns.
52	Bullock Harbour	4 gns.
53	'The Castle of Grace O'Mailie,	70 gns.
	Chieftainess of Connaught in the time of Queen Elizabeth,' Kildownet,	
	Achill Island	
54	'Morning Light'. Dalkey Island and Sorrento from Killiney Bay, County Dublin	4 gns.
55	A Precarious Existence, Mayo Coast	4 gns.
56	A Poor Man's Harvest	4 gns.
57	A Quiet Haven, Grand Canal, Dublin	10 gns.
58	A Mountain Cottage, Achill	12 gns.
59	Brickeen Bridge, Killarney	5 gns.
60	Pontoon, Lough Conn, Mayo	40 gns.
61	At the Boat House, Muckross House, Killarney	7 gns.
62	'When Daisies Pied'	6 gns.
63	The Strand at Dooagh, Achill	4 gns.
64	Kilcool Marshes, County Wicklow	15 gns.
65	A Rocky Coast	7 gns.
66	'A surface dappled o'er with grey'	8 gns.
67	'When the boats come home'	8 gns.
68	An Achill Fiord	3 gns.
69	Spring, Upper Lake, Glendalough	3 gns.
70	On Innisfallen Island, Killarney	20 gns.
71	'Green and Gold'	10 gns.
72	Dooniver Lake, Achill	5 gns.
73	Purple Autumn, an Achill Moor	20 gns.
74	Breanaskill, Achill Island	4 gns.
75	Muckross Abbey, Killarney	5 gns.
76	Hard Times, Mayo	4 gns.
77	'Lovely Summer'	15 gns.
78	A Bright October Morning, Killarney	7 gns.
79	Ruins of the Black Castle, Wicklow	4 gns.
80	Snipe-land, Achill	5 gns.
81	Showers, Lower Lake, Killarney	6 gns.
82	A Poor Widow's Home	5 gns.
83	Mac Gillicuddy's Reeks from Cloon Lake, Kerry	10 gns.
84	The Bank of Ireland	5 gns.
85	A Poor Man's Garden, Achill	4 gns.
86	River Bundrouse, Lough Melvin, County Leitrim	5 gns.

87	In Kenmare Demesne, Killarney	5 gns.
88	His Majesty's Post Office at Keel, Achill Island	5 gns.
89	Strand near Pontoon, Lough Cullen, Mayo	5 gns.
90	Canvas Fishing Canoes	5 gns.
91	Mangerton and the Deer Forest, from the Middle Lake, Killarney	12 gns.
92	The Minaun Cliffs, Achill Island	12 gns.
93	Crossing the Bar	7 gns.
94	Looking up Achill Sound	12 gns.
95	The Cliffs of Howth, Dublin Bay, 'Lingering Evening Light'	6 gns.
96	'Blowing Hard', Middle Lake, Killarney	15 gns.
97	The Dublin Hills from Carrickmines	10 gns.
98	'The Tide's White Rush'	8 gns.
99	An Inlet of the Sea, Achill	5 gns.
100	'Know ye the Valley by the Sea'	5 gns.
101	Croaghaun and Slievemore Mountains, Achill	5 gns.

Watercolours

102	Off to the Fishing Grounds	3 gns.
103	Kerrera Sound, on the way to Oban	12 gns.
104	Baldoyle, County Dublin	4 gns.
105	Homeward Bound	3 gns.
106	Carrickmines, County Dublin	15 gns.
107	A Stile	3 gns.
108	Croagh Patrick, Clew Bay	5 gns.
109	A Spanking Breeze	3 gns.
110	Templeogue, River Dodder, Dublin	8 gns.
111	On the Beach	4 gns.
112	Marshy Land, County Dublin	4 gns.
113	Croaghaun Mountain, Achill	25 gns.
114	On the River Dodder, County Dublin	25 gns.
115	Lying-up for the Winter	6 gns.
116	Making for Port	4 gns.
117	A Dublin Bay Trawler	4 gns.
118	Dean Swift's Pulpit, St Patrick's Cathedral, Dublin	25 gns.
119	Milltown, County Dublin	5 gns.
120	A Ringsend Boat-yard, Dublin	6 gns.
121	Tranquillity	3 gns.
122	A Fair Wind	4 gns.
123	Trawlers	4 gns.
124	Dyeing Wool, Achill	4 gns.
125	A Boat-yard, Dublin	4 gns.
126	Loughlinstown, County Dublin	15 gns.
127	At Mornington, Drogheda	4 gns.
128	Lough Melvin, County Leitrim	4 gns.
129	Slievemore Mountain, Achill	4 gns.
130	Nephin Mountain and Lough Conn, Mayo	15 gns.
131	Mouth of the Boyne, Drogheda	5 gns.
132	A Trout Pool, Rostrevor	25 gns.
133	Portmarnock's Links, County Dublin	12 gns.

134	Deserted – A Decaying Dublin Industry	10 gns.
135	The Setting Sun	4 gns.
136	Near Carrick Castle, Loch Goil	20 gns.
137	Malahide Strand, County Dublin	5 gns.
138	In the Dargle, County Wicklow	20 gns.
139	On the River Boyne, near Drogheda	4 gns.
140	Near Malahide, County Dublin	4 gns.
141	Achill Sound. Viaduct and Railway Terminus from the Island.	6 gns.
142	Sunset	8 gns.
143	Minaun Bay	4 gns.
144	Late Autumn	4 gns.

21st Exhibition

at
Leinster Hall, 35 Molesworth St.
January 22 – February 7 1903

[1–6 missing, page torn]

7	Breezy, Achill Sound	50/-
8	Rocky Coast, Achill	3 gns.
9	Croaghaun Mountain	50/-
10	Fine Weather, Achill Sound	50/-
11	Croaghaun, Dooagh	50/-
12	A Gleam of Light	3 gns.
13	Clouds on Achill	50/-
14	Near Pontoon	4 gns.
15	Road to Dugort	3 gns.
16	Summer Weather	4 gns.
17	Arrival of the Boats, Blacksod	7 gns.
18	A Wild Coast, Achill	5 gns.
19	Beside The Railway Station	5 gns.
20	Gossipers, Achill	4 gns.
21	Rocky Cove, Dugort	7 gns.
22	The Valley, Achill	3 gns.
23	A Wild Day at Dugort	4 gns.
24	Fisherfolk, Mayo	5 gns.
25	The Cathedral Rocks, Achill	7 gns.
26	Lough Cullen	4 gns.
27	Turf Boats Weathering a Point	7 gns.
28	Distant View of Keem Bay	3 gns.
29	Breanaskill Bay, Achill Sound	3 gns.
30	A Lovely Day, Achill	8 gns.
31	Glass Island, Lough Conn	50/-
32	Harvest Weather	50/-
33	Clearness before Rain	50/-
34	A Fisherman's Home	25 gns.
35	An Inlet of the Sea	50/-
36	A Bit of Bog	15 gns.
37	The Lake at Ballinlough	3 gns.

38	Ballintubber of the Kings of Connaught	50/-
38A	Four Sketches at Rockingham	5 gns.
39	In Inver Bay	5 gns.
40	Donegal Bay	50/-
41	Near Rostrevor	50/-
43 [sic]	Gloomy Glendalough	12 gns.
43	Old Bridge, Glendalough	4 gns.
44	Footprints of the Saints, Glendalough	20 gns.
45	In The Valley of Glendasson	15 gns.
46	Upper Lake, Glendalough	6 gns.
47	A Peep in the Woods, Glendalough	6 gns.
48	The Boat Harbour	7 gns.
48A	Near Newcastle Station	50/-
49	Close of Day	5 gns.
50	A Sketch	5 gns.
51	On the Beach	10 gns.
52	A Bit of Sea	4 gns.
53	A Distant View of Skerries	6 gns.
54	Cottage and Windmill	4 gns.
55	The Islands	3 gns.
56	On the Shore between Skerries & Balbriggan	20 gns.
57	On Haven Island	10 gns.
57A	Haven Island	3 gns.
58	A Rough Day, Achill Sound	50 gns.
59	Balscadden Bay, Howth	10 gns.
60	Doo Lough, Killary Bay	10 gns.
61	At Bundoragh, Killary	2 gns.
62	Looking down on Killary Fjord	5 gns.
63	Lough Nafooey	2 gns.
63	Lough Nafooey [listed twice with same number]	2 gns.
64	Lough Mask	3 gns.
65	At Delphi, Killary	2 gns.
66	Kylemore Lake	3 gns.
67	A Bit of a Breeze, Killary	3 gns.
68	Doone Hill, Lough Corrib	4 gns.
68 [sic]	Near Doone Hill, Lough Corrib	4 gns.
69	The Pass of Lough Muck	4 gns.
70	The Pass of Kylemore	5 gns.
71	Near Kylemore Castle	3 gns.
72	Near Leenane Hotel	5 gns.
73	Diamond Mountain	4 gns.
74	The Pass of Delphi	3 gns.
75	The Road down to Salrock	3 gns.
76	The Claddagh, Galway	4 gns.
77	A sketch, made with the Raffaelli Colours	2 gns.
78	Sunset, A Sketch	2 gns.
79	Cloon Lake	5 gns.
80	McGillicuddy's Reeks	4 gns.

81	The Entrance to the Black Valley	4 gns.
82	Ross Castle	3 gns.
83	The Reeks from the Up. Lake	7 gns.
84	'Sunset, Innisfallen'	3 gns.
85	'Beauty's Home'	8 gns.
86	Colleen Bawn Rocks	3 gns.
87	'Glena', Lower Lake	3 gns.
88	A Summer Day, Ireland's Eye	20 gns.
89	At Muckross House	7 gns.
90	Middle Lake, Early Morn	3 gns.
91	The Deer Forest	3 gns.
92	Ross Castle, Torc Mountain	7 gns.
93	Lower Lake	3 gns.
94	At Brickeen Bridge	3 gns.
95	McGillicuddy's Reeks	5 gns.
96	The Boat Pool, Glencar	50/-
97	Castlelough, Shannon	50/-
98	Shannon, near Killaloe	3 gns.
99	Holy Island, Lough Derg	50/-
100	Becalmed	2 gns.
101	Early Summer, Dodder	15 gns.
102	Bellingham Harbour, Howth	3 gns.
103	Hauling the Lobster Pots	4 gns.
104	A Bit in Kenilworth Park	2 gns.
105	Howth & Ireland's Eye	15 gns.
106	Balbriggan Shore	3 gns.
107	Howth, South Coast	4 gns.
108	In the Rocky Valley, Bray	3 gns.
109	The Ladies Cove, Tramore	4 gns.
110	Portrush Strand	50/-
111	Carrickfergus Castle	3 gns.
112	The Burnt Islands, Bute	5 gns.
113	Off Tighnabruaich	4 gns.
114	Entrance to Lough Ormidale	3 gns.
115	Arran Island, from Bute	50/-
116	Rothesay Bay	50/-
117	At Duncraggan	50/-
118	Ben Lomond	3 gns.
119	Evening, Loch Striven	3 gns.
120	In the Gareloch Clyde	4 gns.
121	Glen Finlas, Trossachs	3 gns.
122	Arrochar Pier	50/-
123	Carrick Castle, Loch Goil	3 gns.
124	Kerrera Sound, Oban	3 gns.
125	Head of Loch Venachar	3 gns.
126	In Broddick Bay	3 gns.
127	Near Loch Venachar	3 gns.
128	On the Slaney at Ballintemple	7 gns.
128 [sic]	Flowery meadows, Achill	5 gns.

**'The Land of
The Shamrock.'**

**PICTURES & SKETCHES
BY
ALEXANDER WILLIAMS, RHA
(OF DUBLIN)**

CATALOGUE

THE MODERN GALLERY
175, BOND STREET, W.

EDWARD FREEMAN.
LESSEE & SECRETARY.

WILL CLOSE 30TH APRIL.

[1903]

Patrons.

THEIR EXCELLENCIES THE LORD LIEUTENANT
    AND THE COUNTESS OF DUDLEY.
THE DUKE AND DUCHESS OF ABERCORN.
THE MARCHIONESS OF WATERFORD.
THE MARCHIONESS OF HEADFORT.
THE MARCHIONESS OF DUFFERIN AND AVA.
THE MARQUIS AND MARCHIONESS OF ZETLAND.
THE EARL AND COUNTESS CADOGAN.
THE EARL OF SHAFTESBURY.
THE EARL OF DROGHEDA.
THE COUNTESS OF FINGAL.
THE COUNTESS DOWAGER OF ARRAN.
THE EARL AND COUNTESS OF MAYO.
THE COUNTESS OF ANNESLEY.
THE COUNTESS OF ERNE.
VISCOUNT POWERSCOURT.
LORD CASTLETOWN.
THE LADY O'NEILL.
THE LORD AND LADY CLONBROCK.
THE LORD AND LADY ASHTOWN.
THE LORD AND LADY PLUNKET.
THE LORD AND LADY ARDILAUN.
THE LADY FRANCES DOYNE.
MISS FARQUHARSON.

CATALOGUE

1	Lough Shinny, Dublin Coast	8 gns.
2	'The loaded wings bring on the gathering storm'	15 gns.
3	The Harbour and Hotel, Leenane, Connemara	6 gns.
4	Pollanass Waterfall, Glendalough	5 gns.
5	Polranny Hill from Achill Island	3 gns.
6	Glencar, County Kerry, 'Runlets babbling down the Glen'	6 gns.
7	The Claddagh, Galway	3 gns.
8	The Twelve Pins from Killary Bay, Connemara	15 gns.
9	Near Maam Bridge	4 gns.
10	An Early Morning Coast Sketch	8 gns.
11	A Cottage Door, County Waterford	5 gns.
12	Kylemore Lake, Connemara	4 gns.
13	On the Beach at Skerries, County Dublin	12 gns.
14	Skerries, County Dublin	6 gns.
15	Keem Bay, Achill Island	3 gns.
16	Dollymount Links from Raheny, Dublin	8 gns.
17	'There is a Rapture on the lonely shore'	15 gns.
18	Teampull-na-skelling – The Church of the Rock, Glendalough	20 gns.
19	The Colleen Bawn Caves, Killarney	12 gns.
20	Boggy Land, Roscommon	8 gns.
21	Slievemore Mountain, Achill Island	3 gns.
22	On the Grand Canal, Dublin	6 gns.
23	Old Bridge, Glendalough	5 gns.
24	'Shallows on a distant shore'	15 gns.
25	Near Skerries, Dublin Coast	5 gns.
26	Rain Coming on	5 gns.
27	Near the Varsity Boat Club, Chapelizod, Liffey	6 gns.
28	Achill Sound, 'When nature kind with blessings crowns the farmer's hopes'	4 gns.
29	A Bit of Fresh Sea	4 gns.
30	In Donegal Bay	3 gns.
31	'The Strand sea-lav'd, that stretches far beyond the rocky shore'	8 gns.
32	Expecting the Boats, Achill Island	6 gns.
33	Kylemore Lake, Connemara	4 gns.
34	Fine Weather, Achill Sound	3 gns.
35	'In the time of Birds and Flowers'	20 gns.
36	A Fisherman's Home, near Letterfrack, Connemara	15 gns.
37	A Bright Autumn Day	8 gns.
38	Fisher Folk, Achill Island	6 gns.
39	'By the Deep Sea'	4 gns.
40	'When the whisp'ring breeze pants on the leaves'	10 gns.
41	Beside Muckross House, Killarney	20 gns.
42	Humble Tillers of the soil, Salia, Achill Island	30 gns.
43	The Morning Catch, Achill Island	6 gns.
44	A Cold Grey Sea	10 gns.
45	Preparing for Sea, Achill Island, Mayo	6 gns.
46	Mangerton, the Deer Forest and Turk Mountain from Muckross Lake, Killarney	20 gns.

47	A Sketch on the Seashore	10 gns.
48	'A still salt pool lock'd in with bars of sand'	8 gns.
49	A Good Harvest, Glendarary, Achill Sound	15 gns.
50	The Horses Glen, Mangerton Mountain, Killarney	50 gns.
51	A Sunny Afternoon, Achill Sound, County Mayo	5 gns.
52	Glass Island, Lough Conn	3 gns.
53	'Safe are the Seas and Silent'	6 gns.
54	'O'er the dark marsh, bleak hill, and sandy plain'	5 gns.
55	Near Newcastle, County Wicklow	3 gns.
56	Clare Island from Dooega, Achill Island	12 gns.
57	McGillicuddy's Reeks from the Upper Lake, Killarney	8 gns.
58	Hope	10 gns.
59	Achill Sound, Mayo, Autumn	15 gns.
60	On the Slaney at Aghade Bridge, County Carlow	30 gns.
61	Lovely Summer	4 gns.
62	At Low Water	8 gns.
63	'Across a hazy glimmer of the West.'	4 gns.
64	Glendalough, County Wicklow, 'By that lake whose gloomy shore skylark never warbled o'er'	15 gns.
65	A Grey Day on the Coast	8 gns.
66	A Rocky Coast	8 gns.
67	Clouds on Delphi, Killary Bay, Connemara	8 gns.
68	Eagle Rock, Killarney	12 gns.
69	Near St Kevin's Bed, Upper Lake, Glendalough, County Wicklow	15 gns.
70	A peep at Killary Bay, Connemara	7 gns.
71	Washing Day, Achill Island, Mayo	4 gns.
72	The Shelley Bank, Dublin Bay	6 gns.
73	Victoria Rocks, Muckross Lake, Killarney	6 gns.
74	Derry Castle, Shining Shannon, near Lough Derg	4 gns.
75	A Shore Sketch	6 gns.
76	Portmarnock Church, County Dublin, evening	12 gns.
77	A Peep at Mweelrea, Killary Bay	8 gns.
78	Castlelough, Lough Derg, Shannon	3 gns.
79	Seapink and Trefoil, Bray Head, County Wicklow	6 gns.
80	Near Pontoon, Lough Conn	4 gns.
81	In the Ladies Cove, Tramore, Waterford	4 gns.
82	Autumn Sketch, Kylemore Lake, Connemara	6 gns.
83	Inver Bay, Donegal	6 gns.
84	'When winds breathe soft'	10 gns.
85	The Leenane Hills, Killary Bay, Connemara	5 gns.
86	Evening, Doo Lough, Killary Bay, Connemara	7 gns.
87	Old Head, Clew Bay, Connemara	3 gns.
88	A Distant View of the Pass of Kylemore, Connemara	6 gns.
89	Pontoon Bridge, Lough Conn, Mayo	4 gns.
90	Old Leighlin Bridge, County Carlow	4 gns.
91	At Bundoragh, Killary Bay	6 gns.
92	A Golden Strand, Lough Conn, Mayo	12 gns.
93	Pat McGrail's Rock, Dugort Bay, Achill Island	8 gns.
94	Low Water	6 gns.

95	Holy Island, Lough Derg, Shannon	4 gns.
96	Good-bye	3 gns.
97	Tully Strand, Renvyle, Connemara	5 gns.
98	Rocks on the Beach, Skerries, County Dublin	8 gns.
99	Summer Weather, Newfoundland Bay, Long Range, Killarney	15 gns.
100	Sketch in a Roscommon Bog.	8 gns.
101	'The brook that loves to purl o'er matted cress and ribbed sand'	7 gns.
102	'The Bay was oily calm'	6 gns.
103	Ireland's Eye, Dublin Bay	3 gns.
104	Lower Lake, Killarney	3 gns.
105	Evening, Lower Lake, Killarney	3 gns.
106	'As evening grey advances slow'	8 gns.
107	A Sparkling Day	7 gns.
108	The Vale of Glendasson, Glendalough, County Wicklow	15 gns.
109	Howth from Portmarnock, County Dublin	8 gns.
110	'So let the warm winds range, and the blue waves beat the shore'	10 gns.
111	The Middle Lake, Killarney	3 gns.
112	Harvest Time, Achill	3 gns.
113	Glanagivalla, the Weaver's Valley, Leenane, Connemara	5 gns.
114	Stormy Weather, Achill Sound	70 gns.
115	A Windy Day on the Lagan, Belfast	5 gns.
116	Brickeen Bridge, Killarney	4 gns.
117	The 'Devil's Island', Muckross Lake, Killarney	5 gns.
118	Harvest Time, Achill Island	4 gns.
119	Ballintubber of the Kings of Connaught	3 gns.
120	Glanagivalla, Leenane, Connemara	4 gns.
121	Near the Black Valley, Killarney	4 gns.
122	'Ere yet the morn dispels the fleeting mists'	4 gns.
123	Moorland	4 gns.
124	On the Beach	4 gns.
125	The Vale of Glendasson, County Wicklow	7 gns.
126	Where the peat comes from	6 gns.
127	Doo Lough, Killary Bay, Connemara	8 gns.
128	Achill Sound 'and fair is all the land about'	15 gns.
129	Leafy June, the Upper Lake, Glendalough, Co. Wicklow	8 gns.
130	A Breezy Day, Lough o'Flynn, Roscommon	15 gns.
131	Achill Sound, 'Smooth flow the waves, the Zephyrs gently play'	5 gns.
132	A Squatter's Cabin, Achill	8 gns.
133	The Coast of Howth, Dublin Bay	8 gns.
134	The Minaun Cliffs, Achill Island	15 gns.
135	At the Railway Terminus, Achill Sound	4 gns.
136	On Skerries Beach, Co. Dublin	4 gns.
137	Upper Lake, Glendalough, County Wicklow	7 gns.
138	A Breeze from the Sea	6 gs/
139	A Clearing in the Moor, Achill Island	8 gns.

Irish Industrial Exhibition World's Fair,
St Louis
1904

From Handbook and Catalogue of Exhibits Part I

The work and exhibits of
The Department of Agriculture and Technical Instruction for Ireland

The Congested Districts Board

Scenery of the West of Ireland

As illustrating the beauty of the scenery of the West of Ireland, the Congested Districts Board are indebted to Alexander Williams, Esq., RHA, 4 Hatch Street, Dublin, for the exhibit of oil paintings comprising the following, which are hung on the screen near the Donegal Carpet Exhibit at the south end of the Industrial Hall.

Achill Scenery

Rough Harvest Weather, Achill Sound

Clare Island and Innisturk from Dooega

Blacksod Bay, from Achill

Harvest time, Achill Sound

A Mountain Boreen, Achill

Glendarary, Achill Sound

Dwellings of the Poor, Dugort, Achill

A Harvest Field, Achill Sound

The Minaun Cliffs, Keel Strand

His Majesty's Post Office at Keel

There's no place like home

Turf Boats, Achill Sound

Mayo Scenery

A Golden Strand, Lough Cullen

A Mountain Farm, Croagh Patrick, Clew Bay

Waiting for their dinner

A Congested District

Roscommon Scenery

Purple Heather, Ballinlough

An Oat Field near Ballinlough

Connemara Scenery

The Bens of Connemara from Ballinakill

In Killery Bay

Lough Fee

Ballinahinch River

Derryclare Lake

Killarney Scenery

In the Long Range

The Colleen Bawn Caves

Eagle Rock, Long Range
The Deer Forest, Muckross Lake
Ross Castle
Innisfallen
Cork Scenery

Castle and Groves of Blarney

Downdaniel Castle, Bandon River
Blackrock Castle, Cork
Roches Point and Poor Head

Dublin Scenery

Howth Lighthouse, Dublin Bay
The Velvet Strand, Portmarnock, County Dublin
In Killiney Bay, County Dublin
A bit of the ould sod, Ringsend, County Dublin

Wicklow Scenery

Near St Kevin's Bed, Glendalough
The Upper Lake, Glendalough
Pat Murphy's houldin, Wicklow Town
In the Vale of Glendasson, Glendalough
The Meeting of the Waters, Wooden Bridge
The Black Castle, County Wicklow

Shannon Scenery

Holy Island, Lough Derg

25th Exhibition of Pictures
of
Irish Scenery

35 Molesworth Street
23 January – 11 February 1905

1	At Maam Bridge, Connemara	£2.2.0
2	A Break in a Wet Day	£2.10.0
3	Skerries, County Dublin	£3.3.0
4	Ferriters Cove & Castle, Coast of Kerry	£10.10.0
5	A Windy Day	£2.2.0
6	Keem Bay from Dooagh	£2.2.0
7	Rain Clouds, Lough Conn	£2.2.0
8	Rocks at Dugort, Achill	£4.4.0
9	Sunny weather, Aasleagh	£2.2.0
10	Glanagiola [Glennagevlagh] Leenane	£2.2.0
11	The Pier Head, Howth	£3.3.0
12	Strand at Coastguard Station, Ventry	£5.5.0
13	The Cliff Walk, Bray	£3.3.0
14	Old Irishtown	£3.3.0

15	Dugort Strand	£5.5.0
16	Ashleam Bay, Achill	£5.5.0
17	Cabins at Dooagh, Achill	£3.3.0
18	The Scene for a Great Battle, Ventry	£10.10.0
19	The Valley Strand, Achill	£2.2.0
20	Crossing the Sands, Glendarary	£2.2.0
21	'Come back oh setting sun'	£3.3.0
22	Dunmore Head & Gt Blasket, Kerry	£5.5.0
23	Ventry from the Cliffs	£5.5.0
24	A Dull Autumn Day	£6.6.0
25	The Reeks from the Shore	£4.4.0
26	The Cahirciveen Shore	£8.8.0
27	View in Kenmare Demesne	£5.5.0
28	Glena and Tomies Mountains	£5.5.0
	Replica	£4.4.0
29	The Colleen Bawn Rock	£30.0.0.
30	Mahony's Point	£4.4.0
31	The Strand, near Victoria Hotel	£5.5.0
32	Lower Lake, Killarney	£4.4.0
33	Headland at Dingle	£6.6.0
34	A Frosty Morning	£4.4.0
35	View from Talbots Door	£25.0.0.
36	Nesting Place of the Tern	£4.4.0
		£3.3.0
37	Slievemore Mountain	£6.6.0
38	Moor and Mountain	£4.4.0
39	A Grey Day	£4.4.0
40	Achill Sound	£2.2.0
41	Clouds on Eagle Mountain	£2.2.0
42	The Blasket Islands	£10.10.0
43	An Errand of Mercy	£10.10.0
44	A Real Bad Day, Sutton	£4.4.0
45	Ventry Strand	£5.5.0
46	On the North Bull	£5.5.0
47	Croaghaun Mountain	£2.2.0
48	Cabins at Dooagh	£3.3.0
49	The Deer Forest, Killarney	£2.2.0
50	Correymore	Not priced
51	Achill Island from Inniskea	£3.3.0
52	Seal Caves at Parkmore	£10.10.0
53	Eagle Mountain	£5.5.0
54	An April Day on Liffey	£50
55	View at Ventry	£10.10.0
56	A Study of Rocks	£6.6.0
57	Coast of Howth	£2.2.0
57 [sic]	Evening on the Coast of Howth	£3.10.0
58	A Mountain Stream	£6.6.0
59	Low Water at Tramore	£5.5.0
60	Looking across the Moors	£5.5.0

61	Blacksod Fishing Boats	£5.5.0
62	Minaun Mountain	£2.2.0
63	Haven Island	£4.4.0
64	The Coast near Slea Head	£5.5.0
65	The Malahide Shore	£4.4.0
	Replica No. 65	£6.6.0
66	The Coast Looking up Dingle Bay	£10.10.0
67	The Old Causeway, Burnham	£5.5.0
68	Rahanane Castle	£6.6.0
69	A Grey Day, Baldoyle	£3.3.0
70	The Needles, Howth	£5.5.0
71	The Sun is Rising Fast	£4.4.0
72	'Where under low grey skies'	£8.8.0
73	Where the Erriff River Meets thc Sea	£4.4.0
74	A Cornfield at Ventry	£8.8.0
75	A Rocky Pathway	£5.5.0
76	Achill Sound	£2.2.0
77	Mahony's Point, Killarney	£3.3.0
78	View from Rabbit Island, Killarney	£5.5.0
79	Lake Garagarry, Mangerton	£40.0.0.
80	Dugort Strand	£2.2.0
81	The Devil's Rock	£4.4.0
82	Blackstreams Bridge	£4.4.0
83	At Derrynaslygan [Derrynasliggaun, County Galway]	£4.4.0
84	Ventry from the Sandhills	£5.5.0
85	Up Trawl and Away	£4.4.0
86	Near Recess Station	£4.4.0
87	A Bit of Achill Moor	£4.4.0
88	Lough Shinny	£5.5.0
89	Leenane Harbour	£2.2.0
90	Glena and Tomies Mountain	£10.10.0
91	Near the Laune River	£2.2.0
92	Skerries Coast Evening	£4.4.0
93	Impending Storm	£5.5.0
94	A Close Shave	£3.3.0
95	On Ventry Strand	£5.5.0
96	In Balbriggan Harbour	£3.3.0
97	Haven Island Skerries	£4.4.0
98	Kate Furrey's Cottage	£6.6.0
99	Near the Black Valley	£4.4.0
100	Evening on Lough O'Flynn	£6.6.0
101	Near Bulls Mouth	£2.2.0
102	River Inny	£2.2.0
103	Cliffs at Parkmore	£4.4.0
104	Leenane from the Water	£3.3.0
105	Summer in Achill	£2.2.0
106	A Bit of Sea, Tramore	~~£3.3.0~~
		£1.10.0
107	Malahide Shore	£4.4.0

108	Near Blackstreams Bridge	£10.10.0
109	Sunny Hours, Achill	£2.2.0
110	Maam Road	£2.2.0
111	The Minaun Cliffs	£2.2.0
112	Storm on an Achill Moor	£2.2.0
113	A Bit of Sea	£2.2.0
114	Near Kilcool Station, Wicklow	£2.2.0
115	The Maam Valley	£1.5.0
116	Achill	£2.2.0
117	Near Louisberg	£1.10.0

CATALOGUE

of the

26th Exhibition of Pictures of

Irish Scenery,

by

ALEXANDER WILLIAMS, RHA

(Studio – 4 HATCH STREET),

At 35 Molesworth Street, Dublin,

January 15th to February 10th, 1906.

Admission and Catalogue = One Shilling.

10 to 6 P.M. DAILY.

PATRONS

The Duke and Duchess of Abercorn.
The Marchioness of Granby.
The Marchioness of Waterford.
The Marchioness of Headfort.
The Marchioness of Dufferin and Ava.
The Marquis and Marchioness of Zetland.
The Earl and Countess Cadogan.
The Earl and Countess Dudley.
The Earl of Shaftesbury.
The Earl of Drogheda.
The Countess of Fingall.
The Countess Kilmorey.
The Countess Dowager of Arran.
The Earl and Countess of Mayo.
The Countess of Annesley.
The Countess of Erne.
Lord Castletown.
The Lady O'Neill.

The Lord and Lady Clonbrock.
The Lord and Lady Ashtown.
The Lord and Lady Plunket.
The Lord and Lady Ardilaun.
Miss Farquharson.

CATALOGUE

1	Baldoyle Estuary, County Dublin	£2 10s.
2	Granuaile's Castle, Achill Sound	£4 4s.
3	Lough Melvin, County Leitrim	£2 10s.
4	Salia, Achill Island	£2 10s.
5	Old Dromore, Blackwater River, Kenmare Bay	£6 6s.
6	Shenick Island, Skerries	£3 3s.
7	Landing Fish, Achill	£3 3s.
8	An Achill Village	£3 10s.
9	Between Maryboro' and Mountmellick	£2 10s.
10	River Glyde, at Castlebellingham Bridge	£4 4s.
11	The Cahirciveen Hills, from Ventry	£2 10s.
12	On the River Moy, at Ballina	£3 3s.
13	Dublin Trawlers Becalmed	£4 4s.
14	Stormy Weather, near Templenoe, Kenmare	£6 6s.
15	In Ashleam Bay, Achill Island	£5 5s.
16	Baltray, River Boyne	£3 3s.
17	The Gap of Dunloe, from the River Laune, Killarney	£3 3s.
18	Killybegs, Co. Donegal	£3 3s.
19	The Upper Lake, Glendalough, County Wicklow	£12 12s.
20	'Doran's View', Templenoe House, Kenmare	£5 5.s.
21	Achill Sound	£2 10s.
22	An Impression, Templenoe, Kenmare	-
23	The Owenbrin River, Lough Mask, Connemara	2 10s.
24	The Ox Mountains, from the River Moy	£2 10s.
25	The Stags' Leap, Kylemore Lake, Connemara	£3 3s.
26	A Golden Strand, near Pontoon, Lough Conn	£3 3s.
27	Glanleam, the Residence of the Knight of Kerry, Valentia Island	£6 6s.
28	Wormwood Gate, a Bit of Vanished Dublin	£2 2s.
29	Vanishing Dublin, Skipper's Alley	£2 2s.
30	In the Grounds of the Lake Hotel, Castlelough, Killarney	£8 8s.
31	The Dingle Hills, from Ventry Coastguard Station	£4 4s.
32	Ruins of the Black Castle, Wicklow	£4 4s.
33	Showers, Donegal Bay	£4 4s.
34	Ferriters' Castle, Clogher Head, the Great Blasket and Tearaght Rock, from Sybil Head, Kerry	£63
35	A Soft Grey Day, Kenmare Coast	£8 8s.
36	Minaun Mountain, from Salia, Achill	£5 5s.
37	M'Keown's Rock, Killary Bay	£4 4s.
38	Castlelough Shore, Lower Lake, Killarney	£7 7s.
39	Autumn, near Breanaskill, Achill Island	£4 4s.
40	A Breeze from the Sea	£4 4s.

41	A Strong Wind, Lower Lake, Killarney	£6 6s.
42	Clonee, Middle Lake, Kenmare Bay	£5 5s.
43	Near Skerries, County Dublin	£4 4s.
44	Narrow Water Castle, Carlingford Lough	£2 10s.
45	Polranny Hill, Achill Sound	£3 3s.
46	The Mallaranny Hills, from Achill Sound	£3 3s,
47	Slane Castle, River Boyne	£4 4s.
48	The Bridge of Slane, River Boyne	£4 4s.
49	A Bright Autumn Day, Achill	£3 3s.
50	Ross Castle, Killarney	£2 10s.
51	Innisfallen, Killarney	£2 10s.
52	Near St Kevin's Bed, Glendalough	£10 10s.
53	The Motor Track, Velvet Strand, Portmarnock	£5 5s.
54	Sunrise in the Pass of Kylemore	£5 5s.
55	A Bit of Strand, Kenmare Bay	£8 8s.
56	Kylemore Lake, Connemara	£3 3s.
57	View of Blackwater Harbour, Kenmare Bay	£6 6s.
58	A Wild Day, Achill Sound	£31 10s.
59	Inishabroe, Blasket Islands	£10 10s.
60	A Hillside Boreen, Achill	£10 10s.
61	The Deer Forest and Middle Lake, Killarney	£10 10s.
62	A Bay on Ross Island, Killarney	£10 10s.
63	Lion Rocks, Candlestick Bay, Howth, County Dublin	£31 10s.
64	Clare Island and Dooega Beach, Achill	£10 10s.
65	Poor Achill Islanders	£10 10s.
66	Pollanass Waterfall, Glendalough	£4 4s.
67	A Wild Day	£3 3s.
68	On the West Coast	£3 3s.
69	Weeds	£6 6s.
70	On the Laune River, Killarney	£2 2s.
71	Autumn Day: Middle Lake, Killarney	£2 2s
72	A Sheltered Cove, Ventry, Kerry	£6 6s.
73	Comenoole Village, Dunmore Head, and Blasket Island, Co. Kerry	£5 5s.
74	At Marino, Kenmare Bay	£2 10s.
75	Clare Island and Achill Sound	£2 10s.
76	A Calm Day: Castlelough Bay, Killarney	£3 3s.
77	The Close of Day	£10 10s.
78	Cathedral Rocks, Achill	£3 3s.
79	The Gap of the North, from Dundalk River	£3 3s.
80	Croaghpatrick, from Achill	£2 10s.
81	Rough Weather: Youghal Harbour	£2 2s.
82	A Bright Day: MacCarthy's Castle, Killarney	£10 10s.
83	Shadow and Sunshine: Kenmare Bay	£7 7s.
84	A Spate on the Blackwater River, Kenmare Bay	£8 8s.
85	Templenoe House and Meadows, Kenmare Bay	£6 6s.
86	A Queen's County Moor	£3 3s.
87	A Cottage by the Sea: Rush	£2 10s.
88	Holy Island, Lough Derg, Shannon	£2 10s.

89	Bundoragh, Killary Bay: Where the King Landed	£2 10s.
90	Where the Sheen River meets the Sea: At 'Falls', Residence of the Earl of Kerry	£7 7s.
91	The Reeks, from Glencar River	£3 3s.
92	The Bay of Salruck, Connemara	£63.
93	Killiney Bay, County Dublin	£5 5s.
94	Down by the Sea	£5 5s.
95	View at Templenoe, Kenmare	£2 10s.
96	A Peep in the Grounds of the Lake Hotel. Cover of Catalogue.	-
97	MacCartie Mores' Castle, Killarney. Cover of Catalogue	-
98	Windy Gap, between Killarney and Kenmare	£7 7s.
99	The Bay of Dugort, Achill	£3 3s.
100	Moor, near Mountmellick, Queen's County	£2 10s.
101	Snow on Mangerton	£2 10s.
102	The Woods of Dromore Castle and Distant Hills of Derreen, from Templenoe, Kenmare Bay	£10 10s.
103	View at Derreen, The Marquis of Lansdowne's Residence	£2 10s.
104	Delphi Lake, Killary Bay	£2 10s.
105	Breakers, Achill Shore	£2 10s.
106	At Glendarary, Achill Sound	£2 10s.
107	On the Shore of Lough Conn	£2 10s.
108	Lackabane, Derreen, Kenmare Bay	£6 6s.
109	A Roscommon Bog	£10 10s.
110	Dingle Hills, from Parkmore, Ventry	£5 5s.
111	Near Baggot Street Bridge, Grand Canal	£5 5s.
112	Lough Conn, Mayo	£2 2s.
113	Rounding the Bar Beacon	£3 3s.
114	Ballydavid Head, Smerwick Bay, Kerry	£2 10s.
115	One of the 'Sisters', Smerwick Strand, Kerry	£2 10s.
116	At Woodville, Maryboro', Queen's County	£4 4s.
117	Strandtown Shore, Belfast	£2 10s.
118	The Achill Coast	£3 3s.
119	The Valley of Inagh, Connemara	£2 10s.
120	A Silver Strand, Lough Conn	£2 10s.
121	The 'Reeks', from Boughal Lake, Kenmare Bay	£5 5s.
122	A Rocky Point, Ventry	£2 10s.
123	Blowing Hard, West Coast	£2 10s.
124	Bundoragh River and Village, Killary Bay, Connemara	£3 3s.
125	Alexander's Rock, Killarney	£3 3s.
126	Pontoon, Lough Conn, Mayo	£3 3s.
127	At Drumquinna, Residence of Sir John Columb, Kenmare Bay	£3 3s.
128	The Reeks, from the Upper Lake, Killarney	£3 3s.

The last three titles are handwritten additions to the printed catalogue

129	At Drimmin Lough Conn	£3.3.0
130	Near Maryboro Queen's County	£3.3.0
131	At Mount Mellick Queen's County	£2.10.0
-	Caragh Lake	£2.2.0

'A perception of the beautiful and the grand in art is equivalent to the possession of another sense, for it supplies a new power of reading and appreciating the beauties and sublimities of the natural world.' – SIR JOSHUA REYNOLDS

'There is no doubt whatever of the importance of the moods of nature, the great mother and nurse of us all, and that is the reason why a good landscape is never obsolete or out of date, but is as fresh as in the day when the artist caught the outline of hill and depth of dale under the smile of sunshine or the frown of storm. Nor can the artist or the public ever grow weary of studying the myriad varieties even in the same landscape, as it were endless and rich variations upon a great and pathetic melody.'
PROF. J. P. MAHAFFY

'The Exhibition must be seen in order to be appreciated. For freedom and vigour of treatment, beauty of colour and technique, this collection of pictures, from the hand and brain of one man, deserves the hearty recognition of all who love Ireland, of the rock-bound coast, of the towering mountains, of the placid lakes, of the rushing rivers, and of the emerald pastures.' *Daily Express*

MR WILLIAMS' 4TH London Exhibition will be held at the Modern Gallery, Large Hall, 61 New Bond Street, from the 1st to the 30th of May, 1906.

CATALOGUE
OF THE
27TH Exhibition of Pictures of
Irish Scenery,
BY
ALEXANDER WILLIAMS, RHA
(STUDIO – 4 HATCH STREET)
AT 35 Molesworth St., Dublin
January 14th to February 9th, 1907.

Admission and Catalogue . . . One Shilling
10 to 6 P.M., DAILY
Curwen & County, Dublin 65–93

PATRONS
Her Excellency the Countess of Aberdeen.
The Duke and Duchess of Abercorn.
The Marchioness of Granby.
The Marchioness of Waterford.
The Marchioness of Headfort.
The Marchioness of Dufferin and Ava.
The Marquis and Marchioness of Zetland.
The Earl and Countess Cadogan.
The Earl and Countess Dudley.
The Earl of Shaftesbury.
The Earl of Drogheda.
The Countess of Fingall.

The Countess of Kilmorey.
The Countess Dowager of Arran.
The Earl and Countess of Mayo.
The Countess of Annesley.
The Countess of Erne.
Lord Castletown.
The Lady O'Neill.
The Lord and Lady Clonbrock.
The Lord and Lady Ashtown.
The Lord and Lady Plunket.
Lord and Lady Ardilaun.
General Lord Grenfell, G.C.B.

CATALOGUE

1	Near Glanmore Lake, County Kerry	£4 4s.
2	Achill Woman Washing at Dooagh	£4 4s.
3	Cloon Lake, near Killarney	£8 8s.
4	Near the River Flesk, Killarney	£3 3s.
5	The Reeks, from the Lower Lake, Killarney	£10 10s.
6	Near the Suspension Bridge, Kenmare	£3 3s.
7	Muckross Bay, Donegal	£3 10s.
8	Cahirciveen Hills, from Ventry, Kerry	£2 10s.
9	The Baily Light, Howth, Dublin Bay	£5 5s.
10	At Derreen, Kenmare Bay	£3 10s.
11	The Shore at Templenoe, Kenmare Bay	£5 5s.
12	Near Mount Eagle, Brosna, Kerry	£5 5s.
13	Wet Meadows, Templenoe, Kenmare Bay	£5 5s.
14	Near Dookinelly, Achill Island	£3 3s.
15	Mahony's Point, Lower Lake, Killarney	£5 5s.
16	Wintry Weather, Achill Island	£5 5s.
17	Muckross Shore, Killarney	£5 5s.
18	A Summer Afternoon, Kenmare Bay	£6 6s.
19	Queen's County Bog	£3 3s.
20	Down by the Sea	£5 5s.
21	Washing on the Hill-side, Achill	£4 4s.
22	Stormy Day, Minaun Cliffs, Achill	£4 4s.
23	Crowsfoot and Seapink, Bray Head	£7 7s.
24	The Shelly Bank, Pigeon House	£5 5s.
25	Moorland, Queen's County	£3 3s.
26	Castlelough Shore, Killarney	£5 5s.
27	Candlestick Bay, Howth, Dublin Bay	£5 5s.
28	The Blue Hills, of Connaught, Upper Corrib	£30
29	Near Lake Hotel, Killarney	£5 5s.
30	Lower Lake, Killarney	£5 5s.
31	Purple Heather – A Kerry Glen	£5 5s.
32	A Quiet Bay, Lower Lake, Killarney	£5 5s.
33	Blackwater, from the South side, Kenmare Bay	£5 5s.
34	The Dingle Hills, Kerry	£4 4s.

35	Landing Turf, Achill Sound	£4 4s.
36	A Cottage in the Bogs, Achill	£5 5s.
37	The Strand Hotel and Slievemore Mountain, Achill	£4 4s.
38	In Kenmare Bay, Kerry	£5 5s.
39	Mouth of the Vartry, Wicklow	£5 5s.
40	Low Water, Kenmare Bay	£6 6s.
41	Narrow Water Castle, Carlingford	£4 4s.
42	The Upper Lake, Glendalough	£5 5s.
43	On the River at Mount Eagle, Brosna, Kerry	£5 5s.
44	Near Glendarary, Achill Sound	£4 4s.
45	Aasleagh, Killary Bay	£5 5s.
46	Mountain Farm, Kenmare Bay	£5 5s
47	Lough Conn, Mayo	£2 10s.
48	Glenbeagh Sands, Kerry	£5 5s.
49	Early Spring, Queen's County	£4 4s.
50	Cliff Walk, Howth	£5 5s.
51	The Approach of Evening, Kenmare Bay	£30
52	The Landing Place, Lake Hotel, Killarney	£6 6s.
53	Reedy Pools, Lower Lake, Killarney	£5 5s.
54	Doona Castle and Distant Achill, from the Ballycroy Shore, Mayo	£10 10s.
55	Killarney Mountains, from Lower Lake	£20
56	Moll's Cottage, Windy Gap, between Killarney and Kenmare	£40
57	Muckross House, Killarney, Spring-time	£5 5s.
58	The Walton Shore, Lough Caragh	£5 5s.
59	The Valley Strand, Achill	£3 3s.
60	The Nose of Howth, Dublin Bay	£5 5s.
61	Eagle Mountain, Ventry Bay, Kerry	£5 5s.
62	Evening	£2 10s.
63	The River Moy, Mayo	£2 10s.
64	A Peep of the Devil's Rock, Killarney	£5 5s.
65	Near Mount Eagle, Brosna, Kerry	£5 5s.
66	Cloud and Sunshine	£5 5s.
67	At Derreen, Kenmare Bay	£4 4s.
68	The Dingle Coast, Stormy Day	£5 5s.
69	Wet Harvest Weather, Kenmare Bay	£7 7s.
70	Bright Sunny Weather, Templenoe, Kenmare	£6 6s.
71	The Seal Caves, Slievemore, Achill Island	£30
72	The Sheen River Falls, Kenmare	£4 4s.
73	Bridge on the Glanmore River, Derreen, Kerry	£4 4s.
74	A Sunny Day, the Landing Place, Lake Hotel, Killarney	£7 7s.
75	Distant Berehaven Hills, from Kenmare Bay	£8 8s.
76	A Ferry, Achill Sound	£4 4s.
77	A Roscommon Judicial Holding	£5 5s.
78	Bog at Maryborough	£4 4s.
79	Summer Sunshine, Kenmare	£5 5s.
80	Kildownet Castle – Evening	£5 5s.
81	Sea Cliffs at Ventry, Dingle Bay	£10
82	Clonee Lake, Kenmare Bay	£7 7s.

83	In Keem Bay, Achill Island	£3 3s.
84	On the Mayo Coast	£6 6s.
85	Summer Evening in the Garden at Leenane Hotel, Killary Bay	£4 4s.
86	Spring-time, Lake Hotel Ground, Killarney	£5 5s.
87	Muckross Lake, Killarney	£5 5s.
88	Fisher Folk, Mayo Coast	£4 4s.
89	Slievemore, Achill	£2 2s.
90	The Minaun Cliffs, Achill Island	£30
91	Mangerton, from Castlelough Bay, Killarney	£5 5s.
92	The Woods of Dromore Castle, Kenmare Bay	£6 6s.
93	Bright Stormy Weather, Howth, Dublin Bay	£5 5s.
94	At Brickeen Bridge, Killarney	£5 5s.
95	Toward Evening	£3 3s.
96	Boughal Mountain, from Kenmare Bay	£5 5s.
97	In from the Sea	£5 5s,
98	A Sketch	£3 3s.
99	Sudden Storm, Killeries, Connemara	£10 10s.
100	A Sketch	£3 3s.
101	Sea Cliffs, Achill	£5 5s.
102	Groomsport, County Down	£3 3s.
103	On the Glanmore River, Kerry	£4 4s.
104	Old Bridge, Kenmare Bay	£5 5s.
105	Kylemore Mountains, Connemara	£10 10s.
106	The Liffey, at Chapelizod	£3 3s.
107	Colleen Bawn Rocks, Killarney	£6 6s.
108	Poor Achill Folk	£4 4s.
109	Barren Achill	£5 5s.
-	Marino, Kenmare Bay	£3.3.0

PICTURES AND SKETCHES
THE
MODERN GALLERY,
61 NEW BOND STREET,
W.
EDWARD FREEMAN,
LESSEE & SECRETARY.
IN
OIL AND WATER-COLOUR
[1907]

Artists sharing this exhibition with Alexander Williams, R. H. A.
S. Adams
D. M. Anderson
Sophie Beale [spelled Sophia elsewhere]
Arthur Briscoe
H. Caffieri, R.I.
R. M. Chevalier

Harry Clayton Adams
Gerda Crump
Alice B. Ellis
Ada M. Eteson
Augustine FitzGerald
Percy French
J. S. Harrison
Bertha J. M. Hedley
Percival M. F. Hedley
Richard Herbert
Edith S. Houseman
Champion Jones
C. J. Lauder
C. MacIver Grierson, R.I.
W. J. M. Mackenzie
F. F. Ogilvie
Kate A. Parks
W. H. Pearson
J. Poole Addey
Joseph Powell
Alfred Powell
Cecil W. Quinnell, R.M.S., R.B.A.
R. J. Randall
Mary Stevens
Albert Stevens
Ernest Thesiger
George Trobridge
Ada Watson
Pinhorn Woods
The late L. J. Wood, R.I.

Total no. of paintings in exhibition: 223

CATALOGUE
Paintings by Alex. Williams, RHA in this exhibition.
(The lower price, where two are given, is what the picture in question fetched)

1	Near the 'Victoria', Killarney	£3 3s.
3	The Colleen Bawn Rock, Killarney	£3 3s.
5	Red Rock Bay, Howth	£6 6s.
7	Mountain Walk, Upper Lake, Glendalough	£5 5s.
10	Near Ballinlough, Roscommon	£12 12s.
		£10.0.0
15	A Barren Moorland, Achill Island	£6 6s.
17	Ballymore Cove, Dingle Bay	£6 6s.
23	Harvest Weather, Achill Sound	£7 7s.
		£6 6s
24	The Approach to Dookinelly, Achill Island	£10 10s.
27	'There's no Place like Home'	£6 6s.
28	Cloon Lake, County Kerry	£10 10s.
34	The Upper Lake, Glendalough	£6 6s.
36	Cliffs at Bray Head	£7 7s.

44	Reclaiming the Bog	£6 6s.
46	Rising Mists, Muckross Bay	£6 6s.
48	A Peep of the 'Divil's Rock'	£3 3s.
50	MacCarthy More's Old Castle	£3 3s.
51	Fisher Folk, Galway Coast	£6 6s.
52	Kylemore Lake, Connemara	£10 10s.
55	The River Liffey	£3 3s.
56	Groomsport Harbour, County Down	£3 3s.
57	The Approach to the Gap of Dunloe	£26 5s.
60	Washing on the Hillside, Achill Island	£6 6s.
61	The Colleen Bawn Rock	£7 7s.
64	Road to the Shore, Templenoe	£6 6s.
66	Mangerton Mountain	£6 6s.
70	A Sudden Storm, Little Killeries	£15 15s.
74	A Sod Cabin, Achill Island	£6 6s.
76	At Brickeen Bridge, Killarney	£4 4s.
80	Ross Castle, Killarney	£3 3s.
82	MacGillicuddy's Reeks	£3 3s.
83	The Cliff Path, Howth	£6 6s.
87	Salmon Pool, Glencar River	£10 10s.
88	Old Bridge near Killarney	£7 7s.
91	Delphi Lake, Connemara	£10 10s.
92	Bad Weather Coming, Kerry Coast	£6 6s.
95	Sea Coast, Achill Island	£5 5s.
97	Moll's Cottage, Windy Gap	£3 3s.
99	The Upper Lake, Glendalough	£3 3s.
100	The Baily Light, Howth	£5 5s.
103	A Judicial 'Houldin'	£5 5s.
107	Approaching Leenane	£10 10s.
110	Sea Cliff, Ventry	£9 9s.
111	Grannaile's Castle, Kildownet	£7 7s.
112	Howth Head, Dublin Bay	£5 5s.
121	Ross Island, Killarney	£4 4s.
129	Kenmare House, Killarney	£4 4s.
134	Moorland, Achill Island	£3 3s.
137	On the River Moy at Ballina	£3 3s.
165	Holy Island, Lough Derg	£3 3s.
170	Lough Derryclare, Connemara	£3 3s.
172	Near Recess	£3 3s.
180	Fishermen, Dublin Coast	£4 4s.
184	A Peasant's Cabin, Achill	£3 3s.
206	Near New Ross	£6 6s.
210	The Turf Boats, Achill Sound	£6 6s.
215	Spring Time on the Dodder	£3 3s.
217	Vartry River at Wicklow	£5 5s.
220	'The Rosy Glow of Even'	£9 9s.
221	'Soft Southern Clouds'	£6 6s.

VENICE & DORSET by SOPHIA BEALE.
HORSES & OLD HOUSES by ALICE B. ELLIS.
THE
MODERN GALLERY,
61 NEW BOND STREET,
W.

EDWARD FREEMAN,
LESSEE & SECRETARY

MARINE & RIVER by FRED. J. ALDRIDGE.

EGYPT & NUBIA by AUG. O. LAMPLOUGH.

IRISH SCENES by ALEX. WILLIAMS, RHA

[1907]

Artists sharing this exhibition with Alexander Williams, R.H A.

Frederick James Aldridge
Sophia Beale
Alice B. Ellis
Augustus O. Lamplough
Total no. of paintings in the exhibition – 90

Paintings by Alex. Williams, RHA

73	Derryclare	£3 3s.
74	The Baily Light, Howth	£5 5s.
75	Cloon Lake, County Kerry	£10 10s.
76	Fisher Folk, Galway Coast	£6 6s.
77	Moorland, Achill Island	£3 3s.
78	A Peasant's Cabin, Achill	£3 3s.
79	Approaching Leenane	£10 10s.
80	Salmon Pool, Glencar River	£10 10s.
81	Bad Weather Coming, Kerry Coast	£6 6s.
82	At Kenmare	£3 3s.
83	The Cliff Path, Howth	£6 6s.
84	'The Rosy Glow of Even'	£9 9s.
85	A Barren Moorland, Achill Island	£6 6s.
86	Near Recess	£3 3s.
87	Lough, Derryclare	£3 3s.
88	A Sudden Storm, Little Killeries	£15 15s.
89	Delphi Lake, Connemara	£10 10s.
90	Harvest Weather, Achill Sound	£7 7s.
		Sold
		£6.6.0

'Beautiful Ireland' Exhibition
by
Alexander Williams, RHA
Leinster Hall
35 Molesworth Street Gallery
14 January – 8 February 1908

Catalogue

1	Holy Island, Lough Derg, Shannon	£2.10.0
2	Fishing boats becalmed	£3.3.0
3	The Islands of Kane	£2.10.0
4	Kylemore Lake, Connemara	£10.10.0
5	On the Moy at Ballina	£2.10.0
6	Valley of the Liffey, Chapelizod	£2.10.0
7	The Upper Lake, Glendalough, Wicklow.	£2.10.0
8	Cormorants Resting	£2.10.0
9	Looking towards Inch	£5.5.0
10	Road near Recess, Connemara	£3.3.0
11	A Bit of Bog near Achill Sound	£4.4.0
12	The Bay of Shraheens, Achill	-
13	Summer Evening, Upper Lake Glendalough	£4.4.0
14	Early Morning on the Sea Shore	£3.3.0
15	'Come back o setting sun'	£10.10.0
16	Breanaskill Bridge, Achill Sound	£6.6.0
17	Evening Light, Drimmin Wood, L. Conn	£3.10.0
18	A Peep of the Devil's Rock, Killarney	£2.10.0
19	On the Shore of Cloon Lough, Kerry	£8.8.0
20	Heavy Weather Coming Up	£4.4.0
21	A Bit of Sea	£2.10.0
22	The Colleen Bawn Rock, Killarney	£8.8.0
23	Waning Light	£3.3.0
24	Low Tide, Breanaskill Bay, Achill	£3.10.0
25	View of the Lower Lake, Killarney	£12.12.0
26	Road to the Shore, Breanaskill Bay	£3.3.0
27	Afternoon on the River Brosna	£5.5.0
28	Fisher Folk, Achill	£4.4.0
29	Looking Across Kenmare Bay	£5.5.0
30	Wormwood Gate, Vanished Dublin	£25.0.0.
31	A Cottage at Shraheens Bay, Achill.	£6.6.0
32	Autumn Moorland, Achill	£3.3.0
33	Sweet Innisfallen, Killarney	£10.10.0
34	Dingle Hills from Ventry	£4.4.0
35	The Upper Lough, Glendalough	£5.5.0
36	A Cottage at Achill Sound	£7.7.0
37	Reclaimed Bog, Achill	£5.5.0
38	The Rosy Hues of Evening on the Reeks	£8.8.0
39	Hauling the Trawl	£2.10.0
40	A Roscommon Cottage	£5.5.0

41	Slievemore from the Valley	£5.5.0
42	'Achill. There's no place like home'	£4.4.0
43	Sunset from Malahide Golf Links	£10.10.0
44	On the Lonely Shore	£4.4.0
45	Wild Weather, Culfin Bay, Connemara	£8.8.0
45A	MacGillicuddy's Reeks	£15.15.0
46	Windy Gap, Road to Kenmare	£5.5.0
47	A Blackwater Bridge, Kenmare	£5.5.0
48	Glendarary, Achill Sound	£5.5.0
49	A Rough Day, Balbriggan Coast	£15.15.0
50	The Islands of Greenane, Kenmare Bay	£25.0.0
51	The Bay of Salruck, Connemara	£50.0.0
52	The Church of the Rock, Glendalough	£10.10.0
53	A Quiet Bay, Muckross Lake	£25.0.0
54	Coast of Howth near the Needles	£5.5.0
55	At Muckross House, Killarney	£5.0.0
56	Toilers of the Sea	£4.4.0
57	The Evening Hour	£3.3.0
58	Polranny Hill, Achill Sound	£5.5.0
59	Evening on the Shelly Bank	£10.10.0
60	A Bit of Rough Sea	£4.4.0
61	On the Road to Keel, Achill	£8.8.0
62	The Turf Boat, Achill Island	£4.4.0
63	A Sunny Afternoon, Achill	£4.4.0
64	No Wind	£2.10.0
65	The Pass of Delphi, Connemara	£8.8.0
66	Dawn	£10.10.0
67	Coming to Anchor	£2.10.0
68	On Rabbit Island, Killarney	£2.10.0
69	A Bright Autumn Day, Achill Sound	£6.6.0
70	Hazelwood, Lough Gill	£25.0.0
71	A Perfect Calm	£3.3.0
72	Ruins of Castle Lough	£2.10.0
73	A Sunny Afternoon, Glendarary	£6.6.0
73A	Gathering Wrack, Achill	£4.4.0
74	Tranquil Evening	£4.4.0
75	Cormorants	£10.10.0
76	Sunny Hours	£2.10.0
77	Moorland, Achill	£5.5.0
78	A Collier, Evening	£2.10.0
79	MacGillicuddy's Reeks, Evening	£8.8.0
80	The Approach to the Bridge, Achill	£6.6.0
81	Moving the Harvest, Blind Sound	£4.4.0
82	Ross Castle, Killarney	£2.10.0
83	'Now comes still evening on'	£10.10.0
84	A Roscommon Harvest Field	£5.5.0
85	Early Summer, a Cloudy Day	£5.5.0
86	Barren Achill	£5.5.0
87	Lower Lake, Killarney	£2.10.0

88	Sea Cliffs, Ventry	£10.10.0
89	A Bit of Rough Sea	£2.10.0
90	Morning, Bray River	£3.3.0
91	Killary Bay from Maam Road	£8.8.0
92	Keem Bay, Achill	£2.10.0
93	Evening near Aasleagh, Killary Bay	£3.3.0
94	Cloon Lake, Kerry	£2.10.0
95	The Golfers' Lane, Carrickmines	£3.3.0
96	The Colleen Bawn Rocks	£3.3.0
97	On Dalkey Island	£10.10.0

Pictures of Ireland
by
Alexander Williams, RHA
Leinster Hall
35 Molesworth Street
16 January to 6 February 1909

Catalogue

1	Ards House, County Donegal	£3.3.0
2	The Back Strand	£3.3.0
3	Muckish	~~£3.3.0~~
		£2.5.0
4	Sunset, Sheephaven	£10.10.0
5	Near Lily Lough	£3.3.0
6	A Peep of Ards	£3.3.0
7	A Glimpse of Garnamore	£3.3.0
8	The Back Strand	£3.3.0
9	A Summer Evening	£10.10.0
10	Mahony's Point	£12.12.0
11	Glendalough	£2.2.0
12	On Old Bray River	£2.2.0
13	Dollymount Strand	£8.8.0
14	Aasleagh, Killary	£3.3.0
15	The Pass of Doolough	£6.6.0
16	Bog Road, Maryboro	£2.2.0
17	Sunset	£2.2.0
18	Aasleagh Waterfall	£10.10.0
19	Achill Folk	£3.3.0
19	Achill Folk [(19) listed twice]	£3.3.0
20	Bray Head from Greystones	£6.6.0
21	The Claddagh	£2.2.0
22	The Heath, Maryboro	£2.2.0
23	Glendarary, Achill	£5.5.0
24	Salmon Pool, Lackagh	£7.7.0
25	The Minaun Cliffs	£31.10.0

26	Errigal from Gweedore River	£6.6.0
27	View Looking over Creeslough	£7.7.0
28	A Boreen, Abbeyleix	£2.2.0
29	Slievemore, Achill	£2.2.0
30	Looking towards Mountrath	£5.5.0
31	Achill Cottages	£2.10.0
32	The Church of the Rock	£10.10.0
33	An Achill Sketch	£2.10.0
34	Upper Lake, Glendalough	£1.10.0
34 [sic]	Upper Lake, Glendalough	£2.2.0
35	Near Swords	£2.2.0
36	View on Lough Caragh	£10.10.0
37	Candlestick Bay	£6.6.0
38	Rosapenna Head	£2.2.0
39	The Valley Achill	£8.8.0
40	Over the Rolling Sea	~~£5.5.0~~
		£3.10.0
41	Downings Bay	£12.12.0
42	An Impression	£2.10.0
43	View from Railway, Falcarragh	£4.4.0
44	Where the River Leaves the Lakes	25 guineas
45	An Achill Hillside	£10.10.0
46	Doe Castle	£15.15.0
47	Ferriters Cove	£63.0.0
48	Coast of Blacksod	£10.10.0
49	Inniskea	£26.5.0
50	A Summer Sea	£5.5.0
51	Lower Lake, Killarney	£5.5.0
52	Cloudy Weather	~~£5.5.0~~
		£3.10.0
53	Doagrue Mountain	£10.10.0
54	Road to Lough Nafooey	£2.2.0
55	Slievemore & Croaghaun	£2.2.0
56	Summertime, Glendalough	~~£3.3.0~~
		£1.1.0
57	Bathing Strand, Rosapenna	£5.5.0
58	The Old Post Office, Downings	£10.10.0
59	Rosapenna Hotel	£5.5.0
60	A Boreen, Killcool	£2.2.0
61	Lough O'Flynn	£2.2.0
62	The Gates of the Morning	£12.12.0
63	Autumn, Achill	£10.10.0
64	Carrickmines	£2.2.0
65	Inver Bay	£2.2.0
66	Evening Light	£6.6.0
67	Errigal from Altan	£6.6.0
68	A Salmon Pool	£26.5.0
69	On the Road to Nafooey	£10.10.0
70	In the Rocky Valley	£5.5.0

71	Horn Head, Sheephaven, etc.	£12.12.0
72	Near the Bailey	£3.3.0
73	Cottages, Letterfrack	£2.2.0
74	Glendalough	£2.2.0
75	The Reeks	£10.10.0
76	On the Inney	£3.3.0
77	The Great Sand Mountain	£5.5.0
78	Evening	£2.2.0
79	Killary Bay	£2.2.0
80	The Muglins	£12.12.0
81	On Red Island	£8.8.0
82	Sessiagh Lough	£6.6.0
83	Meeting of the Waters	£2.2.0
84	Heavy Showers	£2.2.0
85	In the Golden Eventide	£10.10.0
86	Blowing Hard, Glenveagh	£6.6.0
87	A Right of Way	£5.5.0
88	The Nose of Howth	£5.5.0
89	Marble Hill Strand	£5.5.0
90	Blarney Castle	£3.3.0
91	Caragh Lake	£3.3.0
92	Passage Cork	£3.3.0
93	Spike Island	£3.3.0
94	Kingston Bay	£3.3.0
95	Moorland, Achill	£2.15.0 ~~£3.3.0~~
96	Mornington, near Drogheda	£10.10.0
97	Warrenpoint, Carlingford	£3.3.0
98	Blackstreams Bridge Gap	£3.3.0
99	Doolough, Killarney	£3.3.0
100	At Glendarary	£3.3.0
101	Rough Weather, Achill	£4.4.0
-	Achill Sound	£2.13.0 ~~£3.3.0~~

'OULD DONEGAL'
THE MODERN GALLERY,
61 NEW BOND STREET,
W.

EDWARD FREEMAN,
LESEE & SECRETARY.
WATER-COLOURS & OIL PAINTINGS
BY
ALEXANDER WILLIAMS.
(Member of the Royal Hibernian Academy of Arts, Dublin).
Last Day, Saturday, 10th April, 1909.

CATALOGUE

1	Sessiagh Lake, East Side	£4.4s.
2	A Bog Cabin, Gweedore, Errigal in Distance	£8.8s.
3	Sandhills at Horn Head Bridge	£4.4s.
4	Evening on the Cliffs, Portnablagh	£8.8s.
5	A Peep of Ards House from the Woods	£4.4s.
6	Sheep Haven Strand	£8.8s.
7	The Murder Hole, Melmore Cliffs	£8.8s.
8	A Corner of Lough Sessiagh, Dunfanaghy	£4.4s.
9	Salmon Pool, Lackagh River, Rosapenna District	£4.4s.
10	Muckish Mountain from the Shore of Ards Demesne	£7.7s.
11	Horn Head, Evening Light	£4.4s.
12	Sheep Haven, Horn Head, Downing's Bay and Rosapenna District from the Road to Lough Salt	£36.15s.
13	A Bird's-eye View of the Back Strand, Ards Demesne	£4.4s.
14	Near Lily Lough, Ards Demesne	£4.4s.
15	Horn Head, Sheep Haven, and Downing's Bay from the Links, Rosapenna	£7.7s.
16	Horn Head Bridge	£4.4s.
17	'The Haven under the Hill', Portnablagh	£8.8s.
18	Dunfanaghy	£4.4s.
19	Sessiagh Lake from the West, Dunfanaghy	£8.8s.
20	The Old Post Office over Downing's Bay, Rosapenna	£12.12s.
21	Creeslough	£8.8s.
22	A Fishing Stream	£26.5s.
23	Low-water, Portnablagh, Dunfanaghy	£7.7s.
24	A Distant View of Dunfanaghy from Breaghey Head	£8.8s.
25	A Few Weeds, the Back Strand, Sheep Haven	£15.15s.
26	Errigal from Gweedore	£8.8s.
27	Duntally Wood, Creeslough	£7.7s.
28	Errigal from Lough Altan	£4.4s.
29	A Distant View of Rosapenna, over Sheep Haven, from Ards	£8.8s.
30	A Sketch in the Hotel Grounds, Rosapenna	£7.7s.
31	Errigal and Lough Altan	£4.4s.
32	The Great Sand Mountain, and Horn Head Bridge	£31.10s.
33	A Sheltered Farm, near Marble Strand	£4.4s.
34	A Rocky Cove, Marble Strand, Sheep Haven	£4.4s.
35	The Bathing Strand, Rosapenna, Hotel Grounds	£7.7s.
36	Glen Lough, Rosapenna District	£4.4s.
37	Rocky Coast at Breaghey Head	£8.8s.
38	Showery Weather, Back Strand, Ards	£4.4s.
39	Doagh Bay, Rosapenna District	£7.7s.
40	Ards House, Sheep Haven	£4.4s.
41	An Iron-bound Coast, Sheep Haven	£8.8s.
42	At Bunlin Bridge, Milford	£4.4s.
43	Horn Head from Portnablagh, Evening	£8.8s.
44	The Mouth of Mulroy Bay, St Martin's, Summer	£15.15s.
45	Tory Island from the Cliffs of Horn Head	£73.10s.

46	Rosapenna and Downing's Bay from Marble Strand, Sheep Haven	£4.4s.
47	A Peep at Ganiamore from Ards Demesne	£4.4s.
48	The Harbour of Portnablagh	£4.4s.
49	Blowing Hard, Glenveagh	£8.8s.
50	In Downing's Bay, Rosapenna	£12.12s.
51	Sessiagh Lake from the East, Dunfanaghy	£8.8s.
52	Rocks at Doagh Bay, Rosapenna District	£7.7s.
53	Rosapenna Head	£3.3s.
54	The Bay of Donegal	£3.3s.
55	Glenveagh Castle	£4.4s.
56	Bloody Foreland Hill and Ballyness Bay from Falcarragh Hill	£4.4s.
57	Donegal Town	£4.4s.
58	Horn Head from Muslack Rocks, Rosapenna Hotel	£7.7s.
59	Rosapenna Hotel, Looking Toward the Great Strand	£6.6s.
60	View from Falcarragh Railway Station	£4.4s.
61	Rosapenna Hotel, Carrigart	£7.7s.
62	Doe Castle, the Ancient Fortress of the MacSweeneys	£4.4s.
63	Lough Derevaragh, County West-Meath	£4.4s.
64	On Red Island, Skerries, County Dublin	£12.12s.
65	Sunset at Mornington, near Drogheda, County Louth	£10.10s.
66	'The Gates of the Morning'	£15.15s.
67	Inney River, Derevaragh	£4.4s.
68	Breanaskill Bridge, Achill Sound, County Mayo	£7.7s.
69	Dollymount Strand, Dublin Bay	£8.8s.
70	Evening Light, Cliffs of Howth, Dublin Bay	£7.7s.
71	On Dalkey Island, Dublin Bay	£10.10s.
72	The Hills of Glendarary, Achill Sound, County Mayo	£7.7s.
73	A Fine Harvest Day, Achill Sound	£8.8s.
74	Macgillicuddy's Reeks, and the Gap from the Lower Lake, Killarney	£15.15s.
75	Rough Weather at Seal Caves, Slievemore, Achill Island	£40.
77	Lough Caragh Looking West, County Kerry	£15.15s.
78	A Corner of the Garden, Malahide Castle, County Dublin	£10.10s.
79	Lough Caragh, County Kerry	£3.3s.
80	Blarney Castle, Cork	£3.3s.
81	A Turf Boat, Achill Island	£3.3s.
82	Howth Harbour from the Nose of Howth, Dublin Bay	£12.12s.
83	Mahony's Point, Lower Lake, Killarney	£15.15s.
84	Templeogue Bridge, River Dodder, Dublin	£4.4s.
85	Wrack Gathering on the West Coast	£12.12s.
86	A Bit at Maryborough, Queen's County	£4.4s.
87	Diamond Mountain from Ballinakill Bay, Letterfrack, Connemara	£15.15s.
88	Abbeyleix Church, Queen's County	£4.4s.
89	Fishermen, Achill Island	£7.7s.
90	A Clear Morning, Bray Head, from Greystones, County Wicklow	£7.7s.
91	A Right of Way, Abbeyleix, Queen's County	£7.7s.
92	Macgillicuddy's Reeks from Barfinihy, Lough Kenmare	£15.15s.
93	On the Achill Coast	£7.7s.
94	In the Rocky Valley, Bray, County Wicklow	£6.6s.

95	Aasleagh, Killary Bay, Connemara	£3.3s.
96	The Post Office, Achill Sound, Mayo	£3.3s.
97	Opposite Passage, Cove of Cork	£3.3s.

CATALOGUE
OF THE
31st Exhibition of Pictures of
Irish Scenery,
BY
ALEXANDER WILLIAMS, RHA
(Studio – 4   Hatch Street)
At the Art Gallery,
35 Molesworth Street, Dublin,
January 13th to February 4th, 1911.

MUSICAL AFTERNOONS each Friday,
4 to 5 p.m.

Admission and Catalogue – One Shilling
10 to 6 p.m. DAILY

		£ s d
1	Pass of Delphi	4.4.0
2	A Bit of Old Youghal	2.10.0
3	Doe Castle	12.12.0
4	A Wet Day, Mulroy	3.3.0
5	The Lower Lake, Killlarney	10.10.0
6	The Bay of Wicklow	4.4.0
7	The Walls of Derry	2.10.0
8	Walker's Column, Derry	2.10.0
9	Stormy Weather, Achill	3.3.0
10	At Leenane	3.3.0
11	Road to Minaun Cliffs, Achill	5.5.0
12	Killarney	3.3.0
13	Meadows at Templenoe	5.5.0
14	Early Morning	3.3.0
15	Mount Errigal from Lough Altan	10.10.0
16	The Colleen Bawn Rock	3.3.0
17	Narrow Water Castle, Carlingford	2.10.0
18	The Old Bird Market, Bull Alley	3.3.0
19	In the Erriff Valley, Connemara	10.10.0
20	The Blackwater near Youghal	4.4.0
21	At Breanaskill, Achill	3.3.0
22	Evening near Mountmellick	5.5.0
23	The Balbriggan Road, Skerries	3.10.0
24	The Minaun Cliffs, Achill	10.10.0
25	Tranquil Evening	5.5.0

26	Candlestick Bay, Howth	£30
27	Near Derreen, Kenmare Bay	5.5.0
28	Near the Post Office, Achill Sound	10.10.0
29	Dull Weather, Kenmare Bay	3.3.0
30	A Blue Day, Skerries, Co. Dublin	3.3.0
31	Killary Bay from the Maam Road	8.8.0
32	Kate Kearney's Cascade	2.2.0
33	Horn Head from Rosapenna	4.4.0
34	Autumn Tints, Muckross Lake	12.12.0
35	Narrow Water Castle	3.3.0
36	Bundonagh, Killary Bay	4.4.0
37	A Rough Day, Achill	4.4.0
38	Near Drogheda	3.3.0
39	Clouds on Killarney Hills	2.2.0
40	Road to Tourmakeady – Mask	10.10.0
41	Clonee Lake, Kenmare Bay	5.5.0
42	Evening, Portnablagh, Donegal	5.5.0
43	Harvest Time, Kenmare Bay	5.5.0
44	Clonee, Kenmare Bay	5.5.0
45	Delphi Mountains, Killary Bay	£21.0.0
46	The Vale of Glendassan, Wicklow	10.10.0
47	A Fine Day at Killarney	25.0.0.
48	Departed Glories. Annakeen Castle	5.5.0
49	Sheen River Falls, Kenmare	5.5.0
50	Close of Day	10.10.0
51	At Derreen, Kenmare Bay	5.5.0
52	Killary Bay	3.3.0
53	Achill Sound	10.10.0
54	Lower Clonee, Kenmare Bay	5.5.0
55	Lane off the Dargle Road, Bray	2.10.0
56	Trawlers Becalmed	8.8.0
57	Evening, Glendarary, Achill	10.10.0
58	At the Railway Station, Falcarragh	2.2.0
59	The Evening Hour	5.5.0
60	Sea Cliffs, Ventry, Dingle	10.10.0
61	On the Arklow River	3.3.0
62	The Owen Brinn River Mask	5.5.0
63	The Gap of Dunloe	2.2.0
64	Fine Weather, Achill Sound	10.10.0
65	Chapter Place, St Patrick's Close	4.4.0
66	Upper Corrib from Doone	10.10.0
67	A Fish Market, Achill	5.5.0
68	Ardmore, Waterford	3.3.0
69	Rocky Coast, Achill	6.6.0
70	Lower Lake, Killarney	3.3.0
71	The Reeks from Caragh	10.10.0
72	Beautiful Weather, Killarney	10.10.0
73	On Ards Strand, Donegal	3.3.0

74	Old Merrion Gates, Dublin	2.10.0
75	Ventry Bay	5.5.0
76	In Killary Bay, Connemara	2.2.0
77	Near Maam, Connemara	2.2.0
78	Road to Lough Nafooey	3.3.0
79	On the Inny, Westmeath	3.3.0
80	Departing Glories	10.10.0
81	Bad Weather, Balscaddan Bay	3.3.0
82	Glendarary, Achill Sound	10.10.0
83	'Half a gale' at Skerries	3.3.0
84	Across the Moor, Ballyfin	2.10.0
85	Old Houses in Cork St.	4.4.0
86	Old Houses off Mill St.	4.4.0
87	Old Houses in Cork St.	4.4.0

Replica of No. 14.   Mrs. Arthur Tyndall
                      Hollywood House Glenealy
                      Co Wicklow

BEAUTIFUL IRELAND.

**Catalogue of
the Thirty-second
Exhibition of Pictures
of Irish Scenery,
BY
ALEXNDER WILLIAMS, RHA
(Studio – 4 Hatch Street)
AT THE
Art Gallery, 35 Molesworth St.,
Dublin,**

JAN. 20TH TO FEB. 10TH, 1912.

**MUSICAL AFTERNOONS each Friday,
4 to 5 p.m.**

**Admission and Catalogue – 1s.
10 to 6 p.m. Daily.**

CATALOGUE

Nos. 1 to 48, the original paintings used to illustrate the four Volumes of *Beautiful Ireland* –
Leinster, Ulster, Munster, and Connaught. The exclusive right of reproduction of these paintings
has been purchased by Messrs BLACKIE AND SON, Glasgow, London, and Bombay.

LEINSTER

No.

1	Bay of Dublin from Howth Cliff Walk	£4.4s.
2	Killiney Bay and Bray Head	£5.5.0
3	Near Abbeyleix, Queen's County	£4.4s.
4	The Port of Dublin from Ringsend	£5.5s.
5	A Hawthorn Glade, Phoenix Park	£4.4s.
6	The River Liffey at Palmerston	£4.4s.
7	A Favourite View: Portmarnock Golf Links	£5.5s.
8	The Meeting of the Waters at Woodenbridge	£4.4s.
9	St Kevin's Bed and the Church of the Rock, Upper Lake, Glendalough	£5.5s.
10	On the River Boyne at Trim	£4.4s.
11	The Bridge of Slane, River Boyne	£4.4s.
12	On the River Slaney at Ballintemple, County Carlow	£8.8s.

ULSTER

13	Muckross Bay, Killybegs, Donegal	£4.4s.
14	Narrow Water Castle, Carlingford Lough	£5.5s.
15	Cave Hill, Belfast, from Strandtown, Belfast Lough	£4.4s.
16	Carrickfergus Castle, Belfast Lough	£4.4s.
17	The Giants' Causeway	£4.4s.
18	Fair Head, County Antrim	£4.4s.
19	Londonderry from the Waterside	£5.5s.
20	Tory Island from Falcarragh Hill, Donegal	£4.4s.
21	Muckish and Ards looking from Rosapenna, Sheephaven, Donegal	£4.4s.
22	Mount Errigal from the Clady River, Gweedore, Donegal	£4.4s.
23	Glenveagh Lake and Castle, Donegal	£5.5s.
24	The Entrance to Mulroy Bay, Donegal	£4.4s.

MUNSTER

25	The Old Clock Tower, Youghal, County Cork	£5.5s.
26	The Blackwater at Dromana, Waterford	£5.5s.
27	Blarney Castle	£4.4s.
28	Ferrybank, County Waterford	£5.5s.
29	Shandon Steeple from the River Lee, Cork	£5.5s.
30	Entrance to Cork Harbour. Roche's Point from Church Bay.	£4.4s.
31	Kenmare Bay from Templenoe	£5.5s.
32	MacGillicuddy's Reeks from Barfinnihy Lough, Kenmare	£5.5s.
33	The Gap of Dunloe, Killarney	£5.5s.
34	Muckross Lake, Killarney	£4.4s.
35	Brickeen Bridge, Killarney	£5.5s.
36	Holy Island, Lough Derg, River Shannon	£4.4s.

CONNAUGHT

37	Lough Breenbannia, near Clifden, Connemara	£5.5s.
38	Wrack Gatherers, West Coast	£4.4s.
39	Mweelrea, Killary Bay, from Tully Strand, Renvyle	£4.4s.
40	Pass of Delphi, Killary Bay	£4.4s.

41	The Owen Brin River and the Three Sisters, Lough Mask	£4.4s.
42	Lough Gill, Sligo	£4.4s.
43	The Minaun Cliffs, Achill Island, Mayo	£5.5s.
44	Castlekirk, Upper Corrib	£4.4s.
45	Croaghpatrick from Old Head Strand, Clew Bay	£4.4s.
46	Lowlands, Ballinlough, Roscommon	£4.4s.
47	Fisherman's Home, Ballinakill Bay	£4.4s.
48	Nephin from Lough Conn	£4.4s.

49	Glasslawn Strand, Killeries, Connemara	£25.
50	The 'Needles' and the Bailey Light from the Cliff Walk, Howth	£15.15s.
51	By Killarney's Lakes and Fells	£25.
52	Atlantic Billows at the Blind Sound, Upper Achill	£4.4s.
53	On the Blackwater, County Cork	£3.3s.
54	Approaching Night	£10.10s.
55	At Gorteen Bay, Roundstone, Connaught	£3.3s.
56	Hornhead Bridge, Dunfanaghy, Donegal	£21.
57	The Mouth of Mulroy Bay, Donegal	£10.10s.
58	'My Island Home', Bleanaskill Lodge, Achill Island	No price
59	Shore at Roundstone, Connemara	£3.3s.
60	View from the Nose of Howth	£7.7s.
61	Harvest Time, Achill Sound, Mayo	£2.10s.
62	The Old Bridge, Upper Lake, Glendalough	£4.4s.
63	In the Gap of Dunloe	£4.4s.
64	A Spate in the Glencar River at Lough Caragh	£10.10s.
65	The Cathedral Rocks, Minaun Cliffs, Achill Island	£2.10s.
66	A Peep at the Upper Lake, Killarney	£5.5s.
67	Ireland's Eye, Dublin Bay	£21.
68	A Lacemaker's Cottage, Youghal, County Cork	£10.10s.
69	Early Summer at Carrickmines, County Dublin	£10.10s.
70	The Upper Lake, Glendalough, Wicklow	£4.4s.
70A	Achill Cliffs, Clare Island in Distance	£12.12s.
71	Meenglass, Donegal	£6.6s.
72	Summer Evening at the Upper Lake, Glendalough, County Wicklow	£4.4s.
73	A Rough Day, West Coast of Achill	£4.4s.
74	Evening at Balbriggan, County Dublin	£3.3s.
75	A Moorland Trout Stream	£15.15s.
76	Keem Bay, Achill Island	£2.10s.
77	The West Coast of Achill Island	£5.5s.
78	The 'Divil's Elbow', Gap of Dunloe	£4.4s.
79	Curraune Mountain, Achill Sound	£4.4s.
80	Slievemore and Croaghaun Mountains, Achill	£2.10s.
81	The Wild Coast of Achill	£3.3s.
82	The 'Duke's' Favourite Salmon Pool, Kylemore, Connemara	£4.4s.
83	Skerries from the Balbriggan Road	£3.3s.
84	In Kenmare Bay	£3.3s.
85	'The Stag's Leap' Rocks, Upper Lake, Kylemore	£3.3s.

86	The Hills of Kylemore from Letterfrack	£4.4s.
87	A Purple Moorland, Achill Island	£3.3s.
88	A Salmon Pool, Lower Lake, Kylemore, Connemara	£4.4s.
89	The Distant Minauns, Achill Island	£3.3s.
90	Derryinver Bridge, Kylemore River, Connemara	£4.4s.
91	Cormorants	£3.3s.
92	Old Canon Street in 1895. Now St Patrick's Park	£5.5s.

CATALOGUE
OF THE
34th Exhibition
of Pictures
BY
ALEXANDER WILLIAMS, RHA
(Studio – 4 Hatch Street)

Mills' Hall, 8 Merrion Row, Dublin,
JANY. 12TH TO FEBY. 6TH, 1914.
–
MUSICAL RECITALS EACH FRIDAY, 4 to 5 p.m.
–
Price – Sixpence.

BEAUTIFUL IRELAND
Companion Series to Beautiful England
F'cap 4to, bound in boards, with coloured panel; each volume containing 12 full page illustrations in colour, **price 2s. each net;** *also bound in levant grained leather or smooth lambskin,* **price 3s. 6d. each net.**

THE great success of the Beautiful England series has encouraged the publishers to issue four volumes devoted to the Green Island. These books are uniform in size and format with those of the Beautiful England series, and each volume contains 12 pictures in full colour.

The work of illustration has been entrusted to **Mr. ALEXANDER WILLIAMS, RHA**, the well-known painter of Irish scenes. Mr Williams is an artist of the first rank, and no painter of late has done so much to bring forward to the public the grace and charm of Irish scenery. It has been well said of him 'that no-one of his craft has ever worked so hard with brush and palette to give faithful expression, through all the gamut of their varying moods, to those charms of lake and mountain, of sea and river, of peaceful valley and rugged headland, of which our country possesses such untold wealth'.

The text for these books has been written by Mr. **STEPHEN GWYNN, M.P.** who is one of the foremost living writers on Irish affairs, and his name on the title page at once stamps the series as being out of the ordinary. The following volumes are to be published.

ULSTER   MUNSTER
LEINSTER   CONNAUGHT

BLACKIE & SON Limited: London, Glasgow, and Bombay

CATALOGUE

NO.		
1	Reproductions in colour illustrating 'Beautiful Ireland'	
2	A Lonely Shore	£7.7s.
3	'Return o' setting sun'	£6.6s.
4	Reproductions in colour illustrating 'Beautiful Ireland'	
5	Upper Lake, Kylemore, Connemara	£2.2s.
6	Crosshaven, Cove of Cork	£2.2s.
7	Heavy Weather	£7.7s.
8	In the Heart of the Twelve Pins, Connemara	£5.5s.
9	Salmon Pool, Oughterard, Galway	£2.2s.
10	The Shining Shannon at Lough Derg	£2.2s.
11	At Avoca, Wicklow	£2.2s.
12	'Winds in the trees chant a glad song'	£4.4s.
13	A Gloomy Day, Brickeen, Killarney	£10.10s.
14	The Duke's Salmon Pool, Kylemore	£4.4s.
15	Sunset at Skerries, County Dublin	£5.5s.
16	A View at Skerries	£3.3s.
17	Summer Evening, Lough Caragh	£12.12s.
18	A Tearing Breeze	£3.3s.
19	'A little grey home in the West'	£10.10s.
20	Glenveagh, Donegal	£4.4s.
21	The Rocky Valley, County Wicklow	£5.5s.
22	Glanagirla, Leenane	£2.10s.
23	Aasleagh, Head of Killary Bay	£5.5s.
24	Glen Lough, Donegal	£3.3s.
25	Dalkey Sound, County Dublin	£25
26	Derryclare Lake, Connemara	£4.4s.
27	Ballycastle, Antrim	£3.3s.

SCOTLAND

28	Ben Lomond, from Luss	£4.4s.
29	Off Tignabruiach, Kyles of Bute	£3.3s.
30	The 'Brig o' Turk', Perthshire	£10.10s.
31	Dunolly Castle, Oban	£2.2s.
32	Duneraggan, 'Land of brown heath and shaggy wood'	£5.5s.
33	Scotch Oats	£2.10s.
34	An Evening Glow, Loch Venachar	£4.4s.
35	The Old Pier, Arrochar	£2.2s.
36	Carrick Castle, Loch Goil	£3.3s.
37	Brodick Bay, Arran	£2.2s.
37A	'The flying scud and the frowning night'	£4.4s.
38	A Heather Glen, Kerry	£5.5s.

39	Roundstone, Connemara	£2.2s.
40	Sweeney's Lane, Dublin	£4.4s.
41	Near Leenane	£2.2s.
42	'Heaven's reflex, Killarney'	£25
43	Colleen Bawn Rock, Killarney	£2.2s.
44	Flood in the Glencar River, Lough Caragh	£10.10s.
45	Clouds on the Hills, Killarney	£2.2s.
46	At Lake Hotel, Killarney	£2.2s.
47	McCarthy's Castle, Killarney	£2.2s.
48	Grey Day, Killarney	£2.2s.
49	A Skerries Fishing Boat	£50
50	Middle Lake, Killarney	£25

ENGLAND

51	An Old Bit at Kew, Thames	£4.4s.
52	Shipping at Greenwich, Thames	£4.4s.
53	Haven Sandhills, Poole Harbour	£2.2s.
54	Evening on the Thames	£4.4s.
55	Near Twickenham Ferry	£2.10s.
56	Entrance, Poole Harbour, Dorset	£3.3s.
57	The Vale of Dyserth, N. Wales	£25
58	Hay Barges, Thames	£2.10s.
59	Autumn at Loughlinstown	£10.10s.
60	Showery Weather, Lough Barfinnihy, Kenmare	£10.10s.
61	Easterly Gale, Red Rock Bay, Howth	£5.5s.
62	View from Kenmare Demesne, Killarney	£10.10s.
63	A Bit of Carrickmines, County Dublin	£3.3s.
64	Dull Weather, Killarney	£2.2s.
65	The Hills of Kylemore, Connemara	£12.12s.
66	From our Window, Bleanaskill, Achill	£4.4s.
67	The Stag's Leap, Kylemore Lake	£2.2s.
68	'The golden eventide'	£25
69	The Ballynahinch River, Connemara	£5.5s.
70	Muckross Lake, Killarney	£4.4s.
71	Moments of Peril, Achill	£5.5s.
72	A Bit at Belmullet, Mayo	£2.2s.
73	Windswept [Handwritten note: Replica sold £4.4.0]	£4.4s.
74	Rain Threatening, Killarney	£5.5s.
75	Were the Laune Leaves Killarney	£10.10s.
76	Horn Head Bridge, Donegal	£4.4s.
77	Summer-time	£2.2s.
78	Old Bridge near Abbeyleix	£4.4s.
79	'By the deep sea and music in its roar'	£5.5s.
80	The Groves of Glendarary, Achill	£10.10s.
81	Cromwell's Gate, Youghal	£4.4s.

The last two are handwritten additions to the printed catalogue

82	Upper Lake of Glendalough	
	Replica of No. [2] A lonely shore	£7.7.0

35th Annual Exhibition
Opens Feb. 12 1915

Catalogue of the 35th Exhibition

1	Road to Horn Head	£20
2	Tory Island from Falcarragh	£3.3.0
3	A Portrait	
4	Frame of Illustrations	
5	McGrails Rock	£3.3.0
6	Bad Harvest Weather	£4.4.0
7	A Break in the Sky	£7.7.0
7A	Kew, River Thames	£5.5.0
8	A Bit of Old Dublin	£4.4.0
9	Howth from Raheny	£5.5.0
10	The Distant 'Gap'	£3.3.0
11	Eventide	£3.3.0
12	Lough Derryclare	£10.10.0
13	Bleanaskill Bridge	£3.3.0
14	Summer Morning, Keem Bay	£5.5.0
15	Only Some Weeds	£10.10.0
16	Lough Altan	£3.3.0
17	The Hour of Rest	£5.5.0
18	An Irish Moorland	£3.3.0
19	The Glencar River	£10.10.0
20	Rossdowan	£3.3.0
21	At Malahide	£4.4.0
22	The Balbriggan Shore	£5.5.0
23	Ross Castle	£4.4.0
24	On the Lackagh	£10.10.0
25	A Donegal Salmon Pool	£25
26	An Autumn Day	£3.3.0
27	The Hag's Glen	£3.3.0
28	Islands of Parknasilla	£5.5.0
29	Achillbeg and West Coast	£10.10.0
30	The Evening Glow	£10.10.0
31	Shore of Caragh	£4.4.0
32	Ashleam River	£4.4.0
33	Derryinver	£4.4.0
34	Old Clonskeagh	£3.3.0
35	On the Thames	£5.5.0
36	Brickeen Bridge	£3.3.0
37	Kilbroney River	£4.4.0
38	Heavy Weather Killarney	£10.10.0
39	A Fine Evening in Achill	No price
40	Summer at Killarney	£4.4.0
41	Clonee Lakes, Kerry	£25
42	Blackwater Hills	£2.2.0

43	The Dingle Hills	£2.2.0
44	The Post Office, Achill	£2.2.0
45	Mweelrea	£25
46	Old Canal Trees	£3.3.0
46A	Early Morning	£3.3.0
47	Close Hauled	£3.3.0
48	Sands of Bleanaskill	£4.4.0
49	Vale of Avoca	£10.10.0
50	The Blackwater	£4.4.0
51	Shore at Templenoe	£4.4.0
52	Carantouhill	£5.5.0
53	Dooagh	£4.4.0
54	Derryquin	£4.4.0
55	Evening in Keem Bay	£5.5.0
56	Turfboat Canal	£4.4.0
57	Autumn, Achill	£10.10.0
58	Blarney Castle	£3.3.0
59	Dalkey Sound	£40.0.0
60	Doran's View	£10.10.0
61	At Leenane	£3.3.0
62	April Showers	£4.4.0
63	The Minaun Cliffs	£4.4.0
64	On Dalkey Island	£10.10.0
65	Glendalough	£3.3.0
66	Road to Pontoon	£3.3.0
67	Sweet Innisfallen	£5.5.0
68	Slievemore	£5.5.0
69	Evening, Mulroy Bay	£15.0.0
70	Saula, Achill	£4.4.0
71	Upper Lough Corrib	£3.3.0
72	Hills of Curraune	£3.3.0
73	Kate Kearney Cascade	£2.2.0
74	Upper Lake Kylemore	£2.2.0
75	Crosshaven	£2.2.0
76	Middle Lake Kylemore	£2.2.0
77	Holyhead Harbour	£2.2.0
78	In Clew Bay	£2.2.0
79	New Woodenbridge	£2.2.0
80	Horn Head Bridge	£3.3.0
81	At Loughlinstown	£10.10.0
82	Sea and Shore	£2.2.0
83	Winter in Achill	£3.3.0
84	Killiney from Carrickmines	£3.3.0
85	Middle Lake Kylemore	£2.2.0
86	Flying Scud	£4.4.0
87	Squally Weather	£2.2.0
88	Sheephaven, Donegal	£2.2.0

APPENDIX III: EXHIBITION SALES

Only exhibitions for which financial figures have survived are shown here. Pictures were often discounted against the catalogue price but may not have been shown as such in every case. Pictures were sometimes added to the exhibition after the catalogue had gone to press and every sale may not have been recorded in the catalogues. Nevertheless the figures are believed to provide a good idea of the artist's gross earnings, the number of pictures he exhibited and the number of pictures he sold per exhibition.

The period for which each exhibition remained open sometimes varied from the dates supplied by the press or even the artist. For instance, an exhibition would be extended if the Lord Lieutenant signalled his intention of putting in an appearance after the intended closing date.

1884, 18 & 19 November, Leinster Hall,
35 Molesworth Street, Dublin
50 pictures exhibited, 9 sold, representing
18 per cent of pictures shown   £70.8.0
[Note: artist gives a figure of £80.0.0 but this does not tally with total of the individual prices he gives for the pictures in question]

1886, 6 & 7 December, 9 Merrion Row, Dublin
'A Collection of Recent Water-color Drawings
and Oil Paintings'   £50.14.6
Fifty-five pictures exhibited; number sold: unknown

1892, 15–23 February, Leinster Hall, 35
Molesworth Street, Dublin   £168.5.0
150 pictures exhibited (including 2 not for sale). Sales: 44, representing 30 per cent of the pictures offered for sale.

1892, Tercentenary Exhibition, Week of
4 July, New Gallery, 35 Dawson Street,
Dublin   £77.00.0
Pictures exhibited: c.182; sales: 12, representing 7 per cent of pictures shown.
(One picture sold was unpriced.)
No. of paying visitors: 55
No. of catalogues sold: 23
Takings: £2.5.9

1893, 19–21 December, Leinster Hall, 35
Molesworth Street, Dublin   £159.11.0
Sixty-six pictures exhibited (64 in printed catalogue, 2 more in handwritten one).
Sales: 24, representing 36 per cent of pictures shown.

1899, 26 January–4 February, Leinster Hall, 35
Molesworth Street, Dublin: 'Beautiful Ireland'   £179.17.0
150 pictures exhibited; 50 pictures sold (plus commission for another), representing 33
per cent of pictures shown.
No. of visitors who paid for entry: 556

1901, 29 March–27 April. First London Exhibition,
The Modern Gallery, 175 Bond Street, London W
'Picturesque Ireland'   £179.13.2
144 pictures exhibited; sales: 52, representing 36 per cent of pictures shown
June–July
Total no. of pictures exhibited unknown.
Sales: 14, grossing   £72.8.0

1903, 22 January–7 February, Leinster Hall, 35
Molesworth Street, Dublin   £202.14.0
The value of two of the pictures sold is not included in the above figure, as part of the
first page of the catalogue has been torn.
134 pictures exhibited; sales of 50 pictures, representing 37 per cent of pictures on show.
The exhibition was extended to Monday 9 February.
No. of visitors listed: 836

1903, April, Modern Gallery, 175 Bond Street,
London W   £185.11.0
'The Land of the Shamrock'
139 pictures; 14 marked as sold in catalogue amounts to £139.13.0, but Freeman mentions
additional valuable picture. So 15 were sold, 11 per cent of total, and Freeman's final figure
is given at top.

1903, May, Grundy & Smith, Manchester
'The Land of the Shamrock'   £15.15.0
115 pictures, 4 sold, representing 3.5 per cent of pictures shown.
These figures are based on the wafers and names placed against a handwritten catalogue.
On account of the publicity the exhibition received, the figures scarcely seem credible.

1905, 23 January–11 February, Silver Jubilee Exhibition,
Leinster Hall, 35 Molesworth Street, Dublin   £261.14.0
122 pictures exhibited; 62 sold, representing 51 per cent of pictures shown.
No. of visitors to exhibition: 1,147
Admissions (3 weeks): £19.2.6
Sales of catalogues: £3.14.3

1906, 15 January–10 February, Leinster Hall, 35
Molesworth Street, Dublin   £185.42.0
Total exhibited: 132; sold: 39, representing 29.5 per cent of pictures shown.
Admissions (4 weeks): £25.8.6
Sales of catalogues: £2.17.5

1906, 1–30 May, The Modern Gallery, 61
New Bond Street, London W
'The Green Isle of Erin'   £160.19.0
No catalogue available, but number of pictures exhibited believed to be more than 140.
Freeman in statement of account provides the number against each picture sold, the highest
being No. 141. Twenty-five pictures sold; as a percentage of, say, 145 pictures shown, this
would have been in the order of 17 per cent.

1907, 14 January–9 February, Leinster Hall, 35
Molesworth Street, Dublin   £182.1.0
Total exhibited: 110; sold: 26 or 24 per cent of pictures shown.
Admissions (4 weeks): £17.13.0
Catalogues @ 3d: £3.4.7

1907, The Modern Gallery, 61 New Bond Street,
London W   *see below*
Thirty-five artists contributed 223 pictures, of which 60 were by Alex Williams.

1907, October, The Modern Gallery, 61 New
Bond Street, London W
Total for this exhibition and one above   £67.15.0
Four artists exhibited a total of 90 pictures of which 18 were by Alex Williams; the greater
number were also in the previous exhibition.

1908, 14 January–8 February, Leinster Hall, 35
Molesworth Street, Dublin   £164.5.0
Total exhibited: 99; 25 sold, representing 25 per cent of pictures shown.

1909, 16 January–6 February, Leinster Hall, 35
Molesworth Street Dublin   £113.16.0
Total exhibited: 104; 29 sold, representing 28 per cent of pictures shown.

1909 March–April, The Modern Gallery, 61
New Bond Street, London W
'Ould Donegal'   £183.11.6
Total exhibited: 101; 28 sold, representing 28 per cent of pictures shown.

1911, 13 January–4 February, Leinster Hall, 35
Molesworth Street, Dublin   £81.9.0
Total exhibited: 88; 16 sold, representing 18 per cent of pictures shown.
Admissions at door: £12.1.0

1912, 20 January–10 February, Leinster Hall, 35
Molesworth Street, Dublin
'Beautiful Ireland'   £188.14
Total exhibited: 92; 43 sold, representing 47 per cent of pictures shown.

1914, 12 January–6 February, Mills' Hall,
8 Merrion Row, Dublin   £101.8.6
Total exhibited: 85; 27 sold, representing 32 per cent of pictures shown.

1915, opened 12 February, Mills' Hall, 8
Merrion Row, Dublin, 35th Exhibition   £102.17.0
Total exhibited: 90; 24 sold, representing 27 per cent of pictures shown.

APPENDIX IV: ANNUAL EARNINGS

Discrepancies & figures additional to the original records are shown in square brackets. These records need to be treated with a degree of caution. The artist was not meticulous in his record keeping. So while it is fair to assume that his earnings for 1883 are complete, he says so himself, no such comment was appended to any of the other years. It is quite possible that there were other sales in addition to those he recorded, although these are unlikely to have been extensive.

EARNINGS FOR YEAR 1883	£000.0.0	Summary
Salaries at cathedrals	125.0.0	
All other sources	158.12.9	
Total	**283.12.9**	

Earnings for Year 1911		By month
January & February		
Watercolour 18x10, Sold by Combridge	5.0.0	
2 pictures sold to W. J. Williams	6.10.0	
Proceeds of exhibition	76.9.0	
Receipts at door	12.1.0	100.0.0
March		
Watercolour painting, *Killarney* R. M. Barrington, Bray	5.5.0	
Watercolour drawing, *Glena Killarney* R. Ussher, Cappagh, Waterford	10.0.0	
Received for pictures sold by the Watercolour Society of Ireland at Annual Exhibition	9.13.6	24.18.6
April (blank)		
May		
Received from Miss Blackie of Glasgow for copyright for 24 watercolour drawings to illustrate 'Beautiful Ireland'	52.10.0 52.10.0	
June		
Sold to Col. Baillie, Red House, Strabane Watercolour sketch	2.2.0	
Sold by John Hilliard, Castlelough, Killarney Watercolour painting	1.10.0	
Dividend Dunlop Tyre Co. Less income tax	3.1.6	6.13.6

July

Sold by J. Sheridan, Dugort Hotel
Watercolour of Achill   10.10.0

3 small sketches   6.0.0

2 sketches sold by I. Hilliard, Castlelough   4.0.0
                                                                        20.10.0

August

17 Sold by I. Hilliard, Castlelough, Killarney
One watercolour sketch   3.3.0

Sold by W. J. Manning. Rosapenna Hotel
4 pictures (less commission)   20.16.0

Sold by I. Sheridan, Dugort, Achill
2 oil paintings   14.0.0
                                                                        37.19.0

September

Sold By J. Sheridan, Dugort
2 pictures at £7.7.0   14.14.0

Sold at Portrush Exhibition
Watercolour drawing   3.0.0

Received from Miss Blackie of Glasgow
for copyright of 24 watercolour drawings
to illustrate 'Beautiful Ireland' volumes   52.10.0
                                                                        69.14.0

October (blank)

November

Sold at the Exhib. of the Dublin Sketching Club
Killarney   4.4.0
Gap of Dunloe   3.3.0
Donegal Bay   3.3.0
Achill   2.2.0
Moonlight   3.10.0
                                                                        16.2.0

December

4 small sketches sold by Elliman, Exchequer St.   5.0.0
Oil painting, *Ross Castle, Killarney*
Purchased by C. J. Carroll, Rocklow, Fethard   4.10.0

Oil painting, Salruck, bought by Miss Drury,
Salruck Cottage, Connemara   22.10.0

Watercolour, J. E. Pickering, London   5.5.0
                                                                        37.5.0

Total for year   [366.2.0]   **362.11.6**

1911 Exhibition expenses

Rent of Gallery 35 Molesworth St.	12.15.0
Attendant	4.0.0
Advertisements	5.0.0
Printing, Invitation & other cards and catalogue	4.10.0
Total	**26.5.0**

Earnings for Year 1912	By month	
January & February	177.14.0	
Admissions to Exhibition	15.12. 6	
	193.6.6	193.6.6
March	4.4.0	
	4.4.0	4.4.0
April		
Watercolour design for calendar Temson Collins	3.3.0	
Watercolour sketch Mr McIntosh	2.2.0	
Watercolours sold by W. J. Manning, Rosapenna	8.8.0	
	13.13.0	13.13.0
May		
Sold at Royal Hibernian Academy Exhibition		
Watercolour drawing	5.0.0	
Watercolour drawing	10.0.0	
Sold by Anderson Stanford & Ridgeway Watercolour	3.3.0	
	18.[3].0	18.0.0
June		
2 watercolours sold by Hilliard, Killarney	5.10.0	
Watercolour sold by Anderson Stanford & Ridgeway	5.0.0	
Watercolour sold by Anderson Stanford & Ridgeway	5.0.0	
	15.10.0	29.6.0
July		
Watercolour Sold to Mrs Baillie, Red House, Strabane	2.12.6	
Watercolour sold by Sheridan, Dugort	2.0.0	
Oil painting sold by Sheridan, Dugort	5.0.0	
	9.12.6	9.12.6

August

2 Watercolours sold by Hilliard, Killarney	6.6.0	
One oil sketch and two watercolours sold by J. Sheridan, Dugort	6.6.0	
2 Watercolours sold by Combridge & Co. (less commission)	10.10.0	
	23.2.0	22.16.0

September

Sold by Combridge & Co. Watercolour sketch, *Killarney*	2.10.0	
2 Watercolours sold by I. W. Manning, Rosapenna (less commission)	8.10.0	
One watercolour sold by J. Sheridan, Dugort	2.0.0	
	13.0.0	13.0.0

October

Sold by Messrs. Combridge (less commission) 2 Watercolours, *McGillicuddy's Reeks* and *Glenveagh*	11.5.0	
	11.5.0	11.5.0

November

2 Watercolours sold by W. J. Manning, Rosapenna (less commission)	8.10.0	
Sold at Dublin Sketching Club Exhibition		
No. 31, *Edge of Moor*	3.3.0	
No. 186, *Killary Bay*	3.3.0	
	14.16.0	15.16.0

December

Sold at Sketching Club Exhibition		
No. 261, *Turf Boats*	3.3.0	
No. 120, *Avoca River*	4.4.0	
No. 103, *Glendalough*	3.3.0	
No. 152, *Lough Caragh*	3.3.0	
No. 286 *Bleanaskill Bay*	3.3.0	
No. 284 *Blackwater*	3.5.0	
	20.1.0	25.6.0

Total for the year	**[336.13.0]**	**[356.5.0]**

1912 Exhibition Expenses

Rent of Room, 35 Molesworth St.	23.5.0
Attendant	4.0.0
Advertisements	5.0.0
Printing Invitation cards & catalogue	4.10.0
Total	**36.15.0**

ENDNOTES

CHAPTER 1

1   Diana Athill in interview with Maureen Cleave, *Daily Telegraph*, 7 January 2009.

2   Audrey Baker, to whom the author is indebted for her recollection of her godmother.

3   'Achill Natural History Notes & Diary', 9 July 1911.

4   An enquiry with Minnesota Historical Society which have papers of and relating to John Fletcher Williams drew a blank on the memoirs of Samuel Williams that John Fletcher used in his own account (see below).

5   John Fletcher Williams, *The Groves and Lappan: An account of a pilgrimage thither in search of the Genealogy of the Williams Family.* Privately printed for the family, Saint Paul, MN, 1889, p. 39.

6   Ibid., pp. 39, 40.

7   Ibid., pp. 43, 44.

8   The will of John Williams, dated 9 March 1795, which Fletcher Williams quotes in full, p. 24.

9   Williams, *The Groves and Lappan*, p. 52.

10 Ibid., p. 31.

CHAPTER 2

1   'Memoirs written by Alexander Williams, RHA, Volume I', p. 24 (hereafter MMI; see Appendix V).

2   Ibid., pp. 50, 52.

3   Ibid., p. 50.

4   Ibid., p. 53.

5   Ibid., p. 30.

6   Ibid., pp. 42–5.

7   Ibid., pp. 36, 38.

8   Ibid., pp. 26, 28.

9   Ibid., p. 28.

10 Ibid., pp. 16, 18.

11 Ibid., pp. 54, 56.

12 Ibid., pp. 40, 42.

13 Ibid., p. 55.

14 Ibid., p. 12.

15 Records of the period are scant and there appears to be no documentation in the Natural History Museum as to what William Williams and R. J. Montgomery contributed. So it is not possible to determine if any of the early material is theirs.

16 *Boy's Own*, vol. V, p. 157.

17 MMI, pp. 14, 16.

18 Ibid., pp. 47–9.

19 W. G. Strickland in *A Dictionary of Irish Artists* (Dublin: Maunsel & Co., 1913) describes Bernard M. Tumalti (or Tumalty) as a portrait painter only.

20 MMI, p. 32.

21 Ibid., pp. 45–6. The quail is a scarce summer visitor, more often reported in spring than autumn. It has been said that if the bittern were less frequently shot, it might again become a breeding species. See Eric Dempsey and Michael O'Clery, *The Complete Guide to Ireland's Birds*, 2nd edition (Dublin: Gill & Macmillan, 2002).

22 MMI, p. 34.

23 Ibid., pp. 2, 24.

CHAPTER 3

1   MMI, p. 60.

2   R. Lloyd Praeger, Some *Irish Naturalists: A Biographical Notebook* (Dundalk: Dundalgan Press (W. Tempest, 1949), p. 15.

3   Eugen Sandow (1867–1925), celebrated Prussian strong man, sometimes described as the 'father of bodybuilding'.

4   MMI, pp. 67–71.

5   Ibid., p. 88.

6   Ibid., pp. 88–9.

7   Ibid., p. 59.

8   Ibid., pp. 61–2.

9   John J. Watters, *The Natural History of the Birds of Ireland indigenous and migratory containing descriptions of the habits, migrations, occurrence, and economy, of the 261 species comprised in the fauna* (Dublin: James McGlashan, 1853).

10 'Ornithological Notes & Shooting Diary', 18 November 1867.

11 Ibid., 5 May 1867.

12 Ibid., 25 September 1867.

13 Ibid., 20 March 1869.

14 Ibid., 3 February 1868.

15 Ibid., 1 September 1868.

16 Ibid., 12 April 1869.

17 Ibid., 13 September 1867.

18 MMI, pp. 63, 65.

19 MMI pp. 63–64. An examination in 2009 of the old houses adjacent to Annesley Bridge did not succeed in identifying the building in question.

20 'Ornithological Notes & Shooting Diary', 18 November 1867.

21 Ibid., 22 September 1868.

22 Ibid., 26 September 1868.

23 Ibid., 11 October 1867.

24 MMI, pp. 93–4.

25 Ibid., pp. 92–3.

26 This anecdote was told to the author by an elderly metal worker living in Bray who had known the 'culprit' from boyhood days.

27 MMI, pp. 91–2.

28 Ibid., pp. 86–7.

29 Ibid., pp. 87–8.

30 Ibid., p. 87.

31 Niall Hatch, Development Officer, BirdWatch Ireland, in correspondence with the author, 9 June 2009.

32 MMI, pp. 97–8.

33 Ibid., p. 98.

CHAPTER 4

1 MMI, p. 99.

2 Evidence to the enquiry, *The Irish Times*, 13 June 1866.

3 *The Irish Times*, 27 June 1866.

4 MMI, pp. 107–8.

5 Ibid., p. 96.

6 Ibid., p. 109.

7 Today the Natural History Museum is one of the four branches of the National Museum of Ireland. When Alexander and Edward first submitted material to the museum it was known as the Dublin Museum of Science and Art. When it was taken over by the government act of 1877 from the Royal Dublin Society, the founding institution, it became known as the National Museum of Science and Art.

8 This quotation exists in two versions; the one given here is from MMI, p. 127. The same quotation, with some small differences, appears in Barrington's obituary notice for Edward Williams, published in the *Irish Naturalist* (February 1906). The differences between the published version and the artist's may possibly be accounted for by Barrington supplying Alexander with a draft copy to check.

9 Montague Browne, FZS, *Practical Taxidermy* (London: L. Upcott Gill, 1884), p. 66.

10 Barbara and Richard Mearns, *The Bird Collectors* (London and San Diego: Academic Press, 1998), p. 21.

11 Williams & Son, memo to the Natural History Museum, 17 September 1909.

12 Williams & Son to R. F. Scharff, 10 April 1906.

13 *Irish Naturalist* (December 1906), for example.

14 Williams & Son to R. F. Scharff, 26 March 1902.

15 Williams & Son to R. F. Scharff, 5 May 1902.

16 Williams & Son to A. R. Nichols, 24 August 1905.

17 Williams & Son to A. R. Nichols, 23 April 1907.

18 Samuel Houghton to R. F. Scharff, 11 July 1911.

19 Williams & Son to museum's storekeeper, 1 July 1907.

20 In conversation with Willie Williams' daughter.

21 Lord Headley to R. F. Scharff, 23 January 1911.

22 C. Douglas Deane, 'Taxidermy now and then', *The Irish Times*, 16 May 1963.

23 British Museum, 13 December 1894.

24 *Irish Naturalist* (January 1894), p. 24.

25 Ibid., (January 1900), p. 22.

26 *Irish Naturalist* (May 1911).

27 Ibid., (March 1915), p. 63.

28 Ibid., (June 1908), 'Wild Bird Protection in Co. Dublin', pp. 119–22.

29 'Ulster Diaries', Volume II, Sunday 20 November 1910.

30 R. Lloyd Praeger, *Some Irish Naturalists: A Biographical Notebook* (Dundalk: Dundalgan Press (W. Tempest, 1949), p. 177.

31 R. M. Barrington uses this quotation in his obituary notice of Edward Williams in the *Irish Naturalist*, XV, 2 (February 1906).

32 C. Douglas Deane, 'Taxidermy Then and Now', *Stream and Field: A magazine of the Irish countryside*, 3, 7 (Autumn 1974).

33 C. Douglas Deane mentions only one daughter, Eileen, as helping her father (*The Irish Times*, 16 May 1963) but the author remembers two daughters being present during his visit.

34 Eric Fuller, *Extinct Birds*, revised edition (Ithaca, NY: Comstock Publishing Associates, 2001), p. 19.

35 *Irish Society and Social Review*, 17 February 1906.

36 *The Irish Times*, 21 January 1911.

37 Mearns and Mearns, *The Bird Collectors*, p. 3.

38 Roger Lovegrove, *The Silent Fields: The Long Decline of a Nation's Wildlife* (Oxford: Oxford University Press, 2007).

39 Mearns and Mearns, *The Bird Collectors*, p. 13.

40 Fuller, *Extinct Birds*, p. 14.

41 MMI, p. 97.

CHAPTER 5

1   Holograph letter from Fassaroe, Bray, County Wicklow, signed RMB, dated 9 March 1911.

2   Holograph letter from R. J. Ussher, Cappagh House, Cappagh Sub Office, County Waterford, 13 February 1911.

3   Enquiry to J. N. Halbert, National Museum, 9 August 1910.

4   Holograph letter from C. J. Patten, The University, Sheffield, 14 June 1910, pasted into the 'Ulster Diaries', Volume II.

5   Holograph letter from C. J. Patten, The University, Sheffield, 6 August 1910, pasted into the 'Ulster Diaries', Volume II.

6   'Ulster Diaries', Volume II, 2 May 1910.

7   'Ulster Diaries', Volume II, Warren's letter quoted and dated 21 May 1910.

8   'Ulster Diaries', Volume II, 23 January 1910.

9   Ibid., 12 June 1910.

10   Ibid., 24 July 1910.

11   Ibid., 25 March 1910.

12   Ibid., 12 June 1910.

13   Ibid., 29 May 1910.

14   Stephen Moss, *A Bird in the Bush: A Social History of Birdwatching* (London: Arum Press, 2004), p. 271.

15   The letter is quoted by the diarist in his own entry for Sunday 2 April 1911 and gives the date of the letter as being the same.

16   It was in an entry for 12 March 1911 ('Ulster Diaries', Volume II) that Alexander mentions being told by Willie of the nuthatch, although in the *Irish Naturalist* Willie gives 26 March as the date he first identified the bird in Trumbull's garden.

17   See P. G. Kennedy, *The Birds of Ireland* (London: Rutledge & Scroope, 1954), p. 330.

18   'Ulster Diaries', Volume II, Sunday 17 July 1910.

19   Robert Patterson, Glenbank, Holywood, County Down, 29 May 1910, letter to A. W.

20   'Ulster Diaries', Volume II, 29 August 1909.

21   'Ulster Diaries', Volume II, 23 March 1913.

22   'Ulster Diaries', Volume I, 18 June 1911.

23   'Ulster Diaries', Volume II, 5 December 1909.

24   Niall Hatch, correspondence with the author, 28 July 2009.

25   Sunday 29 August 1909. Nelson's Pillar formerly stood in the middle of O'Connell Street where now stands the 'Spire'.

26   'Ulster Diaries', Volume II, 3 April 1910.

27   Ibid., 17 April 1910.

28   Ibid., 28 May 1910.

29   Ibid., 22 May 1910.

30   'Green flaggers', more usually referred to as yellow flaggers, the native *Iris pseudacorus* which has yellow fleur-de-lys flowers, often with striking dark venation.

31   'Ulster Diaries', Volume I, 7 May 1911.

32   'Ulster Diaries', Volume II, 16 April 1911.

33   Ibid., Sunday 12 December 1909.

34   Ibid., Sunday 16 April 1911.

35   'Ulster Diaries', Volume I, Sunday 30 April 1911.

36   'Ulster Diaries', Volume II, 3 April 1910.

37   Ibid., 31 July 1910.

38   Unidentified newspaper, but the letter signed and dated R. J. Ussher, Cappagh House, Cappagh Sub Office, County Waterford, 18 November 1909.

39   'Ulster Diaries', Volume II, 8 March 1910.

40   Roger Lovegrove, *The Silent Fields: The Long Decline of a Nation's Wildlife* (Oxford: Oxford University Press, 2007).

41   'Ulster Diaries', Volume II, 1 July 1910.

CHAPTER 6

1   MMI, p. 121.

2   MMI, pp. 113–14. Apart from hearing the stage ventriloquist, Alexander said he had been reading a book entitled *Valentine Vox the Ventriloquist* which pointed out certain conditions that needed to be observed by anyone attempting the art.

3   Robert Duke Williams in fact was dismissive of Alexander's talent in this direction, but it is doubtful that he ever heard him perform as a ventriloquist.

4   MMI, p. 114.

5   Ibid., p. 115.

6   Ibid., p. 123.

7   Ibid., pp. 123–4.

8   Ibid., p. 126.

9   O. J. Vignoles, *The Memoirs of Robert Prescott Stewart* (London: Simpkin, Marshall, Hamilton, Kent & Co., 1899), p. 90.

10   'Memoirs written by Alexander Williams, RHA, Volume II', p. 9 (hereafter MMII; see Appendix V).

11   Ibid., p. 8.

12 MMI, pp. 143–4.

13 Paul Arbuthnott, 'A Survey of the Vicars Choral of St Patrick's and Christ Church Cathedrals during the Nineteenth Century', unpublished MLitt thesis, Trinity College Dublin, 2007, p. 63.

14 MMII, p. 1.

15 Ibid., pp. 6–7.

16 Ibid., pp. 97–8.

17 MMII, pp. 22–3 Walter Bapty was yet another member of the Vicars Choral of St Patrick's Cathedral. It was a very close-knit world.

18 (John) Sims Reeves in his *Recollections* gave his year of birth as 1821 but other sources, as they give the earlier date, are likely to be more reliable.

19 Reeves is said to have lost more money through non-appearances than any other singer in history. He himself put the figure at a staggering £80,000.

20 MMII, p. 99, Reeves had made his debut in *Guy Mannering* and must have known the opera inside out.

21 MMII, pp. 18–19.

22 This unique cylinder is in the possession of the National Sound Archive, London, formerly known as the British Institute of Recorded Sound. The conductor on the occasion in question was (Sir) August Manns (1825–1907) and the composition Handel's oratorio, *Moses and the Children of Israel*. Manns is said to have conducted some 12,000 concerts at the Crystal Palace over a 42-year period and was the conductor of the Handel Festival, 1883–1900.

23 *The Irish Times*, 13 November 1882.

24 *The Irish Times*, 20 January 1881.

25 *Irish Life*, 27 June 1891.

26 Cormac Lowth drew the author's attention to the fact that a Bougham Leech lived in Clontarf. The artist appears to have confused the two names.

27 The banquet at the Gresham Hotel was held on 10 December 1877.

28 *Freeman's Journal*, 23 April 1888.

29 *The Irish Times*, 23 April 1888.

30 Written at the beginning of 1882 in his 'Chronicles & Memoirs'.

31 'Chronicles & Memoirs', March 1880.

32 MMI, p. 124.

CHAPTER 7

1 MMI, p. 118.

2 Ibid., pp. 111–12.

3 Ibid., p. 112.

4 Ibid., pp. 118–19.

5 Ibid., pp. 120–1.

6 In his memoirs he says he submitted only six, but eight are listed in Ann M. Stewart's *Royal Hibernian Academy Index of Exhibitors* 1826–1879 (Dublin: Manton Publishing, 1987).

7 MMI, pp. 106–7.

8 James Haswell Burke, a drawing mounter and photographic framemaker, and Henry Bennett, a carver and gilder, are both listed in *Thom's Directory* for 1870 as being at 34 Wellington Quay, along with William Farrell, a trunkmaker.

9 MMII, p. 52.

10 MMI, pp. 127, 129.

CHAPTER 8

1 Jonathan Beaumont, *Rails to Achill: A West of Ireland Branch Line* (Usk, Gwent: Oakwood Press, 2005), relates the history of the railway with many illustrations.

2 Report to Congested Districts Board by Major Robert Rutledge-Fair, inspector, Achill 1892, reprinted in *Muintir Acla*, vol. 4 (Summer 1996), p. 27.

3 Alexander Williams RHA, *Something about Achill*, picture catalogue, 1897, pp. 5, 6.

4 MMI, p. 131.

5 *The Irish Times*, 31 January 1903.

6 MMI, p. 131.

7 Ibid., pp. 132–3.

8 P. J. Joyce, *A Forgotten Part of Ireland* (Tuam: 1910), pp. 91–2.

9 MMI, pp. 131–2.

10 Ibid., p. 131.

11 This captive eagle was something of a celebrity and appears in Sir Ralph Payne-Gallwey, *The Fowler in Ireland* (London: Van Voorst, 1882), p. 305.

12 Quoted in a profile of the Rev. E. Nangle by T. McN [full name not given], *Muintir Acla* (June/July 1995), p. 14.

13 As of writing in McDowell's Guest House, Dugort, 2010

14 MMI, pp. 134–5.

15 Ibid., p. 135.

16 Ibid., p. 132.

CHAPTER 9

1   MMI, p. 136.

2   Ibid., pp. 137–8.

3   For an illuminating essay on the RIAU see Dr Eileen Black, 'Practical Patriots and True Irishmen: The Royal Irish Art Union 1839–59', *Irish Arts Review Yearbook*, vol. 14 (1998).

4   MMII, p. 52.

5   Ibid., p. 105.

6   Ibid., p. 54.

7   Ibid., p. 101.

8   Annual Report of the Dublin Sketching Club for 1886–7. The handwriting appears to be that of A. W., while the report is signed off by M. A. Boyd.

9   Minutes, 1 June 1887, from the Dublin Sketching Club Archives, National Library of Ireland (hereafter NLI).

10   Minutes for 30 July 1887, signed by W. Sterling, 3 August, Dublin Sketching Club Archives, NLI.

11   Open Night, 29 February 1888.

12   *The Irish Times*, 11 November 1924.

13   Leinster Hall, Molesworth Street, 8–27 November 1886.

14   *The Irish Times*, 6 July 1886.

15   *The Irish Times*, 30 May 1887.

16   *The Irish Times*, 11 November 1924.

17   Minutes by W. Sterling, 3 August 1887. Dublin Sketching Club Archives, NLI.

18   Cormac Lowth, in correspondence with the author, 2009.

19   *The Irish Times*, 7 March 1887.

20   *The Irish Times* in its review of Williams' solo exhibition on 31 October referred to his having exhibited the picture at the RHA 'last year'. But there is little doubt that the reviewer meant the picture exhibited at the RHA's last exhibition, i.e. in 1887, not 1886.

21   Cormac Lowth, in correspondence with the author, 2009.

CHAPTER 10

1   MMII, pp. 25–6.

2   Ibid., p. 31.

3   Ibid., p. 30.

4   Ibid., pp. 33–4.

5   Ibid., pp. 46–7.

6   Ibid., pp. 31–2.

7   Ibid., pp. 41–2.

8   Ibid., pp. 52–3.

9   Ibid., pp. 100–1.

10   Ibid., p. 88.

11   Ibid., p. 76.

12   Aaron Edwin Penley, Associate of the New Society of Painters in Watercolours (ANWS) (1807–70), a portrait and landscape painter who painted frequently in Scotland. He wrote a number of books including *A System of Watercolour Painting*, 1850.

13   Ibid., p. 74.

14   Ibid., pp. 93–4.

15   Robert Duke Williams, who knew Kitty Gray as his aunt-in-law, had a rather distant relationship with her, but he had no hesitation in describing her as a 'Dublin beauty'.

16   This was said by Robert Duke Williams.

17   MMI, p. 122.

18   The mean average winter temperature for 1879 was 1.80 °C; 1880, 4.10 °C and 1881, 2.80 °C, a spectacular drop compared with 1878 when the winter mean was 60 °C and 1877 when it was slightly higher at 6.40 °C. The mean winter temperature in recent years has been between 50° and 70 °C. (Ref: Met Éireann)

19   'Chronicles & Memoirs'.

20   Jonathan Beaumont, *Rails to Achill: A West of Ireland Branch Line* (Usk, Gwent: Oakwood Press, 2005), p. 10.

21   Figures taken from Fergus D'Arcy, 'Wages of labourers in the Dublin Building Industry 1667–1918', *Saothar: Journal of the Irish Labour Historical Society*, no. 14 (1989).

22   Quoted in *The Irish Times* during the coroner's enquiry into the fire at 19–20 Westmoreland Street in 1866.

23   Figures for St Patrick's Cathedral are taken from Paul Arbuthnott, *A Survey of the Vicars Choral of St Patrick's and Christ Church Cathedrals during the Nineteenth Century*, M Litt thesis, 2007.

24   The figures are taken from an unpublished, personal account book 1868–76, kept by J. Alfred Ledbetter, who occupied the positions of both audit clerk in 1866 and assistant cashier in 1874.

CHAPTER 11

1   *The Irish Times*, 18 November 1884.

2   Ibid.

3   *The Irish Times*, 6 March 1893. The eviction scene referred to by Lady Elizabeth Butler (1846–1933) was exhibited at the RHA in 1892. She lived in Wicklow and had witnessed the event for herself.

4   'Chronicles & Memoirs', activities for 1884.

5   The titles he gives in his chronicles do not correspond exactly with those in the printed catalogue.

6   'Chronicles & Memoirs', activities for 1884.

7   *The Irish Times*, 18 November 1884.

8   *Daily Express*, 31 October 1887.

9   *The Irish Times*, 31 October 1887.

10   *Daily Express*, 31 October 1887.

11   The public meeting at the Mansion House was held on 4 April 1895.

CHAPTER 12

1   A Native [Percy Fitzgerald], *Recollections of Dublin Castle & of Dublin Society* (London: Chatto & Windus, 1902), pp. 2–7.

2   'Chronicles & Memoirs'. Lord Cowper viewed the exhibition on 30 October 1880.

3   The six regulations are listed in his exhibition book for 1891.

4   *Thom's Directory*, 1895.

5   *Irish Society*, 20 February 1892.

6   *The Irish Times*, 15 February 1892.

7   *National Press*, 15 February 1892.

8   *Irish Daily Independent*, 22 February 1892.

9   *The Irish Times*, 15 February 1892.

10   *Daily Express*, 4 July 1892.

11   Sixty-four in the catalogue. He may have added one or two that were not listed.

12   *The Irish Times*, 19 December 1893.

13   Carla Briggs, 'The Landscape Painters', in Jim Larner (ed.), *Killarney History & Heritage* (Cork: The Collins Press, 2005), p. 146.

14   Letter dated 31 October 1905, signed J. Hilliard, Lake Hotel. It is not known who Mrs B was or if she was persuaded to buy the other two pictures.

15   *The Irish Times*, 19 December 1893.

16   *The Irish Times*, 27 January 1912, review of second musical recital, held on Friday 26 January.

17   *Irish Society and Social Review*, 17 February 1906.

CHAPTER 13

1   Letter to the editor of *The Irish Times*, from Hugh P. Lane, dated 20 January 1904.

2   Printed letter from City Treasurer's Office, Municipal Buildings, Dublin, dated September 1897.

3   Alderman Pile's comment quoted in *The Irish Times*, 7 September 1897.

4   *Daily Express*, 26 January 1899.

5   Handwritten letter from William Williams, 19 Garville Road [Dublin], dated 8 April 1901. The letter was probably dictated to one of the three children still living at home as the handwriting seems far too firm and fluent for a man of eighty-eight. Indeed he ends the letter by saying: 'I am too tired to write.'

6   Holograph letter from Lord Mayo to the artist from Palmerston, Straffan, County Kildare; 5 March 1901, when giving permission for his name and his wife's to be used as patrons of the London exhibition.

7   *Art Record*, 30 March 1901.

8   *The Irish Times*, 29 April 1901.

9   Signed article: A.F.W., *Brighton & Hove Society*, 6 April 1901.

10   Receipt from B. McGlade, Bill Poster, Poster Writer and Street Advertiser, 42 Middle Abbey Street, 11 February 1905.

11   *Daily Express* receipt, 28 February 1905.

12   There may have been sales after Freeman wrote this letter. At any rate the artist's records suggest gross sales of £202.14.0 (see Appendix III).

13   In his 'Chronicles & Memoirs' Alexander puts this exhibition down mistakenly as having taken place the previous year, 1905.

14   The printed catalogue for the first exhibition has 'sold' written against nine pictures, but only eight are listed in the handwritten accounts in which both exhibitions are combined.

15   Holograph letter from Edward Freeman to the artist, dated 31 December 1907.

16   Holograph letter from Edward Freeman to the artist, dated 14 February 1908.

17   *Standard*, 31 March 1909.

18 *The Irish Times*, 11 February 1901.

19 *The Irish Times*, 21 January 1901.

20 'Chronicles & Memoirs', 1877; precise date uncertain but this quotation is written under a paragraph dated 26 August.

21 Holograph letter from Mrs L. Webb, Spring Gardens, Naas, County Kildare, date 20 February [no year].

22 Postcard from M. Ross, Summerfield, Dalkey, County Dublin, dated 6 March 1913.

23 Holograph letter from M. Ross Graham, 400L Archibald Street, Fortwilliam [Ontario], Canada, dated 6 August [1920].

24 *The Irish Times*, 24 January 1905.

25 Holograph letter from Kathleen Corry Hodgson, dated 13 February [1912].

26 Holograph letter from A. E. Goodbody, headed [Sunnybank] Killiney, 19 February 1904.

27 Holograph letter from A. E. Goodbody, A&L Goodbody Solicitors, 30 College Green, Dublin, dated 9 February 1906.

28 Holograph letter from Amelia Kennedy, Dalguise, Monkstown, County Dublin, dated 16 February 1906.

29 Holograph letter from Amelia Kennedy, Dalguise, Monkstown, County Dublin, dated 10 February 1905.

30 Holograph letter from Amelia Kennedy, Dalguise, Monkstown, County Dublin, dated 3 March 1905.

31 Holograph letter from Amelia Kennedy, Dalguise, Monkstown, County Dublin, dated 7 February 1912.

32 Holograph letter from Gertrude Hamilton, Killiney Castle, 8 March 1912.

33 Holograph letter from Miss P. Neville, Weston, Enniskerry, County Wicklow, undated but the picture in question, *The 'Divil's Elbow', Gap of Dunloe*, the artist's accounts show she bought at his thirty-second exhibition, 1912.

34 Holograph letter from J. J. Fuller, printed crest, no address, dated 19 January 1909.

35 Ann O'Dea, *Anatomy of an Irish Country House and Garden c. 1730–2004: The Altamont Estate Co. Carlow*, Fine & Decorative Arts diploma course thesis, May 2004.

36 The artist's nephew Robert Duke Williams in conversation with the author

37 Letter from The Castle, Walter Callan to the artist, Dublin dated inadvertently 9 Feb 1904 when it should be 1905 (Alexander Williams Papers).

38 Holograph letter from Sophia C. White [date illegible] February [1905].

39 Illustrated article entitled 'The Countess of Dudley's Irish Nurses', *The Lady of the House*, 15 March 1905.

40 *The Irish Times*, 13 January 1911.

41 *Selling at De Veres*, 2008 brochure.

42 *Freeman's Journal*, 20 January 1912.

43 National Census, 1901. Among the photographers, 183 were male and 131 were female. The ratio among painters was almost equal, with 113 males as against 109 females.

44 *The Irish Times*, 20 January 1912.

45 Dr Brendan Rooney in correspondence with the author, 14 August 2009.

46 *Irish Society and Social Review*, 31 January 1903.

47 *The Irish Times*, 11 March 1925, article headed 'Beautiful Ireland: Pictures by a Veteran Artist'.

48 *The Irish Times*, 8 February 1907.

49 Holograph letter from Nan Doyne, 29 Wellington Court, Knightsbridge SW, 11 February [1906]

CHAPTER 14

1 He mentions the lease twice, briefly in his *Memoirs* and there is a longer note at the end of 'Chronicles & Memoirs'.

2 National Census 1911.

3 'Achill Natural History Notes & Diary', 18 September 1910.

4 Hatch Street is divided into upper and lower; No 4 is in Lower Hatch Street.

5 'Achill Natural History Notes & Diary', 8 September 1909.

6 Ibid., 6 April 1907.

7 Ibid., 22 October 1907.

8 Ibid., 8 April 1907.

9 Ibid., 14 October 1910.

10 'Achill Natural History Notes & Diary', 11 October 1909.

11 Ibid., 10 August 1907.

12 Ibid., 27 September 1909.

13 Ibid., 22 August 1907.

14 Ibid., 17 August 1907.

15 Ibid., 10 August 1907.

16 Ibid., 29 August 1907.

17 Ibid., 6 October 1909.

18 Ibid., 28 June 1911.

19 Ibid., 9 July 1911.

20 Ibid., 12 October 1907.

21 *Cordyline australis* is a New Zealand species, introduced to Britain in 1823 (*Hillier's Manual of Trees & Shrubs*, 5th edition). It is widely used in Ireland.

22 Measured in 2005 by Aubrey Fennell of the *Tree Register of Ireland*.

23 Introduced to the British Isles from California about 1838.

24 'Achill Natural History Notes & Diary', 30 October 1912.

25 Ibid., 11 April 1907.

26 Ibid. He writes the dates here as a cluster, 12,13 & 14 August 1907.

27 Ibid., 27 August 1907.

28 Ibid., 15 July 1911.

29 Ibid., 8 September 1909.

30 'Achill Natural History Notes & Diary', 24 June 1913.

31 *Irish Society and Social Review*, 19 January 1907.

32 'Achill Natural History Notes & Diary', 8 September 1909.

33 Ibid., 22 June 1911.

34 Ibid., 12 April 1907.

35 In conversation with Ita Hackett who was a regular guest at the Valley Hotel every year during this period.

36 Ibid., 15 August 1907.

37 Ibid., 27 September 1909.

38 Ibid., 22 June 1911.

39 'Achill Natural History Notes & Diary', 22 September 1907.

40 Ibid., 15 September 1907.

41 Keel Strand at the foot of the Menaun Cliffs is treacherous for swimmers. The council in recent years has erected large warning notices, indicating that the centre of the bay is safe from currents but not either end.

42 Sea Spleenwort, *Asplenium marinum*, a fern found in rock crevices by the sea.

43 'Achill Natural History Notes & Diary', 15 August1911. The temperature he quotes refers to Fahrenheit; in Centigrade 44.4 ° and 33.3 ° respectively.

44 Ibid., 11 November 1912.

45 'Our Office Table', *Building News*, 10 April 1903 in reference to his 'The Land of the Shamrock' exhibition, Bond Street.

46 According to Brian Sheridan, grandnephew of John Sheridan, in conversation with author. None of the headed notepaper appears to have survived.

47 'Achill Natural History Notes & Diary', Thursday 26 September 1912.

48 Ibid., 25 August 1912.

49 Ibid., 26 August 1912.

50 A remark made at a public lecture at the National Gallery of Ireland, 2009.

51 According to Brian Sheridan, in conversation with the author.

52 Ibid., Sunday 4 August 1912.

53 Ibid., 29 June 1911.

54 Elizabeth Morgan JP, in conversation with the author, 2008.

55 In conversation with the author. By a strange coincidence, when Lady Bevir was widowed she went to live in Greystones, County Wicklow, just doors away in the same street where Alexander Williams had taken a house.

56 Hilary Heron taught art at St Stephen's School, Goatstown, Dublin where the author was a pupil. Apart from her teaching, Hilary was memorably associated with her 'Model T' Ford which was painted bright yellow and blue, at a time when, in Henry Ford's words, you could have any colour as long as it was black.

57 In conversation with the author at Bleanaskill Lodge.

58 'Achill Natural History Notes & Diary', 11 July 1911.

CHAPTER 15

1   *The Irish Times*, 24 February 1914.

2   S. B. Kennedy, *Paul Henry: Paintings, Drawings Illustrations* (New Haven, CT: Yale University Press, 2007), p. 38.

3   *Athenaeum*, 24 May 1913.

4   *Morning Post*, 21 May 1913.

5   *Observer*, 25 May 1913.

6   Sir James Jebusa Shannon, RA (1863–1923), an Anglo-American painter noted for his fine society portraits.

7   'Chronicles & Memoirs', 24 April 1916.

8   *The Irish Times*, 5 July 1919.

9   'Chronicles & Memoirs'.

10 *The Irish Times*, 5 July 1919.

11 C. Douglas Deane, 'Taxidermy Then and Now', *Stream and Field: A magazine of the Irish countryside*, 3, 7 (Autumn 1974).

12 R.D.W. in conversation with the author.

13 R.D.W. mentioned that it was a timber structure and did not think much of it. It has long since gone; the orchard has disappeared too, having been built over.

14 From the probate document, 12 January 1931.

15 *The Irish Times*, 26 October 1926.

16 In reporting Alfred Grey's death on 19 January 1926, *The Irish Times* stated that 'With the exception of Mr Alexander Williams, Mr Alfred Grey was the oldest member of the Royal Hibernian Academy.' In fact Grey was born a year earlier than A.W.

17 *The Irish Times*, 9 April 1928.

18 *The Irish Times*, 16 April 1928.

19 *The Irish Times*, 27 March 1926.

20 R.D.W. in conversation with the author.

21 Ibid.

22 Introduction by Aidan Dunne to the *Smurfit Art Collection* 2001, Smurfit Communications, p. 6.

23 Written, in fact, during his yachting cruise to Scotland, but the sentiment would have applied just as much when he painted in the west of Ireland.

PICTURE CREDITS

Kind permission to reproduce pictures from the following sources is gratefully acknowledged:

John O'Shea: pp. 2 (top), 134, 160, 230 (top), 268

François Augereau: p. 2 (second from top)

Larry Martin: p. 2 (bottom)

De Veres Fine Art: p. 13

Captain Martin Donnelly, Drogheda Port Company: p. 26

The National Museum of Ireland: p. 27, 56 (bottom), 57 (l&r), 61

Whyte's Fine Art: pp. 29, 35, 80, 91, 110 (bottom), 223, 244, 269 (bottom)

Veronica and Gerald Roden: p. 45

The Trustees of National Museums Northern Ireland: p. 48, 50 (bottom) © National Museums Northern Ireland 2010. Collection Ulster Museum Belfast. Photograph reproduced courtesy of the Trustees of National Museums Northern Ireland: p. 50 (top)

Dr P. A. Morris: p. 52

Adam's Fine Art: pp. 56, 80, 120, 161, 182, 196, 267

Dublin Zoo: p. 68

Gerard Grogan: p. 84, 193

David Britton: p. 93, 114 (top), 115, 123, 131, 183

The Dean & Chapter, St Patrick's Cathedral: p. 95

John F. Tierney: p. 111

The Cynthia O'Connor Gallery: p. 119 (top)

Frederick G. Pfeiffer: p. 139, 150, 166, 167

Patrick Grogan: p. 149

The National Yacht Club: p. 151 (top)

The Dublin City Gallery, The Hugh Lane: p. 152

The Ferrycarrig Hotel: p. 153

The Bridgeman Art Library: p. 157, 243, 264

Tom & Rosemary O'Reilly: p. 162, 230 (bottom), 256

Grogan & Co.: p. 181

The late Dr Philip Smyly: p. 184, 215, 225

The Lake Hotel Killarney: p. 198 (all), 199

Patrick Munnelly: p. 212

Willem van Goor & Doutsje Nauta: p. 253, 254

Dr Colum Breslin: p. 229

The Gorry Gallery: p. 270

INDEX

In this index, AW is used as an abbreviation for Alexander Williams. Paintings are listed under oils, pictures mentioned in the text, sketches and watercolours. Locations in Dublin are listed individually, rather than under Dublin.